Overzealous prosecutors led justice astray as their lust for an unjustified conviction of two innocent men caused a bizarre nightmare to unfold and greatly affect the judicial integrity of our legal justice system.

Within the first pages of *Journey Toward Justice*, Dennis Fritz grabs the reader's attention. His vivid descriptions recall memories of a time when Ada was stunned by the brutal murder of a young woman. At last, Mr. Fritz tells his side of an event that changed his life and this small community forever.

Riveting and provocative . . . a heartfelt journey about truth, determination—and justice.

This heartbreaking and true story is a must-read for anyone interested in the perversion of justice.

Dennis's book is simultaneously entertaining and horrifying. *Journey Toward Justice* is a story of great impact and great importance.

> —**Mark Barrett**
> Defense Attorney

Nobody wants to believe our courts are capable of serious and tragic mistakes, let alone systemic corruption. But the evidence suggests that while most people in law enforcement operate decently, others repeatedly place conviction rates above justice. *Journey Toward Justice*, one innocent man's story, reads like a detective story, with numerous twists and turns, racing toward a conclusion. Not only does it offer an authentic sense of life in prison, it should serve as an admonition to anyone who serves on a jury: Take the "beyond a reasonable doubt" with deadly seriousness, and don't allow yourself to be railroaded.

> —**Alan W. Bock**
> Senior Editorial Writer
> Orange County Register
> Author, *Waiting to Inhale*

FASTEN YOUR SEAT BELTS! Dennis Fritz's "Journey" exposes serious potholes and detours in the convoluted road toward justice. It's an emotionally breathtaking ride you'll never forget.

> —**Don Lasseter**
> True Crime Author

Journey Toward Justice clearly brings to fore the immense burden upon any civilized society to prove the guilt or innocence of its citizens beyond a reasonable doubt so that the framework of justice can prevail.

> —**Judge Issac Shimoni**
> Vice President Central Court
> Jerusalem, Israel

Journey Toward Justice sheds a light on the grim reality that lurks in the shadows of the American justice system. This powerful saga spins a dramatic web of intrigue that is even more chilling because it is true. Were it not for Mr. Fritz's fortitude and the watchful work of *The Innocence Project*, this innocent man would still be rotting in jail.

> —**Margaret Burk**
> Founder, Round Table West
> The largest book club on the West Coast

Journey Toward Justice is a classic example of how real life can be stranger and more frightening than fiction. Dennis Fritz's tale of the true life nightmare visited on him by often-times corrupt and other-times incompetent law enforcement officials will frighten the reader more than any novel can.

> —**Joseph Badal**
> Author, *The Pythagorean Solution, Terror Cell*

JOURNEY *TOWARD* JUSTICE

JOURNEY *TOWARD* JUSTICE

DENNIS FRITZ

SEVEN LOCKS PRESS

Seven Locks Press
P.O. Box 25689
Santa Ana, CA 92799
(800) 354-5348

Individual sales: This book is available through most bookstores or can be ordered directly from Seven Locks Press at the address above.

Quantity Sales: Special discounts are available on quantity purchases by corporations, associations and others. For details, contact the "Special Sales Department" at the publisher's address above.

Cover and Interior Design by Kira Fulks   www.kirafulks.com
Photographs courtesy of *Ada Evening News*

Printed in the United States of America

Library of Congress Cataloging-in-Publication Data is available from the publisher

ISBN: 1-931643-95-4

Dedication

*To the Lord for giving me the emotional strength and
perseverance to endure, and to my mother, Aunt Wilma,
and Elizabeth for their continued strength and support—*

FOREWORD

Barry Scheck
The Innocence Project

When Dennis Fritz testified before the Senate Judiciary Committee in support of the Innocence Protection Act—legislation that ultimately passed that supports efforts to get post-conviction DNA testing for those claiming innocence—I actually saw tears in the eyes of worldly politicians who for decades had heard an endless stream of moving stories from a multitude of witnesses. Among them were Senator Patrick Leahy, Democrat from Vermont and the legislation's sponsor and great champion, and Senator Orrin Hatch, Republican from Utah. Indeed, Senator Hatch said with unmistakable sincerity that he was humbled by what Dennis had to say. I thought that phrase deftly captured what everyone was feeling—a sense of awe that this man could survive and recount his incredible, hair-raising life story passionately, modestly, and thoughtfully all at once.

And what a life story it is—the literary equivalent to the wildest hardest-of-hard-luck, happiest-of-happy-endings country-and-western song one could imagine. It is a yarn that Hank Williams at his darkest and brightest and on LSD could not have conjured. The wrongful conviction, as you shall see, is only part of the story.

As happens often with Innocence Project clients, I didn't meet Dennis face to face until April 14, 1999, the day before the exoneration court appearance that would result in his release from prison. Notwithstanding years of correspondence and telephone calls, I will never forget it. The encounter took place in Ada, Oklahoma, in the Pontotoc County jail, the local lockup across the street from the courthouse, where jailhouse snitches twelve years earlier had solicited, importuned, and wheedled Dennis in a vain effort to get admissions from him about a crime he didn't commit. One snitch, who testified against Ron Williamson, Dennis's co-defendant, was by an amazingly ironic coincidence in the Pontotoc County jail that morning.

Dennis was dressed in a black-and-white striped prison outfit that resembled a barbershop pole—garb I had only seen in Keystone Kop movies. He was still understandably worried something would go wrong and that his promised release would somehow be sabotaged. I asked how he was being treated, how he was eating. He told me he was on the Zone Diet! At that time, the Zone Diet was all the rage among the sophisticated weight-loss-obsessed of America. It seemed a highly unlikely pursuit for someone confined in a medium-security Oklahoma prison.

I told Dennis that I had arrived with Jim Dwyer, a wonderful Pulitzer Prize winning columnist then writing for the New York Daily News, and Alexandra Pelosi, a smart, wisecracking producer from NBC Dateline. (Alex was wearing the same vermillion glasses that later charmed Presidential candidate George Bush in her HBO campaign documentary, Journeys with George.) Both Jim and Alex were going to cover Dennis's exoneration. Jim and Alex were off trying to find Glen Gore, the real perpetrator of the murder for which Dennis and Ron were wrongly convicted. Gore, in state prison on another charge, was cutting grass out on a road with a prison work crew, a sweetheart job.

Soon, Dennis, Ron, Ron's lawyer Mark Barrett, and I were permitted to meet together in a small antechamber to the county jail where we all had to sit on the floor. Ron and Dennis had not seen each other in twelve years. We could peek out a window at the courthouse across the street. And at one point we could see the county prosecutor, Bill Peterson, on the courthouse steps, where he was giving an interview to a television reporter. Ron began to whoop and holler imprecations at Peterson. Dennis just kept smiling. Then my cell phone rang. It was Jim Dwyer, and he was thunderstuck – Glen Gore had escaped! Apparently Gore had read a story in the Ada evening paper that Ron and Dennis were getting out of jail based on DNA testing and he realized it was long past time to run. Incredibly, his work release status gave him the opportunity.

An indescribably delicious joy and pandemonium ran through us in that small, grim corner of the Pontotoc County jail. For Dennis and Ron, Gore's escape was public vindication they were innocent, even more than the DNA tests on semen and hair that had excluded them and identified Gore as the murderer of Debbie Sue Carter.

The meeting between Dennis and his beautiful, altogether-marvelous daughter Elizabeth the next day in court was one of those sublime and tender moments that all present would remember for their lifetimes. For twelve years Dennis and Elizabeth had written and talked on the telephone constantly but they had not actually seen each other. Dennis, out of love and concern for his daughter, had not wanted her to see him in prison.

In January of 2000, Jim Dwyer, Peter Neufeld, and I wrote about the Fritz and Williamson case in our book, *Actual Innocence*. That short chapter was penned before a successful civil rights lawsuit revealed an underside of misconduct in the case that was truly shocking. And there is still much more to learn and more books to be written about this remarkable case. Some of the same law enforcement officials and jailhouse snitches were involved in the Denice Haraway murder case, an Ada prosecution based in large part on a "dream-statement" confession that put two men on death row and resulted in a very disturbing 1987 book, The

Dreams of Ada, by Robert Mayer. There is no DNA evidence to test in that case. That case keeps me up nights whenever I think of Ada, Oklahoma. One can only be comforted by the venerable consolation of Rev. Martin Luther King, Jr., that truth crushed to earth will rise again, no lie can live forever, and the arc of the moral universe is long but it bends toward justice. That arc covers Oklahoma, too.

As I write these words, there have been one hundred eighty-one post-conviction DNA exonerations in America. In sixty-three of the exonerations the real assailant has been identified. There are thousands of cases since 1989 where people have been arrested, indicted, and then cleared by DNA testing before their trials took place. The reverberations from all of these cases, the causes of wrongful convictions and the remedies to correct them, are the work of what can now fairly be called an "innocence movement." The exonerated and their families, many crime victims and their families (including the Carter family from the Fritz and Williamson case) are the heart and soul of this movement. In this unique and brave community of survivors, there is no more decent and dignified a man, nor a more gentle soul, than Dennis Fritz. For eight years he has unstintingly supported our work in every way possible, re-living what are often very painful memories in service to a just cause. And now he has had the fortitude to tell his whole story. As always, I am in awe of his courage and humbled by his efforts.

FOREWORD

Mark Barrett
Barrett Law Office

Dennis Fritz was far more educated and intelligent than most prisoners. Yet he got nowhere as an innocent man trying to win his own appeal. His book is foremost an account of what it is like to be arrested for and convicted of a murder you did not commit. But it is also an indictment.

First, it is an indictment of the law enforcement techniques that got Dennis put in prison. Second, it is an indictment of an appeals system which in theory is a double-check against injustices, but which in reality places enormous roadblocks between a prisoner and a serious reexamination of the evidence in his case.

Many prosecutors, and sometimes other politicians, have a penchant for complaining about supposed endless appeals in which the inmate is given chance after chance. These complaints are abominable lies. The truth is that when an Oklahoma prisoner gets past his first appeal (and his conviction is presumed to be a valid conviction even in the first appeal), his claims are generally considered to be unworthy of even being analyzed.

As Oklahoma's Court of Criminal Appeals has said, "Claims which could have been raised in previous appeals but were not are generally waived, and claims raised on direct appeal are *res judicata* [already decided and thus not subject to being reopened]."

In other words, with a few rare exceptions, you're out of luck if you either raised the claim or didn't raise the claim in your previous appeal. As harsh as this sounds, most states have similar provisions of law.

Once the case gets into federal court, any prior state court decisions are presumed to be correct, only federal constitutional issues can be considered, and a number of types of procedural mistakes can knock you out of court.

After all, we can't make getting judicial relief too easy because everyone knows that courts are out of control granting relief to undeserving criminals. Right? Well, you would think so if you just listened to the political hype and if you just watched the evening news.

But what they're telling you is not the truth. The truth is that for every Dennis Fritz there are scores more like him who were convicted on similarly shoddy evidence but who have no critical piece of evidence that can be subjected to the magic of DNA testing.

Yes, Dennis's case and others like it expose the awful truth that what we're using day after day to put people in prison for the rest of their lives is unreliable. Yet non-capital defendants, such as Dennis, almost never even get help trying to fight their cases.

After his first appeal, Dennis, for many years, had no lawyer or expert or investigator in his corner. If it were not for the fact that there was DNA in his case, nothing would have changed for Dennis. If it were not for DNA, the snitches and corner-cutting cops would still have Dennis in prison.

I, like many others I know, was brought up to believe that it was central to our American values to uphold the rights of our citizens when they are up against prosecution by their own government. So important were these values that it was better to free a hundred guilty men than to convict one who was innocent. I don't know how many people still believe in these basic American values. Everyone should.

There are in fact many Dennis Fritzes without DNA evidence. How many? Truth is, I don't know and you don't know.

But the truth is almost nothing is being done to find out.

However many innocent people may be incarcerated, those who make claims of innocence deserve to have lawyers and investigators helping them and they deserve to have the doors of our courthouses open to hear their claims.

Anything less would be un-American.

Norman, Oklahoma

PREFACE

Dennis Fritz

Journey Toward Justice is a true account of the injustice, turmoil, and suffering that I endured during my wrongful conviction and incarceration in a state prison. It is the story of my ordeal from the day of my arrest through the day I walked free twelve years later. It tells of the heartache and anguish that also affected my mother, aunt, and daughter as we wrestled with something we didn't understand, and how for many years we struggled to restore our lives to normal.

I undertook the writing of *Journey Toward Justice* with the intention of sharing my horrific experience with others so they might better understand the staggering implications when the justice system goes wrong. My story must not be minimized or dismissed. It is part of a much larger story that begs acknowledgement. Wrongful convictions are pervasive in our justice system. They shatter futures and destroy lives. Their existence tears at the very core of American societal expectations—that each of us is innocent until proven guilty beyond a reasonable doubt. No one should ever be subjected to a wrongful conviction.

In my case, it was an ordinary day in 1987 when I was arrested for murder and rape—charges that stemmed from the senseless and violent death of a young woman in Oklahoma. The state filed a petition seeking the death penalty against me and my co-defendant, Ronald Williamson. Ronnie's defense and mine took separate paths. Ronnie was appointed a well-known criminal attorney. Like a lamb going before the slaughter, I was forced to settle for a court-appointed civil lawyer who specialized in bankruptcy and personal injury.

I had no knowledge of the crime or who committed it, but that didn't stop the unscrupulous prosecutor who was bent on conviction. Using archaic methods of hair and body fluid identification, the prosecution relied on flimsy, circumstantial evidence to create the illusion of possibility. Outright lies in the form of jailhouse snitch testimony completed the state's circle of deception during my trial.

The jury returned after twelve hours of deliberation. I was pronounced guilty and sentenced to life in prison. At a separate trial, Ronnie was also found guilty and sentenced to death. He was assigned to death row. Our lives were forever altered.

For the next eleven years I lived in a stark twelve-foot by fifteen-foot cell, enduring the brutality and horrors of prison life while I struggled to make my declarations of innocence heard. I taught myself about the legal system by researching materials in the prison library. I learned to write legal briefs and requests for appeals. I wrote letters, I made phone calls, I did everything I could think of to create my own second chance. At the moment when I believed I had exhausted my options, someone suggested that I plead my case to the Innocence Project in New York. What could they do, besides tell me *no*? That letter was my last hope when I wrote it in 1997.

Fortunately, the Innocence Project was able to help Ronnie and me regain our freedom. While Barry Scheck, Peter Neufeld, and the staff attorneys couldn't give us back the years we lost, they were able to clear our names and help us start over. For that, I am grateful and I thank them every day.

Since my exoneration in April 1999, I have worked with the Innocence Project in New York and in my hometown of Kansas City. My intent is to give back in some small way what Barry, Peter, Gille Ann Rabbin, Jane Siegel, Nina Morrison, Vanessa Potkin, and Elizabeth Vaca gave to me—another chance, a new opportunity, a sense of hope for the future. I have met other men and women who, like me, were convicted on faulty evidence and lost years of their lives behind bars before someone really listened to their cries of innocence and did something to help them. I have met other people who are still calling out for vindication of crimes they did not commit.

Even now, as a free man, my own journey toward justice continues to play out every day. I awaken each morning to the recycled theme of survival, bearing the burdens of anxiety, caution, and an unrelenting fear of the unfamiliar. A knock on my door, a police car driving past my house, the ringing of my phone—each stirs up old memories of a message I don't ever want to hear again.

For these reasons, I was compelled to write *Journey Toward Justice.* I wanted to purge my soul of the emotional poison that has been embedded deep inside me. I also pray that my experiences and this memoir will serve as a guide for other unjustly convicted men and women and their families.

It is to these people, my family, and the Innocence Project, that I dedicate my journey. Many thanks to my editor, Susan Ferguson, for her expertise, forthright nature and disciplined advice. She is my teacher and friend who is always there with guidance when I need it most. Special thanks to Mark Barrett and the entire Carter family for their lasting friendship. My deepest gratitude to John Grisham for his friendship, inspiration and encouragement to write my story. Thanks to Dan Lux who started the wheels in motion by his insightful referral to Kevan Lyon at the Dijkstra Literary Agency. Last but not least, thank you, Indock, for your continued support and patience that helped to propel me forward.

Kansas City, Missouri, May 28, 2006

Dennis Fritz escorted to court during preliminary hearing
11/17/1987

PROLOGUE

On the morning of December 8, 1982, in Ada, Oklahoma, Peggy Carter, the mother of Debbie Sue Carter, a twenty-one-year-old waitress, asked her husband, Charlie, to go to Debbie's apartment to check on her because she had received a phone call from one of Debbie's friends that something wasn't right.

When Charlie climbed the steps to Debbie's second-floor apartment on Eighth Street, he found that the screen door and front door to her apartment were standing open. Broken glass lay on the ground inside and outside of the front door. He called out Debbie's name. No one answered. He peeked inside. In the living room, sofa cushions and a nightgown were strewn on the floor. The words "Jim Smith next will die" were scrawled in some odd sort of paint on one wall. In the kitchen on the table, in the same mysterious substance, was the lettering, "don't look fore us or ealse."

Charlie stepped carefully through the apartment and made his way toward the bedroom door, where he discovered that the bed partially blocked entry to the room. He shoved the door open. The room was in disarray. Clothing, sheets, blankets, and stuffed animals were scattered about on the floor. His daughter's body, nude except for a pair of white socks, lay face down in a space between the bed and the wall. Written in catsup on her back were the words "Duke Gram." He touched her shoulder and started to roll her over. That's when he saw the blood-soaked washcloth stuffed into her mouth. He called her name several times. When she didn't respond, he called the police.

Officers investigating Debbie Carter's murder scene would later find the word "die" written on her chest in fingernail polish—the same substance used to make the writings in the living room and kitchen. An electric cord and belt were found underneath her. An autopsy would reveal numerous bruises on the face, arms, and body, and a number of puncture wounds on her nose and cheeks. The inside of her mouth was cut, and a semi-circular ligature mark was found on her neck. An internal examination revealed internal bruising and a small metal bottle cap inside her rectum. A couple of hairs that were not Debbie's were found on her body, as was a semen sample. A representative of the Pontotoc County medical examiner's office would later testify in court that the cause of death was due to suffocation as a result of the washcloth in her mouth and a ligature tightened around her neck.

Not long after Debbie's death, Peggy and Charlie buried their daughter, but the ramifications of her murder would touch many lives in the decades that followed. Ada in 1982 was not a big city whose collective societal mind was numbed to the horrors of murder. It was a small town, with barely more than 16,000 residents, where death at the hand of another was not commonplace. Many of the people that lived there were descendents of families who had called Ada home for several generations. While the town's history included its share of lynch mobs and killings, and residents' sensitivities weren't always perfect and pure, the cold-blooded murder of Debbie Carter sent ripples of shock and fear throughout the community. People wanted answers. They wanted to go on with their lives.

Ada was an industrial center in a region otherwise primarily rural and agrarian located barely a couple of hours southeast of

Oklahoma City. The town's factories and feed mills provided jobs that demanded physical labor in exchange for unexceptional wages. The business district thrived, thanks to old-fashioned sensibilities and service, and numerous churches and schools did their share to keep people connected. So did the bars and honky tonks. The presence of East Central University was the town's concession to cultural and intellectual advancement.

In 1982 Ada's resources and manpower in the area of law enforcement were still in the dark ages, technologically speaking. Regional law enforcement laboratories had the capability to run scientific tests on evidence, but the high-tech, state-of-the-art forensic criminology of the 21st century seemed—and was—light years away then. Crimes were solved by whatever means available. In the case of Debbie Carter's murder, those means would come back to haunt.

CHAPTER 1

The jangling of the phone ripped through the dark of the living room. Mom, in her recliner in front of the television, glanced back toward me and Aunt Wilma on the couch. We all looked surprised, but none of us made an attempt to get up. We were too stiff and sore from a grueling day of house painting.

"Now, I wonder who that could be this time of night?" Aunt Wilma asked, glancing at the ceramic clock on the nearby desk.

"Remember what you used to say about late-night phone calls?" I reminded Mom. "How they were always news so terrible that it couldn't wait until morning?"

Mom chuckled as the phone rang a second time. I was perfectly content to stare at the television screen while one of them answered the phone. After all, it was their house. I was just visiting. Whoever was calling was going to ask for one of them, anyway.

"Just let it go, Dennis," Mom said to me. "It can go into the answering machine."

"But what if it's bad news?" I asked as the phone rang again.

Mom fanned herself in the recliner. "I'm betting it's someone who wants to hire us to clean something, but maybe you better go get it, seeing as how you're the only one worried."

I rose from the couch, stepping unsteadily over Aunt Wilma's outstretched legs on the footstool and squeezing past Mom's chair. Navigating the cramped bungalow was tough enough in the daytime. At night, with just the glow from the television to light the way, it was like wearing a blindfold to run an obstacle course. The five beers I'd drunk in short order didn't make it easier.

"Dennis," Wilma called as I strode toward the bedroom, "if that's anyone wanting us to clean their house, just tell them to call back in the morning."

"Okay," I hollered back. In the hall, a lanky black cat darted out from the darkness and scared the daylights out of me. Then it disappeared somewhere into Wilma's room, where the phone was on the table by the bed. I turned on the light and lifted the receiver. In my most courteous tone I said, "Hello."

No one responded.

I listened, unsure anyone was on the line. I thought that I heard someone breathing. I started to restate my greeting when a firm yet feminine voice inquired, "Is Dennis at home?"

I didn't recognize the caller. A thought raced through my mind that maybe it was Sherry, my ex back in Ada. Maybe she was disguising her voice to be funny, or maybe she'd put somebody up to checking on me.

I answered curtly, "Yes, he is," still listening for any noise in the background that would tell me who the woman was. All I heard was an eerie silence.

Then the woman asked a second question: "Am I speaking to Dennis Fritz?"

Without hesitation, I replied, "This is he. Who am I speaking with?" My heart began to beat wildly. Who else knew I was here at Mom's in Kansas City? It had to be Sherry.

In a twinkling, I caught wind of another sound, a breath being taken in quickly, followed by the click of the telephone being hung up. That gentle click and the silence that followed reverberated in my eardrums like someone had struck a gong beside my head. I stayed on the line to detect any sound that might illuminate a clue about the mysterious caller, but there was only silence.

I put the receiver back in the cradle and stood for a moment next to Aunt Wilma's bed. My thoughts stayed stuck on Sherry. She hadn't made any effort to contact me in the year we'd been separated, but Ada, Oklahoma, was a small enough town that everyone knew everybody else's business. Maybe somebody had told her that I was visiting in Kansas City and she was trying to dig up some dirt. Not that it mattered. Our short-lived roller-coaster relationship had been a disaster and was pretty much over.

As I was turning out the light, the black cat skittered out from under the bed. I tripped over it in the doorway as it scrambled into the hall. I stubbed my toe on the nightstand. Regaining my composure, I went to the kitchen and grabbed another beer from the fridge. I braced for the interrogation I was sure Mom and Aunt Wilma would give me. After all, it was their phone, and it was late. I made my way back to the couch.

"Son, who were you talking to on the phone? You didn't seem to stay on very long," Mom asked. She cocked her head around to look at me in that way she had. The side of her face was bathed in the flickering blue light from the television.

"I don't know, Mom. Some woman asked me if I was Dennis Fritz, and when I said I was, she hung up. That's really odd, don't you think?"

Straightening in her chair so she could face me and decipher my expression, she answered, "Do you think it had anything to do with Sherry?"

"To tell you the truth, I'm not for sure." I didn't want to get into that discussion again. Mom and Aunt Wilma were full of all sorts of well-meaning advice, but they'd given it to me so many times since the break-up that all it did now was make me crazy.

"Son, I would be careful from now on, and watch what you

say on the telephone. You never know, she might have a recorder hooked up to her phone and try to use something you say to her as ammunition in the divorce."

Aunt Wilma began speaking in her drawn-out monotone that was worse than listening to a 45 record at a 33 speed: "Dennis, I know what— that woman is capable of— and I don't mean to get in— the middle of your business —"

I tuned her out. Aunt Wilma's stammering was hard enough to listen to. I didn't want to get any deeper in her tedious, meandering conversation about a situation that wasn't hers to start with. I stood up.

"I'm going outside for some air," I told them. I didn't say that they were smothering me with concern.

As I was walking out the door, Aunt Wilma got in one more capturing instruction: "Now, remember, Dennis, don't stay up too late— We've got a lot of fishing to do tomorrow. I'm going to set my alarm— and get you both up early— so we can get a good start— and catch some— big ones. Good night. I love you, son."

By the time I stepped out onto the porch, I was stressed out. Standing there, looking at the other houses on that block of Lister Avenue, I realized I was more than a little drunk, too. It was May 8, 1987, a little too muggy, and the moon was a little more than half full. The street, though, was dark and mostly quiet at this hour.

I puzzled over the phone call and the fact that, had I done what I wanted to do when we'd gotten home from the painting job, I would have been out at a bar somewhere, having fun instead of answering the phone. I stewed about the way Mom and Aunt Wilma vetoed my plans, how they had argued that it was the last weekend of my visit, and they wanted me to stay home and rest up for fishing. I was thirty-seven years old, for goodness sake. I'd been on my own since I was sixteen. Coming home to help Mom and Aunt Wilma paint a house was supposed to be enjoyable and to help me look at life more clearly from a distance. All it had done, though, in the past several days was make things more distressing, for any number of reasons—none of which made sense.

I missed Sherry, and I missed Elizabeth who, at thirteen, reminded me so much of her mother, my first wife, my beloved Mary. I missed Mary. Even now, twelve years after a crazy teenaged neighbor broke into our house and shot her on Christmas Day, I still missed her. That kid didn't know how many of my hopes and dreams died on the day that he killed her or how hard it had been to come back from that loss and raise Elizabeth all alone. As a teenager, Elizabeth was better off now living with her maternal grandmother, but that didn't stop me from thinking I was missing some of the best days of her life. I wasn't sure I missed Ada—life had been pretty rocky—but I wasn't sure I belonged in Kansas City, either.

As I stood there in the dark, the strange recurring feeling I had been having for the past couple of weeks crept back into my psyche. I couldn't quite put my finger on it but I was acutely aware that it seemed on the evil end of some apocalyptic scale—like when you're a kid running from the bogeyman in the dark but he only gets closer, no matter how fast or far you run. That's where I was—running as fast and far as I could but getting nowhere.

I savored the peace and quiet on the porch while I drank my beer. After several minutes of staring out into the street, the closeness of the air started to bother me and I made my way back inside to the fridge where another can of brew waited at a temperature cold enough to chill the day's problems. I popped the top and strolled back to the living room. The television was still on, but Mom and Aunt Wilma had headed for bed.

I glanced at the clock on the desk. I was scarcely able to make out the time—11:25. For a moment, I stared at the old sturdy upright desk with its slanted hinged cover. It had been in our family for years. Some silly sentimentality welled up in me. My feelings turned maudlin. Holding that seventh can of Bud in my hand, I had to admit I was not coping well with the stresses in my life. I was perplexed about all the demands and things that kept changing—my marriage, my family, my future. And for the first time, I had let myself slip into the insidious bonds of alcoholism—following in Mom's footsteps—and that scared me. But the thing that bothered me the most was that feeling of falling victim to something momentous but without definition. I just couldn't shake the feeling that I was losing control.

I settled down in the recliner and stared at the television screen. Someone exited the bathroom and stood in the doorway behind me.

"Son—"

"Yes?" Mom's interruption annoyed me, and I didn't bother turning around to look. I thought she and Wilma had finally gone to bed and I had the living room to myself. Or maybe I'd drunk just enough to resent anybody's intrusions. I braced for one more round of conversation before Mom went to bed.

"Son, I'm going to miss you so much after you leave," she said. "I just wish I could have done more for you during your stay."

Reeling from the thoughts I was having, I turned to her and replied, "I love you, too, Mom, and will miss you very much after I'm gone."

For a second, a wave of unexpected longing rose in me. Mom had had numerous health problems in her life, some of them stemming back to when I was born, and I felt badly that I wasn't able to do more to make her feel better physically. Ever since I was a kid, I had felt responsible—a sense she had certainly reinforced over time—and that feeling had only grown stronger as she got older. I wanted so much to stay near her if and when that time came for her to find out what was on the other side. I shook my head. Not wanting the both of us to end up in a crying jag, I fought off the odd mix of resentment and melancholy as I told her, "Mom, I will always love you and remember the good times till the day I die. You get on to bed now and get your beauty sleep. We've got a long day ahead catchin' all those fish."

"Good night, son," Mom replied in hushed tones. "You get some sleep, too." She turned and went to her room.

At last I had the living room to myself. I lifted my head from the recliner to look at the clock again, but its hands were a blur. I really didn't want to go fishing, but it would be my last day at home and Mom really loved to fish. In my mind's eye, I could see her squatting on the bank with the fishing pole between her knees. She loved fishing so much she would sit there for hours, entranced with anticipation about the slightest tug on her pole.

There was a lull in the sound on the television. I thought I heard car doors slamming outside in the street. I turned my head to listen. Sounds like that were unusual for this neighborhood at this time of night. For the weeks that I had been here, this block had been quiet, certainly not the kind of place where there were street noises, especially late. Beer in hand, I got up to investigate. I strolled to the front door, where I had left the interior door open so that fresh air could flow through the screen door to cool down the house.

I jumped back in surprise as I approached the doorway. There on the porch in the dark stood three men—two dressed in suits, one in casual wear—listening at the screen door. All three wore the same unpleasant, discourteous expression, an expression that didn't change as I neared the door.

Half-dazed and confused, I turned on the porch light and uttered, "Can I do something for you gentlemen?"

There was a moment of awkwardness before the man in the polo shirt, the one closest to the screen door, broke his silence by asking in a deep baritone, "Is your name Dennis Fritz?" His question set my nerves on edge as his look penetrated my face. I didn't recognize him. His straightforward approach puzzled me, as though he may have had some business with me before.

From behind me in the hallway I heard Mom call out, "Son, who is… talking… late." I could barely distinguish her words, let alone give her an answer. I stood riveted in curiosity and fear by the triple set of dagger glares from the men who were awaiting my response.

I pushed open the screen door a few inches and looked beyond the men on the porch. Something moved in the front yard. By the glow of the porch light, I was able to make out a handful of men in uniforms crouching on the lawn. I froze as I counted. There were maybe twenty officers altogether, all pointing what appeared to be automatic weapons at me. To my left, and then to my right beyond the screen, more uniformed officers slid into position as I held onto the door handle. Likewise, their weapon barrels were trained at me. I felt woozy. Courage drained from me in a flash as I stammered to answer the interrogator's question:

"Yes, my name is Dennis." I took a breath and blurted out, "What's the matter?"

Without acknowledging my question, one of the strangers in a suit repeated his partner's question: "Is your full name Dennis Fritz?"

Something—I didn't know what—was seriously wrong with this situation. In the seconds before I answered, I determined that they were making a big mistake. I didn't even live here. Wasn't it possible that there were two Dennis Fritzes in this city, and that they had the wrong one? I hadn't done anything that warranted a SWAT team. My mind struggled to understand what was playing out. Every sound, every motion, every smell, every sensation came to me in slow motion, like I was watching a movie on a giant three-dimensional panoramic screen.

"Yes, my name is Dennis Fritz," I answered. My voice shook as I spoke. "What is going on here? Why are all these police pointing weapons at me?"

The man closest to the door lunged for my wrists, grabbing me and twisting my arm and shaking the beer can from my hand. The can fell and beer splashed on my bare feet as the man yanked me through the open doorway. He slammed me face first against the outside wall. With my head inches below the porch light as the screen door closed beside me, I looked past the glare to see an officer standing inches away, his cold dark eyes and gun barrel aimed at my face.

The man behind me twisted the skin on my wrist and bent my arm backwards against my back. The contortion wrenched my spine and shoulder joints with searing pain. I shut my eyes.

"Slowly bring your left arm around behind your back," the man said.

I did. He grabbed it and twisted it. My shoulders ached from the pressure. The man slapped handcuffs on my wrists, the hard steel mashing and tearing my flesh, their grip crunching against my bones.

"Oh my god, my god, why are you doing this to my nephew?" Aunt Wilma screamed from inside as she and Mom approached the doorway. The other man in a suit pulled open the screen door and stepped into the house. He collided with the women and pushed them back with his body. Aunt Wilma's hand reached out around him toward me. I couldn't see Mom but I heard her crying.

The man who was holding me took hold of my shoulder and jerked me around a hundred eighty degrees so that I faced the street.

"Why are you doing this to me?" I demanded.

"Son, you are under arrest," blared the man who restrained me.

"Under arrest? Arrest for what?"

The man continued to stand close behind me. I could feel his suit coat against my skin. "The big one, boy. You are under arrest for murder in the first degree. You have the right to remain silent, and anything you say may be held against you in a court of law. You have the right for an attorney to be present during questioning. If you cannot afford one, one will be appointed for you. Now, do you understand these rights I have given you?"

"I haven't murdered no one. What is happening here? This is a big mistake. I haven't murdered no one!" I shouted to be heard over Mom's wailing and Aunt Wilma's screaming from inside the house.

The man yanked my arms down straight behind me, wrenching my back another time. Armed officers flanked me.

"Do you understand these rights I have given you?" the man asked again.

"Yes, of course I do, but I don't understand why I'm being arrested. I have never murdered no one."

The detective gave me a shove toward the steps. I glanced again at the street. Beyond the line of armed officers, beyond the row of police cars, neighbors stood in small groups, their heads turning to and fro, their fingers pointing in my direction.

Twisting my head to the side to speak to the detective, I said, "I need my shoes." The motion made my head spin so fast I felt faint, like I might stumble off the porch. I staggered.

The detective pulled me up to a halt and ordered someone to find me some shoes. The officers nearest me, the detective, and I huddled at the top of the steps while someone went into the house to get my shoes.

My heart pounded in my chest. I was sure everyone could see it. What if a major blood vessel burst, creating a big bloody mess that my mother, that everyone could see? I tried to pull myself together, hoping that if I fainted and came to, the bad dream would be over. Behind me, armed officers ran inside and through the house, shouting commands to secure all the exits in case there was someone else inside connected with this monstrosity they were laying on me. The SWAT officers maintained a tight band around me, their handguns and automatic weapons aimed at my head. I looked back over my shoulder for Mom. I could hear her but I couldn't see her. Someone must have been standing between us.

Aunt Wilma returned to the door and handed my shoes to an officer, who held them in his hands. The detective nudged me to start down the steps. I was pushed and half-led down the steep stairs to the sidewalk, where we stopped again while the officers in the yard shifted position. The officer carrying my shoes dropped them on the ground in front of me so I could slide my feet into them.

While we were paused, two new voices entered the fray. From behind the SWAT officers, two men emerged. Their identities were unmistakable, and I felt sick at the sight of them. The man in western garb and a large white Stetson hat was Gary Rogers, an investigator with the Oklahoma State Bureau of Investigation. The bald, goggle-eyed man with him was Detective Dennis Smith, major with the Ada Police Department. I had talked to both of them many times in Ada, but that had been years ago and had long since been forgotten. Or so I thought. Side by side, Smith and Rogers strutted and swaggered, smiles of victory on their faces, as they approached me where I stood handcuffed and surrounded. Fear swept through me in a torrent. At last, I understood what this was about.

Chapter 2

In 1982, when I was a widower living in Ada, a young woman named Debbie Sue Carter was sexually assaulted and strangled in her apartment not too far from the rental house where I lived with my daughter, Elizabeth, who was in grade school, and my mother, who had moved in to give us a hand.

We had lived in Ada for less than a year when news of Debbie Carter's death rocked the community. Accounts of the murder scene and ensuing police investigation dominated the newspapers. When the police didn't arrest anyone right away, residents became edgy and feared for their safety.

I had never met Debbie Carter, but news of her death and the sorrow her family must have felt triggered my own painful memories of loss for my beloved Mary, the love of my life and Elizabeth's mother. Mary and I had been married for six years, six months and twenty-four days when she was shot and killed. Mary's very nature had radiated strength, hope and stability—she had a smile from heaven, a laugh that penetrated my soul, an innocence without compromise. I missed her more than anyone would ever know.

At the time Debbie Carter was killed, I was teaching science and coaching football, track, and basketball sixty miles away at the junior high school in Noble. I spent a lot of time on the road. As the investigation into the young woman's death dragged on through the winter months, I became increasingly protective of Elizabeth and Mom. I had to know where they were every minute. I didn't want to lose the only family I had left.

In March 1983, when the Ada police called me in for questioning, I figured the least I could do was to be helpful. I was nervous and apprehensive when I arrived at the police station. I was directed to a room where two plainclothes officers silently paced. The taller man instructed me to have a seat.

"My name is Gary Rogers," he said. "I'm with the Oklahoma State Bureau of Investigation." He nodded to the bald man who, by this time, had sat down. "This is Dennis Smith, a detective with the Ada Police Department. Dennis, we asked you to come down here today to answer some questions about something you may have some knowledge of."

"I'm willing to cooperate in any way that I can," I replied, trying to appear relaxed.

"Tell us where you live."

"I divide my time between a rental house in Ada, where my mom lives with my daughter Elizabeth, and my teaching job at Noble, where I teach junior-high science. During the day, I teach classes. In the evenings, when I'm not coaching football, basketball, or track, I sometimes work as a private contractor in Norman, where I remove dead trees from people's property. I own a small travel trailer that's parked on the school grounds, and sometimes I sleep there, when I'm not driving back and forth from Ada."

"Do you know a man by the name of Ronald Keith Williamson?"

"Sure. I met Ronnie some time ago."

"When did you first meet him?"

"I believe it was in November of 1981."

"Dennis, tell Detective Smith and myself about the events of how you and Ronnie met, and where you were working at that time, if you were."

"No problem. In July 1981, I accepted a position in Konawa to teach junior high school science and I moved there with my daughter from Durant. Every two or three weeks, I would get a sitter for Elizabeth and drive to Ada to get away from the pressures of teaching. Junior high's not an easy job, and I was raising Elizabeth by myself. One Friday in November, or maybe it was a Saturday, I got a babysitter for Elizabeth and then drove on into Ada. I was going into the Love's convenience store when I noticed a man—Ronnie—sitting in an old green Buick, playing a guitar. We talked a bit about his guitar, and I mentioned that I had my guitar in the backseat of my car. He invited me to his house to play a little music."

"Dennis, let me interrupt you," said Rogers. "Can you tell us if you and Ronnie became good friends after that?"

"Excuse me, but I would like to know what this is all about. Why am I being questioned about Ronnie?"

Smith spoke up. "Are you aware that there was a girl, a young woman, murdered in your neighborhood in December of last year?"

"I read about it in the newspaper."

"Where were you teaching when you read this in the paper?"

"I was teaching at another school, at the junior high in Noble, where I've been working since last August—August of 1982."

"Why did you leave your teaching assignment at Konawa?"

I hesitated before answering. I was embarrassed to tell the truth concerning my termination.

"Dennis, is there any reason why you don't want to answer this question?"

I shook my head. "I just had some difficulties from a few of the students."

"What type of difficulties?" Smith inquired.

"Well, after a couple of students tried to blow up my chemistry class, I had to become a little more strict with these troublemakers, and they retaliated to the point of becoming major disrupters."

"Dennis, did that cause you a great amount of distress?"

"No, I believe I handled it in the right way. I briefly talked to the two male students after class and told them that I could not tolerate this behavior in my classroom."

"Did this seem to eliminate the problem?" Rogers asked.

Red flags flashed in my mind. I didn't answer. They must already know that I fired a ten-gauge shotgun in the air when a bunch of students egged my house on Halloween. That incident, plus other things, only made matters worse and caused me to resign before the end of the school year. They've got to know that, or they wouldn't be asking. I looked first at Smith and then at Rogers.

"My problems at Konawa have nothing to do with Ronnie."

Rogers snorted. "You seem to be evading the question. If you will fully cooperate with us, we can get this over with without taking up too much of your time."

"I'll try my best, but I've never been questioned about a murder before."

"Dennis, have we said anything that gives you any reason to believe that we suspect you of being the murderer? But, as long as you have brought this up, I will ask you: Did you have anything to do with the murder of Debbie Sue Carter?"

"Mr. Rogers, I have never killed nor thought about killing another human being in my life. I won't even hunt animals because I don't want to be responsible for their death."

Smith's gaze seemed to penetrate my thoughts as he leaned dramatically across the table with his thick, fleshy hands clasped and a phony smile curling on his lips. "Dennis," he said, "if there's anything you want to tell us about Ronnie that's been bothering you, we want you to get it off your mind. We are here to help you, and it would also be a big relief for you to tell us what it is that bothers you concerning Ronnie. We believe that you may know something that you've not told anyone else. Please think about this carefully before answering."

I stared at him. I wasn't sure what to say.

Rogers abruptly rose from his seat and placed his palms flat upon the table. Leaning in toward me like Smith had done, he said, "Do you understand what Miranda rights are?"

"Yes, I've heard them mentioned a few times on television," I hastily replied.

"Then, as you are aware, you have not heard us read you these rights here today, so basically this means that you are not under formal interrogation. If you were, we would definitely read you these rights. Consider this, Dennis, before you answer Detective Smith's prior question. Do you remember the question asked?"

"Of course I do, Mr. Rogers, and there's nothing I know about Ronnie that is bothering me in any way. How many more questions are you going to ask me?"

The detectives' faces appeared sullen and grim as their eyes narrowed and their brows lowered. A moment of silence passed before Rogers said, "We want you to know, Dennis, that we are not through with you, and it would be advisable for you not to leave town any time soon. If there's anything that you think of after leaving this office, you can contact us here at the station." He pushed back his chair and stood up. "You are free to leave."

On the way to my car, I thought about Ronnie. Why would they be interested in him? Ever since I'd met him, he'd come across as the life of the party. He was always up, always on, always ready for fun. He could be a little impulsive, but weren't we all a little crazy sometimes? Especially when we were drinking? And Ronnie drank a lot. Still, there was nothing about his behavior I associated with anything dangerous or life-threatening, not like these guys were suggesting.

I recalled one occasion not long after we first met when Ronnie Keith that's what I called him—called me in Konawa on a Friday afternoon and said he wanted to go out and drink beer. Elizabeth had already made plans to spend the night with one of her school friends, so I dropped her off and drove to Ada to pick up Ronnie at his house. To my amazement, he answered the door wearing a double-breasted suit with shoes so shiny I could actually see reflections in them. He was carrying his guitar case in one hand and an open bottle of beer in the other. He put his guitar in the backseat, jumped in the front seat, and off we went.

"Hey, Dennie Leon, what's happenin', man? Listen, I just got back from Dallas after having several attorney conference calls involving a substantial amount of money."

I thought he was joking. "Ronnie Keith, what were you doing in Dallas?"

"Never mind, Dennie Leon. Right now, let's go down to Love's store and get some beer and talk about getting ahold of some of them good-lookin' college girls."

Ronnie liked going to the campus at Durant to look at the women who attended school there. A couple of times we'd gotten lucky and found gals to party with. It was harmless fun.

"Ronnie Keith, I didn't know you were an attorney," I said, trying to tease out an explanation.

"Oh, Dennie Leon, I've got good deals comin' your way and I've got the bucks tonight to make them happen."

I laughed it off. He didn't like being questioned outright. He'd get edgy and clam up or want to talk about something else. But what he was saying didn't really matter, anyway. Ronnie's off-the-wall remarks didn't make sense, but they were funny and he made me laugh, and that was all that was important. Besides, I didn't take everything he said to heart. I had responsibilities; I had been a good dad to Elizabeth—I was there for her when she got out of school, fixed supper every night, and tended to her emotional and social needs like a father should. Ronnie was just a friend, somebody who gave me a reason to get out of Konawa every so often, and that was good. I'd been in other small towns, but Konawa made me feel awkward and alienated whenever I was out in public, like the townspeople didn't take kindly to any strangers that moved in.

When Ronnie and I arrived at the Love's convenience store, he reached in his pants pocket and pulled out a fistful of wadded-up bills. His luminous brown eyes sparkled with delight as he turned in my direction and handed me a twenty.

"Here, Dennie Leon, go get us a couple of six packs of that good-tastin' imported beer you like to drink. And get me a pack of cancer sticks 'cause I'm almost out."

"Okay, Ronnie Keith, I'll be right back. Don't you go nowhere."

I went into the store and headed straight back to the bathroom. As fate would have it, there was someone waiting by the door. I had to pee so bad that I could almost taste it, so I reluctantly got behind the man and waited for my turn. Standing there with my jaw tensed and my legs practically crossed, I turned halfway around and happened to notice a few people up in front by the cash register laughing loudly and looking at something outside the store. At this point, nothing short of a store robbery or a car driving through the plate glass window would have budged me out of my hunkered position. When the bathroom door swung open, I waddled inside and forgot about the crowd.

Exiting the bathroom a moment later, I grabbed a couple six packs from the cooler, rounded the aisle, and headed for the register. Nearly everyone in the store was standing alongside the windows looking out at Ronnie, who was standing in the parking lot in his fancy suit and strumming his guitar while he serenaded the customers. I rushed to the front counter. In the parking lot, a couple groups of people had gathered to watch Ronnie's sidewalk performance. I shook my head. *Shit.* I plopped the beer on the counter and looked at the cashier whose face was twisted into an angry look.

"Sir, do you know that man out there?" the cashier asked.

"Uh, well, yes, I guess I do," I hesitantly replied.

"I'm fixin' to call the cops if you don't get him out of here. He's causing a disturbance and is bothering the customers. What's the matter with him, anyway? Is he drunk, or is he on some kind of drugs, or is he crazy?"

I had to think fast and come up with something good, because I figured this lady meant every word she was saying.

"Ma'am, I appreciate your concern and I apologize that this has happened. He's only had a couple of beers, but he loves playing his guitar so much and he wants to turn professional so bad that sometimes he gets kind of carried away."

"I don't care what he wants or doesn't want. If you don't get him out of here right now, I'm callin' the cops, and I mean it!"

"Okay, ma'am, thank you. Give me a pack of Marlboros. Here's money for the beer. I'll get him out of here."

I set the twenty on the counter, grabbed the beers and smokes, and rushed out the front door, hollering at Ronnie to get in the car because the cops were on their way. We got into the car and sped from the parking lot.

Ronnie was really pumped up and proud of himself for having given such a fine performance. He appeared undisturbed by the commotion he had caused.

"Ronnie, what in the world were you doing back there?" I asked him when we were a few blocks away.

"Dennie Leon, don't you worry. We're gonna go and make some music tonight and drink a few of those cold beers you got." When he opened a bottle, beer spewed out in all directions, but he didn't seem to notice. He continued, "Let's go to your old stompin' grounds and find a couple of pretty cuties at the college. I need some of that soft feminine touch tonight, Dennie Leon, and I'm in the mood to make some good music and do some of that Bo Jangle dancin'."

"Okay, Ronnie Keith, we'll be there in a couple of hours, so hold on to your hat and don't look back," I declared as I headed toward the highway.

There was magic in the air as we headed south toward Durant. The slanted rays of the afternoon sun were warm and embracing and there wasn't a cloud in the sky. It was the kind of early October day that you wanted to last forever. Ronnie smoked and drank the whole trip. Because I was driving, I limited myself to one beer for every three that he drank. For two hours Ronnie gave a nonstop performance of Top 40 hits. His guitar playing and singing slowed his alcohol consumption a little, but he was still pretty well lit by the time we reached Durant. We cruised around the university to see if there was anything going on. There wasn't. The place was eerily quiet.

Durant was a modest, mostly middle-class town supported by the college, tourists visiting Lake Texoma, and families that worked in the factories and shopped at the businesses downtown. It had another side, too — a redneck element that triggered many barroom brawls in the local taverns. This was definitely a concern for me because Ronnie, in his double-breasted suit with his boisterous attitude, struck me as a magnet for trouble. I most assuredly wanted to stay away from the cowboy bars, so I took Ronnie to a college bar that I used to frequent. After a couple of beers, Ronnie's flamboyancy gained strength as he started telling everyone at the bar that he was a hotshot attorney from Dallas. The tales he told left most of them with their mouths hanging open and their heads nodding. Ronnie could out-bullshit the bullshitter. His effervescent way of communicating, especially after he had downed a little alcohol, elicited confidence and energy, and sometimes Ronnie actually believed his own lies. Usually, though, once he reached that plateau, he became bored and wanted to move to another location. That's what happened.

"Dennie Leon, I'm ready to get out of here and find our little honeys," Ronnie whispered to me after a while. "My guitar is getting lonely settin' by itself in the back of your car. We need to get somewhere and make that good ol' music for all these fine Durant people."

"I'm more than ready, Ronnie Keith. Let's get out of here and find out where it's happenin'."

As we drove past the high-rise dorms, Ronnie said, "Pull over there, Dennie Leon, and let's check that basketball game out."

"What's the deal? I thought you wanted to check out another club and get some of those pretty babes. Isn't that what you said?" Watching a men's basketball game outdoors was the last thing I wanted to do when there was the possibility of meeting a couple of nice-looking gals. But I pulled over and allowed Ronnie his request.

Ronnie got out of the car and retrieved his guitar from the backseat. I stayed in the driver's seat and watched as he approached the basketball court with his guitar strapped around his neck. I was reluctant to join him. I didn't want to interfere with the game. Secondly, all of the players were black and I didn't know how they would react if two white guys, especially one in a double-breasted suit strumming his guitar and singing, walked up and watched their game.

As Ronnie got closer to the court, I got the feeling I should be a little closer to him in case something happened, and I moved my car so that it was about thirty yards away from the court. I got out and leaned against the front fender, hoping there would be no confrontations. That was the last thing I needed—to have my ass beaten to a pulp.

By the time Ronnie made it to court's edge, all of the ballplayers had turned their heads and were eyeing him suspiciously, but they kept playing, and so did he. They did not seem to be overly distracted by him, even when he started walking up and down the sidelines, playing his guitar and doing a musical play-by-play commentary of the game.

Vivid images formed in my mind as to what the players' reactions would be, and I braced for the worst. Instead of becoming annoyed or bent out of shape, however, the players became more aggressive and appeared more confident in their abilities. I would have never dreamed of a better outcome. Minutes later, Ronnie walked up to the car to get another beer.

Shortly thereafter, the game broke up and five of the players came over to us, extending their hands to congratulate Ronnie for his fine-tuned commentator's skills. Ronnie wasted no time. He introduced himself as a criminal attorney from Dallas. All eyes were fixed on him as he eloquently pontificated about his legal expertise: "I am so proud to be here tonight in the presence of such a fine group of aspiring, athletically inclined young men. I am adorned with recourse to politically facilitate to you the most intricate and highly publicized interactions within the law. Needless to say, you fine young men are representative of an enterprise that travels in a circle around the globe without the due respect or favor from our prospective and highly enlightened judicial capacities. I have traveled here today to give birth to a time of astute relaxation but nevertheless to promulgate the truth and formidable destruction tendering the inflexibilities within our crowned judicial systems. It is my great pleasure and reward to bestow upon your personage the wonderfully wet and abundantly flavorful substance existing in a chilled bottle of beer."

With their eyes wide and mouths agape, the players nodded their heads up and down in mesmerized fascination. They didn't realize that Ronnie had just offered them a beer. I had not said a word up to this point—not because I didn't want to but because trying to get a word in edgewise while Ronnie was talking was nearly impossible. When he stopped talking for a moment to take a drink, I introduced myself as Ronnie's friend and asked the players if they would like a beer.

"Sure, man, that would be great. We really worked up a sweat playin' ball," one of the guys answered.

While Ronnie walked around the car to get the guys more beer, the tallest ballplayer stepped slightly forward and asked me,

"Say, man, this cat is really on fire. Is he a good lawyer down there in Dallas?"

I didn't want to perpetuate something that was not true but I didn't want to expose Ronnie as a fake, so I said, "I haven't known Ronnie very long but I know that he considers himself to be a very good attorney."

Ronnie handed out cold beers to everyone and for the next thirty minutes did ninety-nine percent of the talking. The ballplayers were thoroughly impressed with him. Of course, in Ronnie's mind this was nothing more than just having a good time, with no intention of doing any harm or causing any misgivings. On the other hand, there was a strong possibility that at that moment Ronnie himself believed that he was an attorney from Dallas.

That, then, was how I remembered Ronnie. I hadn't seen him in a few months, but I was pretty sure he wasn't dangerous. As I stood in the police station parking lot that morning and tried to figure out what exactly Rogers and Smith had been after, I reassured myself that Ronnie was unpredictable but harmless. There was no reason to believe he was capable of whatever they thought he had done.

A month after my first visit to the police station, I received a second invitation. This time they wanted me to come in because there were some procedures they wanted to discuss with me. I voluntarily agreed to assist them. At the station, I was taken to a room, where Agent Rogers asked me if I was willing to submit hair and saliva samples for comparison testing. I agreed to do so and signed a written consent of approval. Rogers left the room momentarily and returned wearing rubber gloves and carrying several small manila envelopes and a roll of white paper strips.

"Here's the procedure, Dennis. I want you to pull out as much hair as you can get, say twenty or so hairs from each area, starting with your head, then your forearms, armpits, chest, legs, pubic hair, and finally, just a few hairs from inside your nose and buttocks. Then, after we get that done, I want you to lick several of these white strips of paper for me."

"What are the white strips of paper for?"

"They will show whether you are a secretor or a non-secretor."

"What do those terms mean?"

"Basically, Dennis, eighty percent of people are secretors, meaning that they show their blood type in their body fluids. The other twenty percent of people are classified as non-secretors because they do not show their blood type in any of their body fluids."

I was a science teacher, not a scientist; his explanation sounded plausible. For over an hour, I yanked out the requested hairs from my body, using my forefinger and thumb and a firm grip. Rogers took the hairs, placed them in the separately labeled envelopes, and sealed them. Not only was this a painful experience for me but I was humiliated by having a stranger watch as I pulled hairs from the exposed regions of my pubic area and ass. Frustrating, too, was the realization that I was becoming deeply involved in a murder investigation, even though all I was doing was trying to help. I finished licking the paper strips. Rogers thanked me and told me, like before, that I was free to leave.

Throughout the remainder of the week, his words "free to leave" served as a distraction. Even the simplest of things, like going to the store and buying groceries, paying the bills, even going out to eat at Polo's, a popular Mexican restaurant in Ada, became a drudgery as I wondered, *At what point might Agent Rogers tell me I am not free to leave?* Instead of waking up feeling refreshed in the mornings, the first thing I would think of would be the frightening reminder that I was part of an investigation of a murder of a girl I had never met.

On a Tuesday during the last week of April, I was midway through my fourth-hour earth science class when Jess Wilburn, the school principal, opened my classroom door and asked me to accompany him to his office. Another teacher followed him, taking my place in the classroom as I left.

After the principal and I were seated in the office, Mr. Wilburn slowly raised his eyes and said, "Mr. Fritz, after careful consideration the school officials have decided to terminate you from your present position at this school. I want you to know that this is not my decision. Earlier today I met with Bill Martin, the superintendent, and he gave me explicit instructions to immediately inform you of the board's decision."

Stunned, I stammered, "What reason am I being terminated for?"

"From what I understand, Mr. Fritz, a couple of days ago the police authorities in Ada notified Mr. Martin that you are currently under investigation for a murder that occurred near where you reside. It was brought to Mr. Martin's attention that you falsified your hiring application, having been previously convicted of a felony on cultivation of marijuana."

"Yes, that part is true, but the reason I lied on the application was because I needed a job, and the charge was over ten years old." I thought back: I had been twenty-two when I was arrested and convicted for growing a few pot plants out behind the house. I'd been given a two-year suspended sentence, I'd completed my probation, and that was that. Nothing ever came of it after that. It didn't seem like a big deal.

"But as far as me being involved in a murder investigation," I said to Wilburn, "that is also true, but I have no knowledge whatsoever about any murder. From what I understand, the police are investigating a lot of people down there, and I have been unfairly brought in on this."

Wilburn gave no indication that he had any compassion or sympathy for my situation. He looked like he was looking through me as he said, "At this point, Mr. Fritz, it doesn't matter. The board has already made its decision. I was authorized to let you know that we will either accept a formal resignation from you or we will have to outright terminate you. It will be to your advantage to go ahead and resign, since you could get the remaining amount of money in your contract. Mr. Fritz, I will shoot squarely with you and let you know that if you try to fight this decision in court, you will be wasting your time and money because you fraudulently misrepresented information in your application. It's entirely your decision."

"Okay, Mr. Wilburn, I'll go ahead and give you my formal resignation at this time."

After sliding some papers across his desk, the principal remarked, "Mr. Fritz, you need to look these over and sign them if this is your intent. Then you are free to go."

On that day, as I walked through the junior high school hallway toward the exit, I felt like a thick cloud of doom was hanging over my head. As I opened my car door, the words "free to go," like "free to leave," taunted my vulnerable spirit.

Two months later, in early June, I was called again by the Ada police and asked to take a lie detector test in Oklahoma City. The questions that OSBI Agent Rusty Featherstone asked of me had to do directly with Debbie Carter: Did I know her, was I present when she was assaulted, did I know who killed her? I told him the truth—that I didn't know Debbie Carter and I had nothing to do with her death. Featherstone told me after the test that I'd failed it.

Agent Rogers was right there to interrogate me and provoke me to confession. When I told him I had taken a Valium before the test to calm me down, he grew furious and told me I'd have to take the test again. Four days later, I took a second polygraph test, but the result was the same. Featherstone and Rogers told me I failed that one, too, even though I told the truth.

Nothing came of the lie detector tests, though. Nothing came of any of my voluntary visits to the police station to help clear up what I believed was their confusion—except my life was wrecked. I couldn't find work. The next couple of years were hell.

I tried to make ends meet and raise Elizabeth, but my deliberate deception dogged me. I couldn't get another teaching job because I had lied on my application at Noble; that mistake followed me like the plague. I wound up in menial, low-paying, survival jobs as a machine operator at the local plastics manufacturing plant, at a steakhouse as a short-order cook, and as a nurse's aide in a local nursing home. In summer, I even shoveled shit at the rodeo that performed at Ada. Mary's mother stepped up to help Mom and me with Elizabeth, and together, slowly, we started turning our lives around.

In 1984, the state of terror in Ada escalated when another woman, Donna Denice Haraway, was abducted from a local store and presumed dead. Even before her body was discovered, her murder resulted in the death-row convictions of two local men, Tommy Ward and Karl Fontenot, who reportedly confessed. The Haraway murder was highly publicized in early 1987 in the book, *The Dreams of Ada,* written by journalist Robert Mayer. His work turned the floodlights on Ada and the town's law enforcement and judicial systems. The book was also an ugly reminder to the locals that the Carter murder remained unsolved, and that threw people and local authorities into a frenzy to find the person or persons responsible for the death of Debbie Carter.

CHAPTER 3

On Mom's front porch in Kansas City then, on that night, the frenzy reached fever pitch. When Rogers and Smith appeared out of the barrage of gun barrels and uniforms, I understood that they had decided that I—and probably Ronnie—were in some way responsible for the death of that girl I had never met.

I was ushered down the sidewalk by the SWAT team to the open door of a squad car on the street. Straining, I looked back over my shoulder and saw, on the porch behind a detective, Mom standing on one side with Aunt Wilma on the other. As I was shoved into the front seat, my hands cuffed behind me, I heard the grating laughter of Smith and Rogers. Someone slammed my door, and the laughter stopped. For a moment, there was silence.

Then Smith got into the backseat to provide guard for the detective-driver, who got in and steered the car steadily away from the curb. I twisted my aching body around for a final look at my blessed mother and aunt. Only Aunt Wilma was waving. Mom stood stiff and staring, bewildered, a look of fear on her face. I so desperately wanted to free my hands and wrap my aching arms around her and tell her everything would be okay. As I looked at her, I remembered the time she told me about my father. When I was two months old, she had said, Walter Ervin Fritz left her for another woman. When I was twelve, he reappeared in our lives, moving in with us like he had never left. Fritz, as most everyone called him, was not a very expressive person when it came to sharing his feelings. Walt, as I called him, never did any of the things with me that most fathers would do with their sons. He worked twelve- to fourteen-hour shifts in some restaurant each day, and when night came, he hit the taverns and chased women. That left very little time for him to spend with Mom or me. Ultimately, he moved out before the year was over, leaving Mom a second time. Now I felt like I was leaving her, too.

Before I swung back around in my seat to face forward again, I glanced behind me and caught a glimpse of the sinister Detective Smith. There was a way he could look at me that made me shudder—a long, judging stare accompanied by silence. That's what he was doing from his place in the backseat.

When the squad car was a block away from the house, I cautiously advanced a question to him: "Does this have anything to do with Ronnie Williamson?"

Smith answered, "Yes. You know better than to ask a question like that right now. Just be quiet. Everything will be explained to you when we get you down to the police station. Is there something you want to tell me before we get there?"

Inhaling deeply, I proclaimed, "I'm an innocent man. You'll never get away with this. You've made a huge mistake, and before it's all over, you'll be pounding the beat on some street corner."

Before Smith had a chance to respond, the plainclothes detective-driver tilted his head toward me and said, "We're not going to beat you up or nothing. This isn't like in the movies." Continuing in his mocking manner, he added, "We're human just like everyone else, and we can understand when someone makes a big mistake. The best thing for you to do is just be completely honest with us. Everything will go a lot smoother for you if you do.

You seem like a pretty intelligent individual, so I wouldn't, if I were you, try to run a con job on us."

"I don't know what you are talking about," I argued. "I never killed anyone, and I have no intention of admitting to something that I didn't do." Underneath, fear surged through my body and mind. I couldn't believe this was happening. I wanted to believe that this would all be cleared up when we got to the police station. "Smith," I said, "just because you can't solve a crime, you have to pick on innocent people like you did with Ward and Fontenot."

Smith perked up at the mention of the two names. "Fritz, you know they were guilty as hell. As for you, we have strong evidence that will prove your guilt in murdering that girl. You're in big, big trouble, boy. The best thing for you would be to level with us and tell us the whole story before it's too late. If you cooperate with us, then we might be able to help you out."

I stopped talking and looked straight ahead at the dark, near-empty street as we traveled toward the police station. In my wildest dreams, I would have never guessed that I would be in a police car, about to be booked on capital murder charges. Things would get cleared up at the station. I was sure of it. This was all a huge mistake.

The reflected rays of the squad car's headlights cast an eerie glow on the massive multistory building that was Kansas City's downtown police department headquarters. The pain in my wrists and shoulders had intensified to a level of excruciating agony as the slowing car veered and turned into a dimly lit underground garage. Police vehicles of all sizes, shapes, and colors were parked within the suffocating, tomb-like enclosure. My heart pounded as the car came to a standstill.

Smith interrupted the silence by taunting, "Well, now, Mr. Dennis, here we are at your new home—at least until we get you back in Oklahoma, and believe me, we will get you back."

I was wrested from the front seat and forced to wait beside the car while several more police cars pulled into the garage and parked. When the remaining entourage of officers surrounded me, I was escorted toward a door.

"Just walk on ahead, up the entrance ramp very slowly," the detective-driver ordered.

Because of the cuffs binding my wrists and the awkward way I had sat in the car, my body was bent at a forty-five degree angle. My back ached, my shoulders seized in spasms, I could no longer feel my hands or arms. I concentrated on my feet and staggered like a blind man to the dirty entrance door, which was buzzed open.

"Just move straight ahead until you come to the end of the wall," the detective-driver ordered.

I walked forward in sullen silence, all the while screaming inside, *Get these handcuffs off, please!* My mouth felt dry as cotton. Minutes blurred as I stood dazed and stooped with my face toward the wall. After a length of time, someone threw my shirt over my shoulder and removed the handcuffs. I shook off the penetrating pain and stood straight.

"Strip it down, all the way down to your birthday suit, darlin'," a grizzled guard barked. "Give me your clothes, possessions, and any weed you got stuck up your ass."

I handed him my shirt. I took my jeans off and stood there naked in front of strangers while the guard took my wallet, belt, and pocket change and placed the items in an envelope. "We keep these," he said, smirking. He shook out my clothes, dropped them on the floor, and kicked them back to me when he was done. "Okay, put these back on."

When I was dressed again, a second guard approached and said, "Okay, Fritz, we're going to take a little elevator ride, so follow the yellow line around the corner, stop at the set of elevators, and don't turn around."

As I looked toward the corner, Smith appeared with a plainclothes cop I hadn't seen before. The fluorescent light from the ceiling reflected off his bald head. Smiling sadistically, Smith commanded, "Move ahead, Dennis. We're goin' upstairs. It took a long time for us to catch up with you, but now we are going to execute you for what you did."

I was sobering up but I resisted the urge to make some disparaging comment and followed the yellow line instead. The guards and I took the elevator up a floor. The scene in the hallway that led to the booking desk was horrifying. Loud shrieking noises came from inside some office; it was impossible to tell where or why. Stinking drunks on hands and knees hovered low to the tile floor. A trio of what I assumed were prostitutes leaned against the wall. I was led to the booking desk and told to go to the rear office to be fingerprinted.

The officer in charge of fingerprinting was a black cop with a receding hairline and an overhanging beer belly. Without hesitation, he uttered, "Give me your full name and where you live."

"My name is Dennis Leon Fritz, and I currently reside at 2034 Lister Avenue here in Kansas City, Missouri."

"Your age?"

"I'm thirty-seven."

"Mr. Fritz, how long have you lived in Kansas City?"

"I have been at this location for about a month. I'm from Oklahoma originally."

"It says here you were arrested on a charge of first-degree murder charges. Were you in flight or attempting to flee from prosecution?"

"No, sir, I came to Kansas City to help my mother and aunt with a house-painting job. I did not know anything about there being a warrant for my arrest."

"What town in Oklahoma are you from?"

"Is all of this questioning necessary?"

Looking at me from the corner of his eye, as if I had just said something confrontational, he answered me by saying, "This is all police procedure and we don't have time to lollygag around, so let's get on with this preliminary bullshit and get you into your cell."

The sergeant ordered me to the fingerprinting table. He squeezed dark blue ink onto a small pad. Then, working with my fingers one at a time, he flattened each fingertip and rolled it onto the inked surface and then onto a six- by eight-inch identification card. Upon finishing the last roll of my pinky finger, he commented, "Mr. Fritz, I hope you realize you are in very serious trouble, and the sooner you can get an attorney to represent you, the better off you will be. Do you know at this time if you are going to fight extradition charges?"

I vaguely remembered hearing the word *extradition* when I was a kid and watched the *FBI* series that starred Efrem Zimbalist, Jr. My mind was already going through an upheaval of doubts and dismay. In a rambling state of fear and uncertainty, I was barely able to come up with an explanation as to why I shouldn't be in the police station in Kansas City, let alone think so far as to why I shouldn't be extradited to Oklahoma.

The desk sergeant repeated his question, this time with more authority in his tone: "Are you going to fight your extradition to Oklahoma?"

"To tell you the truth, Sergeant, I don't know much about extradition and haven't had time to consider it. What do you think I need to do?"

Looking down at his newly completed identification cards, he hesitantly answered, "Son, I'm not your lawyer. Anything as serious as this should be discussed with an attorney before you make up your mind. I will say this. If you did not commit the murder, you have nothing to fear. It might be to your advantage to go on back and get this cleared up as soon as possible. In a lot of instances, charges have been dropped in cases such as yours. Cooperating with the authorities will always go in your favor. On the other hand, it might also be to your advantage to buy some time by fighting extradition. Like I said, I'm no attorney, and have never been in the position that you are now. Just do yourself a big favor and think it over very carefully before making a decision. From now on, you will have to make lots of important decisions." He led me back to the booking desk.

Following booking, I was placed in a holding cell with two benches and a commode. The air stank of urine and sweat. Several black men sat in one corner, exchanging words filled with hostility and defiance. Beads of perspiration rose on my skin. *Oh Lord, why have you forsaken me like this? What have I done in my life to deserve this? Please, God, take care of my family and bring forth my innocence, in the name of Jesus!*

I paced in the small enclosure, staying as far away as I could from the other detainees. Thirty minutes passed before two police officers came to get me.

"Come on, Fritz, you're wanted upstairs," the heavy cop bellowed as he unlocked the wire mesh door. As I was making way to leave, someone in the cell called to me, "Say, man, bring back some cigarettes." Without responding, I walked out into a hallway filled with fresh air and was escorted into the waiting elevator, where we went to the fourth floor. With a detective at each side, I was ushered into a room with office desks and chairs.

"Mr. Fritz, sit down in that chair," the ruddy-faced cop ordered. He added with a wry smile, "And don't get any funny ideas of tryin' to escape, 'cause we'll be watchin' you like a bug under a microscope."

Yeah, I bet you will be, you fat McDonald's-eatin' fucker. By now, I fully realized what was coming down on me—a mountain of unleashed, flaming granite. I had nowhere to run.

"I would like to use the phone to check on my mother," I demanded. "She was very shaken up over this bullshit arrest, so may I have my one phone call, or do I get shafted on that, too?"

After he had finished emptying his coffee cup, the thinner dark-haired cop finally spoke: "Sir, you may have your one phone call but you are limited to five minutes. Do you understand?" He set a phone down in front of me.

Without answering him, I quickly picked up the receiver

and dialed my mother and aunt's number. My mother immediately picked up the phone and said, "Son, is that you?"

"Yes, Mom," I said in a gentle, affirming voice. Because there was so much that I wanted to tell her, I hesitated before continuing. I know that the sound of strength in my voice would greatly influence her emotional state. "Mom, I want you to know that I'm okay. I'm up here in the city police department and they're getting ready to talk with me, so, please try to keep a clear head and get some rest if you can." Mom's voice started shaking and broke into a daunting series of quivering cries. I had never heard that depth of rending heartache from her. I reached down to the core of my soul and firmly stated, "Mom, you and Wilma and the good Lord know I am innocent and did not commit this murder. You and I have been through hell and back together, and this time will be no different. Don't crumble on me now. We will get this worked out, and the truth will win."

"Son, I love you so much. And you know that if I could, I would take your place without a thought."

"I know that, Mom. I would do the very same thing for you."

"Fritz, your time is up, so make it quick and get off the phone," the fat cop said. "Your boys from Oklahoma are about ready to talk to you."

"Mom, I gotta go," I said. "I love you very much and I'll try to call you tomorrow if I can." Ever so reluctantly, I said goodbye and hung up the phone.

From where I sat, I could easily see the Oklahoma officers in an adjacent glass-framed cubicle. They were shuffling through their briefcases, withdrawing papers, and occasionally glancing in my direction as if I were their prey. Finally, after several uneasy minutes, Smith and Rogers abruptly stood up and exited the cubicle and went into another room. The dark-haired cop nudged me down the corridor toward an open door at the end of the hallway.

"In here, Fritz," he said.

I entered the room, which was neat and clean and smelled of disinfectant. Smith and Rogers stood next to each other. Rogers motioned for me to sit in a chair at the table. I sat down and made myself comfortable. I closely studied the detectives' eyes in an attempt to discern what they might be thinking. Rogers began pacing. Smith sat down across from me. No one spoke. As the moments ticked by, I became very uncomfortable.

In a smooth confident tone, Rogers began the interrogation by saying, "Dennis, there is no need for introductions here. I want you to know that I have worked on this for five years and have put a lot of effort into solving this case. I also want you to know that you have the right to remain silent, and if you so desire an attorney to be present, we will go no further in this line of questioning. Do you fully understand these rights I have just described?"

Answering, I stated, "I certainly understand and I do not desire an attorney to be present at this time."

Rogers walked across the room to a table where a tan briefcase lay open. From it, he retrieved a piece of printed paper. Slowly turning to me, he expounded, "What I have here, Dennis, is a legal form called your Miranda rights. Since you have stated that you do not wish for an attorney to be present, do you have any objection to signing it after you have had a chance to read it?"

I took the form from Rogers and thoroughly read through its contents.

"Do you have a pen?" I asked.

"Sure thing, Dennis. I know you are going to do the right thing in this situation, and personally speaking, I'm very proud of you. I just wanted you to know that," Smith said as he took a pen from his pocket and handed it to me.

I confidently signed the form and handed it back to Rogers.

After replacing the signed form in his briefcase, he briskly turned and advanced toward me, his eyes riveted on mine. Stopping a few feet away from my sitting position, he said, "Dennis, do you understand the seriousness of the trouble you are in?"

A few seconds of silence passed before I spoke. "Yeah, I think I have a pretty good indication of that."

"Sir, I am not going to try and con you or deceive you in any way. As a matter of fact, I'm going to be perfectly honest and frank with you. I am sure you would appreciate that, would you not?" Rogers kept his eyes focused on my face.

"Well, yes, I would greatly appreciate your honesty," I stated.

Smith sat silently, his uncomfortable eyes trained on mine.

Rogers suddenly turned from my direct line of vision and walked back across the room. He removed his Stetson hat and set it on top of his closed briefcase. Rolling up his shirt sleeves, as if to tell me it was time to get into the ring, he bluntly said, "We have filed the death penalty on you in a bill of particulars, and we are going to make it stick." Walking closer to me in cat-like fashion, he persisted by saying, "Did you hear me, Dennis? We have filed the death penalty on you, and we definitely have enough good evidence on you to send you to lethal injection." Stepping nearer to me in breath-close range, he added in a higher-pitched tone, "It took me five whole years but we have got the goods on you, and our evidence is strong."

Finally, leaning even closer, he repeatedly jabbed his forefinger into my breastbone, over-emphasizing each and every word as his lips spat, "We are going to kill you for what you did, and there's nothing that you can do about it. We have a solid case of murder in the first degree against you, so get it off your chest, Fritz, and be the man we think you are. You need to realize that we have been working in this field for a long time now, and both of us understand how someone might get to drinking and let things get out of control. We know from other cases we've solved that murdering someone in the heat of the moment is a lot easier than someone might think. So get it off your chest, Fritz, and tell us how it really happened."

Without a flicker of apprehension, I blurted out, "I didn't

kill anyone, and I don't know anything about what you're talking about. If you want to try and kill me, then go ahead. I'm not scared of anything you can do to me because I am an innocent person!"

The veins in Rogers's neck protruded as he roared, "Fritz, we haven't got time for these games and your lies. Make it easy on yourself and confess, right now!"

"Yes!" I shrieked. "Yes, I will confess at this time."

Smith bolted from his chair and left the room. There was silence. If a pin had dropped, it would have sounded like a sledgehammer hitting the floor. Rogers waited for Smith to return.

When he came back, he carried a small tape recorder in his porky hands. He hastily set the recorder on the table, plugged it in, and switched it on. His sudden movements were a contrast to his earlier placid performance.

Now it was his turn in the ring as he instructed me: "Dennis, this won't take long, and we can get this all cleared up here in a few minutes. As you have surely guessed, we are here to help you out, and your honesty in the form of a confession will keep you off of death row. Now Dennis, tell us exactly how it happened."

I looked at the recorder with its wheels spinning silently and then candidly exclaimed to the waiting detectives, "Okay, I'm going to give you my confession. It's the whole truth in every way and I am not going to leave anything out. Here it is: I am an innocent man and have never in my life killed anyone, and furthermore, I am not going to confess to a murder that I didn't do or know nothing about. What do you guys take me for—a complete imbecile?"

Both detectives' faces flushed red. Rogers angrily wrenched his body around and stomped across the room. He snatched up his Stetson, put it on his head, and said with great resentment, "Fritz, we are tired of fooling around with you. You are not funny. If you want to die on the lethal injection table, that is your decision." Turning towards Smith, Rogers remarked with disgust, "If you would like to talk to him any further, then you can stay. I am going back to the hotel and get comfortable while Fritz suffers with these lies."

"Okay, Gary. I'll meet you back at the room in an hour."

Rogers stormed out.

After several minutes, Smith spoke. "Dennis, we don't really believe that you murdered Debbie Carter."

Because his glare seemed to invite a response, I challenged him by asking, "If you guys don't think I committed the murder, then why have I been charged?"

Smith scooted his chair slightly closer to me as he whispered, "We don't think you were the aggressor in this. We strongly believe that Williamson did the actual killing and was the more aggressive one in the rape and murder. We believe that you were there and Williamson put you in a position to participate in the rape but not the murder. Fritz, I can help you out if you talk to me. As a matter of fact, both Gary and I don't think that you're the kind of guy that would be capable of outright murder. On the other hand, we know that Williamson is. We believe you were there and that is just as bad as you committing the murder yourself. Dennis, we dug up Debbie Carter's body and what we found proves that you were there and participated in the murder."

"Smith, I've heard enough of your bullshit. I've told you both over and over that I didn't commit no murder, so take me to my cell. I'm not going to put up with your crazy insinuations no more. I am ready to go!"

"Have it your way, Fritz. I really hate to see you fall for a capital murder that you did not fully commit. Will you talk to me tomorrow before we leave?"

It must have taken him years to perfect the kind of riveting glare he was projecting upon me.

"Yes, I will talk to you tomorrow," I stated. "Are we going to go back to Oklahoma tomorrow?"

"Just as soon as we get you out of court, we'll catch an afternoon flight and be in Oklahoma City by evening. Tonight, think really hard about what we have discussed. Your decision could very well save your life."

With that, he was done talking. The two Kansas City cops entered through the office door, and the smaller cop announced, "Come with us, Fritz. We're taking you to your new residence."

The ride to the upper floor of the jailhouse was brief and quiet. When the elevator door opened, screams, cries, and wails emanated from the small window in the large steel door in front of us. The jangle of keys shattered my concentration. The heavy metal door was swung open, and one of the cops gave me a shove.

The pervasive putrid stench of bodily odors invaded my nostrils as I cautiously entered. I looked around. Three people slept on metal tables in a bullpen area. Though it was three-thirty in the morning, inmates were pacing, chanting, singing, and talking to themselves. Most of the inmates were black. Their stares made me nervous as I was led down a corridor of adjoining cells.

The jail guard haphazardly fumbled for the key to open the third cell door. "Fritz, you'll be going to court at ten o'clock," he said as he swung open the door. Then he looked at me and nodded toward the doorway.

I said nothing as I entered. On each side of the cell were four bare, steel slab beds. I chose one of the top bunks in the rear, climbed onto its hard, cold surface and looked around. Near the front, two men were asleep. A large black man lay awake on a lower bunk, and a Hispanic guy sat on the bunk opposite mine.

"Say, man, you got some smokes?" the Hispanic asked.

"No, I sure don't. They got my pack when I was booked in." I didn't feel like talking but I knew I was not going to sleep, so I forced myself to say, "How long have you been in here?"

"About three weeks now. They say I tried to sell some cocaine to a nark. Those dirty bastards set me up. One of these days I am going to get out of here, and I'll kill everyone that put me here. What did they arrest you on, man?"

I paused, considering whether to divulge information to the stranger, and then answered, "They arrested me on a burglary charge that I didn't do."

"Yeah, those pigs are like that, all right. I wouldn't be surprised if they didn't set you up, too. I hate cops with a passion. Say, man, how would you like to escape with me? I got a pretty good plan worked out."

I looked at him squarely and answered, "I don't know. I am going to court in the morning. I may not be here very long. I'll just have to wait and see what happens." I desperately wanted for this conversation to end so I said, "Listen, man, I've got to get up early so if you don't mind, I need to try and get some sleep."

"All right, man, but just remember: They will convict you just like they have done with everyone else unless you got the bucks to hire a good lawyer."

By this time, the man on the front bunk had begun snoring. He sounded like a 747 taking off. I turned over and faced the wall and pretended to be asleep. I heard other inmates moaning and groaning. I had an overwhelming urge to scream. My mind felt like it was slipping. Every nerve in my body felt like it had been pulled out and tightly strung. At one point, I got up and twisted wads of toilet tissue to put in my ears to minimize the racket. I climbed back onto the slab.

I was mentally and physically exhausted. My thoughts bounded in so many directions that I couldn't concentrate. I couldn't *not* think, either. I wondered how Mom and Aunt Wilma were dealing with this. And what about my daughter? Will she believe that her daddy is a murderer? How would this affect her after having seen her mother on that Christmas Day, slumped over for over five hours in her favorite rocking chair, her arms dangling lifelessly in a pool of blood? Had Elizabeth been in the same room with her mother when the impact of the bullet had ripped into the back of Mary's skull, violently flinging her forward? I prayed. *Oh God, please! Above everything else, protect my daughter and keep her in sound mind and spirit through all of this. If I have to sacrifice my life for something I didn't do, all I ask is that you let Elizabeth grow up to be a happy person.*

Wishing for sleep didn't make it so. I lay there on my slab, staring at the flecks of paint peeling from the concrete wall. I thought about my father. An alcoholic and a womanizer, he left behind nothing I could admire. I thought about Mom's alcoholism and how I had grown up essentially on my own in a condemned alleyway apartment that was a hop, skip, and jump away from the local pool hall in Lee's Summit. I remembered holding my own with the best of them at the pool table and how I honed my skills in the fine art of cooking cornbread and beans. I was on my own, having fun. So what if it was with the wrong people? I was just a kid.

Tonight's attempt by Rogers and Smith to get me to confess to Debbie Carter's murder was just another bad luck story in a series. The first was in 1983, when they gave me those lie detector tests. That must have been the turning point, I decided as I recalled the details. The first test was in June 1983 at the Oklahoma State Bureau of Investigation office in Oklahoma City. I told myself before I left Ada to drive the eighty miles north to Oklahoma City that telling these guys the truth would put an end to all the police harassment that had turned my life into a nightmare, but I was so nervous before I left that I took a ten-milligram Valium tablet to calm my nerves.

At the bureau office, I met Agent Rusty Featherstone, who was introduced as a duly qualified examiner. Featherstone was six feet tall and beefy, with red hair and ruddy skin. He wasted no time. He placed the electrode monitors on every pulse point of my body and began his interrogation by asking basic questions. He then advised me to purposely lie and then tell the truth to the same question so he could establish a margin of error for the purpose of comparison. Then he launched into a series of questions, finally focusing on Debbie Carter's murder.

"About Debbie Carter's death in December, were you present when she was assaulted?"

"No," I stated.

"About Debbie Carter's death in December, did you kill her?"

"No," I insisted.

"About Debbie Carter's death in December, do you know who killed her?"

"No," I said again.

When the test was concluded, Featherstone gathered the polygraph tapes, instructed me to stay where I was, and left the room. Despite the Valium, I became extremely anxious as I awaited his return.

When he reappeared half an hour later with Rogers at his side, their expressions were glum. My clammy feeling of despair penetrated the room when I asked if I'd passed the test. I could still remember Featherstone's reply: "On a scale from one to ten, you scored an eleven. You totally flunked the entire examination."

I recalled shouting that was impossible, that I told the truth on every question. I told him, "Something must be wrong with your machine."

Featherstone denied that the machine had a problem: "Mr. Fritz, our machine is very sensitive and accurate in its responses to your answers. I have thoroughly reviewed all of the comparative charts, and all three zones show conclusively that you have been totally deceptive in the answers you provided."

I didn't know what to tell him. "All I can say is that I was so nervous before coming up here that I had to take a Valium to calm me down."

Rogers got angry. He immediately uncrossed his arms and, with a scowl on his face, told me I'd wasted their time and that I'd have to take the test over. I remember him saying, "We will reschedule another test some time next week, and you cannot drink or take any type of medication before the test. Do you clearly understand what I am saying?"

I remember being so rattled when I left that I could barely drive back to Ada. Maybe they were right and the Valium had caused me to flunk the first test. But I didn't take anything for the second test a week later, and I told the truth there, too, so why had I flunked that one? Featherstone had sounded so hateful when he told me: "Mr. Fritz, after thoroughly reviewing your polygraph charts, I find that you have again been very deceptive in your responses."

As I lay there in the cell, the whole incident of the second test came back to me like a dream—Featherstone, Rogers, and Smith sitting across from me at a table in an interrogation room in the Ada police station, their eyes filled with suspicion, their faces stern as stone.

"I didn't kill anyone and I don't know anything about this girl's murder," I shouted at them. "On both of the tests, I have been as truthful as I can be."

"Fritz, look up in the corner of the room," Rogers said, nodding. "See that camera? This is called a post-polygraph interview. You're being taped. You need to lay it on the line and tell us nothing but the truth, and I mean everything about your part in this murder. We're not leaving this room until you come clean and tell us everything you know. Do you desire to have an attorney present with you at this time?"

"No!" I shouted. "Why do I need an attorney to tell you the truth? I am not scared of anything I have to say because I didn't do anything wrong. I've never raped a woman and I've never had any thoughts of ever doing such a thing."

Featherstone stood up and soberly said, "Dennis, there is something that you are holding back. If there's something you need to explain, then we need to know what it is so we can understand what caused you to do so poorly on the test."

The feeling of being trapped sent a rousing wave of hot prickly sensations throughout my body. "Okay," I said, grasping at anything in my memory that might have caused the test to go wrong, "there is something. Maybe."

The detectives' startled reactions occurred in unison. They lifted their heads, and their shoulders abruptly straightened as they awaited my statement. Rogers said, "Fritz, take your time and try to relax. Tell us what you have to say. It's very important to not leave anything out."

I drew in a deep breath and began speaking: "The only time that I have ever been in any kind of situation with a woman was last August."

"Dennis, was this August of 1982?" Smith asked.

"Yes, I can't remember the exact night. Ronnie had called me up and wanted to go to a bar at the Holiday Inn in Norman."

"Excuse me, are you referring to Ronnie Williamson?" Featherstone asked.

"Yeah. Ronnie, Ronnie Williamson. We got to the bar and got something to drink, and sat down and listened to the band. Ronnie met a girl that was with the band and danced with her."

"Do you remember the girl's name?" asked Rogers.

"I don't remember her name, and I can't even remember what she looked like because it was dark in the club. I remember that Ronnie brought her over to the table and they sat down for a few minutes and that after the band announced last call, Ronnie started telling her I had a bar in the backseat of my car and he wanted her to take a look at it. Of course, it wasn't true but Ronnie was always coming up with something out of the ordinary. I didn't pay much attention to what he was saying."

"Do you happen to remember what time of night that was?" Rogers asked.

"Maybe one-thirty or two in the morning. It was last call. As we were leaving the club, everybody gathered in the doorway because it was raining. Ronnie was standing beside the girl, talking to her, telling her again that there was a bar in my backseat."

"So, Dennis, you went and got your car," Smith coaxed.

"Yes, I drove around to the front of the breezeway and Ronnie and the girl came out to the car. Ronnie got in front, and she got in the backseat. I remember I had the music up fairly loud. I assumed that we were going to ride around for a while. I pulled out onto the highway and got about half a mile or so down the road when the girl starts yelling and wanting to know where we are taking her. Ronnie turned completely around in the seat and was trying to calm her down while she was trying to open the back door to jump out of the car."

"Do you know what street you were on or what part of Norman you were in while this was occurring?" Smith asked.

"No," I replied. "All that I remember was that it was rainy and we were within two to three miles of the Holiday Inn."

"So, why didn't you immediately stop your car and let the girl get out?" Featherstone asked.

"Everything happened so fast. When she started yelling, I was looking for a place to turn around so I could take her back to the club. But when she started trying to jump out of the car, I was trying to drive and find a place to turn around and at the same time reaching back to keep her door locked so she wouldn't jump out."

"That doesn't make a bit of sense. It sounds more like you and Williamson were going to rape her," replied Rogers.

"That is absolutely not true," I shouted.

"Mr. Fritz, we are trained investigators. You are insulting our intelligence with a story that doesn't add up," remarked Featherstone. "To begin with, when you first noticed that the girl was scared and uncertain as to where you were taking her, why didn't you simply stop the car and let her know you were taking her back?"

"Mr. Featherstone, I don't like where this is going. I'm explaining this situation to try and make you understand why I may have flunked your polygraph, and now, all of you are getting the idea that I wanted to rape her. I never had no thought or any intent to do anything like that. I only believed that she wanted to go for a ride. When things got out of hand, I slowed down the car, trying to find a place to turn around. At the same time, I was having difficulty seeing because of the fog on the windshield. To keep her from jumping out and hurting herself, I slowed the car down, and just as I was stopping, the girl got out the door and ran off across the median."

"What about Williamson? What was he doing while she was trying to jump out?" Rogers asked.

"Like I said, everything happened so fast I didn't even have time to turn my radio down, let alone hear everything Ronnie was saying or doing. I remember I kept telling Ronnie to keep her door locked so she wouldn't jump out of the car. He was leaning over the seat trying to keep her from unlocking the door, and I guess that made her even more frantic in thinking that she was going to be raped. I want to make one thing crystal clear: I never had any intention whatsoever of raping her or harming her in any way."

"Did you or Ronnie physically hurt this girl?" Rogers asked. "Because if you did, we will find out. We can check this out with the Norman police to see if there was a report made."

"Mr. Fritz, did you and Williamson rape her?" asked Featherstone.

"I'm through answering your questions. No, we didn't rape or harm that girl in any way."

"Dennis, I have a question," Smith said. "I hope you fully realize that you are under no duress or coercion to talk anymore if you don't want to, but I want to know what you and Ronnie did after the girl jumped out of your car? Do you want to answer this question?"

"Sure, I don't mind. After the girl got out, I didn't want to try and drive back to Ada because I had been drinking, and I didn't want to be out on the highway if this girl called the police. So, I got off the main road and found a place where some old school buses were parked. I pulled in and parked between two buses. Ronnie got in the back and I stayed in the front and we slept there till morning."

CHAPTER 4

The sound of keys jangling stirred me from sleep. A harsh voice bellowed, "Fritz, get yourself up. You have ten minutes before you have to be in court."

Jerking so hard I almost fell from the bunk, I awoke and lifted my throbbing head off the cold steel. I sat up, and immediately a rush of new thoughts filled my head. *Here I am, thirty-seven years old and what do I have to account for in life? A broken marriage, a beautiful daughter who probably thinks I do not care for her any more, and now, I'm going down the tubes on a charge for a crime I did not commit! Why have they done this to me? Was it possible that Williamson said something to implicate me? After all these years, maybe Williamson has finally confessed and decided to drag me down with him. Why would he do such a thing, especially after I tried to help him time after time by giving him lifts to the grocery store and even loaning him money when he was down and out? Ronnie could have very well murdered Debbie Carter, but why would he now try and implicate me?*

I pictured Ronnie's face and stature clearly as I stood at the metal sink and splashed cold water onto my swollen face. I hadn't seen him for several months. The last time we had talked, he looked pretty ragged—his tall, broad-shouldered frame bore just a shadow of the strength he possessed when he played for the Oakland A's maybe fifteen years back. Many speculated that Ronnie could have been the next Mickey Mantle, but his excessive drinking proved too much for the team's management to tolerate and he was cut from the team. That's when everything started to crumble in his life. He lost his wife, his drinking habit worsened, and he was unable to hold a job. That was about the time I met him. Since then, his life had gone from bad to worse. Once sharp and witty, with the world at his fingertips, alcohol and mental illness had transformed him into a lonely, broken man.

I unwound a portion of toilet tissue and dabbed my face dry. Would Mom and Aunt Wilma be in the courtroom? Would Smith still want to talk? Everyone else in the cell was still asleep as I hopped back on my bunk. I took a breath of stale air and tried to relax.

The same familiar, robust voice that woke me up broke the agony of silence a few minutes later by commanding, "Let's go, Fritz. Time to go to court."

I looked toward the cell door and saw a large, light-complected officer in his forties with heavy bags under his eyes.

"Do you know how long this will last?" I asked.

"You'll probably be there all morning, maybe until noon. Come on. We've got to hurry you down there," he ordered. "We don't want to make the judge mad, do we?"

"No, sir, we sure don't," I replied. As I hastily approached the doorway, I caught sight of two younger guards standing to the right of the officer with the keys. Both were holding chains and several pairs of handcuffs.

"Come on out of the cell, Fritz. We haven't got all day to fool around with you," one of the young guards ordered. "All of you murderers are just alike! You think that everybody owes you something and then your bunch starts screamin' your constitutional rights have been violated. If I had my way, every one of your kind would be instantly put to death."

Instead of telling this smartass what I had on my mind, I kept my thoughts to myself and stepped out onto the run area as the older officer closed the door behind me.

"Turn around, Fritz," the young guard said, "and put your hands behind your back, you murderin' son of a bitch."

His last remark was too much for me to ignore. "Listen, you little smartass prick," I said calmly, "I didn't kill nobody and I'm not going to put up with your lip. I'm sure these other two officers will agree with me." I shot a glance at the other guard and the officer. Their faces showed indifference.

"Fritz, just put your hands behind your back and we'll get this show on the road," the older officer advised.

I did, and the cold circles of restraint tightly clamped into my flesh. Pain surged through my forearms and I shouted, "Loosen these handcuffs up right now!"

"Aw, what's the matter? The big murderer can't take a little pain?" the smartass guard teased.

"Say, Joe," said the older officer, "why don't you go ahead and get Fritz's paperwork ready? We'll pick it up on our way out. We've got five other prisoners to handcuff and shackle before we go."

Joe looked disappointed as he turned away and stormed through the metal door, back toward the booking office.

I was relieved. "What's the matter with Joe?"

"He's kind of new here and hasn't fully learned our procedures yet," the older officer told me. " Are your handcuffs still too tight?"

"Yes," I answered. "Could you please loosen them a little?"

He did. "Does that feel better?"

"That will do."

"Now, let's get these leg shackles on you and we can be on our way." He briskly connected the shackles to my ankles and looped a length of chain around my waist. "Now, Fritz, go to the end of the run by the entrance door and wait for us to return. We've got several more prisoners we have to get ready for court."

It was difficult to walk all bound up like I was, but I got to the entrance door and stood there. I could hear the guard with the robust voice calling out the names of prisoners up and down the run. One by one, each cell door was opened and restraints administered until all of the prisoners were properly bound. Six of us, including myself, were directed to the elevator and taken to the first floor, where we were loaded onto a waiting paddy wagon.

None of us spoke as the van sped steadily from the parking area onto an adjacent side street. The mood around us was thick with gloom. I tried to see the bright side of my predicament: I was enjoying a little fresh air away from the dungeon that Kansas City called a city jail. As much as I hated to admit it, the thought of being in the county jail at Ada seemed like paradise compared to what I had just gotten out of. I had been in the Ada jail for four months on a DUI some years back; the place was smaller and there were fewer inmates. Ada's jail just seemed calmer and more predictable than Kansas City's could ever be.

We had only gone a couple of blocks when we slowed to a crawl. Peering through the mesh wire that divided the inmates from the guards, I watched as the driver guided the vehicle toward a driveway that arched downward toward another underground parking area. The paddy wagon wound its way through the catacombs, the muffled silence of the underground broken only by the jangling sounds of chains dragged across the van's bare metal flooring. The prevailing darkness that yielded briefly and repeatedly to gleams of light from dirty fixtures revealed the uplifted eyes of every inmate.

The paddy wagon came to a stop in a sally port. The two guards quickly stepped from the front and swung open the rear doors. The fat cop shouted, "Okay, men, we are at the county courthouse. Each of you will be going to court shortly. Watch your step as you climb out of the van. Stay grouped together until everyone is out."

When the van was cleared, we were instructed to walk in single file to an entrance door up ahead. My feeling of despair intensified as we were led inside and down a long dull corridor, past cells concealed by solid metal doors with tiny windows. "Cigarette, man? You got a cigarette?" begged someone from behind a door.

No one uttered a word as we made our way to a desk where a Department of Corrections guard sat on the edge of his chair. His glasses hung low on his nose as he eyed us.

Our guard spoke first: "Sam, all of these men are scheduled to be in court at ten this morning."

Sam shifted his glasses higher and looked at a clipboard before he answered, "I have another twelve inmates scheduled for the afternoon court. Thanks for the warning. I don't know where we are going to put everyone if they don't kick a few out. We're going to need another jail built if this keeps up."

Sam took names and pulled file cards, and the guards led us around the corner to a large cell with two concrete benches and a commode shielded by a red metal divider. We were ordered inside. Our handcuffs and shackle chains were left on while we waited for our court appearance.

As I sat on the bench, I noticed that some of us were cuffed behind our backs while others were cuffed in front. My cuffs, in back, seemed to have gotten much tighter. The pain throughout my shoulders was making it unbearable to sit in any one position for long. Two other inmates whose hands were also cuffed behind their backs looked like they were just as uncomfortable as I was.

"Why is it that some of us are handcuffed differently?" I said aloud. My question startled the others, and they began to look around at each other.

An older, bearded black man spoke up. "If you're a security risk and have a red dot on your file card, then you have to wear the cuffs behind your back."

"What does the red dot stand for?"

"If you have been charged with a Class A felony or anything relating to a violent crime, then they put a red dot on your card."

"Oh, I see. Missouri is sure set up differently than Oklahoma."

"Is that where you are from?" the black man asked. "What are you doin' in Missouri if you are from Oklahoma?"

"It's a long story. I came up here to help my mother and aunt on a house-painting job and the next thing I know I'm being arrested on charges of first-degree murder for something I did not do."

"Yeah, man, there seems to be a lot of that goin' on here lately. There's no such thing as justice anymore. If you haven't got any money, then you're screwed. Have you talked to any lawyers?"

"No, I haven't. I was just arrested last night. I looked out my front door and there was around twenty officers in the yard."

"Yeah, they've got some real bastards here in the city. Are you going to sign your extradition papers and go back to Oklahoma?"

"I don't really know what I'm going to do."

"Well, man, you better start findin' out because you're fixin' to go to your extradition hearing."

"I didn't know what I was going to court for. I thought it was going to be some kind of arraignment hearing."

"No, man, you won't be arraigned until you go back to Oklahoma. This'll be about whether or not you'll sign the extradition papers. If you waive your extradition rights and sign the papers, then you'll be transported back to Oklahoma immediately. If you don't waive your rights, they can keep you up here for ninety days."

"If I don't go back with the Oklahoma officers, don't you think that would make me look guilty?"

"Not necessarily, man," he remarked. "There's always two sides to a coin. I sure don't want to be telling you what to do, but if it were me, I would make it as hard as I could for those Oklahoma assholes to get me back there."

"Well, I sure want to do the right thing, because I am innocent and I want to get this cleared up." I felt grateful to this guy. He had told me more in three minutes than anybody else had in ten hours. Shifting from side to side, I asked, "If I choose not to go back to Oklahoma, will the court here appoint me some kind of lawyer?"

"I'm not for sure about that. It looks like they would appoint you an attorney to deal with your extradition proceedings. Don't quote me on this. I seem to remember another case where this cat was fightin' extradition and I believe they appointed him a lawyer. Or you could hire yourself one."

Forty-five minutes passed. I stood up and stretched and paced the floor.

"Man, you might as well sit down and try to make yourself comfortable," the older man suggested. "I seriously doubt we'll get in before noon. More likely it'll probably be the latter part of the afternoon. I've been through this seems like a hundred times. The courts here in Kansas City are so overcrowded. It's always been a long waiting game every time I've been here."

I didn't feel much like talking but I forced myself to say, "What are you in for this time, if you don't mind me asking?" I sat down and examined his eyes while I waited for an answer. They were bloodshot, and the skin beneath them was deeply wrinkled. I guessed he was probably in his fifties. Something about how he had an answer for everything gave me the impression he was a con man.

"They are tryin' to get me to plea bargain to first-degree manslaughter from a second-degree murder charge. I was over at some people's house at this party, right? We were drinkin' and doin' a lot of coke. Well, this chick that I was tryin' to get it on with started freakin' on me, you know? This cat that she was with wants some of my black skin on him and we do a little number there in the house. You know what I mean? Well, man, I get tired of this action and blow the scene and find my own party. To make a long story short, this cat I was fightin' got blown away later that night, and now they're tryin' to blame me for his killin'."

I tilted my head downward, not wanting to encourage another blast of his kind of conversation.

"Naw, man, what they're sayin' is it was my gun in the shootin'. I used to own a piece but sold it and it was never registered. None of my fingerprints were ever found on the gun, if you know what I mean."

"You shouldn't have much to worry about then," I calmly remarked.

"Well, I'm not goin' to take their shit this time. I'll be outta here in a couple of days."

After several moments, I grumbled, "I sure wish they would hurry up and get this show on the road. I'll bet it is already after noon and we'll be here, like you said, till after three o'clock."

The guy did not respond. I was relieved that he didn't. Time dragged by in slow painful silence. I was about to get up and knock on the steel frame door to ask what time it was when I heard the jangling of keys on the other side. My heart started pounding. The guard stepped inside the chamber and said, "Johnson and Griffin, come on. Your Honor is awaiting your presence."

I pushed my back against the cool concrete wall, closed my eyes, and silently started counting backwards from one hundred. I had to relax enough to make a decision about extradition. On the one hand, I didn't have an attorney to represent me. If I were to waive extradition and go back to Oklahoma facing the death penalty without any representation, wouldn't I be digging my own grave? On the other hand, if I stayed here for a couple months, I could see my mom and aunt and maybe buy myself some time to try and find an attorney up here. But I had no savings or available cash to even think about being able to hire someone, and Mom and Aunt Wilma's credit wouldn't be enough to get the amount of money needed for a good attorney.

Maybe I should just go back and get this over with. But

wouldn't they have to appoint me an attorney if I didn't have money? Yeah, I bet they would, but whoever I got would probably sell me out and I'd be on death row until they executed me. I looked over at the old guy slouched in the corner. His eyes were closed. One thing he had said during our conversation stuck out in my mind. Why should I make it easy on these dirty bastards after they filed the death penalty on me for something I didn't do? And, on top of that, my poor mom and aunt are going through pure hell over this.

I looked at him again. *I believe you're right, old man, and that's exactly what I'm gonna do.* Nodding my head, I whispered, "I'm gonna stay here. I'm gonna stay here. I'm gonna ...." I dozed off into a trance-like sleep that overcame the extreme pain and discomfort that had stolen the energy from my body.

When I heard the jingling of keys at the door, I woke up.

"Come on down, Fritz and Franks. The judge has requested your presence," the guard called.

Sleepy and dazed, I lunged forward and staggered sideways in an attempt to gain my balance as the guard grumbled to the old man, "Come on, Franks, get up. This is no time for you to be sleeping. The judge is waiting." He watched as the old guy attempted with great difficulty to untangle himself from his awkward position.

I shuffled over to him with the intention of helping him up, but with my hands cuffed behind my back, that was nearly impossible. The guard ordered me away from him and he pulled Franks up to standing. As we dragged our aching bodies into an open waiting area, Franks lost his balance and fell headlong into the wall. The guard made no attempt to help him as he lay there. I took a step.

"Don't try to help him, Fritz," the guard barked at me. "It's my job, not yours, to assure his safety. We have medical staff on hand if someone gets hurt while in our custody." The guard walked back to the door we had just came through and hollered out, "Man down, man down. Need some help now!"

Two guards rushed through the door and helped Franks to his feet. After questioning him about how he felt, one of the guards determined that the old man would be able to attend court. "There's nothing wrong with him except he's got a hard head," the first guard laughed.

"That's probably what got him in here in the first place," the second guard agreed. "Both of you turn around and we'll give you a little sweet surprise I'm sure you'll like."

The guard unlocked my handcuffs and nodded for me to move my arms around in front of me. A stabbing pain streaked through my shoulder blades as I stretched and overextended my torso backwards. The guard put my cuffs back on, this time with my hands in the front, and then did the same for Franks.

"Straight ahead and through those double doors," he ordered.

We trudged forward, following the lead guard through the swinging doors into the courtroom. I scanned the gallery. Aunt Wilma and Mom sat in the center of the row three or four rows from the front. A look of shock lingered in Mom's puffy eyes.

"Move straight ahead, Mr. Fritz, and have a seat on the front row by the other inmates," the guard behind me instructed.

Upon being seated, I looked over my shoulder several times, catching glimpses of Mom and my aunt. Their expressions were filled with grief and anguish.

The courtroom doors swung wide as Smith and Rogers entered and made their way to the rear of the courtroom, where they sat down. Their presence sent waves of tension rippling through my mind. I felt their eyes upon me as I awaited the judge's call.

The judge was middle aged with grayish hair at his temples. He didn't look around the courtroom or make eye contact with anyone as he ordered the bailiff to hand him our cards. With his red-framed glasses perched low on his nose, the judge read a card, looked up and announced, "In the case of the state of Oklahoma versus Dennis Fritz, case number CRF-87-90, the matter of extradition is now before the court. Mr. Fritz, will you please approach the bench?"

I was escorted to the judge's bench by two guards.

"Mr. Fritz, the state of Oklahoma has charged you with murder in the first degree and with first-degree rape and rape by instrumentation. As the record will reflect, you are currently being held as a detainee in the custody of the Missouri Department of Corrections in lieu of $100,000 fugitive bond. If you so desire, an attorney will be appointed to you in the matter of the extradition proceedings now before this court. Mr. Fritz, at this time do you so desire to have an attorney appointed on your behalf?"

"I have a question, Your Honor."

"What is your question?"

"Judge, I would like to know what the amount of time is that I would have to stay here if I decide to not waive extradition?"

"Mr. Fritz, under the Missouri penal code, the state of Oklahoma would have up to ninety days to invoke their right to return you to your home state. If you decide here today that you do not desire an attorney and you agree to waive your extradition rights, then you will be immediately taken back to Oklahoma. If you so request an attorney, then the court will enter into record that you have made a decision to not waive extradition. Knowing these rights as I have explained them to you, is it your decision to be represented by counsel, thus foregoing the extradition waiver?"

I was taking a chance. I had a feeling that any attorney the court appointed would be less concerned about my welfare than he would be about his own. But this would buy me time, and maybe Mom and Aunt Wilma would know someone who could recommend someone to hire. I asked the judge, "If I hire my own attorney and speak with him, would I still be able to waive extradition if I decide to do so later?"

"Yes, Mr. Fritz, the court will grant you the opportunity to reverse your decision if you decide you want to waive extradition. This charge information sheet that I'm giving you outlines the details of the charges against you. You will be transferred to the

Jackson County Detention Center for the remainder of your time until extradition is accomplished."

The judge handed a sheet of paper to the bailiff, who then handed it to the guards. "Please escort Mr. Fritz to the proper facility," he ordered. My appearance was over. It was time to go. As I shuffled toward the courtroom's exit doors and passed the row where Mom and Aunt Wilma were seated, Mom reached out toward me. That outstretched arm, extended in despair, split my heart in two.

Glancing to the back of the courtroom, I saw Smith and Rogers hurriedly exit. Looking back over my shoulder, I saw my mother and aunt rush to reach me before I was led away. Mom squeezed her way through the crowd and lunged against me, hugging me with all the love she had to give. With her face against my shoulder, she sobbed as she told me she loved me and would be there for me all the way through. I was able to kiss her quickly on her forehead before the guards intervened and separated us.

Outside the courtroom, I was immediately flanked by Smith and Rogers. As we walked briskly down the corridor, I sensed their frustration and anger.

"Fritz, you might be able to hide from us for a while, but we will get you back. I guarantee you that it will be sooner than you think," Rogers insisted. "You have only put off the inevitable. Very soon you are going to have to pay for what you did. You can count on that."

"Donnie, would you still like to have our little talk we agreed upon?" Smith said as he tightened his grip on my arm.

I looked at him with contempt. "I don't have anything to say to you, except that when I get back in Oklahoma, I'm going to do everything that I can do to prove my innocence, and nothing you can say or do will stop that."

I heard Mom call my name. When I looked back, she and Aunt Wilma were waving goodbye. Mom mouthed the words *I love you* and her sorrowful face disappeared in the crowd.

I was transferred to the Jackson County Detention Center to begin plotting my defense. The first couple of weeks were like living in a zoo. I slept on the floor at night with twenty or so other men; the days were filled with fighting and arguments among the inmates. The atmosphere was rife with violence, and I feared for my life.

The cell I was eventually assigned to became my place of refuge as I tried to relax and consider the situation before me. I was completely in the dark as to the extent of the state's evidence against me. The only clue that had been provided to me was the charge information sheet, on which several names appeared: Gary Rogers, Dennis Smith, Donna Elaine Johnson, Charles Carter, Susan Land, and Melvin Hett. Rogers and Smith I knew. Charles Carter's name I recognized as being Debbie's father. But the names Donna Elaine Johnson, Susan Land, and Melvin Hett? I had never heard of any of them in my life.

Chapter 5

Two months later I had accomplished nothing in the Jackson County jail. Extradition had arrived at last, and I was on my way to Oklahoma. From the backseat of the unmarked squad car, I looked out the window at the rolling green countryside as we sped hastily toward the Pontotoc County jail in Ada. The July day was sweltering. Even the cattle in the pastures moved sluggishly, keeping their heads close to the ground.

I had survived the humiliation and disgrace of hobbling through the Kansas City and Oklahoma City airports in leg shackles and handcuffs, though it hadn't been easy to ignore onlookers' stares, pointing fingers, and muffled whispers. At the Oklahoma City airport, I endured the harsh glare of the sun and the suffocating heat in the squad car while the two cops that had brought the car made small talk with agents Rogers and Featherstone, my escorts.

Since leaving Oklahoma City, none of us had uttered a word. Featherstone drove steadily, staring straight ahead. Rogers, in the backseat, glanced in my direction occasionally and smirked, presumably to let me know that he had accomplished his mission in bringing his man back to Ada. He was even dressed like an Old-

West sheriff: western-style blue suit, light blue tie, and polished cowboy boots. His white Stetson hat lay on the seat between us, like it had a life of its own.

As we drew closer to Ada, Rogers reached over and lightly rubbed the hat's soft, felted surface from time to time. He seemed nervous. Near the outskirts of the city, he placed his hands on his knees, arched his thin torso up against the seat, and yawned. As Featherstone slowed the car, the pressure in my chest tightened. I took in the familiarity of Ada. I glanced to my left and caught sight of the old fairgrounds building where I had shoveled horseshit for a month to make a living following the loss of my teaching position. In the four months since I had been away from Ada, nothing seemed to have changed. People still rushed to get home from work without stopping completely at the red lights before turning. A lone pedestrian at the intersection urgently swiped his forearm across his brow, unconcerned that all of the buttons on his shirt were undone and his bare chest was exposed. Everything looked normal and familiar, yet I felt a distinct difference—as if I were not a part of this town anymore and that the community had forsaken me. The traffic light at the intersection of Broadway and Richardson Bypass turned from amber to red. The car came to a halt.

"Rusty, let's go in the back way and try to avoid the crowds," said Rogers. He leaned over and lifted his briefcase from the floorboard.

"You wanna go in around the front of the courthouse on the police station side or down the alley in back?" queried Featherstone.

"Let's just go through the alley since it's after five o'clock. If there's any media at the courthouse, we can pretty much beat them in before they realize who's in the car."

The car accelerated when the light turned green. This scene had played a thousand times in my mind while I was in the jail in Kansas City. I envisioned that there would be a great amount of hostility to deal with upon my arrival. I feared that Debbie Carter's family would be outside the jail. Because I was in handcuffs and shackles, how could I defend myself? These uncertainties added to my mounting tension as we slowly paraded to the jail. Perspiration ran down from my scalp as our car passed one of my old haunts, J.D.'s Café. Mom, Elizabeth, and I had enjoyed their home-cooked meals and meticulous service on many occasions, and for the past two months, my mouth had watered for a well-prepared meal. Even with the windows rolled up, I smelled the savory aromas from J.D.'s kitchen as we passed.

Up ahead, just a block from Main Street, the gray towers of the Evergreen feed mill jutted into the sky. The county jail was two blocks south of Main just off Broadway, east of the Ada police station and the city jail. I recalled stories of how the city jail was used as a backup confinement facility when the prisoner population swelled at the county jail. I wondered which place I would be assigned to. My heart raced. I took a breath. The full impact of countless hours in the Kansas City jail spent worrying about the unknown would soon be unveiled. I knew I had made the right decision to not waive my extradition rights and stay in Kansas City for two months. Staying had given me time to gather my thoughts and better prepare myself for the battle I faced here in Ada. I was ready now to fight for my life.

The cars ahead slowed down. A freight train backing up onto the switching tracks alongside the feed mill blocked traffic.

"Another damned train," Featherstone remarked. He quickly glanced into the rear-view mirror at Rogers.

"Yeah, they back up here several times a day, but I'm sure ol' Fritz here won't mind the wait since this will be his last taste of civilization for a good while," answered Rogers. A look of scorn flowed from his eyes to mine.

I glared back. "If I go down on this, Rogers, then you, Smith, and Rusty up there are gonna have to pay for illegally convicting me. I'm ready for what you got, and I don't think it's much."

"You know, Fritz, you had a little vacation up there in Kansas

City, but it's like I told you before we left: You can hide for a little bit but now it's time for you to pay the price. We gave you more than a chance to help yourself out but you're gonna be a hard-ass and dig your own grave, so, have it your way and we'll see where it gets you."

"It's a wonder to me how any of you can sleep at night knowing that you don't have any real evidence to convict me on. And besides that," I said, nodding toward Featherstone, "when you left the room at the airport in Kansas City, your buddy up there more or less told me that I didn't flunk those polygraph tests."

Featherstone stiffened his shoulders and turned to look at me. He spoke sharply, "Mr. Fritz, you can say anything you want to say but the fact remains that your polygraphs consistently showed you were lying about not being in her house. And on the majority of the other questions, you clearly fell in the deceptive range on your responses."

Featherstone's tone was defensive. His cheeks turned a livid red.

"That sure wasn't how you put it to me before we left the airport, was it?" I taunted.

"You can read anything you want into what I said, Mr. Fritz, but evidently you didn't quite understand the precise phrasing I used," he told me. Then he swung around to face forward again.

"Rusty," Rogers laughed, "we know Fritz's game. He's trying to be his same old smart-aleck self. If he keeps it up, he's going to be at Big Mac down there in McAlester before it's all over with."

The freight train continued to back slowly toward its westbound hookup on the main track. In front of us, the long line of cars and pickups inched forward in anticipation that the signal barricades would reopen. I drew in a deep breath and exhaled, releasing some of the frustration and contempt that I felt for the two agents who I was certain were bluffing about their case against me. Why else would Featherstone have slipped up and revealed to me what I already knew to be the truth? They tried so many times to get me to confess, but despite their best efforts and interrogation techniques, my claims of innocence had left them obviously frustrated and angry.

The barricades lifted, and cars streamed over the tracks. As Featherstone accelerated the car through the Main Street intersection, my thoughts started to fragment. Dread bore down on me as the courthouse came into view. Panel vans bearing the insignia of television stations from in and around Ada were parked near the courthouse. Outside the courthouse doors, men and women with notepads and recorders congregated, intently watching as our car entered the alley. Curious spectators milled around on the sidewalk. Upon recognizing us, the assembly broke into a frantic sprint, rounding the courthouse corner and heading straight toward the gray stucco one-story building that was the jail. A second crowd of reporters and photographers with video cameras waited in the alley in front of the jail entrance.

Our car stopped at the door. Rogers and Featherstone exited at the same time. The throng of reporters and cameramen rushed toward Featherstone as he walked around the car to open my door. The onlookers behind the media strained to get a good look.

"Okay!" Rogers shouted. "Everybody move back and let us do our job. Make way, make way. Move back out of the way!"

As the door opened, Featherstone reached in with both hands and helped me to climb out of the car. I stepped out and stood straight. The sun's glare reflected from the parked vehicles and caused me to squint as I looked directly at the reporters. I wanted it known that I wasn't about to cover my face for something I didn't do.

Over the clamor, a reporter yelled, "Mr. Fritz, give us a statement as to your involvement in this case. Can you say anything about the murder charge against you?"

"Yeah. I'm totally innocent of committing any murder or having any knowledge of it," I hollered over my shoulder as I was escorted to the jail entrance.

"Mr. Fritz," someone else said, "do you have an attorney who will represent you, and if so, what is his name?"

"No, I do not."

"Mr. Fritz, Mr. Fritz, did you know Debbie Carter?" another reporter yelled.

The door to the county jail was swung open. I stepped inside without answering the reporter's question. Before the door slammed behind me, I heard one last question: "Did you kill Debbie Carter?"

I felt as though I had been caught in the middle of a baseball-size hailstorm by the media's frenzied questions. I was fully aware that Rogers and Featherstone didn't want me to have any communication with the press, but I reasoned differently. I had nothing to hide. I wanted the media people to know the truth straight from my mouth. Near the end of my stay in Kansas City, I had placed a call to the *Ada Evening News* and inquired as to whether someone would like to do an interview with me. Immediately, I was connected with a staff reporter who took my interview over the phone. I was able to state my innocence in detail and at the same time try to discover more about the case against me. I learned nothing, but I had the satisfaction of knowing that I had told my side of the story.

The county jail hadn't changed inside since my stay on the drunk-driving charge. I looked down the central corridor that extended to the far wall of the long rectangular building and saw several trusties staring in my direction. Rogers and Featherstone maneuvered me into the cramped booking area adjacent to the drunk tank. Rogers withdrew a set of keys from his pocket and removed the shackles from my ankles that were chafed and aching by now. The jail matron, her graying brown hair in a bun, received my transferred property from Featherstone and filled out the booking information sheet.

Undersheriff Ron Scott, who was head of the jail when I was here before, appeared from around the corner, carrying the white jumpsuit I was expected to wear. He bore a scowl on his pudgy, Indian-featured face as he plopped the jumpsuit on the top of the booking desk and peered over the tops of his wire-frame glasses. Taking the suit in hand, I looked at the chalkboard where the names and locations of inmates were written. I wanted to know where Ronnie was, if he was here. The back two bullpens were fairly full, but the middle isolated cells and the juvenile cells were mostly vacant. The girls' tank—that's what it was referred to—showed just a few names. Just as Rogers told me to turn around, I saw Ronnie's name but didn't have time to see where he was confined. Rogers and Featherstone led me into the drunk tank, where my handcuffs were removed and I changed into my jail garb. I was ready for placement in my new accommodations.

Scott took the lead, with Rogers and Featherstone in the rear, opening the first barred gate that separated the office from the rest of the jail. The air was cool in the corridor. I heard the sounds of men in the bullpen. Just the thought of being put in the bullpen made me cringe. In Kansas City I had had enough of the nerve-racking sounds of inmates snoring, farting, and coughing; two weeks of that before I had been put in a cell had driven me to the edge of insanity. I was hoping for a single cell so I could think without distraction and formulate a plan. In addition, I did not want to be confined with someone who might be a relative or close friend of Debbie Carter. There were already enough unknowns. I didn't need any more stress, especially the kind that might come at the tip of a weapon.

Clanging sounds emanated from the kitchen, where a few inmates gathered in the doorway and stared as we walked by. Trusties talking to inmates in the enclosed bullpens at the end of the hallway froze as they saw Ron Scott and his entourage heading in their direction. The trusties' hands swiftly dropped from the bars to their sides, and the mirrors held outside the bullpen bars instantaneously disappeared into the cells. Glancing behind me, I saw other trusties standing near the set of bars we had just passed through, watching as I was led deeper into the jail. A young trusty with cropped brown hair and pimples scurried by and darted into the laundry room.

After we passed the second barred gate, Scott stopped to open a solid metal door on his left. From across the corridor, someone bellowed a string of profanities from a bean hole. I recognized the voice; it was Ronnie's.

"You dirty no good lyin' motherfuckin' snitch," the bar-rattling voice reverberated, pent-up anger bouncing off every surface. "You're gonna pay for this, you motherfucker. Let me out of here right now. I wanna get you, you lyin' snitch, and you too, Rogers. I'll kill you both for lyin' on me."

I shuddered as I stood there. Ronnie's head bobbed back and forth on the other side of the darkened bean hole, his bone-penetrating voice rattling the bars as his shouts grew more unnerving.

"Dennis, the Lord won't let you get away with what you've done. I am INNOCENT! I'll take all of you down with me, you dirty bastards. You're not gonna do this to me, Dennis, or you, Rogers, and you, either, Featherstone." Ronnie's roars could have matched those of a crowd at Yankee Stadium.

"Come on, Fritz. Get in here," barked Scott. "We haven't got all day to stand here and listen to this crazy commotion from your buddy. I've had all I can take of his day-in and day-out screaming, so get in here and go back to the last cell on the left." He pointed toward a cell across from the girls' tank.

"Why am I being put back here?"

"Just move ahead, Fritz. Don't you worry about where you're at," Rogers remarked. "You're lucky that you've even got a roof over your head after what you did."

Ronnie's screams followed me as I entered the short hallway that divided the empty cells on the left from the girls' tank on my right. Out of the corner of my eye, I saw movement through the bean hole of the solid metal door behind which the female inmates were kept. I was sure that I had seen on the chalkboard that the bullpens were not completely filled. If the jail was not overcrowded, then why was I being locked away back here? Not that I was complaining, but I was curious.

I walked past Scott and entered my new home. The pimple faced trusty appeared, carrying a wadded mattress and woolen blanket. He threw them onto the cell floor and hurried away. Scott slammed the cell door shut, and he, Rogers, and Featherstone gave me a look of finality before exiting the chamber that echoed with the solitude I needed.

Chapter 6

Throughout the time I had known him, I had never seen Ronnie in such a state. Quite the opposite—he always acted docile when confronted with danger. Even that time when a bunch of guys jumped us after we gave a woman a ride to her house, Ronnie froze when the fists started flying. Punches had blurred my line of sight and I had sunk to the ground next to the car, but no one bothered Ronnie. He stood motionless and mute by his passenger door until the men, satisfied they had beaten me sufficiently, meandered back toward their porch. Then Ronnie sprang to life, coming to help me around to the passenger side because I was in no shape to drive. It was Ronnie who drove home, but he never said a word about why he didn't move during the fight. He certainly hadn't seemed aggressive then.

He'd get loud and boisterous when he was drinking, but belligerent wasn't his style, drunk or sober. So his yelling and ranting now was not normal. Why he was doing it was a mystery to me.

I looked around my small cell. Cool air drifted from the vent overhead. A thin, crumpled, plastic pad lay on each of the sagging coil-spring bunk beds. The plastic mirror above the commode/washbasin unit had yellowed with age. I couldn't see my reflection—a fact that I suspected would make shaving a chore.

While pacing from the bunk to the bars, I noticed movement through the shoulder high bean hole on the girls' tank's metal door. This bean hole was bigger than the ones in Kansas City, and every so often, I caught a glimpse of a different woman's face in the tank. One face reappeared several times, staying visible for longer periods each time.

"Your name's Dennis Fritz, isn't it?" the woman asked. She was young and attractive, with blond hair and a big smile.

"Yeah, that's what I'm called."

"We've heard a lot about you. You've been in the papers and on TV almost every night now."

"What's your name?"

"They call me Cissy, but my real name is Cynthia McIntosh."

"I've never heard a name like that before, but it's a cute one. Have you been here long?"

"Oh, a little over a month. I'm waiting for my hearing. How'd they bring you back from Kansas City?"

"They flew me back on a jet. I was handcuffed to that big asshole Featherstone. Felt like I had a mother hen at my side. Believe it or not, I sure am glad to finally get down here. It was pure hell in Kansas City's jail."

"The papers said that you're claimin' you're innocent."

"That's right. I never even seen that girl they're accusing me of killing. I feel like I'm losing my mind, not knowing the witnesses they're going to use against me. Did you know Debbie Carter?"

"Naw, I haven't been here very long. I come down from Illinois to be here around my mother, but look at me. I hate this place and all the bastards and motherfuckers around—"

"What are you in for, if you don't mind me asking?"

"I wrote some hot checks and they're makin' some big deal

about it. Truth is, I had a bank account but some of the checks didn't clear and I forgot to write a couple down. They didn't even give me a chance to try and make it right. It's not the first time that I've been mistreated by these sorry wanna-be cops."

Cissy leaned closer with her head up high in the bean hole and whispered, "Don't say too much to these other bitches. There's only one in here that I halfway trust. Her name is JoEllyn, but I'm even careful with her. I sleep with a protector at night."

The jangle of keys interrupted our conversation.

"Chow out! Chow out!" someone yelled. I strained toward the bars to see who was making the racket. It was the pimple-faced kid that had thrown me my mattress and cover. "Chow out, chow out, you hungry females an... Oh, I forgot, males, too."

"Lloyd, I'm not gonna tell you no more to quit comin' back here and blarin' your mouth," hushed Cissy.

Lloyd passed four trays through the girls' tank bean hole and turned to leave.

"Hey, Lloyd, what about my tray?" I asked.

Lloyd gave me a sheepish look.

"Bring me my tray, Lloyd."

He nodded and rushed away.

"Don't let Lloyd get under your skin," Cissy said. "He's mentally retarded but he'll sneak us back things when he can get away with it. If he don't bring you back somethin' to eat, we'll start raisin' hell. The only good guard that works here is Ernie, but he's only on during the day shift. These other assholes won't give you the sweat off their chicken tenders."

"Hey, Dennie Leon," Ronnie roared, "you know what they do to snitches in the joint, doncha?"

I stared into Cissy's large blue eyes as I waited for him to answer his own question.

"He's been like that ever since they brought him in," Cissy whispered. "He's been drivin' everybody crazy, yelling like that. You need to find out why he's callin' you a snitch, 'cause he's right.

You don't wanna get a jacket on you or you might end up dead."

"I don't want to talk to him, especially when he's crazy like this."

"Come on, Dennie Leon Snitch," Ronnie screamed. "You're gonna get fucked up real soon and you're not gonna know when it's comin', you dirty bastard! I wanna talk to an attorney! Jailer, I wanna call John Tanner! Right now!"

Tanner was an attorney Ronnie had hired to represent him on other charges previously. I didn't know if he was his attorney now.

As Ronnie shrieked, Cissy fluttered her eyes and squeezed them shut. "Please say something to him to shut him up so we can eat our dinner in peace."

The last thing I wanted to do was to talk to Ronnie like this, with everybody listening, but I couldn't let the purported snitch rap go on. Cissy was right. It was too serious to overlook.

"Hey, Ronnie," I hollered, "I'm tired of you screaming me out to be a snitch."

The jail became silent. The seconds ticked by as everyone awaited his response.

"Yeah, Dennie Leon, well, your buddies Smith and Rogers told me that you gave a confession sayin' I killed that bitch Carter, and now you think you're gonna get off without a scratch. There's gonna be recompense."

"Well, whatever Smith and Rogers told you is a bare-ass lie," I yelled. "In the first place, I don't know what you did or didn't do. And secondly, I'm no snitch, and I don't appreciate you threatening my life when in fact I didn't say a word about you to Smith and Rogers. They were trying to mess you up by telling you lies so you would confess. Hell, Ronnie, they don't care whether we did it. Just so they can get somebody to take the rap for this is all they want. Think about what I said and try to calm down. You're dragging on everybody's nerves."

Ronnie didn't answer.

I sat on my bunk. I was exhausted and hungry. I started to holler for Lloyd when he reappeared with my dinner tray. Half melted slivers of ice floated in my Kool-Aid, and the food looked cold and greasy. Lloyd reluctantly came full face with me at my cell door, quickly bent, and slid my tray under the bars. He stood up, looked cautiously to his left and right, then slid his hand into his pocket and produced a small paper sack that he handed to me. It was filled with raisins.

"Gotcha, Lloyd," I responded as he disappeared into the hallway. I sat down on my bunk to eat, and the outer door slammed shut. I ate my supper and stretched out on my mattress. I was nearly asleep when I thought I heard someone say my name.

"Dennis, are you still awake?" whispered Cissy.

I stepped to the bars.

From the bean hole, Cissy flashed a seductive smile. Her eyes sparkled with desire. "Just wonderin' what you were doin'," she teased.

"Just finishing that so-called crap they call food," I responded.

She was flirting with me. Her eyes darkened as she tossed her hair seductively from side to side. It had been a long time since I had seen a woman, and her swaying rhythmic motions definitely had an effect.

"I wrote this here little letter for you to read so you can go to sleep tonight with me on your mind," she purred. She flipped a folded piece of paper toward my cell. It landed on the floor. She backed up from the bean hole and stepped up on something. Possibly it was the table; I didn't know how the girls' tank was laid out. She opened her shirt. Her breasts were bare, and thin nylon panties hugged her hips. Then, like an erotic dancer, she writhed in circles across the table, flailing her hair and showing off her bare body.

I was spellbound.

Some of the other women in the tank sang strains of a Supremes song and clapped while Cissy did her thing and danced.

The performance went on for several minutes, until keys sounded in the corridor.

I reached out and grabbed the folded letter before the door opened. The girls stopped singing, and the star of the show disappeared.

"What's all this noise back here?" the guard said.

I stepped back to my bunk and didn't say a word.

A plump, grinning man in uniform stepped in front of my cell. Beads of perspiration dotted his forehead. His thinning hair and double chin made him look old. "Who's makin' all that noise?" he asked me.

"I wouldn't know. I just woke up when you opened that door. What time is it?"

"It's a little after eleven," he said, looking me over. "I understand you're the Dennis Fritz that everybody's been talkin' about."

"Yeah, that's me. What does everybody call you?"

"My name's Mike, jailer Michael Tenney. What time did they bring you in?"

"Late afternoon, probably between five-thirty and six. It was really hot out still. How long have you been working here?"

"Just a few months. Why do you want to know?"

"No reason. I was just trying to make conversation, if that's all right."

"I hear they got the death penalty filed on you," Tenney said. He turned and glanced at the girls' tank bean hole.

"That's what I understand. Do you know when I might be taken to court to be arraigned?"

"I'm not for sure, but I think it'll be within the next couple of days. Do you have an attorney?"

"No, my family couldn't scrape up the money. I talked to a few Oklahoma lawyers over the phone while I was in Kansas City, but they wanted more than my family could afford. Do you know if they'll appoint me somebody before I'm arraigned?"

"You'll just have to wait and see what happens. It's a big case around here, so if you can't afford an attorney, they might have to appoint you one. I just don't know."

"Thanks. I appreciate the information. I'm an innocent man and didn't commit any kind of murder. Thank you, Mike, for talking with me. You seem like a good person. I would like to talk with you more later but right now I'm dead tired. I need to get some sleep."

"Well, I've gotta make my rounds. If you're awake later, we can talk more. I'll tell you this right now: You sure don't wanna go before a death penalty jury. Maybe you can make some kind of deal if they appoint you a public defender."

"No, Mike, I can't make any deals. I'm an innocent man and I'll take it all the way if necessary."

"Well, you just think about it. Don't be foolish and overlook the chance to make some kind of a deal, especially when you're facing the death penalty. If you've lived around here very long, then you must remember what happened with Ward and Fontenot. The prosecutors didn't even have a body, but they both got convicted and sent to death row. You need to start thinkin' about yourself and forget about Ronnie. He's crazier than a bedbug, anyway, and truth is, they're gonna get a conviction in this case one way or the other, and you don't wanna end up with him on death row, do you?"

"Of course I don't, but I'm not about to lie on Ronnie just to save myself from getting the death penalty when in fact I don't know whether he's guilty or not."

"You think about it. Ronnie don't care about you in the least. He's been talkin' real bad about you ever since they brought him in."

"What's he been saying?"

"I don't have the authority to reveal that to you. All I can say is that he is very upset with you and has been makin' life uncomfortable for everyone around here." He twisted his keys in his hand. "I gotta make my rounds. I'll talk to you later on."

I lay back down on the crumpled mattress and tossed the scratchy woolen blanket around my legs. I wondered how my mom and aunt were coping. They were torn with despair when they realized I had to be moved here and they wouldn't be able to visit me regularly. I wanted to call them and let them know everything was all right, but I let it go. My heart ached for them.

I thought of Elizabeth. I still didn't know how she was dealing with the shock of having found out that her daddy had been arrested for such a terrible crime. I had only talked to her once, not too many days after I was arrested. Her grandma Mary had answered the telephone and didn't want me to talk to her, even when I told her I was innocent and didn't know anything about the murder. I couldn't blame her. After all, we had grown apart after Mary died, and she had always acted like she held Mary's death against me. I asked Me Ma Mary if Elizabeth knew that I had been arrested. She informed me that she had called her minister, who came to her house and delicately told Elizabeth what happened. She said Elizabeth had wept and sobbed throughout the night.

After hearing me out, she said she would only allow me to speak with her if I agreed to not upset her any more than she was. I assured her that I wouldn't.

When Elizabeth got on the phone, I did most of the talking. I told her that I loved her very much and that a big mistake had been made. I assured her everything would be all right. I told her that I did not do what people said I'd done. I asked her to believe in me and to pray that my innocence would be brought forth. Her voice quavered as she said, "I love you, Daddy. I believe you didn't do what they're saying you did." Her courage melted my heart. I found the strength to remain calm as I shared with my daughter the reminder that Jesus had suffered greatly for something he was innocent of. Her crying abated. We said our goodbyes.

Unfortunately, I had just arrived in the jail at Ada and didn't know if I could use the phone. And it was late. I figured I couldn't call Elizabeth, anyway. I couldn't talk to anyone. I could pray, though. That's what I did.

CHAPTER 7

I awoke during the night. The jail was quiet except for occasional laughter resonating from the bullpens. The steady rush of cool air from the vent filled the dark, lonely silence within my cell. Fear and anxiety gripped me. Why had I been put in the juvenile area, across from the women? Something didn't feel right about that. And why was a jailer so intent on trying to persuade me to plea bargain and sell out Ronnie? Wasn't it enough that I was facing the death penalty, let alone have a guard I had just met be brazen enough to expose me to horrid thoughts of the death chamber?

My thoughts shifted to the preliminary hearing and the witnesses that I had never heard of. Because it was Thursday, I doubted anything would happen this week. At least I had my own private air-conditioned cell. In an odd way, I felt secure in my little cubbyhole, the metal door to the corridor protecting me from the harsh, cruel world that wanted to end my life. At the same time, I understood that I had to compose myself some way for all of the upcoming courtroom experiences. I prayed for the strength and courage to make it through this hellish nightmare. I felt Cissy's folded letter in my pocket. I would read it in the morning. Everything would be clearer in the light of day. I rolled onto my side and closed my eyes again.

Some time later, I awoke to a new volley of obscenities from Ronnie. The content of his verbal harangue was unchanged. I turned over in my bunk and faced the concrete wall, pulling the rough blanket over my head in an attempt to block out his screams.

"Shut up, you crazy motherfucker," a voice retaliated from the bullpens. "Guard, guard, shut his ass up or we're gonna flood these commodes. Get off your lazy asses and do somethin' about his bullshit or we're gonna make some real trouble for you back here. He's driving all of us crazy. Shut that crazy fucker up. Where's the chow, where's the chow? Trusty, bring us our chow."

I guessed the time to be around six in the morning. *Finally, someone has the balls to wake these assholes up and make them do their job.* I listened for the sound of a guard. The girls' tank was silent, but everyone else had to either be awake or in some delirious dream of escaping Ronnie's tantrums. I heard the faint jingling of keys unlocking something and footsteps that stopped just outside in the hallway.

"Williamson, if you don't shut up, we're gonna move you over to the city jail, where you can scream yourself silly if that's what you want," the guard's voice echoed.

"I'm innocent!" Ronnie roared. "You can take me over to the city jail if that's your decision, but I'm not gonna stand for that snitch bein' over here and hidin' out like a weasel. I wanna call my attorney, John Tanner, right now. Do you hear me? Right now!"

"You can talk that over with Ron Scott when he gets here. I have no authorization to allow you to make any calls this early in the morning, so be quiet. You'll get your chance to ask Ron when he gets here."

I got around to reading Cissy's letter, which consisted of information regarding her daughter, how much she believed in my innocence, and how she would love to be over in my cell to make me feel "completely satisfied," with her hot body next to mine. Needless to say, the idea sounded appealing, but I had to be concerned with more important things. Although her presence was distracting, I appreciated hearing someone tell me that they agreed with my declaration of innocence. It made me feel like a dry sponge that had been thrown into water.

A couple hours after breakfast chow was served, a new female inmate was brought back and placed into the girls' tank. Later in the afternoon, she appeared in the bean hole and introduced herself as Billi Jo Beverlin. She stated that she was from a nearby town called Roff. She did not volunteer what she had been charged with.

Billi Jo seemed like a nice girl with a clean-cut appearance, shoulder-length brown hair, and smooth skin. She had a pleasant, outgoing personality. I guessed her to be somewhere in her mid-twenties. She said that she had read about my case and believed in my stated innocence.

"Is the other guy here that got charged with you?" she asked.

"Yeah, he's over across the hall. You'll probably be hearin' him before the day's over with. He's been going off the deep end ever since they brought him in. He thinks I told the cops that he murdered that girl, and he won't accept the truth that the cops lied to him to get him to confess."

"Do you know if he is innocent?"

"I have no idea. The only thing I know for sure is that I have no knowledge whatsoever of any murder."

"Well, I've got some friends who know that girl's family, and what they tell me is that her family thinks the other guy was the one who killed her. Most of the talk that I've heard seems to mainly center around him. You seem like a pretty nice, level-headed guy. I can usually tell a lot about people by what their eyes tell me, and your eyes are kind and caring."

"Well, thank you. I just wish the police believed that, but

they're looking for someone to take a fall for this, and I guess I just happened to come along at the right time."

Our conversation was interrupted by the sound of the key opening the outer door. Ron Scott came to my cell, accompanied by a deputy bearing the nametag of *Christian* pinned over his left shirt pocket.

"Come on, Fritz, your attorney is here to talk to you," Scott muttered. "Don't try any funny business or we'll have to put the cuffs on you. You'll probably be out there about thirty minutes or so. Go ahead, John. Lead the way."

I was led down the hallway toward the main entrance of the jail, following Christian as he turned down another short hallway that led to an open door. As I walked in behind him, I saw an unfamiliar, well-dressed, barrel-chested, white-haired man with a pooched belly standing by the side-entrance glass door.

"Greg, do you want someone to stay out here with you?" Christian asked.

"No, that's okay, John. I don't think Dennis will try to escape."

"Well, I'll leave this inner door open where we can keep a close eye on him."

"Thank you," said the man.

As Christian walked through the doorway, the man smiled and introduced himself.

"Hi, Dennis, please have a seat. My name is Greg Saunders, and I've been appointed by the court to represent you on the charges filed against you." Stepping to a table where his briefcase lay, he withdrew some papers and placed them before me. "Dennis, before we proceed, I want you to read very carefully the document before you. It is a pauper's affidavit with an attached form showing the various income ranges that fit your financial status. If you fall into an acceptable range, which I think you will, the court will then accept my entry of appearance, and I will officially be your attorney of record throughout all of the legal proceedings. After you've read the attachment, we'll bring in a notary who's waiting outside, and you can sign your name at the bottom of the affidavit."

I hurriedly reviewed the documents and checked the lowest income range on the attachment, then signed my name.

"That was pretty fast," the attorney commented.

"I'm a fast reader, Mr. Saunders, and besides, I have no income to my name or any property to claim. My mom and aunt are at the bottom of the barrel financially. They scratch out a living by cleaning houses and odd jobs that they can find. They have to work their tails off just to make ends meet."

"Dennis, you can call me Greg," the attorney offered. "Let me ask you this: How long were you in Kansas City before you were arrested, and what was the exact reason why you left Ada?"

"I was there a little over three weeks, I guess. The reason I left was because me and my wife were separated and I went to Kansas City to help Mom and Aunt Wilma with a house-painting job."

"You are aware that a bill of particulars has been filed on you?"

I nodded, then asked, "You're asking me if I know that the death penalty has been filed on me?"

"Yes. The reason I asked you why you left Ada is that it becomes very important in the legal proceedings if in fact you left to flee or avoid legal prosecution. So, you did not leave because you had any idea that you would possibly be arrested on this charge?"

"No, it's like I told you. I left Ada to help my mom and aunt."

"Okay, Dennis. You have been charged with rape in the first degree, rape by instrumentation, and first-degree murder. Your preliminary hearing will begin this coming Monday on July 20. I've been talking to Barney Ward and Frank Baber, who will represent Ronnie, and we all believe that the rape charges against you will have to be dropped because of a three-year statute of limitations."

"What does that mean?"

"Essentially, Dennis, it means that the prosecution has three years from the time of the murder to have charged you and Ronnie with the rape. Since five years have elapsed from the time of the murder, you are exempt from being charged with the alleged rape. There are some exceptions to that rule, but we think that you fall outside those exceptions. And one of those exceptions coincides with whether or not you were fleeing prosecution when you left Ada. I don't believe that they have any evidence that would show your prior knowledge of a pending arrest."

"Well, that's good to know. When will you know for sure whether or not the rape charges will be dropped?"

"We are going to check this out very thoroughly before we proceed to attempt to get the charges dropped. As far as I know right now, we're going to go ahead and start the preliminary due to the fact that I don't have much time to prepare and we want to find out what evidence the state will put on. I will try and get a continuance, but there are no guarantees to that. I have to ask you, Dennis, because you are my client and I must abide by your final decisions: Do you want to waive the preliminary hearing and take this on to trial?"

"What would be your advice on doing that?"

"Well, in this situation, since I have not been fully informed as to who the witnesses are and what their testimonies will include—I know that they plan to introduce a doctor, Fred Jordan, and someone named Glen Gore—it is my opinion that we need to have the preliminary hearing to find out as much as—"

"I don't know about them. Do you know who Donna Elaine Johnson, Susan Land, and Melvin Hett are?" I interrupted.

"Where did you hear those names?"

"They were at the bottom of the charge information sheet that the judge gave me at my extradition hearing."

"I'm not sure about Donna—who'd you say?"

"Donna Elaine Johnson."

"I'm not sure who she is but Susan Land and Melvin Hett

work with the Oklahoma State Bureau of Investigation. They were the ones who analyzed the hair comparisons."

"Hair comparisons? Listen, Greg, I want you to know that I am innocent of this murder. I never met Debbie Carter in my life, and I only read about her murder in the newspaper after it happened. I never heard her name even mentioned before her murder occurred. Smith even told me that he didn't believe that I committed the murder but thinks that I was there that night with Ronnie."

"He told you that? When and where did he say that?"

"It was the night of my arrest when they—him and Rogers—were trying to get me to confess. Rogers left the room momentarily, and Smith got close to me and told me that, in a very low voice like it was some sort of secret. I couldn't believe that I had been arrested on a murder that I knew nothing about, and Smith said he didn't believe I had participated in it. And Featherstone—while we were at the airport in Kansas City getting ready to come back here to Ada—told me that I had done bad only on one lie detector test question."

"And what was that question, Dennis?"

"He had asked me if I had ever been in Debbie Carter's apartment. I can remember when he asked me that, and I had some doubt because I was trying to remember if maybe I had had too much to drink and had totally blacked everything out. But, Greg, I have never been so drunk that I couldn't remember where I had been the night before."

He nodded. "I just met with District Attorney Bill Peterson, and his assistants, Nancy Shew, and Chris Ross. They are being very tight-lipped about everything. We'll have to see what kind of case they've got before I can file the necessary motions. That always comes during or after a preliminary hearing. Listen, Dennis, right now, the most important thing is for you to not talk to anyone about anything. It can only do you damage, so above all else, don't talk about your case with anyone. Understand?"

"Yeah. Greg, can you tell me why they put me in the juvenile area, across from the girls' cell?"

"I don't know. Maybe the jail's too crowded, or maybe they're intent on moving you as soon as the hearing is over."

"I just thought I'd ask. It seemed a little strange, especially since I looked at the jail roster when I first got here, and there were still empty bunks open in the bullpens and some of the other isolated cells were empty. I don't mind it. At least I'm away from all the noise and confusion in the bullpens. I should be thankful that I've got a cell to myself. And one other thing, Greg. Ronnie is back there, cursing and yelling and calling me a snitch. He believes I ratted him out while I was in Kansas City. He is really flipping out."

"Don't even respond to him. He's obviously wrong, isn't he?"

"Absolutely. I have never snitched out on anyone, let alone try to save my own self at the expense of another person. I don't know one way or the other whether Ronnie committed the murder."

"Were you with him on the day of the murder or sometime shortly before that?"

"No, not that I can fully remember. I hadn't seen Ronnie for several months. I was teaching school in Noble and didn't have the time or motivation to hang around him. He had gotten pretty far out there, with extreme mood changes and times where he was loud and demanding one minute and really sullen the next. I'm still having trouble remembering exactly where I was at on the night of that girl's murder. I spent countless hours up there in the Kansas City jail, going over and over in my mind where I was at."

"I understand, Dennis, how difficult it might be to remember where you were five years ago. I probably couldn't remember where I was a month ago, let alone five years. But actually, weren't you interrogated a few months after the murder occurred?"

"Yeah, that's true, but I never really felt like I had a reason to remember where I was on that night. In my wildest dreams, I would never have guessed that I would have been charged with a murder that I never knew anything about. I'm still not one hundred percent for sure, but I believe I was in Ada on the night that girl was killed. The reason I can pin it down is because I had been seeing a girl by the name of Sharon Hill there in Ada. Every now and then during the weekdays, I would drive from Noble to Ada after my classes were over. Sharon had called me in Noble the night before and invited me to come over to her apartment the next night. After basketball practice that next afternoon, I believe I drove to Ada and went to Sharon's apartment and spent the entire night with her."

"Excuse me, Dennis. Let me get this straight," said Greg. "You're saying that you might have been in Ada on the night that Debbie Carter was murdered?"

"Well, like I said, I can't be totally for sure but I'm almost certain that it was during the early part of December back in 1982."

"What apartments did Sharon live in?" asked Greg, his eyes meeting mine.

"The Oxford Square Apartments up behind the Village Inn. Of course, I'm not sure whether she still lives there, but she worked as a nurse at the Valley View Hospital, if that helps any."

"I am going to try and locate Sharon Hill and see if she will be willing to provide you with an alibi defense. If for whatever reason she does not agree to do so, then our defense will be limited to the mere fact that you are innocent and had no involvement in the murder or rape," Greg said.

"Greg, y'all have another five minutes to wrap it up," Christian announced from the hall.

"Okay, John, we're about through. Listen, Dennis, I would like to spend more time with you but they've got their rules, so I will try and get back over to talk with you before the hearing starts. I believe it starts at nine o'clock. I might be able to get over here around eight or so to let you know what to expect."

"I appreciate that, Greg. I just have one other question. Are you a criminal attorney?"

"My practice is in civil law but I have been involved in a few criminal cases in the past. Some time ago, I was assigned as one of the attorneys in a pretty big murder trial."

"What kind of civil law do you do?" I asked.

"Right now, Dennis, I do personal injury and civil litigation ranging from divorce to bankruptcy and other types of civil liabilities."

"Time's up, Greg. We need to get him on back so he can eat some chow," Christian instructed.

I didn't get a chance to ask Greg several other things that were on my mind. After I was locked down, Ronnie started yelling that I must have been snitching to the cops again. He wouldn't shut up. I wasn't in any mood to listen to his bullshit. Despite Greg's warnings to not talk to him, I let Ronnie know that I had talked to my newly appointed attorney and was not snitching him out to any of the cops. He became quiet. Either he lost interest or became preoccupied with eating. For whatever reason, his silence was a small miracle.

As I ate, I mulled over the multitude of questions that I didn't get around to asking. Why did they have to dig Debbie Carter's body back up after five years? Wouldn't her body have decayed after that long? Why did they have to wait five years before they arrested me? Were any fingerprints of mine found in her house? Surely, I would have remembered something—even a glint of a memory—if I had been in her house. Or do I have amnesia and not know it? I had no way of finding any answers.

The jail's air conditioner broke down during the weekend. Inmates were climbing the walls due to their discomfort, dispensing their dissatisfactions with boisterous threats of lawsuits and destruction to the jail. It was impossible to sleep, concentrate, or remain in any state of tranquility, especially in the isolated cells where Ronnie and I were, where we had no showers to cool off in.

The heat escalated through the weekend, and I woke Sunday lying in a pool of my own sweat. The skin on my buttocks and lower back shriveled and then blistered in the heat. Ronnie's maddening screams grew to deafening proportions. Cissy continued her sporadic performances of topless erotic dancing, and more folded letters containing graduated descriptions of her raging sexual desires arrived air express at the foot of my cell door. The trusties grew despondently inactive, staying close to their box fans in the kitchen, rarely responding to the aggravated pleas echoing from the bullpens. The food we were forced to eat went from bad to worse as we sweltered in our cells. I had thought jail in Kansas City was bad. Jail in Pontotoc County that weekend was hell.

Chapter 8

The rank odors of misery and suffering that permeated the jail all weekend gave way on Monday to streams of cool air circulating once again through the cells. I shivered with anxiety as I swung my feet from the bunk to the floor, knowing that this day was my day in court and that it would likely be filled with surprises. I would finally get to see Ronnie in person and maybe find out just how much the cops had lied to him. I would also get to meet his attorneys. I knew Barney Ward's reputation: He was the best criminal attorney in Ada, despite the fact he was blind. Barney was a large man who commanded an audience's attention. In the courtroom, he got to the point of any matter and did not react well when someone tried to pull one over on him. He was well liked and respected—a "true defender for the working class." He loved the challenge of defending an underdog. Frank Baber, on the other hand, was not someone I'd ever heard of. Maybe he did all of Barney's legal legwork because Barney was blind.

Something that had bothered me just under the surface really grated on me, now that I thought about it. It just didn't make sense that Ronnie got Barney, the best criminal attorney around, while I got a bankruptcy lawyer. Why wasn't I getting a criminal attorney, also? We were both charged with the same crime. We both faced the death penalty. Why the difference? What was the deal?

Muffled voices, footsteps, and rustling keys sounded in the corridor outside the metal door, but the retarded trusty didn't say a word as he entered the hall between the girls' tank and my cell to deliver our trays. As he slid my tray under the bars, I heard other footsteps—short, choppy ones—in the outer hall. I bent down to get my tray. Ron Scott appeared at the cell door.

"Let's go, Fritz," he mumbled. "We gotta get you showered and ready for your preliminary hearing at nine."

I looked at the grits on my tray. "Can I eat my chow while it's still hot?" I asked.

"Don't worry, you'll be right back. You've got ten minutes to shower. Your chow'll still be hot when you get back," Scott said as he unlocked my cell door and glanced around the cell. Apparently he had already eaten breakfast and wasn't hungry. It was no skin off his nose if I missed mine.

"Go on up and use the shower in the laundry room. You walked past it when we brought you in. Shampoo and soap's already there, so make it snappy and don't be foolin' around."

I hesitated. He was sending me off to the shower alone?

"Go on. You're wasting time," he said. He took the tray from my hands.

I walked past him into the hall. The glare of the overhead lights reflected off of the white walls. So this is what a mole must feel like when he first comes out of his hole. The forty-watt light bulb in my cell was hardly an adequate source of light, but my privacy was more important than having a cell all lit up like a carnival. I walked to the laundry room. No one was waiting there to jump me.

Upon returning to my cell, I heard Ronnie roar out a new string of vocalizations about how he was going to vindicate himself through the will of God in all of His strength and glory. His attentions seemed to be more focused on himself, amiss from his usual projections of anger and hostility towards me. I was glad. I paused briefly in the outer corridor and glanced at Ronnie's cell door. His face appeared briefly in the bean hole as he paced in his cell. Our eyes locked for a second. His expression looked empty.

"Move on, Fritz," Scott commanded from the hall.

"Do you know what time it's getting to be?" I asked, stepping past the metal door and into the cell again.

"It's time for you to get ready to go. It's eight-thirty."

Upon being locked down, I picked up my tray from my bunk. The chow was cold. I ate a few bites, but it wasn't worth it. Just the sight of the food — the lifeless, lumpy grits slung beside two pieces of stale white bread and a small scoop of peanut butter — made my knotted stomach churn. I felt like I needed to vomit. As I sat there, Ronnie's rich baritone broke into a rendition of *I'll Fly Away* with all the sanctified fervor of a gospel singer. Despite his extreme accusations, I couldn't help but feel Ronnie's wrenching pain and duress. He too was charged with this hellish murder, and he was screaming to no end that he did not commit it. As Ronnie screamed, I realized I was trembling. My heart ached to hear his agony and torment. We may have drifted apart these past couple of years, but Ronnie was my friend — my friend to the end.

I pulled a small paper sack from my jumpsuit pocket — the raisin sack Lloyd had given me on Friday — and cupped it around my mouth and nose. I inhaled and exhaled with measured breaths — a technique I had learned many years back that always seemed to stabilize the effects of hyperventilation that occurred when I was stressed.

I sat on my bunk and waited. Ronnie's singing had ended. He hadn't made so much as a peep for several minutes. Evidently, he had either refused his shower or had been taken to the courthouse before me.

Ron Scott and the jailer, Mike Tenney, entered the hallway in front of my cell.

"Let's go, Fritz," Scott said as he unlocked the cell door. "Time to get this show on the road."

When I stepped from my cell, I could see the main corridor. Ronnie was shuffling forward toward the central corridor, his hands cuffed in front of him, a guard following him just a few steps away. I caught a glimpse of shackles around his ankles. A second guard, someone I hadn't seen during the weekend, was following Ronnie's guard. He turned the corner and headed toward my cell. He carried a set of shackles in his hands. When he got close enough, I read his badge: Self.

"I don't think we'll need the shackles on Fritz, Ernie," Scott asserted as he shot me a quick glance.

"I definitely am not going anywhere but the courtroom," I assured him.

"Ernie, go ahead and get his cuffs on and pat him down good. I'll be up front tendin' to Williamson. We need to get him over there first in case he stirs up a commotion."

The girls were peeking around the stacked food trays left unattended in the bean hole as Ernie locked the cuffs around my wrists. He patted me down easily, like he sensed the stress in the situation. He cracked a joke about the air conditioning, glancing at Tenney like he wasn't sure how he'd react. He seemed like a pretty good guard.

Ernie stepped just beyond the outer door into the corridor and stood there for a few seconds before he signaled to Tenney to bring me out. With Ernie in the lead and Tenney in the rear, we slowly walked to the office area at the front of the jail and stopped. Ernie disappeared as he rounded the breezeway toward the side door of the booking desk. A moment passed before he reappeared and gave the go-ahead to start the half-block walk to the courthouse.

As we exited through the door of the jail, reporters with cameras on their shoulders or microphones in hand bombarded me with questions.

"I'm innocent! I'm innocent," I openly declared as I passed, looking directly at the cameras.

Spectators packed the alley behind the courthouse, the east lawn, and adjacent sidewalks. Inside, the corridors were lined, too. Everybody wanted to get a first-hand look at the killers finally being brought to justice. Whispers and remarks flew like feathers on a windy day as the guards moved me quickly through the masses to the concrete stairway that led to the courtroom. We walked to the third floor. The hallway outside the courtroom was packed with curious onlookers. I didn't recognize anybody, which was probably good.

Though I had mentally prepared myself for this moment, I was taken aback as the courtroom doors swung open and I saw the packed benches of the gallery. People twisted, swung their heads, and shifted from side to side as I entered. In the back of the courtroom stood more onlookers, who stared and grew silent as I passed. I walked down the aisle, searching for and finally seeing the back of Ronnie's head in the front of the chamber. He sat at a long oak table on the left side of the room with his back to the gallery. One of his attorneys, Barney, sat directly across from him, with his back to the witness stand. Greg sat at the other end of the table as far away from Ronnie as he could; there was an empty chair between Greg and Ronnie that I figured was supposed to be mine.

On the right side of the room, District Attorney Bill Peterson and his assistant Nancy Shew stood between the prosecution's table and the railing that separated the gallery from the court. The jury box was empty. At the judge's bench sat a well-groomed, dark-haired man dressed in an elegant black robe. He looked several years younger than me. The plaque on his desk bore the name Judge John David Miller.

"Here's my man," said Saunders as I approached the defense table.

Before I was seated, the guard removed my handcuffs. Saunders picked his chair up and moved it nearer to mine at the right side of the table. Ronnie's hands were still cuffed. He held them on his lap. I didn't look to see if he was still in shackles. Saunders handed me a sketch of a human figure with arrows pointing to multiple locations of injury. The name, Debbie Carter, was printed at the bottom of the page. Out of the corner of my eye, I saw Ronnie glance at the sketch and then at me.

"Dennis, you are a lousy, no-good motherfucker for what you did to me!" he shouted at the top of his lungs. From out of nowhere and without any warning, he heaved the solid wood table up into the air and out into the room, violently knocking Barney backwards and out of his chair. The attorney rolled over a couple of times on the floor. Greg stood up behind me. Next to me, Ronnie stood up and looked down at me with a madness that I had never seen before. I bolted to my feet as he lunged for me.

"You son of a bitch!" he screamed. "You lousy, lying, motherfucker son of a bitch."

He rushed toward me like a grizzly bear gone berserk. I scrambled over the upturned table to the other side, and with my back to the witness stand, squared off with my fists clenched, ready to take Ronnie on if he came at me. People in the gallery froze as the horror of the situation unfolded.

"You'll pay for this, you—!" Ronnie shouted, staggering as he tried to take steps in his shackles. The three guards and bailiff uncoiled from their stations and rushed at Ronnie from all directions. Tackling him, they knocked him down. The floor shook when he fell. Still screaming, he lay on his stomach with his cuffed hands beneath him and wriggled as he tried to stand up. It took every bit of the guards' strength to control him. Grabbing Ronnie by the shoulders and arms, the guards dragged him from the courtroom, his still-shackled feet kicking wildly as he bellowed and cursed everyone's existence. Spectators standing near the path of egress slammed into each other like dominoes as they leaned away to be as far from Ronnie as possible.

Greg helped Barney to his shaky feet. The overturned table

was placed in its original position and the chairs put back in place. I stooped over and picked up the only chair that hadn't been righted and scooted it to the back of the table so that I faced the crowd of spectators. I sat in the chair and looked at everyone. I wanted them to see clearly my unafraid expression. I wanted them to know that I was not intimidated or ashamed for anyone—especially the Carter family—to see my face.

The hysteria in the courtroom leveled off to looks of great distress and wide-eyed relief. Simultaneous exhalations and sighs took place throughout the courtroom. The tensed muscles and looks of exasperation all but disappeared in the assembled congregation as Ronnie's shouts faded away out in the hall.

Barney straightened his coat and tie and turned toward the judge's bench.

"I want the record to show I am now making application to withdraw," he proclaimed to Judge Miller. His voice was quaking. "That boy won't cooperate with me at all. If he was paying me, I wouldn't be here. I can't represent him, Judge. I just can't do it. I don't know who's going to, but I can't. And I'm—if I can't get relief here, I'm going to see if I can't get it from the court of criminal appeals—I'm not going to put up with this. I'm too damned old for it. I don't want anything to do with him, not under any circumstances. I have no idea about his guilt or—that has nothing to do with it, but I'm not, I'm not going to put up with this. The next thing you know, he'll be thumping on me, and when he does, he's in bad trouble, and I'll probably be in worse trouble."

"Counsel's motion will be overruled," the judge quickly responded. "I need to see counsel in chambers, please."

After a brief recess, the proceedings continued. The judge spoke to everyone present: "I'm going to ask at this time that the courtroom be cleared of all spectators. Nobody is to remain but counsel and counsel for the defendants and the defendants. I'm going to ask that there be no— I'm going to reconvene the hearing at approximately eleven o'clock. There are some preliminary matters that have to be addressed. I would ask that if you're going to stay around the courthouse, you either go down to the first floor or the second floor. The third floor will be kept clear. And I'm going to attempt to reconvene the hearing, but at this time I'm going to ask that you clear the courtroom."

Chapter 9

"Let's go, Fritz. It's that time," Christian blared as he stood at the cell door at what must have been a few minutes before eleven. In his hand were the handcuffs I would have to wear.

This time, the walk to the courthouse was quieter. The multitudes of media and onlookers had dispersed for the time being. Once inside the building, though, I realized that nothing had changed. When the courtroom doors were opened, the crowd of spectators turned to look at me with awe in their eyes. In the courtroom, Ronnie was already seated in the same chair, and Greg was at the end of the table again, to Ronnie's right. Barney was standing at the other end of the table, out of Ronnie's reach; Frank was next to him, and the judge was already seated at his bench.

"Soon as he walks in," Ronnie was bellowing, "I'm going to get—all right, I see him—Fritz, you're going to settle this now—you and me is going to settle it."

"Mr. Williamson!" the judge shouted.

"Me and you is going to settle it. I ain't never killed nobody," Ronnie continued.

"Hold him there," the judge commanded Christian as we

passed the railing. The deputy led me over toward the prosecution counsel's table, where we waited out of Ronnie's reach while the judge continued, "Mr. Williamson, if there are any further outbursts, this hearing will be conducted without your presence."

"That will be fine with me," Ronnie said.

"Okay, you understand—"

"I said I'd rather not be here, Judge. If you don't mind, I'd rather go back to my cell."

"You wish to waive your right to be present at the preliminary hearing?"

"Yes, I do."

"Nobody's threatening or forcing you to do this? This is your own personal..."

"I'm threatening," Ronnie said.

"Has anybody threatened you, or is this your own personal decision to waive your—"

"I said I'm threatening!"

"Okay. You do not wish to appear at this hearing. Is that correct?"

"That's correct."

"Okay, you may take him back to the county jail," the judge said to the bailiff and guards standing just a few feet away from Ronnie. "Court record will reflect that the defendant Ronald K. Williamson does waive his right to appearance in this courtroom due to his outbursts of anger and total disruption. And the court finds that this hearing cannot be conducted with his presence based on his current statements to this court and outbursts. The court has deemed him to waive his right to his personal appearance. Counsel that has been appointed to him will be here and present, and the court will now take a brief recess for twenty minutes."

The judge stood and stepped from the bench.

I remained standing while Ronnie was escorted from the courtroom and was then led to my seat next to Greg.

"How are you holding up, Dennis?" Greg asked nervously as he watched Ronnie being led through the courtroom doors.

"Have you had a chance to find out what all the police told Ronnie?" I eagerly asked.

"No, I haven't. I don't think they would tell me anyway, and more than likely, Peterson may not even know himself. Even if he did, he wouldn't admit to it and probably would give me crap about it being under protected work product, which is not discoverable. But it's very obvious that the law enforcement officials probably told him you snitched him out to try and extract a confession from him. The main thing right now, Dennis, is for me to find out just exactly what the state's evidence is. You do understand that the prosecution is not required to put their whole case on at this hearing? They only have to present enough evidence to show that there is probable cause that you and Ronnie committed this crime. So, whatever they present I will file motions later on during the discovery process, which will force the state to give me a list of all the remaining witnesses and what their testimonies will be at trial. It's a procedural thing that the judge will have to grant for me to adequately prepare for trial."

I could do nothing more except nod with approval. I had never heard of a discovery process and what it encompassed. Everything that my attorney was saying sounded like he knew what he was doing. Except for today, the closest I had ever been to a trial was having watched Perry Mason on television. Still, the fact bothered me that my attorney was a civil lawyer and had only handled a few criminal cases, especially since the death penalty had been filed on me, and he only had minimal exposure of a murder trial in his past.

I leaned closer to Greg and whispered, "Do you know any of the Carter family? Are they the kind of people who might decide to shoot me here in the courtroom?"

Greg looked at me oddly.

"When you get a chance, look over on the right end in the center section, third row, where the three men and two women are sitting," I whispered.

Nonchalantly, Greg turned his head toward the rear of the courtroom and quickly surveyed the seating section in question with a broad sweeping glance.

"Do you know if they're—?"

"I can't say for sure, Dennis, but I believe the white-haired man is Debbie's father, Charlie Carter. I suspect that the entire row of people are probably Debbie's kinfolk."

"Yeah, I've been getting some real bad looks from them," I told him. "I used to have a backyard neighbor over where I lived on Eighth Street, who told me that there were a lot of Carters, and most of them were pretty mean."

"I wouldn't worry too much about that, Dennis. I don't know if you noticed it or not, but all the courthouse entrances except for the one we came through used metal detectors on everyone coming in."

"Well, I would just feel better if I were facing them head on, eyeball to eyeball."

At that moment, Judge Miller pushed aside the black curtains that shielded his private chambers and reentered the courtroom, and with an air of confidence took his place and began reading: "Comes now this 20th day of July 1987 the matter of case number CRF-87-90, State of Oklahoma versus Ronald Keith Williamson and Dennis Leon Fritz, charged by way of information by the state with three counts: Count One, rape in the first degree; Count Two, rape by instrumentation; Count Three, murder in the first degree, set for preliminary hearing at this time."

He asked District Attorney Peterson and the three defense counselors if they were ready to proceed. They all agreed that they were ready.

At last the time had come. I would get a peek at the strength of the state's evidence against me. Greg said they weren't required to present everything. How could there be anything to present? The more I had thought about it, I was sure I'd never even met or seen Debbie Carter. How had they connected dots between me and a girl

I'd never met? Feelings of helplessness and apprehension shivered through me as I stared at the judge.

"You may call your first witness, Mr. Peterson," the judge announced.

Leaning on the arms of his chair and taking a dramatic breath, Peterson stood up slowly, stepped from between his chair and the prosecution's table, and swaggered confidently toward the podium. His walk, combined with his unyielding, stone-cold glare when he glanced at me, caused goose bumps to form on my arms. His air of conceit projected the impression that he was in possession of a powerful great secret and that he was waiting for the perfect moment to unleash it.

"Your Honor, at this time I would call out of order Dr. Fred Jordan," Peterson announced.

A tall, slender man approached the witness stand at a relaxed gait and was sworn in by the bailiff.

"State your name for the record, please."

"Fred Jordan."

"Are you a duly licensed physician and surgeon?"

"Yes, sir."

"Dr. Jordan, did you have occasion on December 9, 1982, to conduct an examination of one known to you as Debbie Carter?"

"Yes, sir, I did an autopsy examination ordered by Dr. Cartmell, the medical examiner here in Ada."

"And would you relate to the court your findings of that autopsy, please?" Peterson stated.

"Yes, sir. The body was that of a young white female. She was clad only in white socks at the time that I saw her. Received with her was a length of electrical cord attached to a rheostat and a belt that had the name *Debbie* inscribed on it. Externally, the body had what appeared to be catsup smeared over parts of her upper legs and her back. On the front area below the breasts and the upper part of the abdomen was the word *die, d-i-e,* in some type of material different from that. It was dried. It looked like it might have been nail polish or something of that nature. There were multiple bruises about the head and the arms and the legs. There was a greenish-colored apparent washcloth which was firmly impacted into the mouth and the back part of the airway. There were linear abrasions around the neck. There was bruising around the vagina. There was bruising around the rectum, and there was a bottle cap found inside the rectum. There were also small hemorrhages about the eyes and the whites of the eyes."

"Now, you said that there was a ligature mark around the throat of the deceased?" Peterson asked.

"Basically, on the front side of the throat and partially on the sides, yes, linear abrasions consistent with a ligature mark."

Peterson walked slowly away from the podium and stood before the expert witness in front of the witness stand.

"Dr. Jordan, did you also take some slides or recover some material that you looked at under slides to determine whether there was any spermatozoa?"

"Yes, sir."

"Would you tell the court what your findings were, please?"

"I took swabs from the mouth, anus, and rectum at the time I first examined Debbie Carter. The slides made from the swabs of the mouth did not show any spermatozoa. However, intact sperm were present on the slides made from the rectum and from the vagina."

"Thank you. Dr. Jordan, with reasonable medical certainty do you have a conclusion as to the cause of death of Ms. Carter?"

"Yes, sir, I do. Ms. Carter died as a result of asphyxia, or in other words, not obtaining enough air, a form of suffocation that was caused by the ligature strangulation and the washcloth in the mouth, and probably the two in combination."

"Your witness," Peterson announced abruptly. He returned to the prosecution's table.

There was a hint of reservation in Judge Miller's eyes when Barney stood to cross-examine the witness.

Barney stayed near the defense table and held his cane in his hand, his dark glasses placed on the ridge of his nose. He painstakingly grilled the physician about the date and time that his facility received the body and where the results of the test of the victim's drawn blood could be located. His questions were delivered with the precision of a drill sergeant performing morning inspection. Jordan hesitated frequently as he answered, stating that he would have to refer to his notes but he did not have a complete set of them because his secretary didn't get everything copied. Gruffness started creeping into Barney's voice after Jordan made several evasive responses concerning the exact date and time that he had last viewed Debbie's body. Barney didn't miss a beat. His intelligence was mirrored in his directness and spontaneity. Jordan's facial color was slowly turning ashen.

"When you last viewed the body, what type of work did you do on it?" Barney stated.

"I didn't do any at that time. The body was exhumed at the request of the OSBI because they — I understood they had wanted to take palm prints, so I did nothing directly. It was a police matter."

"You personally saw the body?"

"Yes, sir, after they had opened the casket. As I say, I wasn't directly involved in this except for the use of our facilities so they could take palm prints."

"Can you describe the hands to me?"

"No. I didn't look at them carefully, Mr. Ward."

Looking at Greg to get his attention, I slid a handwritten note to him to ask him if he could ask Jordan what condition the body was in when he viewed it last. Greg looked down briefly at the note and then stuck it inside his file full of papers. Greg was heavily focused on Barney's cross-examination and did not acknowledge my request with an immediate answer.

"I don't have any further questions," Barney concluded.

"Mr. Saunders, you may cross-examine," the judge announced.

At last, I would finally get to see my bankruptcy attorney in action. I'd already made my mind up that if he didn't do well, I would ask the court for another attorney. I didn't know what legal process it would involve, but there was always the media if everything else failed. To my surprise, Greg came out like a roaring lion, with a lot of energy and well-articulated questions.

He had a vastly different approach than Barney. He was not as blunt or straightforward in his delivery of questions to Jordan. He used the nice-guy approach by introducing himself first and then trying to make the witness feel that he was under no pressure but to tell the truth and answer his questions to the best of his ability. He seemed to be able to get to the same point as Barney did, but he did so in a more roundabout way without intimidating Jordan. I hoped that his style would be just as effective as Barney's when the heat was turned up.

Greg moved from the front of the witness stand and back to the podium, never staying in any position longer than a few seconds.

The color gradually returned to Jordan's face. He explained that he had copies of everything that Greg needed and he would furnish all documents, including the history of the case and anything that was contained in the examiner's file, to the defense. Momentum was building on each and every question that Greg asked.

"Doctor, were you able to form an opinion as to the approximate time of death?"

"No, sir, when I saw the body, it was in full rigor, and— but of course, the body had been put in our refrigerator, which kind of slows things down, but the stiffening of the body was complete."

Greg concluded his cross-examination by asking questions concerning the procedures that were done to preserve the fingerprints and palm prints just prior to Debbie's death. Jordan's office was not involved in the actual fingerprinting of the victim. As he stated before, that was a matter for the police.

"No further questions, Your Honor," Greg stated.

"If there is no redirect, the state may call its next witness," the judge stipulated.

"The state calls Glen Gore," Peterson declared in his calm and bold manner.

Gore was short and stocky with a plump face and black wavy hair. He was sworn in and sat nervously in the witness chair as he waited for Peterson to speak.

The district attorney asked Gore to name his past felonies for which he had received convictions.

"Objection, Your Honor. The state doesn't have the right to impeach its own witnesses," Barney argued.

"Overruled, Mr. Ward. There's an evidence code, and if he's a hostile witness, I think it's for your own behalf. I will allow him to proceed."

Gore had recently been brought back from the penitentiary after he had been convicted of kidnapping, first-degree burglary, and shooting with intent to kill. He had a string of other felonies but he only named the convictions he received time on. He was a smooth talker once he got started. His answers were straightforward and without hesitation. His dark, ominous eyes shifted from side to side as he purported the events of December 7, 1982, the eve of Debbie's murder.

"I went out to the Coach Light nightclub a little before midnight with this guy named Ron—I can't remember his last name—and had a few drinks. Well, we was all sittin' at a table, and I can't remember who all was sittin' there with us—well, anyway, I went up to get me another drink and seen Debbie talkin' to Williamson, and right after that she came up to me and asked me if I would rescue her. You know, just like most girls do when a guy would ask them to dance, they'll say no and then when somebody comes along that they know, they'll ask them to step in. Debbie said that Williamson was bugging her so we went ahead and danced. I had quite a bit to drink that night but I remember him because I served him before when I was a bartender out at Harold's. Shortly after that, they started flickin' the lights on and off for everybody to leave, so I got a ride and got somethin' to eat before goin' home."

I leaned over to Greg and whispered, "Greg, he didn't say a word about me."

Nodding his head, Greg turned slightly and softly said, "Our turn's coming right after Barney, so be patient."

Be patient! How could I be patient when Peterson's witness never even said a single word about me? Why would Peterson be waiting to implicate me when he never even asked Gore if I was with Ronnie that night? There must be something huge that he's saving for me.

Gore's cross-examinations by Barney and Greg dumfounded everyone in the courtroom, including the judge. Barney squeezed out key information. Gore said he first talked to the police shortly after the murder, telling them the same thing he had just related. Barney's glasses almost slipped off his nose after finding out that Gore didn't talk to the police again until two years after that first visit. Gore said that a couple of years later he was asked by Smith to give hair and saliva samples, along with a second statement because the police had lost the first one. He also said that the police told him that they needed his hair and body fluid samples because he was the last person to be seen with Debbie. Barney squeezed even harder. Gore tensed up before finally stating that there were lots of people there at the nightclub but he didn't think that he had seen me there that night.

My mouth dropped open. Greg looked at me out of the corner of his eye and smiled. The courtroom crowd was flabbergasted. The bailiff dropped his eyes and turned his head to look at the judge. The sound of Peterson tapping his fingers against the prosecution table was heard throughout the courtroom.

"Did they take anything else from you besides hair samples?" Barney ventured.

"No, that's about it."

"Did they ask you for anything else?"

"They asked me if I would submit to a polygraph test, and I said yes."

"Did you?"

"No."

"Why not?" Barney sounded angry.

"They never come forth to me again."

"They just asked you if you would?"

"Yes."

"Did they lose interest, then?"

"I don't know. They come back and— It was around the day before you talked to me this last time."

"You mean two or three weeks ago, Glen?"

"Yes, and they got— they asked me to give them some more samples because they lost the other ones, and—"

"They took hair samples from you twice?" said Barney in an exaggerated voice.

"Yes, yes, three times, I think."

"They took a statement from you twice because they lost one of them, took hair samples from you at least twice and possibly three times, and told you the reason was that they had lost the first samples?"

Gore nodded.

"I believe that's all, Glen."

"Mr. Saunders," Judge Miller directed.

Greg stood up and stepped to the podium. He didn't stay still long.

"Glen, other than seeing pictures on the news and maybe seeing him around town, you haven't ever had any contact with Mr. Fritz, is that true?"

"No, he tried to talk to me the other night in the jail through a girl in between us by the name of Cissy, asking me what I—if I was down here for this case and everything. I told him I wasn't supposed to talk about it."

"Okay, but other than that, you've never had any contact," Greg confirmed.

"No."

"You may redirect, Mr. Peterson," said Judge Miller.

"Mr. Gore, have you ever seen this defendant and Ron Williamson together?"

"No."

"Not at the Coach Light?"

"They might have been, but it—I—I couldn't directly say."

"No further questions," said Peterson with a look of disgust. It was obvious that he was upset over Gore's testimony. He walked briskly back to the prosecution's table and in a state of irritation fumbled through a stack of folders. Nancy Shew rose from her seated position and whispered something to him. Peterson shook his head.

A tall, middle-aged, thin man named Tommy Glover was the prosecution's next witness. Led into the courtroom by an attending deputy, Glover had an awkward, timid presence. He testified that he knew Debbie Carter by having worked with her at the Brockway Glass plant and the Coach Light Club. In brief testimony, he stated that he had gotten off work that night around midnight, drove to the club, had a couple of beers, and left around one on the morning of December 8. As he was leaving, he said, he saw Debbie and Glen Gore talking out in the parking lot by Debbie's car. Glover indicated to Peterson, Barney, and Greg that he hadn't noticed anything unusual while Debbie was talking with Gore. In response to Greg's round of cross-examination questions, Glover stated that he had never seen or heard of Dennis Fritz in his life.

What was his testimony all about then? Other than the fact that Glover had told Peterson that he had seen Debbie leave by herself, what relevance did that have with me and Ronnie? I looked over at Greg. He looked like he might be wondering the same thing but then he turned toward me, and I saw a look of confidence in his eyes. At the same time, I realized that Peterson still hadn't played whatever card he was holding that I guessed was supposed to implicate me in this mess. Whatever it was, it had to be a surprise out of hell in a wrapping of lies and deliberate misrepresentations. I shifted in my seat as I awaited the next witness.

"Your honor, the state calls Charlie Carter," Peterson proclaimed.

Upon seeing Mr. Carter ushered to the witness stand, my heart turned over in my chest. I knew the pain and sorrow that he had experienced over the death of his daughter. I deeply sensed his every reaction: his averted eyes, his facial features tightening over the mere mention of his daughter's name, his dejected tone of voice that hit at the very core of my own vulnerability as I thought of my beloved wife, Mary. His brittle white hair and gaunt cheeks identified the hours of suffering that he and his family had gone through for five years—waiting, waiting, and waiting for the veil of justice to be lifted.

Peterson began his direct-examination by asking Mr. Carter how he came to find his daughter in her apartment. He said he had gotten a call from her mother saying that she thought something was wrong after she received a call from Donna Johnson or one of Debbie's other friends. He went to Debbie's upstairs apartment on Eighth Street and found her nude body lying face down with a gray washcloth stuffed in her mouth. Her bedroom furniture and belongings were in total disarray. With one look, Mr. Carter said, he knew his daughter was dead. He reached down and picked her up by her shoulder and called out her name several times. He turned her body halfway over and then laid her back down. He walked out of the bedroom and stopped for a moment and read the bizarre writing on the living room wall and kitchen table.

On that cold, gray morning of December 8, 1982, Charlie Carter's world was turned inside out, without any hope or promise of ever seeing his precious daughter again. Barney and Greg did not cross-examine him, and the judge recessed the court for lunch until two o'clock.

As the spectators were departing from the courtroom, I spoke to Greg before being taken back to the jail. He seemed to be in a good mood, and I was full of questions that needed to be answered. We were still seated at the defense table when I quickly asked him, "Is there anything that you know that I should be aware of on any of Peterson's upcoming witnesses?"

"I'm not really for sure what you mean, Dennis, but, so far there's been nothing that has implicated you in any way. To be truthful with you, I don't know exactly what Peterson's got up his sleeve but we've got quite a ways to go so try and be as calm as you can. If you have any questions at any time during the hearing, use your notepad to write them down and I will try to present them if it's relevant to the case. How are you holding up?"

"Well, I'll tell you, Greg, right now I'm a bundle of nerves and I'll sure be glad when this day's over with. Do you know who will be the next witness after we get back from the lunch break?"

"Actually, it's just up to how Peterson wants to proceed with the order of his witnesses. Barney told me a while ago that a fingerprinting expert by the name of Jerry Peters will be up some time this afternoon. Anyway, they're fixing to take you back over to the jail, so don't breathe a word to nobody, and try to stay as cool and collected as you can. Okay?"

I nodded as the handcuffs were loosely clamped around my wrists. While walking back to the jail, I thought, just how calm and collected am I supposed to be? Maybe I should be a little more expressive about my innocence and not worry about what everybody else is thinking. Here I am in the middle of a preliminary hearing where the death penalty's filed on me, and I don't even know what the girl looked like that I was supposed to have killed.

After lunch, at the onset of the hearing, I told Greg that I wanted to look at the crime scene pictures to determine whether or not I had ever seen Debbie Carter. A dubious look passed over Greg's face. I explained to him that I would not continue this hearing without first seeing her face, even if her family didn't agree with my decision.

Greg stood up. "Your Honor, my client has made a pertinent

request to look at the crime scene pictures that were introduced with Fred Jordan's testimony."

Judge Miller cleared this throat and looked out toward the section of the courtroom where the Carter family was seated.

"For what purpose does your client base his request?" Judge Miller inquired.

"Your Honor, my client's request is predicated on his own curiosity as to whether or not he ever saw Debbie Carter. Mr. Fritz is laying claim that he has never met or seen Ms. Carter in his life."

The judge sighed and granted the request. He asked the bailiff to go and see if Dr. Jordan was still in the building. While the whole courtroom waited, I felt the Carter family's hateful stares boring into the back of my head. I didn't want to offend the Carter family but at the same time, I was not going to subject myself to any more unsettled feelings at the expense of my own emotional health.

The bailiff returned with Dr. Jordan, who held the photos in his hands. The bailiff took them and handed them to me. I looked at the gruesome and grotesque photographs one by one. I almost vomited at the sight of Debbie's lifeless, violated body. At that moment, without a doubt, I knew that I had never been to her apartment or ever seen her in my life. I handed the photos back to the bailiff.

As Barney had predicted, the state's next witness was Jerry Peters, a fingerprinting expert with the Oklahoma State Bureau of Investigation. Peterson's direct-examination was brief. In his suave, swaggering style, Peterson moved for the admission of a paper sack containing several articles that had undergone fingerprint comparisons after they were removed from the crime scene. Ward roared his objection to the motion, arguing that the chain of custody had not been established for the unidentified contents in the sack. Miller overruled his objection and noted his exception.

Jerry Peters was unusually nervous during Barney's lengthy, detailed, often abrasive cross-examination. In a staggering description, he explained that he had initially failed to obtain a complete inked palm impression of the victim's left hand before she had been buried. He also stated that a minute, bloodstained piece of Sheetrock that had later been removed from a wall in Miss Carter's bedroom could not be adequately compared to her palm impression because he had missed a small ridge detail on her palm print. Under intense scrutiny from Ward, Peters indicated that his oversight in 1982 was the reason that Debbie's body had been exhumed in early 1987 for another comparison.

"Your opinion four and a half years ago was that that bloody palm print was not Debbie Carter's. Is that right?" Barney asked.

"Yes, that's— According to my report at the time, I said it was not identical," Peters told him.

"Mr. Peters, have you compared the palm print which was taken in 1987 with— from the body of Debbie Carter, with the palm print that was taken in 1982. Have you made comparison between those two prints?"

"Yes, I have, and I determined that the inked palm impression of Debbie Carter in 1982 was identical to the latent print found on the Sheetrock."

Ward hammered away at Peters after that. The fingerprinting expert divulged that the unidentified articles in the paper sack were common household items that his laboratory had used to compare prints. Of the twenty-two latent prints removed from the items, Peters testified that nineteen were determined to have been the decedent's, two prints were never identified, and one print lifted from the kitchen table matched the inked impressions of Dennis Smith of the Ada Police Department. He surmised that Smith must have touched the table by accident while at the crime scene.

"Mr. Peters, let me ask you this: Of all the fingerprints that you examined and tested from the decedent's apartment, were any of the prints connected to either Dennis Fritz or Ronnie Williamson?"

"No, sir, there were no identifications made to Mr. Fritz or Mr. Williamson."

"No further questions, Your Honor," Barney said with a smooth, satisfied voice.

Saunders reiterated many of the details that Barney had already drawn out of Peters, including Peters's statement that none of my fingerprints were found at the crime scene. Peters agreed to supply Greg with the names of the thirty-five people who had previously submitted their prints for the sake of comparison, but he unearthed no new information. On redirect, Peterson reemphasized the high points of Peters's original testimony, cementing the alleged fact that the expert's mistake was no fault of his own because Ms. Carter had already been buried by the time Peters had received the piece of Sheetrock.

Judge Miller continued the hearing until nine o'clock the next morning. It had been a long, difficult first day filled with rollercoaster anticipation. I still didn't know what Peterson's ultimate surprise would be.

Chapter 10

The county jail was unusually quiet upon my return. The odor of cooked hot dogs and the sporadic sounds of dominoes being slapped down on the tables in the bullpens told me that chow had already been served. As I made my way back to the cell, an unfamiliar trusty eyed me suspiciously and then handed me my plate of chow. I purposely avoided eye contact and tried my best to not show any signs of the emotional upheaval that the stressful day had imparted.

Cissy's face appeared in the bean hole. Her curiosity was wide eyed, and she was all ears.

"What happened? They brought Ronnie back early," she said.

I gave her a broad rundown of Ronnie's courtroom threats and ended it with mention of the overturned table and Barney rolling on the floor.

In a mesmerized state, Cissy conveyed how Ronnie had screamed out all day worse than ever, over and over, that he was innocent—until just a little while ago—and that everyone in the jail had been shouting and pounding on the walls, bars, and tables to get him to shut up. Her description reinforced my sense of the pain and suffering that Ronnie was dealing with. Even with the massive dosages of Thorazine that Barney had told the judge that Ronnie was receiving, he was still in incredible pain and frustration.

Cissy grew silent. Her look of inquisition suddenly switched to a look of seduction, and she smiled longer than usual and licked her upper lip in that way she had.

"Maybe you'd like to talk about something else? Is there anything I can do to make you happy?" she asked.

I was about to decline her offer when I heard Ronnie's gravelly monotone.

"Hey, Dennie Leon, are you over there?"

I stared at Cissy and didn't answer.

"Come on there, Dennie Leon. Has the pussycat got your tongue?" queried Ronnie.

"Ronnie, you know I'm over here. What is on your mind?"

"I'm perplexed as to what went on at the inquest today, Dennie Leon."

Shaking her head, Cissy said in a whisper, "Don't get him started up tonight."

I ignored her admonishment and cautiously offered to Ronnie, "Peterson put on a couple technical witnesses—a doctor named Fred Jordan, and Jerry Peters, who is a fingerprinting expert with OSBI."

Cissy stared at me with her lips pursed in irritation.

I was not about to get into Glen Gore's testimony, and I desperately needed to get some sleep to withstand a second day in the courtroom Twilight Zone. The one thing that I did not want to share with Ronnie was that the judge, at the close of the day's hearing, announced that he wanted to have Ronnie brought back in the courtroom to inquire one more time whether he still wished to not be present. I waited for Ronnie's response but there was none. *Thank God.*

"Yeah, Ronnie," I volunteered, "I seen the crime scene

pictures today and they were absolutely horrifying. Whoever did that to Debbie Carter has to be a totally deranged psychopath, after what I seen."

"Was she still on the floor or on the bed?" Ronnie asked.

His words froze in mid-air. Cissy's mouth fell open. I dared not respond. I could only stare into her disbelieving eyes. Pandora's box had been opened.

I shut up and sat on my bunk. I couldn't believe what I had heard. I wondered, was it just a slip of the tongue that caused Ronnie to incriminate himself, or did Ronnie let the cat out of the bag without realizing it? How many people in the jail had overheard Ronnie's question, which sounded a lot like an inadvertent admission? I lay down to sleep, the implication of Ronnie's question gnawing at my soul.

The next morning, the courtroom was packed again with spectators, each of them wedging, side-stepping, and shoving their way in for a better view of the second day of the hearing. The atmosphere was charged with expectations from a hundred different sources. The entourage of guards led me to the defense table where Barney and Greg were huddled together in a focused, discerned discussion. Upon noticing my presence, D.A. Peterson grinned in my direction, as if to say, "This is the day I'm saving for you."

My stressed mind retaliated: *Well, bring it on, you bastard. I'm ready for whatever you've got!*

Judge Miller opened the proceedings by asking the defense and prosecution if they were ready to proceed. As before, they were in agreement.

"The record will reflect that Defendant Ronald Keith Williamson is not present at this time due to his continued disruptive and disrespectful conduct, and after three times of trying to start the proceedings, Defendant Williamson has made the statement that he does not wish to be present. This morning prior to this hearing, a hearing was held, with Mr. Williamson disclaiming his right to be present. Mr. Williamson would not promise to be respectful and orderly and continued to state that he did not wish to be present at this hearing. Therefore, the court is proceeding without him. The state may call its next witness."

"The state calls Dennis Smith," Peterson proclaimed.

My heart stopped. Sweat beaded on my forehead and oozed into my scalp as I watched him swear in. Smith and Rogers were my enemies—they were treacherous masters of deception.

For thirty minutes, Peterson questioned Smith about the state's exhibits that included photographs of the decedent's body, her apartment and various articles within, the disarray of her bedroom, and the writing on the kitchen table, living room wall, and her body.

"Mr. Smith, let me show you State's Exhibit No. 14, which is a close-up photo of the writing on the kitchen table. For the record, would you read what it says, please."

"Yes. On the kitchen table was the words printed in fingernail polish. It says, 'Don't look for us—for, f-o-r-e—us or else—e-a-l-s-e.'"

"Now, Mr. Smith, let me show you State's Exhibit No. 8, which is the body of Debbie Carter. Is there any wording on her?"

"Yes, sir, there is. The word *die* is written across her chest in fingernail polish, and in this other picture, the word *Gram* is written in catsup on the decedent's back."

"Once again, Mr. Smith, would you identify the wording of State's Exhibit No. 7?"

"Well, the words on the wall—well, it says, 'Jim Smith next will die,' and that's on the west wall of the living room of the apartment, also written in fingernail polish."

Peterson was at the height of his swaggering glory as he asked Smith about his initial interviews with Williamson and me. Smith stated that both of the defendants denied any involvement in the Carter murder. The pounding in my chest eased to a racing pace when Smith said that, but then he continued to implicate Ronnie and me as he responded to the D.A.'s questions. He stated that he, along with Gary Rogers, had collected hair and saliva samples from both defendants, who had voluntarily agreed to cooperate. He described in detail concerning the Miranda-issued interrogations that he and Rogers administered to me throughout the course of the investigation. Peterson's persistence in drawing out the details concerning the interrogations caused me to shudder with every response that Smith gave. I sat on the edge of my chair for most of the time.

"And would you relate to the court what Mr. Fritz told you when you interrogated him about the death of Debbie Carter?" Peterson asked.

"He denied knowing Debbie Carter and denied any knowledge of the killing—of the death. He denied ever seeing her before. He denied any knowledge of ever being in her apartment."

"Do you recall, Mr. Smith, whether there was a hair sample recovered underneath the body of Debbie Carter, and who found it, if you remember?"

"I think either I did or Agent Rogers," Smith replied.

"I yield the witness," Peterson said.

Barney's and Greg's cross-examinations yielded little new information. The thrust of Greg's examination focused upon obtaining reports that neither Smith nor Peterson had immediate possession of. Greg was specifically interested in gaining access to all of the investigative reports that had been taken from all of the individuals who had submitted head hair, pubic hair, saliva, and handwriting samples.

Smith was evasive in his responses and appeared totally unprepared for the hearing. Of course, veteran that he was and having testified in hundreds of trials, he knew the tricks of his trade. With no reports in hand, he could play dumb. Greg, with his smooth, good-guy approach, was no match for him, though he did set the stage for Barney's more rugged sort of questioning.

Dressed in a black pinstriped suit and holding his cane in his hand, Barney stood out like an unwavering old oak tree as he began his interrogation of Smith.

"What type of an investigation did you conduct insofar as that individual named Gram, or Graham?"

"Well, the man gave a statement and, of course, I can't remember exactly what it was he said, but we checked his story out and were satisfied with it."

"Are you meaning to say that he had some type of alibi?" Barney inquired.

"Yes."

"Did you collect hair samples from him?"

"I'm not for sure if we did or not. We may have."

"Well, it's obvious we'll be back here tomorrow. Do you have your files with you?" Barney asked.

"No, sir, I don't have all of that information, but I will bring it in tomorrow."

"Do you know anybody by the name of Jim Smith?"

"Yes," answered Smith with a slightly embarrassed look.

"Do you know where he was on or around December 8, 1982?"

"Yes, sir, he was in the penitentiary, behind the walls in McAlester."

Barney was meticulous in his questioning. The sudden urge to laugh out loud billowed in my throat at the sight of Smith squirming in the hot seat with his face blushing red. The words *Go, Barney, go!* flashed in my mind.

Barney asked Smith how Ronnie and I first became suspects. Smith shifted uneasily in the witness chair as he stated that a trusty inmate at the county jail contacted him concerning an incident where Ronnie had gone berserk and attacked him while he was asleep after he had talked to Ronnie about the Carter murder. Smith added that the police's attentions "then turned to Fritz because he and Williamson had been seen together on many occasions" prior to Debbie's murder and that their personalities had changed, according to a witness that the police interviewed.

Barney changed the subject abruptly.

"Did you get a report back on the handwriting samples that you acquired from Williamson and Fritz?"

"We did not submit it," Smith said frankly.

"Did not submit it?" Barney blustered. "Wouldn't it have been important to let an expert look at this to make some kind of determination?"

"Well, there were similarities in the handwriting based on our observations."

"Then, you don't have anything that could possibly eliminate Williamson or Fritz."

"Well, we were doing it for our benefit. We wanted to know in our own minds—"

Barney cut him off. "I bet that's right, Dennis," he said. "Well, now, you're not trying to tell this court there's a possibility that these two boys took turns with that fingernail brush, are you?"

"No, but I think it was our opinion that both of them had a hand at the writing, not necessarily on the same writing, but there was, you know, several different writings in the apartment."

"Did you submit the saliva samples of Williamson or Fritz, saliva test or— no, that's what you do on a race horse. Strike that! What— what— whatever you refer to the saliva, did you submit that—"

"Yes, sir, we submitted it to the OSBI in Oklahoma City."

Barney scrutinized Smith by asking him about the number of times that he had submitted hair samples from Gore. Smith's hard, bulging eyes glared contemptuously at Barney before answering. It was obvious to everyone in the courtroom that Smith felt intimidated by Barney, and perhaps more so, he was being shamed by a blind man about things he had seen. Dumfounded, Smith stated that he and Rogers had to obtain the second set of hair samples because it had been so long they had forgotten that they had already sent the first samples for testing. Upon hearing

Smith's profoundly negligent reply, Barney shifted into high gear and hammered him further, demanding to know why it had taken the OSBI lab two years to do the hair comparison testing.

Regaining some of his composure, Smith squeezed in the excuse that it must have been the caseload of the lab people.

"Oh, come on now, Dennis. We know better than that," Barney said with a patronizing tone.

Peterson stood up abruptly. "Your Honor, I'm going to object to counsel being argumentative with the witness. He's already answered his question!"

"Objection sustained," Miller announced with his eloquent, deliberate manner. "I will allow you to inquire, Mr. Ward, but if that's all he knows, you —"

"Okay," replied Barney. "Is that the only thing that caused the two-year delay?"

Having recouped his shaken rhythm, Smith rambled on about the intricate, eye-straining process that the lab people had to contend with to check hundreds and hundreds of hairs, not only in this case but from other unsolved cases over the state.

Barney didn't buy Smith's meandering opinions, and his patience was once again challenged.

"If you learned this in December of 1985, about the hair samples or exhibits or whatever, why was there a delay during all of 1986 and four months plus of 1987 before anything was done about it?"

"Well, the —"

"Do you understand the Constitution of the United States?"

"Your Honor — Your Honor, just a moment, please," Peterson lashed out. "I object. He won't let him answer."

"All right, I'll withdraw. I don't care what he objects to," Barney said. "All right. Now then, tell me why there was a seventeen-month delay from December of 1985 to May of 1987, when this information was filed?"

Smith shot a quick glance in Peterson's direction before answering.

"Well, we had the unknown palm print on the wall and we didn't know who it belonged to. We thought there was a remote possibility there was a third person involved. We knew that the palm print didn't belong to either Mr. Williamson or Mr. Fritz, and we were trying to locate this other person if there was one. Had we arrested Williamson or Fritz back then, we were afraid that it would have run the third person off. We just didn't know whose palm print that was."

"Well, I know that, but do you have any other information involving a third person, other than that handprint on the wall?"

"No. No, we don't," answered Smith, staring straight at Barney.

Barney concluded his examination of Smith by asking him why the exhumation of Debbie Carter's body couldn't have been done sooner, since Peterson had the piece of Sheetrock shortly after Debbie was buried.

Smith's cocky attitude returned as he explained that the Carter family had already gone through one traumatic experience, and to dig the body up and have them go through it again would probably have been more than they could stand.

Barney had no further questions.

The courtroom spectators were restless. Up to this point, none of the testimony had remotely implicated me or implied any participation on my part in the murder. From time to time, audible whispers, muffled coughs, and heavy sighs blended with the sounds of shifting feet and popping bones brought on by the unpadded courtroom benches. Everyone in the crowd had one thing in common—they were ready to hear some of the stuff that the D.A. hadn't thus far put into action.

"Where's the evidence on Fritz?" a faint voice murmured from the rear of the courtroom.

As far as I knew, there wasn't any, but the courtroom battle continued between the prosecution and defense—each with very opposite personalities and expectations. Back and forth, from re-direct to re-cross, to further re-cross, Peterson, Barney, and Greg battled for more information using every legal trick they knew. Peterson defended his already-gained ground. Barney shuffled, pried, toyed, and dismantled any and all information that was pressed out of Smith. Greg, with his criminal courtroom inexperience and good old-boy demeanor, continued to question Smith in his pomp display of flowing mannerisms.

After several hours, not a shred of incriminating evidence had been gained from Smith's marginal testimony. Under the table, I crossed my fingers for good luck.

CHAPTER 11

The state called Gary Rogers, who stated that he was a special agent for the Oklahoma State Bureau of Investigation. Rogers's account of the crime scene was very similar to Smith's. He first noticed that the glass window in the door had been broken and that equal amounts of glass were strewn inside and outside the residence. He said that the living room looked undisturbed except for a couple of cushions and a nightgown and some writings on the wall, and that there were similar writings on the kitchen table. He said he observed upon entering the bedroom that the victim's body was face down on the floor with a rag or washcloth protruding from her mouth. Rogers said the bedroom was in disarray and that several articles were strung over the floor—an indication that a great struggle had taken place. He then explained to the court how he later cut out the piece of Sheetrock from the bedroom wall.

"In your gathering of evidence at the crime scene, Officer, did you ever find an empty or used bottle of fingernail polish?" Peterson asked.

"No, sir, we did not," Rogers responded. "There were two items that we did not find. One was the house and car keys, which were supposed to be on a small silver cowboy-spur key ring, and also, the bottle of fingernail polish."

Without question, Rogers was a smooth operator on the witness stand. He had been an OSBI agent for eleven years and had interacted in numerous murder cases. His answers were direct and without hesitation. He did not give the appearance of trying to impress anyone.

The D.A.'s questions to Rogers focused on the collective identification of the vast number of articles removed from the apartment. Barney immediately stood and objected, forcing Peterson and Rogers to go through each and every article individually. Peterson showed his irritation about Barney's request by being exceptionally painstaking with each item.

Thank you, Barney, I said under my breath, cracking a slight smile for the first time in hours. Because Rogers had been in the courtroom while Smith gave his testimony, he knew what he would be up against when it came time to be cross-examined by Barney.

Each of the evidence articles was introduced—sheets, a pillow, a bedspread, a multicolored blouse, an afghan, a pair of torn purple panties, an electric blanket cord, a stuffed animal toy, a plastic drinking cup, and the Mickey Mouse telephone that had been ripped out from its wall jack.

Was Peterson using this time-consuming questioning as a bluff, or was he building to the point of getting Rogers primed for a blast of lies? I wondered. I fidgeted in my chair, looking over at Greg for some indication of his reactions. There were none.

"And in essence, Agent Rogers, would you tell the court, in relationship to Debbie Carter, what Mr. Fritz said about his knowledge of that?"

"Well, all along the defendant has denied ever knowing Debbie Carter. He's denied ever having contact at, near, or inside her residence. He denied ever having contact with her in any way, shape, or form. He denied even knowing what she looked like and further stated that he did not know who she was from his trips to the Coach Light Club. He said he had never been in her vehicle or apartment."

I let out an audible sigh of relief. What was this all about? Two of the state's main witnesses had announced my innocence, and yet here I was under the onus of a first-degree capital murder charge. *This is impossible!* my mind screamed. *What else can there be? How much more of this can I take? Lord, please! Let this end.*

Peterson abruptly changed his line of questioning, asking Rogers about the dates and number of times that he had interviewed Ronnie Williamson. Peterson was specifically interested in an interview that occurred on May 9, 1987. Rogers responded by saying that Williamson started talking about a pretty girl that he had seen at the Coach Light Club on December 8, 1982. He thought he would follow her home but paused and started talking about a stolen stereo. When asked if Williamson had ever said anything about a dream that he had had, Rogers stated that Ronnie had described a dream where he was in Debbie Carter's apartment and was strangling her with a cord pulled tightly around her neck and that he thought he had stabbed her. In a casual tone of voice, Peterson asked Rogers if Williamson had said anything about his intentions when he went there. With a funny look on his face, Rogers said that Ronnie had said Ms. Carter had been mean to him. He added that Agent Featherstone, who was also present at that interview, had questioned Williamson further as to what he meant by the meaning of *mean*, Williamson said something to the effect that Debbie had made fun of him. Without hesitation, Peterson quickly asked Rogers as to whether Williamson had stated if Dennis Fritz was with him in the dream. Rogers said *yes.*

Greg sprang from his chair so fast that it caused me to flinch.

"Your Honor, I certainly want to object to that as being pure, raw hearsay in reference to Mr. Fritz and ask that the statement not be considered by this court as any evidence against Mr. Fritz. And we do want to preserve the record on the objection."

"Objection overruled, exception noted," Miller stated. "Is the prosecution through with this witness?"

The D.A. nodded.

At the onset of his cross-examination, Barney's temper flared. Rogers admitted that it was not Eddie Deatherage but Eddie's brother Robert who informed him about the incident where Ronnie had allegedly attacked him in the jail. Barney wanted to see a written report concerning the incident but Rogers was difficult and evasive.

Barney demanded to see it.

Peterson stepped up and stated that it was work product of his office. Miller saw what was coming and suggested that Barney ask Rogers if he had used the report to refresh his knowledge prior to his testimony. Rogers said that he had not reviewed the report for some time.

"Well, I can tell from the testimony that you haven't done a hell of a lot of reviewing by anything," growled Barney.

Bolting out of his chair, Peterson demanded, "Your Honor, I'd ask that Mr. Ward be admonished."

"I know, I know. I sure don't want to cause him any trouble, Judge. I don't want to ruffle his feathers," Barney said.

Before Barney could take a breath to speak again, Miller reminded everyone—mostly Barney—that they were professionals and should be held to a strict standard of conduct that meant sticking to the rules.

"That's exactly what I thought until about fifteen minutes ago," declared Barney.

"Well, okay. That's— We're not— I'm going—" stammered Miller.

"That's what I thought until this morning, Judge," repeated Barney. There was no stopping him. He was in one of his moods that his point was going to be heard, one way or the other. Everyone in the courtroom, except for Peterson and Miller, was deathly quiet. Barney jumped back into the ring with Rogers and asked him when he last saw Deatherage, and if his report would reflect that.

Rogers paused.

"Is Mr. Peterson now refreshing your memory about it? Is that what you're hesitating for—to let him nod you *yes* or *no*?" Barney stated.

"I resent that, Mr. Ward!" proclaimed Rogers.

"Oh, I don't care whether you resent it or not," Barney fired back.

Miller sat up stiffly and told Barney that the witness was answering the question as best he could and that he had not noticed him looking over at the district attorney.

"What did you hesitate for, Gary?" Barney inquired.

"To answer you truthfully as best I could, Mr. Ward."

"Wouldn't it help matters out a little bit if you would look at your report?"

Rogers didn't respond.

Barney didn't care. He had driven his point home and everyone knew what its intended meaning was—especially Peterson. For the next hour, Barney scrupulously questioned Rogers over the chain of evidence and how it was labeled, tagged, numbered, where it was sent, how long it stayed there, and who identified it. On and on it went. The circuits in Barney's brain were lit up. I could almost visualize the wheels in motion as he continued his grilling of Rogers. Miller overruled all of Barney's objections as to Rogers's incomplete identification of the evidence being introduced.

Barney's interrogation then moved in another direction—to the subject of Ronnie's rendered custodial statements. Rogers unclasped his hands and straightened his slumping shoulders in the witness chair. Barney wasted no time. He asked Rogers if he had a tape recording of his client's statement? Before Rogers could answer *no* to his question, Barney fired back, wanting to know if his client had signed the statement. Once again, Rogers said *no*. Upon further questioning, Rogers admitted that he had a tape recorder in his office, where the questioning took place, but didn't understand what Barney was getting at.

"I don't think you're telling the truth is what I'm getting at, and I'm trying to be able to prove it," snapped Barney.

"Well, I resent that statement," Rogers said, with a twinge of emotion creeping into his voice.

"I don't care whether you resent it. You wanted to know. Now I'm telling you. Would it have been too much of a chore to have recorded his statement?"

"I wouldn't think so," Rogers responded.

"Don't have to be a Rhodes Scholar to do it, do you?"

"I wouldn't think so."

"Can you give this court any idea why, in a case that has a man charged with three capital offenses, you didn't find it necessary to record this so-called confession?"

With his head lowered and eyes widened, Rogers forced out an explanation that law enforcement has had problems with defendants admitting to other crimes on tapes and that it is very difficult to get them admitted into evidence.

Like a brick in mud, Barney wouldn't budge, wanting Rogers to tell him if he had asked his client to sign or read his confession statements. Another familiar *no* resonated from Rogers, followed by the question, "Why should I?"

"Do you understand that as a police officer you're working for everybody concerned: the defendants, the victims, the district attorney? You're working for everybody. Do you understand that?" Barney implored.

Small beads of perspiration glistened on Rogers's forehead as the overhead lights seemed to glow with increasing intensity.

"I understand that fully, Mr. Ward," replied Rogers.

"Do you have any reason at all, instead of asking me 'Why should I?' to give to this court, why you didn't ask Ron Williamson for his signature?"

"What would he have signed? Rusty Featherstone's handwritten notes?" taunted Rogers with an added resurgence of sarcasm.

Barney's face flushed crimson. Apparently, Barney had a low tolerance for know-it-alls and smart alecks, and at the moment, Rogers was topping the list in both categories. Still, he continued — aiming straight for the jugular. Objections flew from Peterson's mouth, and the cross-examination ended abruptly when Miller banged his gavel. Barney and Peterson returned to their respective tables without saying anything, and Miller advised both attorneys that no further outbursts would be tolerated in his court. After the dust settled, Barney continued to chip away at Rogers, extracting a statement that the agent hadn't even signed or initialed Ronnie's purported confession.

After Barney passed the witness, Greg began his cross-examination.

Rogers, still visibly shaken, seemed to relax as he viewed Greg approaching the podium. The dark cloud of Barney's presence lifted. Rogers settled back in his chair as Greg's soft-stance inquiry focused on procedures, methods, and locations of the hairs retrieved during the crime scene investigation. Greg's work-around approach sifted no additional information about the broken front-door glass.

Rogers said he could not make a determination as to whether there had been a forced entry into the apartment. The chain lock and the door lock appeared to be intact, he said; therefore, he could not technically say whether the perpetrators were let in or whether they broke in, because he didn't know whether the victim had her doors locked or had the chain lock on.

Greg inched ahead by asking Rogers about the significance of a belt found under the victim's body. Did the decedent's body, he asked, show any evidence of physical restraint around her wrists or arms?

Rogers indicated that there were no restraint marks on the victim, and that no on-the-scene determination could be made that the belt was used for the strangulation because the skin on the victim's neck was folded in a way that the width of the ligature mark could not be fully seen.

Greg was a clever attorney. He had a special way of presenting himself that made a witness feel relaxed. Then there were times when Greg played dumb and coaxed the witness into revealing too much information. But with Rogers, Greg's tactics were in vain. His questions yielded very little information, though Rogers was very forthcoming in answering his questions about the makeup of his files, narrative information from submittal reports, and written memoranda as to the investigative flow of the case.

"Agent Rogers, have you testified to substantially everything you know about the case that you anticipate you would be called upon to testify to at a trial?"

"I can't think of— Nothing stands out in my mind at this point in time," Rogers answered with ease.

"All right, sir. So, pretty much everything that you know about the case has been testified to here today and discussed to some degree?" Greg confidently asked.

"I feel it has, yes, sir."

I didn't even hear Greg state that he was through with the witness. Upon hearing Rogers's last response, a rush of thoughts came up and smacked me in the face again. The familiar feeling of utter dismay crept over me. I was bewildered as to why I had been arrested if this was all that the state could present. I turned my head sideways and glanced at Peterson and his assistants. I felt a burning bitterness well up inside as I watched his insidious mannerisms. His haughty look ripped through my soul. How could a man even think of prosecuting another human being with the type of so-called evidence that I had seen so far? My attentions snapped back to the protective sound of Barney's voice saying that he was now ready for his re-cross of Agent Rogers.

Again, Barney started nailing Rogers concerning the piece of Sheetrock. When was it submitted, how was it labeled, when were the results finalized, where was the lab report, and why wasn't it in his possession?

This time, Rogers's response was markedly improved. The

agent appeared to have learned the finer points of compliancy and detail, which Barney greatly preferred. Rogers also indicated that he had gained a little wisdom about the word *assume*. Barney re-explored the elements of rigor mortis with Rogers and how it related to Jerry Peters's failure to have adequately secured a complete ridge roll of Debbie's palm print. Driving Rogers back to the reason for the lengthy delay in the arrest, Barney hammered on the fair and speedy trial rights afforded by the Oklahoma and United States constitutions—this time without objection.

The crux of the examination had shifted. Barney was allowing Rogers to speak without restriction about the professional difficulties involved with a lengthy delay in charging a suspect. Rogers rambled on, giving his insights, observations, and clarifications when he was questioned about the dream Ronnie had described—a situation not unlike Tommy Ward's dream-state confession in the book, *The Dreams of Ada.*

Following lunch, Dennis Smith returned to the stand. Both Barney and Peterson questioned him concerning the admission of hair evidence retrieved from the crime scene. Barney and Greg objected that the evidence had neither been properly identified nor had any probative value because the chain of custody had not been properly established for its proper admission. Miller sustained the objection and advised the D.A. to lay a more thorough foundation. Shortly thereafter, the judge released Smith from the stand and the prosecution called its next witness, Mary Long, an OSBI criminologist whose specialty was serology.

My heart thudded as I listened to Long's recounting of her credentials and the training she had received over the past seven years of her employment. Peterson was running out of time to show whatever smoking gun he had up his sleeve. Maybe this woman was it.

Long seemed unusually nervous as she answered Peterson's questions, stating she had received whole blood, vaginal swabs, scalp and pubic hair, trace evidence, and saliva samples from the body of Ms. Carter, Ron Williamson, me, and a long list of other suspect donors. Wearing larger-than-normal red-framed glasses, her gaze was solidly fixed upon Peterson. The only time she averted her eyes was to glance down when identifying the state's offered exhibits. Her testimony indicated that everything she had collected except for the body fluids evidence was sent on to Susan Land, a criminologist with the OSBI.

There was that name again. From Long's testimony, I gathered that Susan Land was some kind of big wheel in the Bureau who dealt with some facet of hair identification. Who knows? She may be the next upcoming witness against me. At this point, I braced myself for anything Peterson had to offer.

Peterson, now in a state of grandeur, presented every exhibit item that had semen on it for Long's reported findings. The torn purple panties, the swabs, the fitted sheet—all tested positive for the presence of semen, and in Long's opinion were donated from a non-secreting individual who had no antigen content in his blood. Additionally, Long stated that eighty percent of the people in the world were secretors, and the other fifteen to twenty percent were non-secretors.

"Mary, did you have an opportunity to do a test on the saliva samples submitted to you that belonged to Ron Williamson and Dennis Fritz?" Peterson asked.

"Yes, I tested for secretor substances or the antigen—the blood-type antigens in these saliva samples. I did not detect any in either one of these samples."

"So, would that indicate to you that Mr. Williamson and Mr. Fritz would be non-secretors?"

"If there was an adequate sample there, yes," Long submitted. "If there was plenty of saliva on there, then about the only conclusion that I could draw was that the person whose saliva it is is a non-secretor."

"Yield the witness, Your Honor," Peterson stated as he gallantly strutted back to the prosecution table.

"Mr. Ward, you may cross-examine," invited Miller.

Barney's opening question focused on how many other people were tested for their secretor status. One by one, Long read through the list of nineteen people who had submitted saliva samples for testing. Out of the nineteen, eleven people showed to be non-secretors—with no antigen activity—and the other eight showed various antigen activity in their blood. At Barney's request, Long went on to explain that antigen activity was synonymous with a person being a secretor. Secretors are able to show their blood type in their water-based body fluids, whereas non-secretors cannot.

Barney's whole demeanor softened with Long. He was less aggressive and took a smoother approach with a lot more tact. Long seemed at ease with Barney's persuasive inquiry. When asked why her test results showed a higher-than-twenty-percent number of people as non-secretors, she said she could only give two possible explanations: It could just be by chance that there were that many non-secretors in the tested group, or there just wasn't an adequate amount of saliva on the submitted sample.

Barney moved the court that Long's testimony be stricken from the record on the grounds that it was inadmissible due to its lack of definition. Peterson vigorously argued that the validity of Mary Long's test results went to the credibility of the weight of the evidence instead of its admissibility. Greg countered that before the test could be admissible, it must be a valid test, and by Long's own admission the results were not necessarily valid because of a variable not controlled by this witness—to wit, the sample that was taken.

Barney and Greg combined forces against Peterson. Their agitation weighed heavily on the D.A. His first star witness's testimony was being torn to shreds by both defense attorneys. Peterson fired back to the judge that prior testimony was given that the strips of paper were wet when they were collected.

Miller disagreed, stating that he did not recall Agent Rogers testifying that the test strips were wet when he retrieved them from Ronnie and me.

For the first time, Peterson was at a loss for words, saying over and over, "It goes to the weight of credibility, Judge!"

The courtroom temperature was beginning to heat up at an alarming rate. Not a peep could be heard from the spectators.

Ignoring Peterson's broken-record ravings, Barney and Greg stated to Miller that in order for Long's test to be valid, she had to presuppose that there was an adequate sample of saliva on the test strips, which she had no control of. A new spring of life force ebbed its way back into my existence. The tables were beginning to turn in the direction that I had hoped for.

Since the beginning of the hearing, Barney had been the conquering warrior—always with no holds barred. Out of form and without requisition or recompense, a subtle change surfaced within Barney. He now became the rescuer for Judge Miller, who was caught having to exercise his bridled decision-making process too fast, too soon, and without the security of notice.

Barney threw water on the flaming fire and simply stated, "If the court please, let me withdraw that objection just a moment and ask a couple more questions."

The only thing that Miller could say was, "Okay."

Barney proceeded with his inquiry of Long: "How would you take a— How would you know whether you had enough of a sample? Is there any way that you can tell?"

"With the naked eye, no," Long stated.

"Well, with all the equipment you have at your disposal, can you tell?"

"I can now. At the time when I ran the tests, I did not have the methodology, and the technology would not have been advanced enough at that point in time for me to be able to do that. Now, I could go in and quantify an amount of amylase, which is an enzyme in the saliva, and you know, see if there was some there."

"Now, you can do that and— Is that because of additional

equipment that the State of Oklahoma has purchased or additional know-how that you have obtained?"

"Additional know-how," Long agreed in a regrettable tone.

"Okay. You had the equipment all along," Barney remarked.

Barney asked Long about the swabs that had been used to collect the semen found in the decedent's vaginal tract and whether her test results showed that the donor was a non-secretor. Long's reply was that it was possible because there was no antigen activity there. The first thing that came to her mind after concluding her test was that the donor was probably a non-secretor.

Dissatisfied with her answer, Barney asked Long if there was more than one thing that came to her mind in reaching her determination.

She looked away from Barney with her eyes to the ceiling and slowly stated that she had also considered that the semen donor could have been a secretor whose level of antigens were so weak that they could not be detected.

Barney's face looked confused. In a point-blank manner, Barney asked Long if she was here today to show that these boys were the ones who committed the offense.

Long blushed.

All in one motion, Peterson slapped the palms of his hands on his table, stood up, and objected to Barney being argumentative in asking the witness to draw a conclusion.

Miller intervened. No ruling was made, except for providing Barney with the explanation that the reason she was here was to testify to her results.

Most of the time, Barney was well practiced in brushing off the judge's comments, always saying *okay* or *all right* in an acknowledging yet direct way. Before ending his cross-examination of Long, Barney drew yet another objection from Peterson for being argumentative. This was the second time that the serology expert had given an "oranges-and-apples" answer in her response in comparing sperm to saliva.

"Judge, I tell you again. If the district attorney had furnished us with these tests back when we asked for them, this wouldn't be necccoary," Barney complained.

"Well, that's true, but—"

"Mr. Ward would be just as confused today, Your Honor," swiped Peterson.

"Now, wait. Let's—" Miller said before being interrupted.

"Well, I sure as hell wouldn't get you to clear it up. I'll tell you that," Barney erupted.

"Counsel, approach the bench right now, please," Miller commanded.

From my vantage point, I could hear drifts of Miller telling Barney and Peterson that this was a very emotional situation, but the unprofessional comments would not be tolerated in his courtroom. He said something after that about very technical evidence—not being required by law to turn it over up to this point—and not gaining any ground by being argumentative. Miller asked if there were questions. Since Barney's voice carried like the wind, I easily overheard him denying any attempt to gain any ground with the judge or the district attorney, saying that he was only here to protect his client—"…his guilt or innocence didn't make a difference, and every time I ask a question that's a little embarrassing or I strike a nerve over there, he bounces up like a jack-in-the-box and starts arguing with me." Following this comment, Miller recessed the court for a fifteen-minute break.

Chapter 12

The climactic events of the day showed on Greg's face during the recess. Barney remained seated at the defense table while Frank Baber exited the courtroom to fetch amenities for himself and his co-counsel. As I was about to speak, Barney started telling Greg of his personal feelings for Peterson and how those crooked bastards would go to any extent to railroad someone just for a conviction, even without having any evidence.

"If it was left up to me, I would fire everyone of those sons-of-bitches and put 'em out on the street corner sellin' tamales," cajoled Barney. He sat in a relaxed position with both hands clasped on the top of his cane.

Greg laughed at Barney's remark while quickly glancing around the courtroom. Many spectators had shuffled out into the waiting area to refresh themselves before another round. In a bold voice, Greg told Barney he believed Peterson had already exhausted his case and asked Barney if he'd caught wind of who the next witness was going to be.

Barney chuckled as he told Greg that Baber had heard that Melvin Hett, the OSBI's top gun in hair identification, would be the state's upcoming attraction. Greg said that he had heard his name before from some of his criminal lawyer buddies and that he was a very tough witness to deal with.

"Oh, hell, Greg, most of those OSBI assholes have got their heads so far up their assholes they don't even think that their own shit stinks."

Greg started to say something when I interrupted him.

"Greg, I've been setting here for the past two days now, and I haven't heard anything that connects me to this crime in any way. What I want to know is why they charged me with this murder if they have no evidence to back it up?"

As Barney was about to dish out a comment, Greg spoke up and said, "That's a very good question, Dennis, because we're wondering the very same thing. We've got Mary Long to finish up with, and if there's time left today, we'll get to see who their next witness is."

"Greg, don't you and Barney think that if they had somethin' up their sleeve, they would have already put it on by now?" I asked.

"Oh, hell, they would start their own forest fire just so they could say that they were the ones who put it out," Barney interjected.

"So, what you're saying is that they don't care one way or the other whether I'm guilty or not?"

"Shit, that damn whatchamacallit Peterson thinks the whole world's guilty of something," said Barney. "And hell, he'd kill a garden snake before he'd take time to see if it had any rattlers on it."

"More or less, Dennis, what Barney's trying to say is that we're beginning to think that Peterson has no other evidence stronger than what he's put on," Greg explained.

"Hell, there's no trying to say about it at all. It's as obvious as the sun sets in the west that he's runnin' some kind of a two-ring circus out there," Barney groused.

"Well, what I'm concerned about is if it turns out that there's no stronger evidence than what's been shown, can I be bound over for trial on this kind of crap?" I asked.

"They're coming back in, but we'll have more time to talk about that in greater detail after tomorrow," assured Greg. "Right now, I'm going to see what I can do to tear down Long's testimony a little bit more. I know it's hard, but just try and be patient."

Barney's sardonic smile seemed to mirror his fixed expectations of what was to come. Miller appeared from behind the black curtains and gazed over the courtroom. Mary Long stepped up into the witness stand with a reserved look on her face.

"Mr. Ward, I believe you were cross-examining the witness," stated Miller.

"That's all I want to ask right now," Barney calmly said.

"Okay. Mr. Saunders, you may cross-examine."

There seemed to be a different feeling in the courtroom as Greg walked to the podium. I felt a surge of rejuvenation running through my body after talking to Greg and Barney. Maybe this nightmare would soon be over and they would have to release me for lack of evidence.

Greg came out of the gate like a charging bull kicking dust, questioning Long about her examination of swabs taken from other parts of Carter's body. In her detached manner, Long indicated that there was no sperm found. Greg reiterated Dr. Jordan's testimony that intact spermatozoa had been found in both the vaginal and rectal tracts of the victim. Long differed in her opinion, stating that she had found no sperm in the rectal tract of the victim, which could be caused by a number of factors, such as the destructive effects of bacteria, the time the sample was deposited, the length of time between the deposit to the time the swab was taken, and the interval of time the swab was placed in the vial to the time that it was examined.

Greg changed the direction of his questioning and asked the witness if any of her tests indicated whether the victim had been raped by more than one assailant. Long said *no.* Greg asked her if she could conclusively state that Dennis Fritz had no antigen activity in his saliva sample. After several attempts to answer the question, Long reluctantly admitted that her results were based upon the assumption that a sufficient quantity of saliva was needed to have rendered a valid test result. Greg said he had no further questions for the witness, but Long remained on the stand while he and Barney engaged in a series of prolonged pleadings to Miller concerning the accuracy of the serologist's test results. Peterson fought back for every piece of ground that he could gain.

Miller asked Long several detailed questions about the validity of her test results, how the absence or presence of saliva could have affected the outcome of her tests, whether saliva could be seen by the naked eye on a piece of paper, and about the high percentages of non-secretors in the case. At closing, after a multitude of challenges, conjectures, re-crosses, re-directs, and further re-directs from both the defense and prosecution, Miller reserved his admissibility ruling on Mary Long's testimony for a later scheduled time. The next witness was called.

As Long exited the chamber, a tall, lanky, intelligent-looking man in a navy blue suit and tie entered the courtroom. The sounds of shuffling feet and muffled whispers came to an abrupt halt as he confidently made his way to the front of the courtroom. All eyes were upon him. There could be no doubt in anyone's mind that he was a man with a mission.

"State your name for the record, please," voiced Peterson.

"Melvin R. Hett."

"What is your occupation and where are you employed?" the D.A. asked in an overly confident voice.

"I'm a criminalist, what's more commonly known as a forensic chemist. I work in the Enid Regional Laboratory of the Oklahoma State Bureau of Investigation."

Replying to Peterson's questions, Hett gave the court a complete accounting of his special studies and training qualifications that he had earned in the field of evidence comparison. By contrast, his long-winded listings of academic accolades made Mary Long look like a mere apprentice in her field of serology.

Peterson moved for admission of the state's marked exhibits following Hett's identification of the envelopes containing both sets of known and unknown hair samples retrieved from the crime scene, Williamson, and me. Greg was the first to object, then Barney, on improper identification without an accounted-for chain of custody. Miller interceded, and after a long interlude of extensive questioning by the judge, prosecution, and counsels for the defense, Miller allowed the items to be admitted under his guidelines that a sufficient chain had to be established during Peterson's examination of Hett, and only then, if Detective Smith were brought back to re-testify to lay the proper foundation.

Miller was not leaving any stones undisturbed. I knew that this was going to be a long afternoon. I gathered that Hett's testimony would be the biggest obstacle for Greg and Barney to overcome. I could feel the cold, clammy sensations of despair and uncertainty creeping over me as Hett settled in his chair.

Peterson asked Hett from whom he had received the state's hair exhibits.

"From Susan Land," Hett responded.

I immediately wrote on my notepad, "Who is Susan Land?" and passed it over to Greg. He acknowledged it with a nod of his head. Again, he was in deep concentration while my mind was screaming from within, *Who in the hell is Susan Land?*

Peterson didn't waste any time. One by one, hair by hair, he asked Hett to give his scientific opinion as to the results of his microscopic comparisons made between the unknown crime scene hairs to the hairs that Ronnie and I had submitted. Peterson spent a majority of time in his direct examination of Hett, attempting to impress Miller through his tactic of creating a crescendo before having Hett announce his findings on each of the individual microscopic hair comparisons.

Peterson's methods wore thin, though, as Hett delivered his expert opinions as to each of the individually examined hairs. At the conclusion of his comparisons, the well-trained criminalist found that eleven of my pubic hairs were microscopically consistent with one hair found on the washcloth removed from Carter's mouth, one hair found on the floor under the body, two hairs taken from the panties, and seven hairs removed from the sheets. In addition, Hett determined that a total of two scalp hairs—one taken from the bedding and a second removed from Carter's body—showed to be microscopically consistent with my scalp hair. It was his overall opinion regarding both the pubic and scalp hairs tested that they "could have" originated from the same source—meaning me! Hett added that two pubic hairs from Carter's bedding and two scalp hairs from the washcloth were microscopically consistent to that of Williamson's known hair samples and "could have" originated from the same source.

Peterson yielded the witness, and Greg began his cross-examination. He addressed Hett cautiously, questioning him with a kid-gloves approach. Greg carefully wove his array of questions around each of Hett's scientifically stated responses that described the physical structures, variations of color, length, thickness, shape, and other unlimited combinations in the science of hair comparison. He allowed Hett the latitude to do most of the talking without any feeling of being pressured or manipulated—at least to any noticeable degree.

Hett's formality and aloofness, combined with his irrefutable scientific jargon, perplexed everyone in the courtroom. He explained in minute detail his complicated considerations of how he made his determinations of how a comparison between known and unknown hairs would be classified as microscopically consistent.

"Is there any quantification, or is it purely a subjective evaluation?" Greg asked.

"It depends on what you call— In the way of quantification, in the way of saying that did I measure the exact diameter of a hair, no, that's not part of what I do. But it is compared side by side on a comparison microscope, a questioned sample to a known sample. The eye can detect small differences in diameters on a comparison microscope. I did not measure the exact diameters and then compare those measurements. What I do is a direct comparison between the known and the unknown."

"All right," Greg continued, "is there any quantification that's available to you to show how many people will have exactly the same characteristics as exhibited by Mr. Fritz's scalp hair?"

"Sir, I know of no scientific studies that have been done looking at particular characteristics among the general population. These are generally not available."

With patience, Greg questioned Hett about the meaning of the phrase "could have come from the same source."

Hett, without wavering, stated that there were no hair examiners that would routinely say that a hair sample came from another individual.

Greg wanted to know why they would not.

Without blinking an eye, Hett said because there was a possibility that another individual could have exactly the same characteristics.

My heart jumped into my throat upon hearing Hett's statement. Down to my toes I tingled with the elation of realizing that if this was the state's last witness and this was the best that Peterson had to offer, the chances had now greatly increased that I might get to go home. Even though the light switch of freedom had just been turned on, I forbade entertaining any further thoughts, knowing that there was still another day left in the hearing for this nightmare to unfold itself. I bit my lip and focused back on Greg's examination, which ended uneventfully shortly thereafter. Still, my heart raced—but with a rejuvenated beat of hope.

"Mr. Ward, you may cross-examine," Miller announced.

From the very beginning of his examination, it was inevitable that Barney and Hett would clash. Hett's somber, unrelinquishing attitude marked the type of witness that could totally unnerve Barney even in his calmest moment.

Barney began his interrogation of Hett with a twinge of demand in his voice, wanting to know how many known hair samples from Ron Williamson had been submitted to him and by whom. Glancing down at the emptied envelopes, Hett informed Barney that there were three bindles before him that had contained the known hairs of Mr. Williamson. With a stir of impatience in his voice, Barney wanted to know who had collected Williamson's samples. Hett said he didn't know. Unsatisfied, Barney knocked on Hett's door again, asking the same question, still getting the same tenuous response. Hett stubbornly read off to Barney the submittal date and the written name—D. Smith—at the bottom of the manila bindle.

The tension was building. Barney asked Hett if there was another method, other than microscopic examination, to examine hairs with. Hett responded by saying that microscopic comparison is the generally accepted method for examining hairs.

"That's not what I asked," Barney corrected the witness.

Miller didn't let a second go by before telling Barney to please allow the witness to fully respond before cutting him off.

Hett repeated his answer but with an added redefinition as to each of the physical characteristics found in a hair sample.

Barney's frustration was nearing the end of its fuse. Slight rustling sounds of anticipation could be heard from the audience in the rear of the courtroom.

"Okay, but all of that is from looking at it, isn't it?" asked Barney.

"Yes, sir, that is required to open one's eyes to look through a microscope, yes, sir."

"I beg your pardon?" Barney asserted.

"Yes, sir, it is required to open one's eyes to look through the microscope," Hett reiterated.

"It would help, wouldn't it?" Barney shot back. He was

making an extra effort to keep his cool, using another approach on Hett, ot wanting to know if measurements on a hair could be calibrated in the same way that striations on a bullet are measured.

"Sir, if there were striations, I would do that. There are not striations on hair capacities," Hett smugly stated.

Barney looked at the judge. "If the court please, I want you to advise—I don't care how smart this witness is, just ask him to answer my questions, if either he does or he doesn't. That's all I ask. I don't want a lecture from him."

Peterson voiced his opinion to Miller that Mr. Hett had answered Mr. Ward's questions by telling him that there were no striations.

"No, he's not trying to. He's telling me if there were striations on there— If I had wanted to know if there were striations on a hair, that's what I would have asked him," argued Barney.

Miller had learned one thing about Barney—that the sooner he stepped in on one of his mounting disputes, the sooner he would be able to regain control of his courtroom. Miller ruled that he would allow the witness to answer and instructed Hett to be responsive to Barney's initial question. Hett answered by simply stating that any measurement he made was based on the individual characteristics exhibited by that hair.

Seeing that Hett was trying to outfox him, Barney maneuvered into another area by asking him if he had any photographs made in connection with his examination.

Hett started to reply as to the reason why he did not take photographs.

Barney interrupted and told Hett that he didn't ask for a reason. He only wanted to know if he had any photographs. "Just say yes or no," Barney said with a stiff lip.

"No, I did not photograph the hairs," Hett arrogantly replied.

Barney was not gaining any ground. Their personalities were too much alike—stubborn and cavalier with a driving ego as big as

Dallas. Even a simple question from Barney, when he asked Hett about his terminology and his meaning of microscopically consistent, ended in another scuffling match fighting for dominance.

"But that's what you just said, that it could be inconsistent microscopically and therefore it probably did not have the same source?" countered Barney.

"Sir, I said that they are not consistent microscopically. I did not use the word *inconsistent*."

"What's the difference?"

"There is a difference to me," exclaimed Hett.

"Well, what is the difference?" Barney asked, raising his voice.

"The difference is that I use the term *not consistent*."

"And I used *inconsistent*. Now, is there really any difference in that, or are you just trying to show how much smarter you are than me?" Barney quipped.

Again, Miller stepped between the dueling parties and issued a directive that it did not make any difference and to continue without argument.

Barney continued questioning Hett about his microscopically consistent conclusions and whether the expert had mounted his own hair slides. Hett stated that he had mounted some of the slides but had received several already-mounted slides from Susan Land.

My ears perked up. Hopefully, Barney would find out just who this Susan Land is. Sure enough, that was Barney's very next question.

Hett briefly stated that Susan Land was a criminalist currently employed by the OSBI and had helped in the initial mounting procedures, but he was unaware of her exact job responsibilities.

I wondered why Susan Land's name had been important enough to show up on the charge information but she was not important enough to testify at this hearing. Although I knew nothing about the law, I found it to be sort of odd that her testimony was not included, unless they were saving her for the trial.

Barney's flared temper had calmed down somewhat, not for the reason of being influenced by any threat of Miller's authority or Peterson's position but because he realized that Hett was one tough nut to crack. For Barney, the integrity of his intelligence was on the line, and no witness was going to get the best of him. In a gruff tone, Barney questioned Hett about being able to gain possession of the hair slides if so ordered by the judge, and why it took him well over two years for the completion of his examinations.

"Did you know that you were working on a murder-rape case? Wouldn't such a case take precedence over other lesser important cases, creating a need to hurry for the results?" Barney pushed.

Hett was unmoved in his responses and gave logically evasive answers for everything Barney asked.

"Judge, I give up," Barney said after several minutes. "I yield to the superior intelligence of the witness. It's obvious he doesn't want to answer my questions, so—"

"Well, I'd like to take a stab at it again if I could," Greg spoke up with a sense of urgency in his voice.

"You've already yielded," said Peterson.

"Oh, I understand that. I ask the court's permission to allow me to—"

"Mr. Saunders, how many more questions do you have?" Miller asked.

"I've just got four areas I've written down here I'd like to ask him about. I'll be very brief."

In his first area of concern, Greg asked Hett if Ron's name and mine had been mentioned to him early on as being major suspects in the case.

Hett agreed that the names had been brought to his attention but would not state that he had been predisposed to look at certain individuals more than others.

Secondly, Greg asked Hett if he could make a color comparison of someone's hair that had turned partially gray to an unknown hair that was brown or red.

Hett stated that he could get a reliable result, but he needed approximately twenty to thirty known hairs taken from different parts of the head to test against the unknown hair sample, despite its color.

Next, Greg asked Hett if the reliability of his test results was dependent on the labeling accuracy of a mounted hair slide. The expert admitted that he had not mounted the majority of the hairs in this case, and that in some instances, improper mounting could affect his results.

In his final question to Hett, Greg asked him whether the passage of time between the deposit of the unknown and the taking of the known sample had any effect on the validity of his tests. Without waiting for him to speak, Greg described a hypothetical situation where collected hair samples from a crime scene had not been examined for a period of several years. "Are you still going to be able to make some sort of reliable test?" Greg asked.

Hett stated that it was still possible to get a result but that the passage of time did have an effect as to the reliability of a test result. He admitted that even a few days could make the difference in getting a reliable result.

"So, it depends on other variables?" Greg asked.

"Right. If an individual shaves their head completely, there is not hair to have a comparison of," Hett articulated.

"Absolutely," said Greg. "Finally, we agree upon something. Thank you."

There were no further questions. Miller excused the witness and called Dennis Smith back to the stand.

Peterson re-directed his examination of Smith on the chain of custody procedures that were used in the mailing or transporting of the evidence to the proper facility heads. On re-cross, Barney and Greg briefly examined Smith with a little more expressiveness concerning his exact drop-off points and origins of mailing. With no further questions, Peterson moved the court for the admission of the state's hair exhibits.

Miller granted his request.

Wasting no time, Barney and Greg objected to the admissibility of Hett's testimony on the grounds that an assumption had to be made that the hair evidence was properly handled and properly mounted. Between the prosecution and defense, a series of back-and-forth disagreements commenced, with each side giving its legal interpretations concerning the control factors involved in the processing and labeling of the hair slides and whether or not the chain of custody was or was not broken due to the absence of the one who facilitated its direction—namely, Susan Land.

Miller abruptly stated that the hearing was continued until ten in the morning.

CHAPTER 13

One of the guards approached me and slapped a set of handcuffs on my wrists. On my brisk march back to the jail, neither of the guards that flanked me said a word. I was led to my cell and the door was shut.

I retraced my steps while I waited for my supper. On previous days, I had been allowed to visit with Greg before leaving. Today, though, I was shuttled from the courtroom without so much as a nod. Even if the hearing had lasted until 5:40 and everyone was tired and the guards probably had a lot of work to catch up on, that didn't excuse my gut feeling that something was different. The guards' eagerness and aggressive behavior was out of place. Something had changed, and not necessarily for the better. I wished I knew what and why.

I recalled the last minutes of Hett's testimony. He had obviously wavered in his remarks, which should have been good for me, but I wasn't so sure. I had noticed as the guards shuttled me from the courtroom that several spectators had glares of disdain and hostility and that even when I met their challenging stares, they continued to look at me with contempt. The guards' expressions had changed, too, and the grip of their hands on my arms had felt tighter and more urgent. I expected that kind of abrasiveness from John Christian; his personality was that of a pseudo-commando. But Ernie Self was a likeable guy whose humor made everyone in the jail feel equal. As I thought about the way he hung his head and averted his eyes, his out-of-character transition reinforced my suspicions. Something *was* different.

A trusty brought my tray. The food was cold. As I ate, I recalled the plot of an old sci-fi flick, *The Invasion of the Body Snatchers*. Was this that—a repopulating of Ada by unfeeling alien pod creatures who took over the bodies of humans while they slept? Was I the one person who, at the end of the movie, was supposed to make an escape and warn other cities of the alien invasion? It was silly but in a weird way, this sci-fi fantasy mirrored my predicament: Changes were taking place in the way people reacted to me and I didn't know why or what caused it to happen.

I swallowed the rest of my unseasoned beans and cornbread and stretched out on my bunk. The din from the bullpen lulled me to sleep. Some time later, the sound of the outer metal door being unlocked awakened me. I figured it was the trusty returning to retrieve my food tray, and I rolled over to face the wall to avoid conversation.

"Well, Fritz, I see you're causin' quite a stir over there in the courtroom," Tenney called out.

I sat up and swung my feet to the floor. Tenney stood outside my cell with a grin out of place for a guard talking to a prisoner. I studied his expression. He glanced backward once or twice toward the girls' tank, presumably to see if anyone was listening.

"Hello, Mike," I responded. "I'm not quite sure what you're referring to."

His beady eyes reflected a twinge of nervousness. He waited several seconds before he replied. "There's some talk circulatin' around that you might not make it to trial," he mumbled.

"What exactly does that mean, Mike?"

Leaning toward the bars, he whispered hoarsely, "Well, I'm not for sure if I should be even tellin' you this, but there's been some loose talk out there that some people are getting the idea that you might somehow beat this rap and get your case dismissed."

I made no reply.

Seconds ticked by. Tenney's eyes shifted from side to side. His voice was nearly a squeak when he spoke again: "Seems as though there's some people out there that don't take too kindly to the rumor that you might be released in a few days. Personally speaking, I don't put too much trust in any of the rumors, especially when it comes on beatin' a charge like yours at the preliminary hearing."

"Are you tryin' to say that there has been some kind of a death threat made against me?" I asked, trying to understand what he meant.

He glanced again toward the girls' tank. "Now, don't go and get yourself all worked up over something I never said. You know as well as I do that if you walk outta here by gettin' your case dismissed at the preliminary hearing, there's gonna be a lot of folks out there that will still believe you're guilty and think you got off on a technicality."

"Well, to tell you the truth, Mike, I don't care too much what those other folks think. It's like I told you before, I'm innocent of this crime and I'm gonna take it all the way, if that's what it takes. If I do get released, it won't be on a technicality because the state hasn't put on any evidence that even comes close to proving that I did this. You just said something about people not taking too kindly to me getting out of here. Were you referring to anything you heard that might involve a threat against me?"

"Listen to me, Fritz. All I can say is that if you don't walk at this hearing, you best start thinkin' about makin' some kind of deal, because there's a lot of people that think you're guilty, and you already know how hard it is around here to beat a murder charge in a trial. I gotta go, so don't go gettin' your hopes all up about walkin' outta here because it probably won't happen. Just remember what I said."

As Tenney locked the metal door behind him, Cissy's face appeared in the bean hole. She had that little smirk and that sparkle in her eye that let me know she had overheard what the guard said.

"What was that about?" she asked in her little-girl tone.

I shook my head. "I'm tired. I don't really feel like talking."

She licked her lips. "Is everything okay?"

I knew what she was trying to do. "Everything's— I'm just tired."

I backed away from the bars and lay down on my bunk. I turned Tenney's words over and over in my mind as I drifted in and out of sleep, tossing and turning, and now fearing for my life. Now I understood why everyone was behaving so differently towards me.

The impatient voice of Ron Scott roused me out of a dream. He ordered me up and to the shower. Chow was served—cold cereal and bread. As I ate, I thought about the hours ahead. Nothing—not even a death threat—was going to stop me from proclaiming my innocence. I had come too far to let an unfounded rumor rob me of my pride and dignity. No matter how long this took or what the outcome was, I would hold my head high and not let these people break my spirit.

On the walk to the courthouse, I was flanked by four guards instead of two, all of them unusually quiet and acting more alert than they had during the two previous days. I looked around. Nothing looked suspicious. Cars were parked, people were standing around to watch the morning procession to the courthouse, reporters were waiting on the sidewalk to film that day's tape. Still, I felt uneasy. I realized that I too was alert and ready to react—even in handcuffs— if anything out of the ordinary were to happen. Fortunately, nothing did.

The courtroom was again filled to capacity. People whispered to one another as I made my way to the defense table, where Greg, Barney, and Frank Baber awaited. The tension in the air was thick. I noticed the same glares and judgmental stares when I tried to make eye contact with a person or two in the gallery.

Miller announced that Ronnie had once again been brought to the courthouse prior to my arrival and vehemently disclaimed his right to be present during the proceedings. In a firm, deliberate tone, Miller overruled—with exception noted—defense counsel's objections to the testimony of Melvin Hett and the request that it be stricken from the record on the basis that the prepared slide exhibits he used in making his comparisons laid no foundation for evidence. Miller issued an additional finding that the state should fully disclose to the defense the names of the persons that aided in the preparation of the mounted hair slides. Next, Miller ruled that Mary Long's testimony specific to the saliva test should be stricken from the record; her remaining testimony in regard to the semen evidence would be allowed to stand. All distraction and noise in the courtroom abruptly ceased when the judge finished speaking.

Peterson's confident expression fell from his face. Miller asked Peterson if the state had anything further to present. "No," replied the district attorney. "The state of Oklahoma rests."

Anger and relief churned in my gut. The burden of fear that had weighed on my shoulders for months lightened as I realized Peterson had been bluffing all along. Thoughts of supreme contempt and outright disgust filled my head for this arrogant and pompous son of a bitch who had taken an oath to be an unequivocal advocate for justice. My stomach reeled at the sight of him and at the thought of his pretentious behavior. At that moment, I despised Bill Peterson more than anyone I had ever known—as a man, as a professional, and for the power that he unjustifiably possessed and unfairly wielded. I looked at Greg. Was Peterson running for reelection? Was that what this was about? I didn't want to ask.

Following a conference at the bench, Greg and Barney objected to the state's offered evidence in the rape, rape by instrumentation, and first-degree murder charges on the grounds that there was not sufficient evidence to prove a violation of the applicable statutes and that the statute of limitations on the rape counts had expired. Greg and Barney individually argued that the state's ability to prosecute for the rape expired three years after the date of the commission of the crime, which occurred on December 8, 1982. Barney reminded the court that prior testimonies of Rogers and Smith showed that neither Ronnie nor I had left or fled the state, which would have provided an exception to the limitations statute, while Peterson argued that the ability to charge arose in May of 1987. Since the charges were filed within a week of May 1, his contention was that the state was within the timeframe provided by the statute of limitations.

For the first time, Frank Baber spoke out and cited the specific state statute to the judge: "In Section 152, Section 3, the statute says that in all other cases, none of which pertain to this case, a prosecution for a public offense must be commenced within three years after its commission, period."

Immediately, Peterson asked Miller to give him some time to research the issue. Miller granted his request and informed the parties that he would take the issue under advisement.

"Any other motions on behalf of the defendant Williamson?" Miller asked.

Barney stipulated before Miller that he had yet to receive any of the nine fingerprinting reports made by Jerry Peters that the district attorney had promised to turn over to the defense. Peterson gave his agreement to turn them over. With no further motions coming forth on behalf of his client, Barney stepped aside for Greg to deliver his motions. Greg wasted no words in moving that the court dismiss the murder charge on the basis that prosecution for such an offense cannot rest on the sole evidence presented by hair examination.

"I don't think that they can bind him over on that, and I've listened very carefully. There is no other evidence that has been produced by the state of Oklahoma other than that of the hair examiner that puts Mr. Fritz either there or committing any of these offences," Greg stated sternly. "About the rape charge, there is no evidence that links him to a charge of rape or rape by instrumentation other than these hairs. And taken in their best light and giving them full credence, which I don't think the court can do, this evidence certainly does not make out those two charges. Consequently, I move to dismiss all counts against the defendant Fritz."

Peterson fired back, "Your Honor, the standard is to prove at a preliminary hearing that those three crimes were committed and that there's probable cause to believe that the accused committed those crimes. Based on that burden, I believe that this court even issued a warrant, which is a probable cause warrant based on the very same allegations, and therefore, I think the burden of the state of Oklahoma has been met at this hearing."

Greg dug in, reminding the judge that he and Barney had carefully asked each witness if that was all they knew about this case, and if there was anything else they could be asked at trial that wasn't testified to. He emphasized his point when he told Miller about a recent case where it was determined that the committing magistrate must make an assumption that the state will improve its case prior to trial. "I don't think you have to make that assumption in this case. I think you've seen it because, by their testimony, they've indicated that you cannot be required to assume they're going to improve their case because you've got evidence in the record to the contrary," Greg firmly argued.

Miller smiled politely.

Recharged by the force of Greg's statement, Barney orated to the judge that both he and Greg had filed prior motions seeking a list of prosecution witnesses. Citing a familiar case authority statute, Barney attempted to persuade Miller that the defense had in fact been entitled to a complete list of witnesses before the beginning of the preliminary hearing. Inching his way closer to the judge's bench, Barney stated that was what the court ordered him to do at that time, and also, that was what he told the court he would do.

"We assume that's all the witnesses they're going to use. So, if they've used all their witnesses, and all those witnesses say 'I've testified to all that I can testify to and everything I know about this case,' then I don't know how you can be put in a position to assume that they're going to improve it. Improve it with what?" Barney concluded.

Peterson staunchly held his ground by telling the judge that his order was to endorse all witnesses that he intended to call at preliminary hearing and at trial, but at this time he did not know what other witnesses he might or might not call at trial since that trial decision had not been made.

Miller diverted the flow of the issue by asking Greg, Barney, and Peterson what day on their calendar would be good to reconvene for his rulings on all of their objections and motions to dismiss. All agreed that Monday morning at nine was convenient. Miller instructed them that any case authorities accompanied by briefs should be in his office by no later than eight-thirty Monday morning.

It was time for the defense to call the witnesses on their list. All ten were jail officers, each of whom gave testimony for the sole purpose of stating whether or not they had overheard Ronnie or me make culpable statements while in custody. Each witness rendered testimony that they had not heard any incriminating statements from either of us during their employment hours at the jail.

"This matter will be continued until nine-thirty Monday morning, July 27," Miller concluded.

CHAPTER 14

The guard wasted no time in securing the handcuffs around my wrists. As I stood up, Greg stepped around the table and told me to try to relax and to not talk to anyone about my case. He assured me that it would be no later than Monday, or Tuesday at the most, when Miller would issue his bind-over decision. As I was being led away, Greg nodded his head and told me to hang in there.

That afternoon, time came to a standstill.

The next four days were a living hell. I couldn't stand the pressure that built in my chest from the worry that was building in my mind. I paced for hours between my bunk and the cell bars. I couldn't sleep. I ate just enough to have the energy to be able to think clearly, but all I could think about was the way the events of the past three days had unfolded.

The harder I tried to think of anything else, the more my mind padlocked my thoughts. I tried praying. I prayed on my hands and knees, like I'd learned to do as a kid. I prayed while I paced. I prayed while I sat. I prayed flat on my back on my bunk before trying to sleep. Resolution dangled at the end of an imaginary string, swaying like a pendulum before me, as the unmerciful hours crawled forward at turtle speed. Only my prayers comforted me through the agony of waiting.

On top of everything else, Lloyd the trusty crept up to my cell several times without showing himself and let out a hideous yell that nearly jolted me off the commode—the only other chair in the house besides my bunk. Lloyd's outbursts created an opportunity for the girls to yell, as well, usually at him, and then try to strike up a conversation with me. I followed Greg's advice, though, and avoided talking.

By Friday, I was frazzled by emotional and physical stress. My efforts to unravel my predicament and forecast my fate ended when I collapsed in a haze of despair and exhaustion. Lying in my bunk in a delirium, I surrendered my will to the open arms of the Lord and His grace and mercy upon me. I moved only to use the toilet and then returned to my meditative state, with my face toward the wall, to seek the solace and protection that I so longed for. Without budging, I prayed through the afternoon for strength, perseverance, and edification.

As the trusties began delivering supper trays, someone called out my name. I looked over my shoulder and saw Greg standing outside the cell.

"How are you holding up?" he asked.

I shook my head and rolled over. "Don't ask," I said, sitting up. My body felt like lead.

"Don't get up," Greg said. "I just wanted to let you know that Barney and I have found some cases that will be most helpful in convincing Miller not to bind you over for trial." He raised his eyebrows as he spoke, and then a somber look replaced his enthusiasm. "But I think we have to be realistic, too, and understand that it's rare to overcome probable cause for bind-over purposes. I don't want to get your hopes up but I wanted you to know that there's precedent. We're doing what we can."

His words, or maybe his intentions, contradicted themselves. I wasn't sure what he was trying to tell me, so I nodded.

"Are you doing okay?" he asked again.

"I'm doing the best I can do."

"Well, try not to stress out too much," he said, adding, "if that's possible."

"Thanks, Greg," I said. My smile was more like a grimace.

"I'll see you later," he said, and he was gone.

"Yeah, thanks," I called out.

I sat up and moved over to the commode—my thinking chair. As I wondered about the cases Greg had mentioned, a loud voice reverberated in my head and I heard clearly the words, "Trust me!" I turned my head toward the bars, thinking that the loose-minded trusty was up to his tricks again, when I realized that I had not heard the spoken words with my ears but from within. A warm, tranquil sensation radiated throughout my chest as I arrived at the realization that I had just heard—within—the voice of Christ. Hot tears of joy and happiness streamed down my cheeks as I silently reveled in the spirit of the Lord with a rekindled sense of awe and exuberance. Never in my life had I experienced such a spiritual encounter. His words penetrated to the deepest part of my soul, chasing all the worry, fear, and apprehension from my mind and body for the rest of what would have otherwise been a wretchedly long weekend.

Monday morning arrived, and the courtroom buzzed with people awaiting Miller's rulings. After I was seated at the defense table, Greg turned to me with a big smile on his face and informed me that Miller was going to throw out both of the rape charges. My brain mulled his words, and I trembled with elation. Glancing over at Barney, I noticed that he didn't share Greg's enthusiasm. Leaning close so Barney couldn't hear, I asked Greg what was wrong.

"When they brought Ronnie over a little while ago, he started shouting all kinds of obscenities and came close to shoving the table over again, near where Barney was sitting. Don't worry about Barney. He's okay. Just relax and— Miller's here," he said, interrupting himself as the judge entered the courtroom. "Forget about what I said. Just stay calm. If you have any questions or comments, write them on your notepad."

As Miller took his seat at the bench, Peterson stood and announced to the court that the state was withdrawing the rape charges as to counts 1 and 2 in the charged information on the grounds that the three-year statute of limitations had expired for prosecuting the offenses.

"If they had embezzled Ms. Carter's money, the statute of limitations would be seven years. If they had cheated on their income tax, it would be five years," said Peterson in a begrudging manner. Pausing dramatically, Peterson then admitted wearily to the court that the language of the law was obvious on its face and described how the state was legally bound to drop the rape charges. Pausing again, Peterson then proffered new murder charges to the court, amending the previous third count so that it became Count 1, murder with malice aforethought, and a new second count of murder while in the commission of a felony. Both of the dismissed rape charges were included as the underlying felonies in the newly amended charges.

Barney and Greg requested additional time to review the district attorney's verbal amendment to determine if the statute of limitations applied to felony murder. Miller granted the defense's request and gave them until nine the next morning to find precedent-setting case authorities to back up their challenge. Miller expressed his doubt that any such cases existed.

Barney argued before Miller—who had also been the committing magistrate in the Ward-Fontenot case—that, when he dropped the rape charges against Ward and Fontenot and his decision was later reversed on the grounds that Miller should have assumed that the state would improve its case before trial, it stood to reason that Peterson should not be allowed to call witnesses in a trial that he did not use in the preliminary hearing because the Ward-Fontenot decision was made after the Carter murder occurred. Miller sat mute and did not address Barney's statement but granted the defense's motion to get a completed list of Peterson's intended trial witnesses.

As the morning wore on, Greg reasserted his argument that the state could not improve its case because all of the expert witnesses who had testified had stated that they had testified to everything they knew. He embellished the previous day's argument that no testimony except for Hett's, which he said was questionable, could link me to the crime. He made a motion that the court grant a new preliminary hearing because he had not had the proper amount of time to prepare, having been appointed on the Thursday before the hearing had begun on Monday. Greg told the judge that my constitutional right to adequate counsel as set forth in the Sixth Amendment had been violated.

The judge overruled the motion but went on to grant the defense's pending motion to receive a copy of the preliminary hearing transcript at the county's expense. He concluded by stating that he would announce his bind-over decision tomorrow. Greg told me before I was returned to my cell that there was probably not a snowflake's chance in hell that Miller would bind us over. He qualified his remark, though, with the statement that the probable-cause requirement carries a much lower burden of proof than the trial standard of guilt beyond a reasonable doubt. Those were the thoughts I took with me as I was led back to my cell. All night long, I tried to imagine that I would be reunited with my family in the morning.

The next day, Judge Miller bound Ronnie and me over for trial and set the district court arraignment date for August 20. His decision was not a surprise, though the sting and humiliation of defeat left its devastating impression on my enthusiasm and faith in the judicial system. Throughout the morning, Barney and Greg argued before the judge about Peterson's enlistment of the second murder charge.

"Peterson is coming in the back door because you and the court have closed the front door," Barney insisted. "Besides, the punishment for murder can only be done once."

Both defense attorneys slammed the way that the charges were written, with Barney specifically objecting to the mention in the new charges of any offense barred by the expiration of the statutes of limitation. Both attorneys emphasized that the statute for felony murder did not include rape by instrumentation as an optional underlying felony. Miller overruled the defense's objections and ordered Peterson to reconstruct the charges to show what acts occurred during the rape that led to Debbie Carter's death.

"I can see how the washcloth in her mouth and the ligature around her neck could be construed as resulting from attempts to keep her from screaming, or it could have been premeditated. But the count is not drafted properly," Miller told the district attorney. He then ordered Peterson to amend the second count to show that the death resulted during the commission of a forcible rape and that any reference to rape by instrumentation be deleted on the redraft.

Barney requested that the state furnish a copy of the notes of any statements taken during Williamson's arrest. Peterson objected. Miller instructed Barney to file a written motion to be heard by Judge Jones in the district court, banged his gavel, and ended the preliminary hearing proceedings.

While Frank and Barney gathered up their notes and documents, Greg and I talked briefly. The guards didn't seem like they were in quite so much of a hurry today.

"It's not over yet, Dennis," Greg said. "I'm going to file what they call a motion to quash the information as to the insufficiency of the evidence and several other procedural motions before your arraignment. If the motion to quash is denied, then I may have the option to appeal the ruling to the Oklahoma Court of Criminal Appeals. I firmly believe with all my heart that they didn't have enough to bind you over. Hett's testimony was purely subjective, and there was no other evidence to put you at the scene of the crime. So, like I've said before, no matter how strong the temptation is, don't talk about your case to anyone, and I'll be over to the jail to see how you're doing. I'll let you know of anything I hear." He sounded sincere as he stacked his papers.

"Above anything else, Greg, I want you and Barney to know that I'm totally innocent of committing that murder and have no knowledge of who did." I told him, rushing my words in case the guards decided that I was just supposed to be listening.

"Dennis, Barney and I have spent a lot of time going over this case, and both of us wholeheartedly believe that you're innocent. I promise you that I will do everything in my power to try and clear you of this charge. You're going to be stuck over there in that jail for a few weeks before your arraignment, so do your best to stay as calm as possible. Don't cause any trouble or talk to anyone, because these people are out to take your life, and that's as serious as it gets." With that, he put his papers in his binder.

The guards moved swiftly toward me, cuffed me, and led me to my cell. Back in the jail, days turned into weeks, with little variation in my daily routine. I could count on three square meals of crap each day, a shower once a week, a steady stream of sexually suggestive notes from Cissy, regular outbursts from Ronnie, hours spent pacing or attempting to sleep, and most of all, daily visits from Mike Tenney.

It was late on a hot July evening, when the air conditioner wasn't working right, when Tenney paid me a visit. Sweat streamed down my face as we talked at the bars.

"Well, Fritz, it doesn't look too good for you from what I hear. I've heard that death row down there in McAlester is a very tough place to be, with all those killers waitin' to die." He looked around suspiciously and leaned over to half-close the small metal swinging door that covered the bean hole of the girls' tank. His voice was quieter when he spoke again. "Seems like to me that makin' a deal would be greatly in your favor at this point."

I didn't answer. In the silence, I realized that I hadn't heard Ronnie screaming for a good part of the evening.

"Look, Mike, I'm not scared of death row because I know that the truth is gonna win out. I'm gonna walk outta here a free man. I've told you a hundred times before that I'm innocent, and sooner or later my innocence will be proven. Besides, my attorney has already told me that if I wanted to make a deal, that the D.A. would probably offer me some kind of plea bargain. Whatcha think?"

Tenney shook his head. "You know that if you wait too long, the chances of gettin' a deal go way down. Like I told you before, you gotta start thinkin' about your own self and quit worryin' about Williamson. Bein' in jail is better than bein' dead."

"Well, you might be right there. I wish I could help the D.A. but I'm not gonna rat on Ronnie when I don't know that he's guilty. I'm not the kind of person who would lie about someone else just to save my own ass. But I'll think about what you said, and we'll talk later," I said and turned away. I wanted to cut the conversation short.

Tenney opened the door on the bean hole of the girls' tank and walked away.

He was getting on my nerves—with his constant attempts to scare me with the death penalty and always talking about making deals. He always tried to talk quietly so the women wouldn't hear him, but they always told me after he left that they had heard every word he said. He might be pretending to be my friend, but I was onto him. I wondered what kind of game he was up to. The more I thought about his disturbing comments, the more irritated I became.

One night when I heard his voice outside the metal door, I called to him and asked him if he would come and talk. I wanted to set the record straight with him because I didn't want him to get the idea that I would consider a plea bargain.

"Yeah, whatcha want?" Tenney grumbled.

"I just want you to understand something. If I hadda been up there in Carter's apartment that night, and let's say I went ahead and got a little, and Ronnie got carried away and killed her, don't you think that I would go ahead and take a plea bargain instead of takin' a chance of dyin' on death row?" Before Tenney could respond, I continued by saying, "But I didn't see Ron kill Debbie Carter because I wasn't up there, so how could I tell the D.A. something I didn't see?"

"Fritz, all I can say is that you better think everything over very carefully because it's gonna be your ass on death row and not mine. I'm not your attorney and I can't advise you what to do, so you'll have to make up your own mind."

"No, Mike, there's nothing to make my mind up about. I didn't kill that girl, and I don't know whether Ronnie did or not. It's as simple as that."

Tenney shrugged and walked away. I felt better now that I had gotten my point across as to why I wouldn't consider taking a plea bargain. Although Greg had told me not to talk to anyone about my case, I was sure that I hadn't said anything that was even close to sounding incriminating, nor had I given any factual accounts of anything Greg and I had talked about. And besides, the girls across the way knew I was always telling Tenney that I was an innocent man. They had also heard it from me at least a hundred times over the course of the time I had been locked up.

A couple of weeks later, Tenney came to my cell. He partially closed the girls' tank bean hole cover and drew close to my cell bars. In a near-whisper, Tenney said that he could testify favorably for me if I could have my family send him five hundred dollars to someone at another name and address that he could give to me. I told him that I didn't think that my family could afford it but I would ask them and see what they said.

On several occasions after that, Tenney came to my cell and asked if my family had sent off the money. I told him that I had contacted them but they had told me that they didn't have the cash to spare. Each time, Tenney closed the conversation by saying that I might get the death penalty and should consider some kind of a deal where I could turn state's evidence and get seven or eight years. As he turned to leave, he always remembered to open the girls' tank bean hole cover and to tell me in a normal tone that we would talk later.

"Hey, Dennis," beckoned Billi Jo one evening.

"Haven't heard from you in a while. How are you doing?" I responded.

"We heard most everything Tenney was tellin' you, especially about the five hundred dollars. If I were you, I'd be careful with him 'cause he's the police and he'll take your money and probably turn everything around in his favor."

"Yeah, I know he's on the take. Besides, my family's broke and they told me that they wouldn't do it, even if they had the money. Would you be willing to make out a statement on everything that you've been hearing him say to me?"

"No problem. I don't like these cops down here and I'm sure not scared of them. I don't live in this town anyway. I think you're innocent and believe you're gettin' a raw deal all the way around. You seem like a nice guy, so I'll be glad to help you out."

"Well, I appreciate it very much, Billi Jo, and if there's anything I can ever do for you, just let me know," I told her.

Chapter 15

August 20 was a copy of every other listless and boring day I had spent in jail so far, with two exceptions: Today was the day for arraignment in district court, and it was also my birthday. Except for the steadfast support of my family, I felt alone and very dejected on my thirty-eighth birthday.

Greg met with me first thing and outlined the different motions that he was preparing. In addition to requesting a severance and seeking designation of the state's witnesses, he said he was in the process of working on a brief in support of his motion to quash based on the insufficiency of the state's evidence. He said there would be an upcoming hearing where he would give his oral arguments but he didn't know whether it would be before or during the arraignment. He went on to explain that Judge Jones had been on the bench for quite a while and had a reputation for being a hanging judge.

"He shows very little mercy, Dennis, but don't get me wrong," Greg told me while we sat across the table in the visitors' room. He had a notepad in front of him as he spoke. "Jones goes strictly by the book and shows no favoritism for either side. He's a tough judge, very difficult to persuade if the issue before him is the least bit controversial. For example, trying to get a change of venue, where another court would hear your case, would be futile at this point, despite all of the news media coverage. Unless there have been death threats made against you, which I have not heard of, Jones would never grant a change of venue. I want you to know that I'll do my very best in the oral argument hearing, but I also want you to be aware that the possibility of getting Jones to grant the motion to quash is very slim to none at all." There was a hint of reluctance in his voice as he lowered his eyes to his notepad and continued to speak, "Dennis, as you know, you are in very serious trouble, but I am going to do everything humanly possible to fight for your acquittal."

His visit left me feeling uncertain—about my fate, about Greg's ability to persuade, about the judge's reputation, about my future. I mentally prepared myself for whatever lay ahead by thinking of my mother, aunt, and daughter and imagining my freedom.

The moment of reckoning arrived. In front of the judge, Greg and Barney informed him of several pending motions that they had filed prior to the hearing. Jones, with no emotion in his voice, said that he was aware of them and recessed the arraignment till September 4. I was immediately removed from the courtroom and returned to the jail.

I felt like a yoyo on a short string. At the least, I got some fresh air and viewed what used to be a normal, everyday sight for me—civilization and people moving about freely. But it was all so short-lived and then I was back in the doom and gloom of my cell. Jealousy and anger collided in my mind, fueling a wretched and unfathomable sense of loneliness. When the trusty handed me my lunch chow, he also gave me two postmarked envelopes—one from my blessed mother and aunt, and the other from Elizabeth. Upon reading my birthday cards, I could not stop the flood of tears. Sadness and joy ripped my heart in two.

On September 4, Jones rescheduled my arraignment proceedings for the following Tuesday at one in the afternoon. Ronnie's arraignment was to start ninety minutes later. I was marched back to the jail again to wait, and wait, and wait longer. The saving grace, if there was one, was that my skin felt fresh from the lukewarm shower I'd taken earlier and my hair was combed. I felt physically good.

At the beginning of Tuesday's proceedings, Jones announced to the defense and prosecution that the court was ready to hear oral arguments on the defendant's filed motion to quash. I studied the judge's face. He looked to be in his early fifties, with neatly combed gray hair. His glasses were positioned near the tip of his nose, and when he spoke, he looked out over the tops of the frames. His expression was dull and disinterested. I could easily see why some people called him the hanging judge. If for no other reason than his appearance was a reflection of his judging abilities, then I was in powerful rushing water without a paddle. Jones's tired, worn-out facial features cast a look of indifference as he slowly read in a monotone the newly amended Counts 1 and 2.

Greg argued that the prosecution's case was predicated solely upon the testimony of OSBI chemist Melvin Hett, whose comparisons were inconclusive and could not be used as incriminating evidence against me. Greg also stated that Mary Long's expert testimony had been ruled inadmissible and that the testimony of OSBI agent Gary Rogers suggested that Williamson might be guilty but, Greg added, "not my client, Mr. Fritz."

Greg and Peterson battled back and forth for more than an hour as to whether Hett's testimony was sufficient enough to show that I had been involved in committing the crime. Jones ordered the state to have additional blood samples taken to determine my secretor/non-secretor status.

As I stood alongside Greg, the judge stated that before he accepted my plea, he was required under the law to advise me of my rights. Never looking up, he stated that I had the right to a retrial/appeal upon conviction, the right to testify, the right to call witnesses in my behalf, the right to confront and cross examine witnesses, and that the state was required to prove guilt beyond a reasonable doubt, with or without my testimony. Jones's voice was so low that I didn't fully hear the last couple of rights I was being afforded. As the hearing neared a conclusion, the judge overruled Greg's motion to quash, and upon my plea of "innocent" entered by Greg, Jones announced that the arraignment was completed and that a trial date would be set shortly. I was escorted back to my cell.

Stress and indecision would fill the weeks ahead. I wanted to know exactly what was going to happen, but Greg didn't tell me. The only thing I was sure of was that I faced a jury that would decide on the death penalty. I wanted to believe that Greg would do everything that he could do, but there lurked in the back of my mind the doubt that it might not be enough. I asked myself again and again whether I was strong enough to withstand the strain of this formidable madness, or would I suddenly short circuit and lose my mind? That fear whirled constantly through my head. I kept coming back to those words, *Trust me,* that I had heard weeks ago. They filled my vulnerable spirit with consolation and peace of mind when I needed it most.

Late one night, the sound of the outer door woke me from a deep sleep. A night guard I didn't recognize opened the door to the girls' tank and escorted Cissy out. I heard the guard say something about the front of the jail. After the outer door was closed, Billi Jo's face appeared in the bean hole. When I asked her what had happened, she said she didn't know.

I awoke again a couple hours later, when Cissy was returned to her cell. Chow was served maybe an hour or so after that.

During the day, Cissy didn't say a word to me about her interrogation. Again that night, at approximately the same time, she was escorted from the cell by a guard, someone I didn't know. As the sound of the cell bars toward the front of the jail clanged shut, Billi Jo came to the bean hole with a bewildered look on her face.

"What's going on?" I whispered.

"They're questioning her about her case," Billi Jo said. "Or at least that's what she told us."

"In the middle of the night?" I asked.

"Yeah, we were wondering about that. She was really disoriented when they brought her back, like she was on something," Billi Jo said. "I think there's more to it than what she's saying. You might want to be careful what you say to her."

I agreed. I lay back down on my bunk and went to sleep. When the guard brought Cissy back a few hours later, she was wearing a pair of jeans and a shirt instead of the normal jail whites, which indicated to me that she had done more than just talk about her case.

Several days passed without Cissy so much as even tossing a note across to me. Even Billi Jo seemed somewhat distant during the couple of occasions that we had conversations. Again one night, like clockwork, Cissy was taken from the cell, but this time by a county cop I had never seen before. I was on my bunk, pretending to sleep. He looked suspiciously in my direction after shutting her cell door.

Billi Jo appeared in the bean hole after hearing the front gate lock. In a low whisper, she told me that she had overheard Cissy telling JoEllyn that she was working with the cops and that Bruce Johnson, a one-time cop turned special investigator for Peterson, had put a wire under her shirt and sent her out to make drug buys at local residences.

"She's even braggin' that they gave her a new Trans Am to drive over to the people's houses and that she's gettin' in real good with that Johnson cop. She really thinks she's hot shit now with that goody-two-shoes attitude she's carryin' around. She's nothin' but a lousy snitch in my mind, and she's probably thinkin' that she can work some kind of deal to get her ass outta here," Billi Jo grumbled.

"And, on top of that, she's trying to get JoEllyn to work some deals on her own with the cops." JoEllyn was one of the women that Billi Jo didn't trust.

"What's JoEllyn and the other girls doin' right now?" I whispered.

"They're all asleep over here, or at least I think they are. I better get away from the window, or JoEllyn might get suspicious and try to cause trouble."

I waited up until Cissy was returned to her cell. This time, I stood at the bars to get a good look at her. Even with the guard beside her, she turned and gave me a big smile. Her eyes looked glazed and her hair was matted to her head. I returned to my bunk to go to sleep.

I vaguely heard chow being called but didn't get up. I was in no mood to eat. It was early October, and they still hadn't turned off the air conditioning. It was cold in the cell. I just wanted to cover up and sleep the morning away. I rolled over and dozed off. Deep sleep found me for the first time in a long while.

Ron Scott's loud voice rudely invaded the small space of my cell, jarring me awake. I turned over. He was yelling at me, "Fritz! Get up and get your shit packed and bring your mattress. You're goin' back to the bullpens."

I groaned in retaliation. "Why are you movin' me back there? I wanna stay where I'm at," I demanded.

"I don't wanna hear none of your complainin'. You're not runnin' this jail so get a move on and get your shit and let's go. I'm not gonna stand here all day waitin'," Scott said.

Another guard appeared at the bars. It would do no good to argue.

"If anything happens to me in the bullpens, you are totally responsible," I said to Scott, glaring at him as I walked through the open doorway into the hall.

Scott said nothing. The impatient look on his face told me that he could care less.

"Goin' to the bullpen on the left," the other guard instructed me.

I had stayed in the bullpens during the DUI conviction and hated them. My list of complaints was long: They were almost always overcrowded past their eight man capacity, there was no privacy—you had to take a crap in front of everybody, guys stayed up to all hours slamming dominoes on the metal picnic table used for eating, the lights stayed on all night, the filthy language was inescapable, as were the ever-present sounds of day and night farting, snoring, or someone screaming from the D.T.s or other deliriums. The only good thing was that I could take a shower whenever I wanted. In my opinion, the bad greatly outweighed the good and I would have forsaken a daily shower any time to be in a cell of my own. But that wasn't up to me. I found a temporary bunk by the top vent, threw my mattress on it, and climbed aboard the loft of lunacy.

No one in the bullpens knew who I was, and the first few days passed without any confrontations or verbal exchanges. I was wary at first, because I wasn't sure if there might be someone back here that was related to the Carters. I slept with one eye open. I adjusted gradually to the harsh surroundings.

One afternoon, a guard appeared at the cell door.

"Where's Fritz?" he yelled. "Your attorney's here waitin' to see you."

I immediately jumped off my bunk and rushed toward him. The jailer led me to the same small visiting area where Greg and I had first met. Upon entering, I noticed that Greg was jubilantly smiling. He told me to have a seat.

"Dennis, I have great news for you!" he said excitedly. "I just talked to the judge. He is going to order another preliminary hearing based upon a couple of new cases that were just heard by the Oklahoma Court of Criminal Appeals that could have a direct effect on your case. They are exactly on point with the argument I made, with only some slight differences—that Hett's testimony cannot stand alone in binding you over without further independent evidence showing that you were at the scene of the crime."

I was speechless but bursting inside.

"Anyway, Jones is going to vacate his prior bind-over order and remand it back to Miller for further preliminary hearing. What's the matter? Has the cat got your tongue?" Greg asked and then giggled.

"Greg, I can't believe what I just heard you say. I know you're not bullshitting me, but would you pinch me so I'll know this is not a dream?" I said.

Greg laughed with the enthusiasm of a kid. So did I.

"When is all of this going to happen?" I asked as a smile spread over my face.

"Well, from what I understand, the hearing will be some time in the middle of November. Do you know what this means, Dennis?" Greg asked with exhilaration in his voice.

I didn't answer. I was still too much in shock to venture a guess.

"What it means, Dennis, is you're gonna walk out of here because the state has no other evidence against you."

Free to go. I imagined putting on my jeans and shirt and shoes and walking out without looking back. Then a thought crossed my mind that Greg ought to know about.

"Greg, I can't begin to tell you how happy I am inside, but I guess I just don't want to get my hopes up too much and then be let down again. I need to tell you about something kinda odd that happened a few days ago. They moved me back in the bullpens. Just out of the clear blue."

"Beyond everything else, Dennis, do not, and I'm dead serious about this, do not talk about your case to anyone. Are we in agreement on that?" he insisted.

"Of course, of course," I said as I nodded vigorously.

"I'll keep you posted," he assured me.

Back in the bullpen, I moved to a bottom bunk in a cell in

the front where it was warmer and rejoiced to the Lord well into the evening for bringing about a miracle that I had prayed for since my arrest. In just a little over a month, I'd be out of this hellhole, and I'd be free! At evening chow, I ate at the table with some of the other inmates. As I anticipated, a couple of guys asked some general questions about my case. I sidestepped their questions by stating my innocence, but one of the inmates, a fellow named James Harjo, asked a lot of specific questions. I sensed that it was his way of opening up to me.

As the days dragged by, I got to know James better. He was a Native American, with a slim build, long black hair, and acne blemishes on his face. James could not read or write very well, so I helped him write letters to his wife, and we played chess to pass the time. He was part of a little group of us that got together around the table once a week or so for Bible study. James was a little slow-witted, and I wasn't sure how much of what he said was truth or lies or just misunderstanding, but he was just a kid. I told him one day that getting his G.E.D. might help him get out of whatever rut he was in, but he didn't seem interested. James became more and more curious about my situation. On occasion, he came into my shared cell area, sat on the back of the commode, and pretended to be a detective trying to solve my case. I always told him, and everyone else in the bullpen, that I was totally innocent of the charges against me.

After a while, I noticed that James's curiosity got the better of him, usually after I returned to the bullpen after visits from Greg. James, who seemed borderline mentally retarded, would ask me what Greg and I had talked about. He was convinced that he was a private detective, or at the very least, he liked imitating how the detectives had questioned him in his own case, when he admitted his guilt to them after being charged with first-degree burglary and possession of stolen property.

Greg asked me at one visit if I knew anyone named Gary Allen. I did not recognize the name. Greg said that he had learned through Peterson that Allen was going to testify at the upcoming remanded hearing that he had seen me and Ronnie, late at night, using a water hose in the backyard to wash blood off ourselves. Greg eyed me closely as I explained to him that I could not remember anyone by that name and had never been in my backyard late at night using a water hose for any reason, let alone washing off blood.

"When was this supposed to have happened?" I asked.

"I don't have all the details, but it's my impression that it happened on the night of the murder," Greg responded, his look grim.

"You've got to believe me. I have never done whatever this Gary Allen guy is saying. Please don't let this lie from hell make you think I'm involved with that girl's death," I implored.

"I believe you. I'll let you know what else I find out," he assured me. "By the way, the judge has granted my motion to sever the trials. You and Ronnie will be tried separately. The remanded preliminary hearing has been set for November 13. The trial date is April 21. And the test results are back on your blood work."

"And?"

"The results show that you're a non-secretor."

I returned to the bullpen burdened by doubt. One of the inmates noticed that I looked troubled and asked what was wrong. I told him. I also asked him and a couple other inmates if they had ever heard of Gary Allen. No one knew his name. That evening, James came into my cell, sat on the back of the commode, and asked if I had a water hose in my backyard. He must have overheard my conversations. With pencil and paper in hand, James asked again about the water hose. To get rid of him, I said that I really couldn't remember but I may have had one hooked to the water faucet on the back of the house. James drew something on the paper. While he was drawing, I told him that I had a lot on my mind and needed to sleep.

Reluctantly, he left.

Before falling asleep, though, I realized that every time I talked to James, or anybody else for that matter, I was divulging information about my case, and I'd promised Greg I wouldn't do that. I decided that I should collect from all of the inmates handwritten statements acknowledging the fact that I had never said anything incriminating while I was in the bullpen. Though I was continually proclaiming my innocence to everyone, these handwritten statements would be a backup safeguard against anyone who might want to snitch in exchange for leniency favors in their case. I decided that I would start asking in the morning for people to voluntarily submit their statements.

Not many days after I had started collecting statements, including one from James, the jailers put a guy by the name of Harlan Shields into the bullpen. From all indications, James and Shields had known each other on the streets, and now they were thick as syrup together. Shields, also a Native American, was a massive man, well over three hundred pounds and nearly six and a half feet tall. It was obvious to me, and probably anybody else, that James considered Shields his personal bodyguard. I was glad that James had a friend by his side because it meant that I would have less contact with him, but there was something about the two of them that didn't seem quite right. The situation gave me a feeling of pending danger.

Over several days in mid-October, the inmates in my bullpen were taken one by one to the front and questioned as to whether they had heard me say anything about my involvement in the murder. Upon returning, every man except James told me that the questions they'd been asked were about me. James agreed to write a new statement for me but would not admit that the police had talked about me with him. He said they asked him about his own case, but the way he acted toward me told me a different story. He avoided me, and that only made me more suspicious. Tension built between us.

On Halloween night, the accumulated stress began to

overwhelm me. I lay in my bunk with my face to the wall, and for a while tears flowed from my eyes onto the coverless, plastic pillow. I wanted a smoke, and everyone had gone to bed in my shared cell area, so I got up and walked to James's cell area. I whispered his name and asked if he had a Marlboro. From his bunk, he handed a cigarette to me without saying a word. I thanked him and went to the eating table, where I sat down with my back against the bars.

Harjo approached and stood at the foot of the table.

"Fritz, I think you're guilty of killin' that girl," he said, his voice flat and dry.

All I could see was his face illuminated by the dim light shining from the rear of the cell. I shook my head and said, "To tell you the truth, I don't care what you think. Your little detective game has gone far enough, and you're wrong, so don't even put that bullshit on me right now." I felt a fight brewing, so I got up and returned to my cell, where I lay down on my bunk. Harjo followed me and sat down at my feet.

"I figured it out, Fritz. I know that you and Ronnie killed that girl and you need to confess right now."

"This is the last time I'm gonna tell you, Harjo. You best get outta here or we're gonna have some trouble. I've suffered over this more than you will ever know, even to the point of my own daughter maybe thinking that I'm a murderer. Leave my cell right now!" I exclaimed.

Harjo jumped to his feet in a stance of retaliation. In a breath, I leapt from my bunk. I was ready to fight. Harjo backed away. Our eyes locked in anticipation of the slightest movement.

"I'll make up something on you as pure as gold," Harjo said and he turned and walked away.

CHAPTER 16

The trusty called out about morning chow, but I wasn't interested. Only a handful of inmates ate breakfast, anyway, so I would not be missed. I rolled over on my bunk to face the wall and eventually drifted back to sleep. Some time later, I was awakened by Ronnie's voice blaring through the bullpen.

"Where's that Dennie Leon at and that little Karl Fontenot?" Ronnie asked in a frisky tone.

I opened my eyes and looked around. There was Ronnie, standing just on the other side of the bullpen bars, holding a pot of steaming coffee. I sat up and stretched, grabbed my cup, and made my way toward him. Karl, who was back in the Ada jail following his overturned conviction, was just a few steps behind me.

"What are you doin' out, Ronnie?" I asked, squinting and rubbing the sleep from my face.

"They told me I could get out and get a little exercise, so I decided to run a few bases before going back to the dugout and bring some of this finely brewed coffee to this elite group of highly educated criminal offenders," Ronnie said.

Before he could fill my cup, he glanced over my shoulder. I turned around.

Harjo and his big buddy had walked to the table and were standing there, glaring at me. Harjo had said to me yesterday, before our confrontation, that he was going to be transferred to the penitentiary some time around the first of November, so it was better that we have as little contact as possible. But last night's tension hadn't lifted. I felt instinctively that another confrontation was right around the corner. I spoke out.

"Hey, Ron, Harjo here thinks that you and me murdered that Carter girl. Says he solved this crime by drawin' somethin' on a piece of paper."

Ronnie stood silently at the bars. A baffled look spread across his face. Harjo rounded the table and took a few steps my way. His fists were clenched. Anger contorted his expression. I braced myself for a fight. It was time to clear the air. I was ready for the storm to hit.

Shields didn't move. "Ron, you and your buddy killed that girl, didn't ya?" he called out from his place by the table.

Harjo stopped in his tracks when Shields spoke.

"Dennie Leon," Ronnie warned me in a hushed tone, "don't do nothin' stupid that you'll be sorry for later. They're only guessin'. We both know we didn't do it, so let's let it be, and they can think what they want."

"You raped her, didn't you, Ron?" Shields taunted.

Ronnie stood motionless, holding the coffeepot. His mouth gaped open but he didn't speak. After a moment, a nearby inmate intervened and told everyone to break it up because it would only bring the guards back and everybody would get shaken down.

Still holding the coffeepot, Ronnie walked away from the bullpen and meandered through the hall toward his cell. I returned to my bunk and left Harjo and his bodyguard standing at the table. The day progressed without further conflict. The next day, Harjo and Shields were transferred out to prison.

After their departure, I collected statements from Fontenot and another inmate in the other bullpen, who verified that they had heard Harjo state that he "would make up something on me as pure as gold." I also got into a fistfight with a black guy who was charged with raping a white woman. He called me a punk, and I took a swing at him. He swung back. I raked my knuckles across his teeth and sliced my hand open, and that resulted in a high-security hospital visit to treat my wound. Even after I returned to the bullpen, the pressure continued to build.

At Greg's next visit, I gave him the inmates' statements and told him what had happened. Greg was disappointed and reprimanded me for not keeping my word to not talk about my case. Greg had heard nothing new about any other witnesses against me. He said that Peterson had a couple more weeks before the hearing date and he was being real tight-lipped about everything. That in itself made Greg nervous and fearful of what the D.A. was considering.

A few days before the hearing date, Greg told me that Tenney was listed as a witness to give testimony that I had made some sort of a confession to him and that he had a written account of everything I had been telling him. I was astonished. What Greg said after that, though, pushed my blood pressure nearly through the roof.

"Tenney has been working through Rogers to gain information against you, Dennis," Greg said. "What do you know about that?"

"Damn it, it's all lies," I shouted. "Those dirty bastards will do anything and everything to get a conviction on me."

Greg asked me to settle down but I was at the breaking point. I didn't even want to finish his visit.

"All I can tell you, Greg, is that Tenney is a no-good son of a bitch, and if you don't believe me, I don't give a damn. I've had it up to my ass with all these motherfuckers here trying to railroad me for something I don't know about. I'm ready to go back now. Is there anything else you need to tell me?"

"No, Dennis, that's all I've heard, but I do need to know

what all you've said to Tenney," Greg said. He put his hands on the table and leaned toward me.

I collected my thoughts. "All I told Tenney, and I told him this hundreds of times, was that I was innocent and that if I had been up there that night, which I said I wasn't, then I would go ahead and make some kind of deal with Peterson instead of going before a death penalty jury. That's the extent of most everything I told him. You've got the statement that I gave you from Beverlin to back up what I've told you about him. You've looked it over, haven't you?" I said. I looked at him, eyeball to eyeball. I had my doubts.

"Yes, I've read all of your statements, and I want you to know that I believe everything you've said, but what I want to get straight before I leave is, did you ever say anything, and I repeat, anything, that might have sounded incriminating in any way?"

"No, Greg, it's like I'm telling you. He bugged me so much about the horrors of the death penalty and making deals with the D.A. that I had to tell him several times that I wouldn't ever consider making a deal just to save my life, with me being innocent and not knowing whether or not Ronnie was guilty."

Greg looked at me. "Okay, Dennis, now try your level best to calm down and relax, because this is not over until the fat lady sings, and I've not seen or heard a fat lady sing for some time now."

I couldn't help but laugh at Greg's attempt at humor. I felt some of the stress ease from me. I took a couple of deep breaths.

"I'll keep you posted," Greg said. With that, he left.

That evening, two guards came to the bullpen and told me to pack my stuff because I was being moved again—this time to the isolation cell adjacent to where Ronnie was housed. I didn't know if it was because of the fistfight or because of Tenney's involvement, or some other reason, or all of the above. It didn't matter. I was ready to be alone and out of that crazy bullpen.

The next morning, after a shave and a much-needed shower,

I entered the courtroom dressed in my whites. Unlike the previous preliminary hearing, where the room had been packed, this time the benches were full but only a handful of people lined the back wall. Many of the faces were familiar. Charlie Carter sat with his family. I recognized him, and them, when I walked in.

As I sat down at the defense table, Greg grabbed my hand and whispered an instruction to me: "Don't say a word while the testimonies are being given. There is a chance you might walk out of here, so be cool."

I nodded in reply. I wondered if Greg could hear my heart pounding. I took a deep breath and tried to regain my calm as Miller approached the bench and made his beginning introductions. I glanced over at Peterson and Nancy Shew. Catching my eye, Peterson gave me a smirk. All that did was add to the resentment of him that was building within me. No doubt about it, Peterson was going to do everything he could to get me bound over for trial.

Peterson called Gary Allen.

As Allen made his way to the witness stand, I recognized him as the guy who had lived in the upstairs garage apartment directly behind my house. Dressed in a red and blue plaid shirt tucked into his Levis, Allen, who looked like he was in his thirties, answered Peterson's question about why he remembered the tenth day of December in 1982.

"That's the day I got paid," Allen responded without hesitation.

"And do you recall some time during that week in the early morning hours of a day that week, something unusual happening?" Peterson asked.

"I don't know whether it was that week. It was before the tenth."

"Do you recall something unusual happening around the first of December?" Peterson asked.

"I was awakened around three-thirty in the morning. I could hear Mr. Fritz and somebody raising Cain outside, and they had a water hose out," said Allen. He had a look like he was seeking approval.

Peterson asked Allen what he had seen.

"It looked like they was having a water fight or something, you know, with the water hose. I could see that they didn't have their shirts on," Allen said.

Again, Peterson asked Allen to describe to the court what he saw.

In a shaky voice, Allen stated that "they were behind, between me and his car, and I couldn't see who he was with. I just noticed Mr. Fritz when he turned the water faucet off."

Peterson asked Allen what they were doing with the water hose and if he ever got a good look at the other person.

"Just looked like a water fight, just hitting each other with the hose." Allen went on to say that he did not see the other person because he was behind the car.

"Did you overhear any conversation or anything else while this was going on?"

"They were just cussing and raising Cain," answered Allen.

Peterson yielded the witness.

Greg rose from his chair and tried to make Allen feel that there was a bond of trust between them before he began his cross-examination.

"And I will make a deal with you. I'll try not to ask any question that's intended to confuse you."

"Okay," Allen said, and his posture relaxed just a little.

Greg asked Allen about his employment at the time in question. Allen explained that he was self employed and contracted roadwork on oilfield roads. He said that he had moved to the garage apartment in 1980 and had only talked with me on two or three occasions before December 10, 1982.

Greg asked Allen why the tenth of December stuck in his mind.

Allen answered that he specifically remembered that date because he hadn't worked for a couple of weeks and that he had taken his roommate to Oklahoma City Saturday morning after he got paid.

During further questioning, Allen admitted that he had informed Smith and Rogers about the incident only last summer, four and some-odd years after the murder. Allen told Greg that he had checked his dad's diary to reconstruct the time that he had been out of work during those particular weeks, but he was positive that the date of the water fight was between the first and the tenth of December. He apologized that he could not remember the exact date.

"Was there any exterior lighting in the back of Mr. Fritz's house?" Greg asked.

Allen shifted in his chair before saying that there was only one light on at his downstairs neighbor's apartment. Seeing that Allen had become fidgety, Greg asked if he had only seen me one time when I was turning the water faucet off.

Allen replied, "Yes, when he was turning it off."

"And you did see Dennis?"

"Well, I just caught a glimpse of him as he walked past the front of the car and over to the water hose," said Allen as he glanced over at Peterson.

"Could it have *not* been Dennis? Or are you pretty sure it was Dennis? Which way do you recall it?" Greg asked.

"It sounded like Dennis and it was his car down, parked between us."

"But you didn't see him long enough to identify him as the person that you saw. Is that also correct?"

"I couldn't swear to it that it was him," Allen stated. He lowered his eyes.

My heart skipped a couple of beats upon hearing Allen speak the truth—that he wasn't sure who he saw. Now my fate hinged upon the testimony of one more witness—one who in my opinion had the potential to lie. I sighed heavily as Greg finished with Allen by asking him to repeat several times, over Peterson's objections, his admitted truth. Greg released the witness. The next witness was called.

"State your name for the record, please," said Peterson.

"Michael Tenney."

Upon being questioned, Tenney said that he had been a trainee jailer and acknowledged that I had been in his care and custody. When asked if he had had a conversation with me on the second day of August, Tenney told the court that I had engaged him in conversation by asking him to come back to my cell, wanting to know about making a deal.

"And the conversation went on like this: Fritz said, 'Well, what if it happened this way? Maybe Ron broke into the— Debbie Carter's apartment. I went in and got a little, and Ron got a little carried away. He was going to teach her a lesson. And she died. But I didn't actually see her die, or him kill her, so how could I tell the D.A. something I really didn't know?'" When Tenney was finished speaking, he looked at Peterson.

Peterson yielded the witness to Greg.

On cross-examination, Tenney confirmed that he had numerous conversations with me, that I had always insisted "hundreds of times" that I was innocent.

"Did he ever tell you that he had anything to do with the Debbie Carter killing?" Greg asked him.

"All he ever said was, 'What if,' 'maybe—'" Tenney answered.

"Again, that's a little bit different than what you said earlier, but 'what if, maybe,'" Greg said with authority in his voice.

"Uh-huh," responded Tenney.

"In fact, I talked to you earlier, and you said 'thousands of times.' Isn't that correct?"

"Yes," replied Tenney.

Upon further questioning, Tenney revealed that he had

developed an ongoing relationship with me and said that I would call out to him to come back and talk when he checked on the other prisoners.

I couldn't believe my ears. Tenney was actually telling the truth. I had a glimmer of hope that the charges would be dropped and I would go home. I looked over at that son of a bitch, Peterson. Desperation showed on his face.

Greg continued. "All right, sir. Was the sum and substance of the conversation then that, 'if I had committed these acts, I'd work out a deal, but I can't because I didn't.' Isn't that basically what he was saying?" Greg said in a smooth and very eloquent manner.

"Basically, yes," answered Tenney.

"More specifically, wasn't what he was saying was that 'Even if I wasn't involved in the killing but was just involved in the other crimes that occurred up there, I'd work out a deal. But I wasn't so, consequently, I can't testify to something I don't know anything about'?" queried Greg.

"Yeah, he said that."

"So, really, what he's saying during the course of this conversation was, 'If I had done some of these things, *if* I had gone there, *if* it happened this way, *if* I had gone there,'" Greg said, emphasizing every *if*, "and I, I think he used the term 'got a little, and Ronnie got excited and killed her,' I'd work out a deal. But I can't, because I didn't do any of those things."

"Right," Tenney agreed.

Before yielding the witness, Greg elicited further information from Tenney that he had contacted Rogers and told him of the conversations and that Rogers told him to write down anything that he heard. Greg had no further questions.

The prosecution rested.

Greg moved that the case be dismissed upon the grounds that the state's evidence was incomplete and totally insufficient to sustain probable-cause bind-over. Miller listened to Greg's motion and to the prosecution's argument and then continued the hearing until Tuesday, when he would give his ruling on the defense's motion to dismiss.

The next several days, stretched out over the course of a weekend, were the longest days of my life. In my relocated isolation cell, I paced the floor like a nervous lion—back and forth from wall to wall, unable to sit for any length of time on the concrete slab that supported my thin, plastic mattress. Through the bean hole of my solid metal door, I saw Ronnie's head from time to time silhouetted in the bean hole of his cell door. He peered at me but didn't speak. I was in no mood to talk, let alone watch his glaring, mute stares every time I walked past the bean hole. As I continued to pace, I quit looking out toward him. I avoided eye contact altogether. After several hours, Ronnie asked what had gone on at my hearing. I told him about the testimony by Allen and Tenney and said that Miller was going to make a decision Tuesday on Greg's motion to dismiss. Ronnie wished me luck.

Hundreds of fleeting thoughts raced through my mind over those long days. Mom called to tell me that she and my aunt were coming from Kansas City to hear Miller's decision. It was their first time to come to see me and I worried about their safety. I thought about what Tenney had said about the possibility of threats, or even worse, an attack on their lives. Again and again, the words *Trust me* wouldn't leave my mind.

On Sunday a guard awakened me when he hollered through the bean hole, "Hey, Fritz, you got a visit from your attorney." I slipped on my shower thongs and stepped toward the doorway, past the guard, and into the hall. It had to be afternoon. My lunch tray still sat on the sill of the window to my cell.

"Hey, Dennie Leon's got a visitor. Tell Saunders I wanna see Barney," said Ronnie in an unusually subdued voice.

I nodded that I would.

Instead of going up to the front of the jail where I had visited with Greg before, the guard stopped midway through the hall. He opened the door to the regular visiting room, which was partitioned by a see-through plastic shield with a wire-mesh mouthpiece in the center.

Greg was seated on the other side of the partition with a very pleasant smile on his face. After the guard closed the door, Greg put his mouth to the speaker and said, "Dennis, brace yourself. I've had a conversation with Miller and he told me that he is going to drop the charges against you Tuesday."

I must have looked at him suspiciously.

Following a pause, Greg said, "Dennis, did you hear what I just told you?"

I didn't even realize I was speaking as the words tumbled out my mouth,

"Yeah, I think, I, I heard what you said, Greg. Are you absolutely for sure that Miller is going to do that?"

"Miller told me that he had reviewed the entirety of the preliminary hearing transcripts and there was nothing that could independently corroborate Hett's testimony of putting you at the scene of the crime. He said something to the effect that he was bound by the law to deliver this decision in accordance with the fairness of justice. Dennis, you are gonna walk out of here a free man Tuesday morning. Whadya think about those potatoes?" Greg exclaimed as a huge smile spread over his face.

"I'm either dreaming or I'm in a state of shock, Greg. I am so happy I feel like I've sprouted wings and I'm flying right now," I jubilantly blurted out.

Standing up and putting his hands on the glass, with mine to follow, Greg said that he had to go.

"Above anything else don't tell anyone, absolutely no one, what I have told you today. Are we clear on that point?" Greg said, emphasizing each syllable as he spoke.

"Crystal clear, Greg. I want to thank you so much for what you've did for me, and—"

"Let's never mind about that right now, but thanks. I've

always believed that you were innocent, so do what I tell you, and you'll be in your living room come Tuesday night. Oh, before I forget, your mom called me before I talked to Miller and said that she and your aunt were coming down tomorrow for the hearing Tuesday."

"Yeah, I already got word that they were coming, so it's gonna be one glorious day ahead when I'm out of this hell," I continued to rave. "Oh, Ronnie wanted me to tell you that he needed to talk to Barney, if you can get hold of him."

"Yeah, I'll call Barney and let him know, but don't breathe a word of this to Ronnie, at least not right now." With a thumbs-up gesture, Greg walked out of the room.

Later that afternoon, I got a surprise-of-a-sight visit when I saw Mom and Aunt Wilma sitting behind the plastic partition, their eyes sparkling with tears and with so much love in their hearts. Four months had passed since I had seen them. Mom looked so tired. Aunt Wilma looked grim. I told them what Greg had said, and we whooped, and we danced, and we put our hands and lips to the glass, celebrating our love, strength, and the sheer happiness and hope of being reunited once again as a family!

Chapter 17

I spent the remainder of Sunday and Monday daydreaming about the things I would do after my release. I had always wanted to take Elizabeth, Mom, and Aunt Wilma to Disney World and stay in one of those fancy hotels with an indoor swimming pool and a candlelit restaurant that serves elegant four-course meals on white tablecloths while soft music plays in the background. Above anything else, I just wanted to have a closer relationship with all of my family. On my hands and knees, I gave thanks to the Lord for the miracle he had just performed. For the next two days, I slept like a baby on a feather bed of clouds.

Tuesday morning I awoke to the sound of the breakfast tray being shoved into my cell window. I ate with an appetite and afterward was escorted out of the cell for a shower. I wanted to look my best when I walked into the courtroom. The hearing wasn't until ten-thirty so I had a little time to meditate and prepare.

I tried to talk to Ronnie but he was still asleep, probably from his now-daily dose of Thorazine. I lay back down on my slab and tried to relax. It would be a day of intense emotions, I figured, what with trying to get out of Ada without any danger to me and my family. My mind was dizzy with excitement and the anticipation of celebration as the jailer appeared at the cell door to walk me to the courthouse.

Barely able to contain my joy, I walked with my head high and my spirit soaring. I met Mom and Aunt Wilma outside the courtroom doors and they both hugged me with every ounce of strength and love they had. Tears of happiness streamed down my mother's face as she released me to go into the courtroom. Greg was already sitting at the defense table with his head resting in his hands. I sat down beside him.

Smiling, he turned to me and put his hand on my shoulder and said, "This is your day, and I'm so happy for you."

I felt as if I would float out of my chair.

Miller entered the courtroom and opened the proceedings. Peterson sprang from his chair and delivered the most devastating words I had heard since having been arrested.

"If it please the court, I'd like to ask that the state be allowed to reopen this case on the grounds that information has recently been received, through a rumor, that the defendant made a confession to a certain individual while he was in jail."

The remainder of his statement reeled by in slow motion. Peterson requested that the court allow the state a two-day continuance to question the unnamed individual who was currently incarcerated at the Lexington Reception Center. My ears stopped hearing and my mind went blank when I heard Miller grant permission that the state reopen the case for further investigation.

In despair and shock, I looked at Greg. His reddened face hung low, and he shook his head from side to side. With his cheek muscles clenched, he turned and asked me if I had any idea who it was they were talking about.

I was too numb to think. I told him that I wasn't for sure. I turned and saw looks of horror on the faces of my mom and aunt— the same looks that I had seen on the night of my arrest. Anger and resentment pulsed through me. The thought of my poor mom and aunt having to endure this insanity again tore me up.

Mom was sobbing as I was led from the courtroom. Greg caught up with me and told me he would see me at the jail after he had a chance to find out who it was that Peterson was going to investigate. I realized at that moment but didn't tell him that it could only be one of two people — Harjo or his buddy, Shields. Both had been shipped off to Lexington not too many days earlier.

Greg came to the jail late in the afternoon and informed me that the inmate's name was James Harjo. I told him the entire story as it had happened and emphasized that I wanted some of the inmates who I had collected statements from to testify in my behalf — especially the two who had heard Harjo's "pure as gold" threat. Greg said that he would see what he could come up with. I assured him that I had never made any kind of confession to Harjo and that he was nothing but a lying snitch who was just trying to gain popularity. Greg said that he believed me and would do everything possible to bring down his testimony.

On Thursday Mom and Aunt Wilma were already seated in the courtroom when I was led in. I could tell by their faces that they had not gotten much sleep. My mother mouthed "I love you" as I passed by her. I took my seat at the defense table and immediately turned to Greg.

"Did you talk to anyone at the jail about their statements I gave you?" I asked.

"No, Dennis, there wasn't much time, and besides that, it wouldn't matter anyway because the burden is on the state to put their evidence up to show probable cause. We could put a zillion witnesses on and Miller would bind you over anyway because it would then be a matter for a jury to decide who was telling the truth. Here comes Miller, so I'll talk to you about that later," said Greg in a distracted, uneven voice.

Miller opened the proceeding, and Peterson called his witness. Harjo walked into the courtroom and took the witness stand. After he was sworn in, the assistant district attorney Nancy Shew rose and walked around the prosecution's table to stand directly in front of him.

"Would you state your full name, please?" Shew asked.

"James Cletus Harjo."

"Were you in the county jail before you were sent to the penitentiary?"

"Yes, ma'am, I was."

"And while you were in the county jail, did you know a person there named Dennis Fritz?"

"Yes, I did."

"And were you all friends, and did he help you with anything?"

"Yes, he used to help me write my letters to my wife. I can write, you know, 'and,' 'this' or 'that,' but that's it."

Shew didn't budge from her position during questioning. In her navy blue suit and white blouse, she had the appearance of a nun standing before an altar. Her only movements involved the angle of her head—down as she read from her notes and then back up again as she listened to Harjo's responses.

She asked him what happened on Halloween night that made him not want to be friends with me anymore.

With the voice of a child, Harjo asked for a piece of paper and a pencil, which Shew gave him, and then he said, "Me and Fritz usually talks about his case a lot, and Dennis said this guy named Gary Allen was going to testify against him that he seen him and Ron washing blood off early in the morning. And I asked Dennis, I said, 'Dennis, do you have a water faucet?' And Dennis said, 'No, I don't have one.' And I said, 'Okay.' And then I said, 'Do you have a water hose, Dennis?' And he said, 'Yeah, the one I use, you know, siphoning gas out of my car.' And I said, 'Oh.' And then he said, 'No, there's one, it was wrapped around a pole, or something, you know, right there.' And I put these lines right there, you know."

As he spoke, he drew something on the paper with the pencil. He held up the diagram for Shew to see and then returned it to his lap to make more marks on the paper. "I can't read or write, so I—you know, I just put lines so I could remember them. And then I asked him, I said, 'Do you got a garage or anything around there?'

And he said, 'No, there ain't nothing around there.' I said, 'No apartments or anything?' He said, 'No.' And I said, 'Okay.' And I said, 'Well, all right.' Then after a while he said—I said, 'Dennis, I've did some carpenter work, you know, roofing most the time. And every time we got roofing, we would always go to the people's house and get water out of their water faucet. Every house we went to, you know, they've usually got an outside water faucet.' Dennis said, 'Yeah, there is one behind the house.' And I said, 'Oh.' And I put a little x on top of that, and then put a G up here on the very top of my paper, you know. And then, I said, 'Do you have a— What about this water hose?' And he said that he had a little water hose, and it had that little adapter. So, I put a little x up there. And I said—Dennis said, 'Yeah, this guy named Gary Allen, he's going to testify that he seen them washing the blood off of them.' I said, 'You don't know him?' He said, 'No.' Then he said, 'Yeah, yeah, I think I do. I think he used to be in that apartment right behind our house.' And I put a G up there, like that. And then I just— you know, I just asked him and pointed to those little arrows up there, and then I said, 'It sounds like you're guilty, Fritz.' And Fritz jumped up and he went in his cell, and he came back out and he sat right there in front of me, and we looked eye to eye, and then a chill hit me. When that chill hit me, I just looked at him, and I knew he, you know— So, he got up and he went over there and he got a Marlboro and came back and sat down. And Dennis just looked at me, and tears were coming down his eyes, and he said— He said, 'We didn't mean to hurt her.'"

I bolted from my chair and shouted, "You're lying! You are lying!" My heart was pounding.

"Mr. Fritz!" Miller admonished.

Greg reached for my arm and tugged at it. I sat down.

"Dennis, you are not supposed to say anything during this hearing," Greg scolded me. "Promise me you will not say another word during his testimony. Miller will not put up with this if you continue with any more disruptions."

"Greg, he's lyin'. You think I'm supposed to sit here and listen to this bullshit when he's lying on my life?" I blustered.

"I know this is very hard for you but you can't disrupt the court, or Judge Miller will have you removed like he has with Ronnie."

"All right, all right, I won't say another word, but you better tear him apart when it comes your turn," I sputtered, anger nearly consuming me. Greg turned to the judge and assured him that there would be no further outbursts from me.

Harjo continued by saying, "He said, 'We was drunk' and that they had some beer cans in there, and they took them out and they wiped everything down."

Shew edged closer to Harjo and said, "Can you think, Mr. Harjo, if he said anything else concerning anyone else who was with him? When he said 'we,' did you know who he meant?"

"I guess he meant Ron."

"Did he ever use his name?" Shew asked.

"No, he never used his name. But he used to always get a Bible and say, 'Let's have a Bible study,' you know. And we would say, 'Okay.' You know, me and this other guy named Harlan, we would sit down and read the Bible with him. And he would always say, 'God says "trust me, trust me."' And that same night when I was telling him about that deal, I said, 'If God told you to trust Him, why are you worried, Dennis?' He was going mad, and he tried to fight me twice in there."

"Did he ask you anything after he had told you this, after you all had this conversation? Did he ask—make any requests of you, or anything?" Shew said, coddling him.

"Yeah, he told me that he had a little girl, and what would she think of her daddy being a murderer, you know, and I just—I didn't know what to say."

Like a daycare worker would talk to one of her children, Shew asked Harjo if this had made him nervous and if he did anything different before he went to bed. Harjo said he was very scared to go to sleep and that he had started sleeping at the other end of his bunk, with his head facing the wall instead of the entrance bars. He added that before going to sleep, he would put a pencil in one of his socks and another in his trousers. Shew announced that she had no further questions.

On cross-examination, Harjo told Greg that he was twenty-two years old and had quit school in the eleventh grade. He spent most of his time just running around and drinking. Harjo admitted that he had been convicted of a prior felony and received a preferred sentence, which drew an objection by Peterson on the grounds that it was a *deferred* sentence and could not be used since it was not considered to be a conviction. Greg argued that under the new evidence code it could be used for impeachment purposes, but Miller sustained the state's objection.

Harjo was obviously enjoying all of the attention stirred up over him. Having spent a lot of time around him, I knew that this was nothing more than a game to him, like a kid who reads a comic book and then imagines that he is the hero. How could Judge Miller with all of his legal wisdom even consider using this kind of rigmarole garbage as a source of reliable evidence, especially with no corroboration that the event even took place? I had a suspicion that, if Miller bound me over, it would be solely because he didn't want to have to face the aftermath and criticism of letting what people assumed was a murderer go loose.

"Mr. Harjo, I get the idea sitting here watching you testify that you're angry with Mr. Fritz. Is that the case?" quizzed Greg.

"No, he tried to fight me twice, though."

"I mean, you're not afraid of Dennis Fritz, are you?"

"Yes, after I found out what he did," Harjo answered decisively.

"Did you ever tell him, 'Dennis, I'll get you, I'll get you for this?' Did you ever use those terms? 'I'll get even with you?'"

"No," Harjo said with a hint of teasing in his voice.

"Do you remember going to his cell over there and him throwing you out of his cell?"

"No. I found out right here, by this thing right here," he said, gesturing to his drawing.

"You pieced this together yourself? Let me see what you've got here. Again, what does all this mean, Mr. Harjo?"

Harjo repeated his explanation of his diagram with all the xs and Gs positioned on his paper. Harjo demonstrated great pride in the work that he had completed, which brought on giggling from a few people in the gallery.

"Okay. So, is it your testimony that you figured out on your own by using this analytical method here that Mr. Fritz was guilty? Is that your testimony?" offered Greg.

"Yes."

With Harjo's drawing in hand, Greg walked to the bench and handed the paper to Miller to be introduced as Defendant's Exhibit Number A. On further cross-examination, Harjo admitted that while he was in school he rarely attended classes and made mostly Ds and Fs, and when he did attend he usually copied off other students' papers. Greg shifted the subject back to Halloween by asking Harjo who was in the bullpen and if whoever might have been present was close enough in proximity to have heard the conversation he said he had had with me. Harjo named everyone in the bullpen but wasn't sure if anyone overheard the conversation. Peterson objected at the mention of each name, arguing that Greg was asking Harjo to speculate as to what other people heard or thought they heard. Miller overruled each objection. Meanwhile, Shew had returned to the prosecution table, where she sat motionless and without expression.

While pacing in front of the witness stand, Greg asked Harjo when the near-fights occurred. A look of delight spread across Harjo's face as he explained that it was the "day when we were watching TV, and Ron Williamson was out in the hallway, then Dennis told me in front of Ron that I had said something about them, and Dennis got mad and squared off with me. And then Ron said, 'Don't turn to violence, Fritz.'"

"Now, when you said he said— I didn't follow that," Greg said, stepping closer to Harjo.

"Well, see, I said that he took Williamson over to that house."

"*You* said that—?" Greg asked.

"Yeah, just to see what the reaction was, you know."

"He had never told you that he took Williamson over to that house, did he?"

"No," replied Harjo. "And then, you know, and that's what he said to him. And I looked at Ron, and that's when he—he got up and squared off."

"Well, you accused him of committing a felony crime, did you not?"

"No, I didn't accuse him," clarified Harjo. "I just said he took him over there. I didn't say he did it."

"Why did you not say he did it? Did you ever tell anybody else that you thought that Fritz committed the offense?" Greg asked bluntly.

"No, I knew. You know, just over that one little incident right there, I knew he did, because, see, we used to play chess and he used to help me write letters and stuff. And all that stuff quit."

After retrieving the drawing from Miller, Greg walked to within just a couple of feet of Harjo and said while holding the paper in front of him, "This right here is what made you know that he committed the offense?"

"Yes, he got mad and everything."

"Okay. This is what makes you feel that he committed the offense?"

"That's what I know—" Harjo said.

"But you figured this out by—" Greg asked.

"Just playing around with him, really, trying to play Perry Mason or something, you know."

"So, you were playing detective?" Greg asked, grappling with Harjo's response so that it might make sense.

"Yeah, and when I figured it out, he got all huffy and stuff, and he started messing around, then started smoking cigarettes like crazy."

Greg drew Harjo's attention back to his uncorroborated statement, "We didn't mean to hurt her."

Harjo explained what he had already told Shew, repeating the scenario about the tears "coming down my eyes" and how I had said that I didn't want my daughter to think I was a murderer and how he couldn't eat at the same table with me.

Greg then changed his tactics by asking Harjo if had ever given any tape-recorded statements to any of the police officers.

"They never asked me nothing about Dennis Fritz, and they never put a tape-recorded statement on me yet, that I know of," Harjo said in a dumfounded way, drawing yet another round of chuckles from the spectators. Upon further questioning, Harjo admitted that he had told the police the names of different people that he knew that were involved in drugs but said that he received no favorable consideration for his help.

For the next thirty minutes, Greg went over twice again every detail of every occurrence that Harjo had already described and Harjo told the same story both times. From the beginning to the end of his testimony, Harjo persisted in believing that it was his analytical methods that single-handedly solved the murder—a murder that no one else in law enforcement had been able to solve in five long, difficult years.

CHAPTER 18

Harjo's testimony clinched it. I was bound over and returned to the jail. Distraught over the heart-wrenching disappointment, I sat on my mattress and stared at the stark walls in my isolation cell. I couldn't get Mom's anguished look out of my head. A rush of thoughts tormented me—all because of Harjo's lies. Foremost, I believed that the Lord had abandoned me during a time when I needed him most. *Why, Lord, why have you forsaken me when you know that I am totally innocent? Why? Why? Why, Lord, are you putting me and my blessed family through this nightmare? Have all of my prayers been in vain and have I imagined hearing your voice telling me to trust you? Am I now losing my mind?* From sheer exhaustion, I fell asleep.

Some time later, I was awakened by a guard shouting out my name at the cell window.

"Fritz, wake up. Fritz! Your attorney got you a special visit with your mom and aunt before they head back to Kansas City. You've only got ten minutes so make it snappy," he barked.

Feeling as though I had been hit over the head with a sledgehammer, I walked into the private visiting room and peered through the plastic glass at the sad eyes and swollen faces of Mom and Aunt Wilma. My heart felt as though it would leap from my chest as I viewed the pain and humiliation deeply etched into their faces.

Putting her head to the glass and speaking with the stubbornness that she was known for, Aunt Wilma said, "They're not going to get away with— this crap that they put on today. Dennis, I want you to know— that if they convict you on these bullshit lies, I will go to my grave before I will let you spend the rest of your life— suffering in prison." With a set jaw and eyes as stern as steel, she continued, "I know you told me that you didn't— want me to sell my house, but, I will do anything you ask— to get you out of here. I'm not going— to sit back and let these bastards railroad you on this kind of— so-called evidence! Everyone in the courtroom could tell that— that lyin' Indian was crazier than a bedbug with all of his stupid drawings— and with that stupid smirk on his face, it only meant that he— was enjoying every minute of it. I'm sorry, but I am so upset over having to witness what I heard today. Listen to your mom, Dennis. She's got some good news to tell you and since we don't have— very long to talk, I want you to know that me and Sis will stand behind you in every way we can, because we love you and we believe in you, son, and don't ever forget that."

With tears running down her face, my mother edged over to the meshed-wire mouthpiece, and putting her hand on the plastic glass, in her soft-spoken quivering voice she told me, "I love you— son, so— much!"

The exasperating pain of watching my mother struggle for the words to say as tears dripped from her eyes only swelled my intense hatred for Bill Peterson and everything that he stood for. I put my hand up to the glass where her shaky hand rested and told her, "I will always be there for you, Mom. No matter where I'm at, I'll be there with you." Brushing my hand against my eyes to wipe away my own tears, I looked up into Mom's eyes and told her, "Everything is going to be all right. You've got to believe in that with all your heart or it won't happen. They cannot steal our dignity and the love that we have as a family. No matter what they do or say, we will always be united."

"Son, I feel so bad for you having to be here all by yourself. I know that it must be so hard for you having to be in a place like this for something you don't even know about. Wilma and I know that you could have never done what they've got you charged with, so I want you to also keep your faith strong and never give up on your belief in the Lord." Taking time to regain her composure, my mother added, "There's a man that we work for who is a private investigator. We've been talking to him about your case, and he has told us that he would come down here and investigate on your case, if we wanted. He owns his own company and has a really good reputation, from what we understand. We were just waiting to find out what was going to happen here today before we talked to him further. If it's all right with you, we want to hire him and see what he can find out about your case."

"Did he say how much he would charge you?" I asked.

"All he said was that it would depend on how much time it would take him to do the investigation, and that if it ran over a little, we could pay him out by cleaning his house."

"That would be wonderful, Mom, if he could talk to some of the people who overheard Harjo say that he was going to lie on me at the preliminary hearing. I want you to use the rest of the money that you got from the sale of my car to pay on his bill."

"There's fifteen hundred dollars left. But, son, I don't want you to worry about the money. We'll get it somehow or some way. The Lord has always provided, no matter what. Are you in a safe place, and are they treating you all right?" Mom said, sensing that the time was getting short.

"I'm doing okay, Mom. They've put me in a cell by myself not too far away from where Ronnie's at, so don't worry about my safety or anything like that. Please drive careful on your way back to Kansas City, and watch your back when you leave out of town.

You never know what could happen, so be careful and I'll write you and Wilma every day. I love you with all my heart, Mom."

As the guard was about to end our visit, more tears welled up in my mother's eyes as we prayed together. We waved goodbye, and I was removed and taken back to my solitary confinement. I knew it would probably be several months before I would see them again. I worried so much for their safety. If anything were to happen to them on account of me, I wouldn't want to live.

Unless something changed, I would probably be stuck in this hellhole for several months before going to my scheduled trial, now set for April 6, 1988. I felt a sense of relief that I had gotten the opportunity to visit with them now, before the long solitary ordeal started. The last thing that I wanted was for them to know that I might be stark-raving mad by next spring from living minute to minute in this six- by ten-foot tomb, with no windows and only a forty-watt light bulb to try to read by.

As my hopes and dreams of walking out of here as a free man vanished, the reality of going before a death penalty jury with a court-appointed bankruptcy attorney loomed in my thoughts. I lay on my bunk and tried to reconcile my feelings. The sting of bitterness and muddle of confusion in knowing that I had come so close to regaining my freedom fueled in me a frustration so powerful that I had to do something. I bolted upright and grabbed my dirty, lice-ridden mattress and slung it as hard as I could against the wall. From deep in my throat came a guttural wail that made me feel so good. As I leaned over to grab the lumped-up mattress again for yet another round of battering to release some of my tension, I heard Ronnie's gravelly voice.

"What's going on over there?" he asked.

"Don't talk to me!" I shouted. "I don't want to hear your accusin' bullshit any more, so leave me alone or I will snitch you out for sure, you stupid shithead!" I abruptly turned and stepped to the window and glared at him. His head swayed from side to side and he stared back at me as if I were an inanimate object, like a picture on a wall. I had never talked to Ronnie like I was talking to him now.

"I want to get something straight with you right now, Mr. Ronnie Keith. If you ever accuse me of bein' a snitch again, I will have Peterson brought over here and I will turn state's evidence on you and take my life sentence and let you rot on death row. Do you understand what I'm telling you?" I yelled over at him. I lingered at the window, watching and waiting for some kind of response. After several seconds of silence, it dawned on me that Ronnie hadn't heard a word I had said, or at least it hadn't soaked in enough for him to bother giving me an acknowledgement. I didn't see or hear from him for the rest of the night. It didn't matter to me at this point anyway, except that I was totally fed up with everyone accusing me of something I never did. Yeah, I'd really like to tell that Peterson a thing or two, all right — like just how lowly a maggot he is for stripping me of my freedom on the idiotic testimony of a mentally retarded felon who only craved attention.

After days of going through a depressing period of denial and listening to a cascade of Ronnie's extreme personality changes, I made up my mind that I was not going down without a fight. Despite the terrible light quality in my cell, I started reading every piece of evidentiary material that Greg had given to me throughout the course of the hearings. Over and over again, day after day, for weeks I meticulously reread each of the names of every person who submitted hair and saliva, and each piece of evidence that had been removed from the decedent's apartment, hoping to find some kind of mistake. I wasn't sure what I would do if I found it, but I had to do something. No one else would.

In a matter of time, I was sleeping throughout the day and parts of the night to escape the horrific stress and boredom. With no contact from the outside world and very little company except for the trusties bringing food, I often confused the days and nights and didn't know which one was which. Because I usually skipped breakfast, I never really got to gauge whether lunch was dinner or dinner was lunch. But I could tell when it was Sunday because that was the day, the only day, that the jail served fried chicken.

As each day passed, the thought of facing the death penalty drew me deeper into the escape mode of sleeping, but I made sure that I wrote to Elizabeth, and to Mom and Aunt Wilma, at least three times per week. Their return letters were like a ray of sunshine that filtered through my dark and dismal existence. Their words gave me life and a sense of hope that there might be a chance of being found not guilty at trial. I read them over and over again to keep myself in touch with the reality of what lay ahead.

One letter in particular made me realize that I still had a fighting chance of proving my innocence. In it, Mom told me that they had hired the private detective and he was coming to Ada soon to start the investigation. The next day, Greg visited with me at my cell door and confirmed the good news that the investigator would be down on December 8.

"Who was it that you talked to?" I asked.

"He said his name was Ron Westcott, and he was working for the other detective that your mom and aunt clean house for. He was with an agency called the Kansas City Bureau of Investigation, I believe. I think he will be very beneficial in being able to interview some of the witnesses who overheard Harjo threaten you. Dennis, are you doin' all right? You're not looking very well. I'm sorry I haven't been over for a while but I've been busy filing a lot of preparatory motions in your case, and trying to keep up with my own practice."

"I can't really say for sure, Greg. Things are getting kind of hazy in this sweatbox, but I'm still standing erect and hoping for the best. Did the investigator say how long he would be down here?"

"No, not really, he just said that it might take him a few days to talk to all of the witnesses that you gave me statements from. He sounded like a pretty professional kind of guy and didn't seem to have any pretense about himself. He did say that he was going to tape interviews of everyone he talked to."

"Not meaning to interrupt you, Greg, but one of the trusties told me that he had heard through a source that he wouldn't reveal that a contract had been put on me and Ronnie by the Carter family, and that they were going to pay someone to purposely get arrested and then kill us after they get in the jail."

"When did you hear this, Dennis?"

"It was about a week ago when one of the trusties brought me my food tray. They said they had heard it from someone in the bullpens that had just been brought in, someone that supposedly knew the Carters real well."

"Who was the trusty?" Greg questioned me.

"Greg, I can't tell you that, because I damn sure don't want to be labeled a snitch any more than I already have been. You know what I mean. From time to time, he stops by and gives me the grapevine information he hears in the bullpens."

Ronnie interrupted our conversation and hollered over at Greg as to whether or not he had heard anything from Barney. Greg walked over to his cell window and told him that Barney would be coming over shortly to talk with him.

"You tell Barney I want to know what's going on with my Social Security check and whether I can still get it while I'm in here," demanded Ronnie. "I want to throw a party for everyone in here when my money comes in, so you be sure and get him over here. I'm ready for some of that good chocolate cake and cold, cold ice cream."

Greg assured him that he would convey the message and that Barney would probably be over before the week was out. Ronnie seemed satisfied with that and backed away from the window. Greg came back to my cell window to talk to me.

"Listen, Dennis, the main reason that I came over here is to tell you some news that I think you will find very encouraging, but you have to be quiet about it. A couple of days ago, a guy by the name of Ricky Simmons walked into the Ada police station and confessed to murdering Debbie Carter. From my understanding, they videotaped his confession. Peterson will barely even talk to me about it."

"Say what? That's totally unbelievable! What else did you hear?"

"That's all I can tell you right now. They're keeping it under tight wraps and nobody's talking to any extent. I guess they don't want the media to get wind of it until they've had time to check it out further. I got the impression that they are trying to downplay his confession because he had admitted to overuse of drugs and has a history of mental problems."

"Yeah, and that's exactly who would have committed a crime like that," I said, nodding. "Is there any way that you can see the tape before it gets conveniently lost or destroyed?"

"I asked the same question to Peterson and he hum-hoed around and finally told me he would have to let me know more in a couple of days. That's all I can tell you right now." Stepping closer to the cell window, Greg lowered his voice and said, "Above all, Dennis, do not, and I repeat, do not mention anything about this to Ronnie right now. I know it's been so hard for you with all of these ups and downs you've been going through, but for Ronnie, he's given Barney all he can take, so please keep this on ice for a few days, okay? I'll be back over here, I believe, on Tuesday when Westcott is supposed to get here."

"I promise, Greg, I won't say a word about this to anyone. I don't know how much more of this roller coaster ride I can take, though. This totally blows my mind again, to get my hopes up like I did before, and now this comes along— I already feel like I'm losing my mind. What do they think I am, anyway—a man without any feelings?"

"I know, Dennis. I have lost more sleep on this case than any other case I have ever had. And I know, I'm not the one sitting over here in this piece of shit, but try to keep yourself together and maybe something might come out of this Simmons thing," Greg reassured me.

For a long time after Greg left, I sat on my bunk and let my mind wander. As I thought about the Simmons guy making a confession, I felt like a huge weight had been lifted off me. Hope started to creep again into my soul. I dropped to my knees on the cell floor and asked the Lord to forgive me for doubting Him. Tears streamed down my face. Every emotion spilled from me at once: the sheer terror of having to face the ultimate punishment of death, all of the months of worrying about my daughter's emotional insecurity and dealing with all of the ongoing publicity, and how all of this was affecting my mother's and aunt's health and their overall safety. After my emotions subsided, a sensation of peaceful calm swept over me. I climbed up on my bunk and fell into a deep, contented sleep.

The day Westcott arrived my anxiety level was off the charts. I was shaking as I was escorted toward the visiting room to meet him. Greg introduced us and said that they had just returned from his house, where they had viewed the confession tape of Ricky Simmons. Greg said Simmons seemed to be not completely in control of himself and that he had admitted on the tape to the heavy use of drugs, including LSD.

Then he added, "From what I hear, after I picked the tape up at the sheriff's office, I gather that they're not going to charge him because they sort of figured he was one of those types that will confess to anything just for the attention."

"What are your thoughts, Dennis?" Westcott asked.

"I'd like to view the tape myself," I said, though I was doubtful that would happen. "That way I could judge for myself." I'd seen the crime scene photos. I'd heard the evidence in court. Maybe something Simmons said in his confession would jibe with that and get me and Ronnie off the hook.

Greg said he had to return the tape back to Peterson by the end of the day, but I might be able to take a look at it another time.

Westcott asked what I had been hearing through the jail grapevine.

"Well, like I told Greg, there's been talk that a contract has been put out on me and Ronnie by the Carter—"

"Have you heard anything else?" Westcott interrupted.

"Yeah, I heard something about Debbie having a girlfriend who she had gotten into an argument with who swore revenge against her. I heard that the girl was a tall white female with long dark hair and that the writing on the wall in her apartment was done by a female."

"Just so you know, Dennis, jailhouse gossip can have some reliability but in most cases, it's nothing more than someone's personal opinion," Westcott said. "Greg told me about the situation between you and this inmate, James Harjo. He also supplied me with a list of other inmates who gave you statements after hearing your conversations with him. What I would like to do today is to interview some of the inmates who overheard your argument with Harjo on, what was it, Halloween night?"

"Yeah, it was on Halloween, but the only inmates still here who heard anything are Karl Fontenot and Melvin Love. Kenneth Stepp has already been transferred to the Lexington Reception Center. Can you give me some idea of how your investigation will proceed?" I asked.

"The last thing I don't want to do is to give you any false hopes or undue expectations. First of all, I want you to know that I am here to assist your attorney in whatever way I can to help gain information for your upcoming trial. I would love nothing more than to bust this case wide open and find out who actually killed this Carter girl, but that usually doesn't happen, and I'm working on a limited budget. Is there anything else you would like to tell me before we get on with these interviews?"

"Yes, there is. I'm bein' railroaded for a crime I didn't commit, and as Greg probably told you, I got bound over on the sole testimony of Harjo, without any corroboration as to whether any of the alleged statements were even made. What I would like for you to do is to talk to Harjo and see if you can get him to admit to the truth that he lied on me."

"That's exactly my plan, Mr. Fritz. They are still holding him over in the city jail, so that will be my next stop after we get through with these two interviews. Tomorrow, I plan on talking to this Kenneth Stepp to see if we can get a defense built up for you at your upcoming trial,"

"Dennis, I'll make it a point to come over and see you after the investigation is concluded and let you know what all we found out," promised Greg as they stood and signaled to the guard that the visit was ending.

On Saturday, Greg gave me a rundown of Westcott's accomplishments. I had already heard through the vine that Love and Fontenot had given favorable interviews on my behalf. Greg said that Stepp had also agreed to testify favorably for me under subpoena. He was in kind of a hurry, but he did mention that Westcott had spoken with a woman named Gina Vietta who said she had a late-night phone conversation with Debbie on the eve of her death, first about a man in her apartment who she didn't feel comfortable with, and then when Debbie told Gina that everything was all right and that she would see her tomorrow. Greg said that Westcott had gotten a few names out of Vietta and that he would check them out before he left. Then, inching closer to the window, Greg said that Simmons's confession had hit the papers and was all over the news and that he wouldn't be surprised if a lot of pressure was being put on Peterson to rethink his position of not accepting the confession.

The days and months ahead were grudgingly slow: I had one shower per week; slept most of the day to survive the loneliness, agony, and despair; watched Ronnie shuffle to the beat of his medications as he would name backwards all of the presidents of the United States—and their vice presidents—without ever skipping a beat or ever blinking his eyelids; and, the worst imaginable pain of all—finding out that my precious daughter was being taunted and ridiculed by her school peers that her daddy was a vicious murderer!

Often I drifted off into a hazy world of tormented dreams. When I wasn't sleeping, I paced the floor throughout the night. I didn't know or care what time of the day or date of the month it was. All that seemed to really matter was that I could escape in my dreams into a world where thoughts were without form or image.

One night, late, someone knocked at my door.

"Get up, Fritz, you've got a special visit. Do you hear me? Climb out of that rack or I will cancel your visit," the guard blared out.

"Do you know who it is?" I asked.

"You'll find out when you get in there," he told me gruffly.

A special visit meant that I would be going to the side-entrance visiting room where prisoners got contact visits. I wondered who it could be. No one had alerted me to any such visit. I rounded the corner and approached the door. My heart felt as though it could leap out of my body. There stood my beautiful daughter, Elizabeth, with her grandmother Mary and my mother. I was so shocked I could barely speak.

"Hi, sweetheart, how are you doing?" I asked as tears formed in my eyes.

"Good," Elizabeth responded as she moved slightly away from me.

"Hi, Mom, it's really good to see you, and you, too, Mary. I had no idea that you all were coming down." I wrapped my arms around my mother and hugged her. I stepped to Mary and did the same, but I could feel a tenseness that told me to not linger in my embrace. I turned my attention back toward Elizabeth.

"Lisa, I have missed you so much, and you'll never know how much I have thought about you. How have you been doing? Are you all right, sweetheart?" I asked.

"I guess." Her voice was meek and she lowered her head as tears welled in her eyes.

I stooped to her and wrapped my arms around her. Her

body was trembling. With every ounce of resistance I had, I held back my own tears so I would appear to be unshaken in front of my own child. I stepped back and sat down in a chair. My mind searched for the words to say.

"Lisa, you and I have always been truthful with each other, haven't we?"

Without looking up, she shook her head in agreement.

"You're a big girl now and I want you to listen very carefully to me." I glanced at my mother and Mary before continuing. "The police have made a big mistake, sweetheart. They arrested me for a crime that I did not commit and have no knowledge of. I need for you to believe that because I have never lied to you in any way."

She lifted her head a little but held her gaze toward my legs.

"Lisa, I love you with all my heart and you know that I would never do anything like they said I did. I know this is very hard for you and you must be feeling terrible inside right now, but I promise you that I will prove my innocence and everything will be okay again. Will you believe that for me?" I said, my voice starting to crack.

Lisa raised her head fully and looked into my eyes. Her lips quivered, showing her grief within.

"Yes, Daddy, I believe you and I don't want to be away from you. I miss you so much," she said as giant tears plummeted from her eyes.

The door suddenly opened and the attending guard alerted us that our visiting time was up. Elizabeth rushed toward me and flung herself into my waiting arms. I lifted her up and held her tightly. Tears spilled from my eyes as I told her that I would always love her, no matter what.

"Always believe that, Elizabeth. Your daddy will always be with you even if I'm away. Thank you so much, sweetheart, for coming to see me. And thank you for believing me in what I've told you. Don't ever stop believing that I will one day prove my innocence and be with you again." I was barely able to speak without totally breaking up.

I hugged my mother and told her that I would always love her, too. Her tears rolled down her swollen face. I told her that things would be all right and for her to try not to worry too much. I hugged Mary and gave her all my love. I looked over my shoulder as I was being led out. Lisa was waving goodbye, and there was a smile on her tear-stained face.

CHAPTER 19

The day of my trial dawned with a turn of events as distasteful as bread and water. I was sleeping in my cell when a guard appeared at the cell window.

"Pack your shit, Fritz. You're moving to the bullpens. Come on. We ain't got all day," he yelled, like he was hollering down a tunnel.

His voice rattled through the fog of my isolation, deprivation, and frustration as I slid my feet around to the floor. "What time is it?" I asked, yawning.

"Five-thirty. Come on. Get a move on."

I had expected that Ronnie and I would be separated sooner or later, but waiting until the morning of my trial to move me out was without conscience. I bundled up my papers, letters, blanket, and mattress and walked toward the cell door.

"This must be high on your list of things to do to make people feel totally miserable," I said to the guard as I waited for him to open the cell door.

He didn't answer. He just nodded for me to step out into the hall, and then he followed me as we walked to the bullpens.

He opened the bullpen door on the right, and I stepped inside. The door clanged shut behind me. I was back in the hellhole. I flung my crumpled mattress on the nearest top bunk, climbed up, and turned toward the wall. I despised this luminous, harsh environment with all its farting drunks, multiple personalities, and domino slappers. And on top of that, it was precisely the wrong time to be in this noisy, chaotic place. I needed to be able to concentrate and focus. I needed to face as squarely as I could the reality that I faced either prison or death. Was this just one of many lessons I would learn if I ended up incarcerated for the rest of my life—that just as you start getting used to something, they change it? Was this what prison was about?

As I hunkered in my bunk, I thought about how much I had changed. I was not the man I used to be. I had gained a lot of weight from not being able to exercise, and the high carbohydrate jail food hadn't helped, either. That and the constant stress had robbed me of my emotional and physical health. How was I going to help defend myself in the courtroom when I couldn't even be sure what day of the week it was?

In a few hours, I would be dressed in my suit and seated in the courtroom, watching while someone picked the jury that would decide whether I lived or died. I clenched my eyes closed and said a silent prayer, forcing myself to thank the Lord for being with me the past eleven months and for giving me the strength and courage to make it through this day. I also asked for a divine miracle to be found not guilty—a thought that went against the feeling that had been gnawing at me inside for several weeks that I was going to be convicted and given the death penalty.

I shook my head and sat up. *You've got to snap out of this, Dennis, and face your accusers with your head held high! Be the man that you think you are and walk into that courtroom without showing any fear of anyone or anything. You're innocent and you have nothing to hide from, so get yourself off this bunk and get ready for the battle.* At seven, I took a shower and waited for the guard to bring my suit—the same one I had worn at the preliminary hearings. *I would do this. I could do this. I had run out of options.*

At a few minutes before nine, the guards came to get me to take me to the courthouse. As I stood by the cell door, I realized how nervous I was. I looked back at my cellmates. Several of them yelled out and wished me luck. The one consolation that I had was that I would get to see my mom and aunt again.

As I walked to the courthouse, the media, as frenzied as ever, bombarded me with questions to which I always responded the same way—"I'm innocent! I'm innocent!" As before, the waiting area just outside the courtroom was packed with people, many of whom glared at me. This time, though, the people looked different. They seemed more sullen and acted more nervous. Could it be that they were some of the jurors that would be called to hear my case? When I walked through the swinging doors into the courtroom, I was surprised to see only a fraction of the crowd that had been at my previous hearings. I guessed that there just wasn't as much interest in listening to the probably predictable process of jury selection.

I immediately located Mom and Aunt Wilma seated in the front row right behind the defense table. They turned—Mom had tears in her eyes—and watched me as I slowly made my way down the aisle to sit beside Greg at the table. As spectators chatted in the few minutes before the start of the trial, I listened to the buzz of conversation but I didn't listen to the words. I no longer had any interest in the spectators' reactions. Their familiar stares of fear and contempt just didn't matter.

Placing his hand on my shoulder as he leaned toward me, Greg smiled and assured me that he would do his best to pick a jury that wouldn't convict me on the prosecution's poor evidence. He informed me that the jury selection process was called *voir dire* and that he would be asking the potential jurors a lot of questions to find out who we wanted to sit on the jury. He instructed me to pay close attention to each person's responses, and if there was somebody in particular that I didn't care for, to write it down on my notepad. I could sense nervousness in his voice as he spoke, but I was nervous, too. I figured that was normal.

Judge Jones emerged from behind the black curtains and seated himself like a king on his throne. Quickly scanning the courtroom, he received confirmation from the prosecution and defense that they were ready to proceed. "Call twelve jurors, please," the judge announced. His tone was dull and flat, as though he had little interest in the proceedings.

The first of the possible jurors entered in file and took their seats in the jury box. After the panelists were sworn in, Jones introduced them to the prosecution and counsel for the defense. In his forthright and mechanical manner, Jones specified to the panel their responsibilities of being truthful and honest in rendering a fair and impartial verdict. He explained that if any of them were chosen, they would not be allowed to leave under any circumstances—not even for a death in the family. The jurors listened carefully as Jones drifted into a lengthy, in-depth recitation on a wide variety of legal subjects ranging from media exposure to principles of law—specifically about the presumption of innocence, burden of proof, and assessing guilt—and a barrage of other information that each of the jurors would be obliged to talk about. Jones was deliberate and methodical in his delivery to the panel. Reading off each and every one of the state's witnesses' names, Jones called for a show of hands if anyone recognized any of them.

"I know Charles Carter. He's married to my ex-sister-in-law," voiced one woman.

Another hand shot up. "I know Dennis Smith. He's my mom's best friend who married Jane," another juror spoke out.

Yet another hand flew up. "Yeah, I know Tony Vick," a nameless juror announced.

"Would you be able to evaluate his testimony and not give it any greater or less weight based on the fact that you know who he is?" Jones asked automatically of one juror, then the next and the next, never budging from his stoop-shouldered manner of sitting.

When no more hands were raised, Jones read off the charged offense and gave the qualifications of assessing punishment with regard to life imprisonment, life imprisonment without parole, and death. One by one, Jones asked each of the prospective jurors if they would have difficulty in assessing the death sentence. Several hands shot up at once.

I listened closely to each of their responses. On my notepad, I listed their answers. Four of the women said that they could assess a death sentence, while the other three said no. Four men said *yes,* and one said *no.* In agreement with the prosecution and the defense, Jones dismissed for cause the four people who had said *no.* Four new people were called and sworn in. They were all women who said without hesitation that they each could consider the three options of punishment. I had no idea how this process worked and what cause and preemptory challenge—two words the judge used—actually meant, but I wanted to be as useful as I could without appearing helpless. I instantly scribbled a message to Greg, saying that I wanted more men than women. He nodded in acknowledgement. The idea of a majority of women deciding my fate, especially because the victim was a woman, wasn't what I perceived to be in my best interest.

More people were let go. More were called in. The morning dragged on. Jones asked each of the potential jurors personal questions about their health, where they lived and worked, whether they had ever been the victim of a crime, whether they had ever been a juror, and whether they could give this case the full consideration it deserves. Two more persons were excused because of hearing difficulties, and two new potential jurors were sworn in. Jones initiated his lengthy qualifying process again.

I studied each juror's face and how each person reacted to every question. An older man—a fellow named Cecil Smith—and an unknown-named female juror glared at me suspiciously throughout the selection process, so I slipped another note over to Greg, expressing my dissatisfaction.

I always felt that I had a good knack for reading people, and if there was ever a time for that to be true, it was truly being put to the test today. At the same time, my mind had dulled noticeably during the past several months and I really wasn't sure about anything at all except that I knew I was innocent and that my family loved me and supported that belief. I took a deep breath in and listened to Jones as he asked each of the jurors if they knew anyone in law enforcement anywhere, in or out of the county and state. Many of the jurors responded that they did, and I slid another note over to Greg. This time, he made eye contact and nodded in agreement.

From time to time, I glanced back toward Mom and Aunt Wilma. They would each force a smile and nod a little to let me know that they were there for me. After a while, I began to relax and feel like I was an actual part of the jury selection process, despite the sense that I was drained of my physical and mental energies.

After a five-minute recess, Peterson stood, strutted to the jury box, and launched into his *voir dire* examination. In a discourse that seemed that it would never end, he told the jurors everything that the judge had already mentioned and then added his own explanations about the laws governing jurors' responsibilities. The panel stared blankly at Peterson as he rambled.

Greg interrupted Peterson and requested a bench conference. Their conversations were hushed, but evidently it had something to do with the way Peterson was conducting his examination. After Greg sat down again and Peterson returned to the podium, Peterson's style of communicating with the jurors changed to a form of direct questioning as he gathered every iota of personal information he could think of. "Where did you teach?" he asked one juror. "Do you attend church on a regular basis, Mr. Smith? Mrs. Cope, are you a married lady? Any grandchildren? Get eyeglasses free, Mrs. Hobbs? Pardon me, Mr. Mann, you say you had a brain concussion? Grandson is not spoiled or anything, is he, Mrs. White?"

Peterson focused on one woman who had been in the jury

box for a while. "Mrs. Flowers, when the court was talking to you about the punishment aspect of this case, you stated that you could find somebody guilty and assign punishment if there was no doubt in your mind. You understand that's not the burden? You understand that *no doubt* is not the burden? It's *beyond a reasonable doubt*, okay?"

Mrs. Flowers innocently nodded her head.

"Are you going to require the state to remove all doubt from your mind?"

Nodding her head again, Mrs. Flowers said that she had to have no doubt in her mind. Peterson grimaced and suddenly swung himself around to the judge and asked that she be excused.

Greg leapt from his chair and went to the defense of Mrs. Flowers, asking Jones if he could question her before a decision was made. Without hesitating, Jones said that he would reserve his ruling. Peterson refused to let it drop and continued to hammer on Mrs. Flowers about her refusal to accept the state's requirement of proof beyond a reasonable doubt. Mrs. Flowers persistently held to her belief that all doubt would have to be removed from her mind before finding guilt.

"You understand that the defendant has pleaded not guilty," Peterson harped.

"I didn't know, no," Mrs. Flowers answered, never looking away from Peterson.

"Does that create a doubt in your mind?"

"Objection!" Greg blurted out.

"Sustained," Jones said automatically without looking up.

Seeing that he was getting nowhere with Mrs. Flowers, Peterson shifted his questioning back to the other jurors, then yielded and announced his challenge to Mrs. Flowers for cause. By this time, I had already stopped keeping count of who was being passed for cause because it took away from the time that I thought I should be spending on studying the jurors' reactions.

Jones recessed for lunch until one-thirty and reminded the jurors to not discuss any of the day's proceedings with anyone.

After lunch, when Greg and I were seated again at the defense table, he emphasized to me that Mrs. Flowers would be the key juror for our side and that he would fight Peterson tooth and nail to keep her on the jury. Once the jurors were seated, Greg exploded into action with a volley of questions to Mrs. Flowers to determine the true intent of her declared "no doubt" statement. Without touching upon the definition of reasonable doubt, Greg equated to Mrs. Flowers that she would have to decide in her own mind the meaning of reasonable doubt. She agreed, and she stated that she would be able to follow the law as Judge Jones had handed it down.

When Greg finished his examination, he turned to the judge and asked if he wanted to make a ruling. Jones declined. Greg turned his attention to the other jurors to qualify them with general questions on improper exposure to the media and on the likelihood of them finding me not guilty if there was no substantial evidence available.

Peterson objected to Greg's form of questioning, saying that he was making speeches instead of asking questions. Apparently, he had not forgotten Greg's prior objection on the same grounds and wanted to even the score and put Greg in the hot seat for a while. After several conferences at the bench, the tension between Greg and Peterson became obvious to everyone in the courtroom. Nearing the end of his qualification examination, Greg asked each juror one by one the same question — "Are you of the frame of mind where you can give my client a fair trial?"

Each of the jurors answered *yes,* and Greg announced to Jones, "We'll pass this jury for cause."

Jones wanted to make sure in his own mind about Mrs. Flowers and questioned her briefly about whether her standard of determining guilt was different than that of reasonable doubt. After she stated that it was not, Jones denied Peterson's motion for Mrs. Flowers to be excused.

A smile of victory swept over Greg's face. With a gleam in his eye, he walked back to the defense table as Jones accepted Peterson's first peremptory challenge by dismissing the man who had had the brain concussion.

The afternoon ground on as one juror after another underwent the tedious process of qualification by the court, prosecution, and defense. Peterson and Greg battled back and forth for supremacy. Peterson wanted jurors—he showed a preference for women—that believed in the death penalty. Greg wanted men that expressed a desire to be fair and partial and were willing to render a judgment based solely on the facts. Before passing each juror for cause, Greg conferred with me before declaring his decision to the court. One by one, some were dismissed, and some were sworn in. I began to wonder how long this tug of war could take.

As the hour approached six o'clock, weary looks began to appear on the jurors' faces. Most of the spectators had vacated the courtroom, and the hush of the near-empty gallery further indicated that it was time for an overnight break. Just as Greg passed another juror for cause and the court called for the prosecution's fifth peremptory challenge, Peterson rose from his seat and proclaimed to Jones that the state of Oklahoma waived any other challenges and accepted the panel in place in the jury box.

Jones looked sharply at Greg and told him that this was also his fifth challenge. Greg abruptly told the judge that we also waived any future challenges and accepted this panel as constituted.

Without a second glance at either attorney, Jones turned to the eight women and four men on the panel and instructed them to stand and raise their right hand, and proceeded to swear them in under the laws of the state of Oklahoma. He told the jurors that they could leave for the day and instructed them that they should not tell anyone about their work today, or hereafter, until they were discharged from their duty in this case. Jones cautioned the jury that they could not allow themselves to be exposed to any type of media—no newspapers, radio, or any local television stations. Before releasing the twelve, Jones advised that if anyone made any kind of contact with them concerning this case, they should immediately inform the court. After that, he called for a short recess.

Greg told me he was greatly relieved to have picked a jury that he believed to be the best of the lot. I wasn't wholly in agreement. There were eight women on the jury, several of whom had indicated that they were in favor of the death penalty. Greg sympathized with my feelings but explained that he had a good gut feeling for most of the women that were chosen—especially Bonnie Flowers. I questioned him about one of the jurors, the older man named Smith. I told Greg that I thought the way he looked at me was extremely odd, as if he were trying to psychoanalyze my every thought. I reminded Greg that I had a funny feeling about him during qualification and that one of the notes I had passed to him was about Smith. As court was about to resume, Greg advised me that there would never be a time in which a perfect jury could be picked and that Mrs. Flowers would be our ace in the hole when it came down to someone holding out against the requirement of a unanimous verdict.

The process of qualification for the two alternate jurors could have taken just as long as the events of the day, I thought, as Jones explained this next phase of *voir dire*. I was more than ready to get this boring procedure over with. I was tired, and my concentration had dwindled during the past couple of hours, but I forced myself to pay very close attention to what each of the jurors had to say. A man and a woman were called in, and Jones explained the penalties and principles of law. I felt like we were starting all over again.

Both jurors said they could impose any of the three punishments and they would adhere to the laws. Immediately following their responses, though, they received challenges from Peterson and Greg and were let go. Two more jurors entered and were questioned. This time, Peterson and Greg passed both jurors for cause.

Jones announced that the jurors would act as the first and second alternates in the order that they were called and swore them in. He gave them the same instructions he had given the rest of the jury. He stated a continuance for nine the next morning and adjourned the day's proceedings.

Before the guards put me in handcuffs, Greg mentioned that he was going to meet with Peterson and the judge in chambers and would be over to see me at the jail a little later. He didn't say what they were meeting about.

As I was cuffed and led from the defense table by the guard, Mom hugged me and assured me everything was going to work out. The tired, mournful expression on her face and on Aunt Wilma's told me the day had been long and hard on them, too. When the guard nudged me to move along, I lingered for a few seconds and reassured them. Then I entered the empty courthouse corridor through the tall, heavy doors and headed back toward the bullpen.

CHAPTER 20

Back inside the jail, I changed from my suit to my jail clothes and received instructions from Ernie, the nice guard, to go to the kitchen and get something to eat before returning to the bullpens. If Ron Scott had still been on duty, this would never have happened. I took advantage of Ernie's thoughtfulness, fixed myself a tray of leftover food, and ate in the quiet, dimly lit kitchen.

It had been an exhausting day. I reflected on the expressions and the responses of the people who had ultimately been impaneled as the jury. My gut was nervous, my head and back ached, and emotions rattled around inside me. These were the people who would decide my fate. Live or die. This group of twelve, and the alternates. What had I seen in their faces? Could I even be sure what I saw was sincere? What had they told or not told the lawyers?

As I took the last bites of my cold cornbread and beans, Ernie entered the kitchen. "Your attorney is here in the outer visiting room. I can give you ten minutes, and then you have to be back in your cell," he told me.

I followed him to the visiting room. The minute I entered, I recognized an uneasy look on Greg's face. I wondered what it was about.

He wasted no time in telling me what was on his mind. "Dennis, there's a couple of things I want to talk to you about. Most importantly, I want to let you know that I think it would be a big mistake on our part to try and put Simmons on the witness stand in the condition he's in emotionally. I know we talked about it, and you thought it was a good idea, but his emotional shape would greatly affect his credibility before the jury and give Peterson an opportunity to cast a bad light on your defense. I just wanted you to know that's the reason I have not subpoenaed him."

I was disappointed. I asked, "Is there anything else you can do, like maybe get some kind of a written or recorded statement from him and play it before the jury?"

"No, Dennis. Jones would never allow that, and Peterson would holler all the way to Oklahoma City about not being able to cross-examine Simmons in person. You have brought up a good point, though. There might be a possibility of getting some kind of closed-circuit video TV set-up to tape Simmons's out-of-court testimony, but I would have to get it approved through the court. That might be difficult since Simmons is not on his deathbed or so physically impaired that he couldn't attend court. I'll see what I can do, but it's very doubtful Jones will even go for that."

"Well, Greg, here's the way I see it," I said, still not understanding things quite the way Greg probably wanted me to. "With Simmons supposedly being so crazy, isn't that the kind of person that would be capable of killing someone, and if he was put on the stand, wouldn't that go a long way in creating reasonable doubt to the jury?"

With a look of exhaustion, Greg stood up and paced the floor.

"I understand what you're saying, but there's a lot of risks and a lot of doors that could be opened, and I am just totally against putting him on with his unbalanced state of mind. Trust me on this one, Dennis. I know you want every opportunity to prove your innocence, but this would be too risky. And I wanted to mention to you that I haven't heard back from our hair expert yet about the results of his examinations. I've got a call through to him and we should be hearing something real soon." Greg stood still for a moment and looked at the floor before looking back at me. "I'm gonna have to leave. I am dead on my feet. Is there anything you need?"

"Yeah, there is, now that you've mentioned it. How about a pair of ear plugs so I won't have to use toilet paper, and then maybe I can get some degree of peace back in the bullpen?"

I didn't say anything to Greg about how I felt about the eight women on the jury. As far as the jury selection process went, I had to believe that he had done the best that he could. His day had been just as long and stressful as mine. It wouldn't do any good to get into a big debate about the women jurors.

"I'll see what I can do," he said. "See you in the morning." He left through the outer door, and Ernie, who had been waiting outside in the hallway, escorted me back to the bullpen, where the noise seemed louder than ever.

In the months I'd been in isolation, the lunacy within the bullpens had magnified to deafening proportions. Because I had been away from these loud and unpredictable noises, every slam of a domino or sudden shriek of excitement went through me like an electric shock. I despised those county jail assholes for putting me back here at a time like this. To them, I must have been nothing more than a piece of scum that really didn't deserve such an upscale place like this—especially with the amenities of hot showers and a worn-out air-conditioning system.

During the night, the racket of men and noises crushed my chances for any amount of sleep. Off and on through the hours, I prayed for my family and asked the Lord to deliver me out of this hellish nightmare. Out of sheer exhaustion, I must have drifted off for maybe thirty minutes before I heard someone calling out about chow. I knew it was imperative that I eat something if I was going to have any faculties at all for the stressful day ahead. The only thing the bullpens had over isolation was that you couldn't think about anything in depth because of all of the loud and crazy commotion. If nothing else, it had a way of keeping my mind off the possibility of the dreaded death penalty, but the tradeoff was feeling like I was engulfed in total madness—hardly a fair trade.

My stomach was a tangle of knots as I made my way to the courthouse. With my head hung low, I ignored the annoying media people and the curiosity seekers who stood around on the courthouse lawn and walks. Inside, still more people pointed and whispered as I passed by. I felt the sudden urge to glare back at one or two of them so they could get a sense of what a wild, murdering criminal might look like. Instead, I lifted my head and forced a slight smile. It made me feel better, and it crushed the satisfaction they would have otherwise gotten during gossip at the local coffee shop.

Reporters with cameras hoisted on their shoulders darted in and around the courthouse crowd, positioning themselves so they could capture the award-winning shot for the evening news. The guards seemed undaunted by their presence and employed their usual directives, telling the reporters and the crowd to "stand back," "clear the way," and "give us some breathing room." My guess was that, underneath, they were enjoying every second of their spotlight exposure.

The crowd at the courthouse seemed larger than any that had attended the preliminary hearings. Everybody and their uncle was squeezed in among the mass of people standing just outside the courtroom, all waiting to catch a close-up glimpse of Dennis Fritz, the notorious killer.

There was hardly any standing room left in the courtroom itself. As I made my way down the aisle to the defense table, I spotted the Carter family to my right, along with other familiar faces whose names I didn't know. Their expressions taunted me with anger and hostility. I looked away. Near the front row, I spotted Barney. Next to him sat a woman, an assistant, who was shuffling through a sheaf of papers in a briefcase. Barney sat motionless in his usual manner, with his hands propped on top of his walking cane. His brows, knotted with concern, expressed the apprehension that circulated within the courtroom. Mom and Aunt Wilma sat in the same front-row position as they had yesterday. Neither of them looked like they had gotten a wink of sleep.

As I took my seat next to Greg, a wave of fear ripped through my gut. I had no doubt that Greg's night hadn't been restful, either. His cheeks looked pale, his eyes were reddened, and the glare of the overhead lights exaggerated the puffiness that was already noticeable beneath his eyes.

He cleared his throat and leaned toward me. In a whisper, he said, "Before the jury comes in, I want to tell you that I talked with Jones in his chambers, and he is being really hard-nosed about letting the Simmons tape come in because Peterson's hollering, like I told you, about not being able to cross-examine him. I would like to put Simmons on the stand but it would be too much of a risk in the shape that he's in. Peterson isn't cooperating at all, but that's par for the course. I have just been so busy in preparing all of the motions and talking with all the people that I haven't had time to turn around, let alone—" He stopped in mid-sentence as the first member of the jury entered the courtroom. "Here comes the jury. We'll talk later."

Members of the panel, dressed in their best Sunday clothes, entered the courtroom in single-file fashion and without expression took their seats as the bailiff looked on. In the gallery, the chatter of the crowd ended abruptly as Judge Jones made his entrance through the black drapes and sat down in his black leather chair.

Turning to the jury box, Jones spoke without hesitation, addressing the somber-faced jury members again about the principles of the law and how they pertained to their obligations and responsibilities in rendering a verdict. No one on the panel gave any indication of reaction as they listened to Jones's delivery.

As he spoke, I stared into the faces of each juror,

contemplating which ones would be for me and which ones would be against me. Greg had said during yesterday's proceedings that a jury foreman would be selected. I gazed across the rows of jurors, trying to determine who would be the most likely candidate. More than likely it would be a man. I shuddered to think what would happen if Cecil Smith would be designated to lead the jury, since he had stared at me yesterday like he was itching to push the syringe himself. His name, along with the names of Mrs. Flowers and Mr. Sanders, were the only ones I could remember. It seemed that all of them were purposely avoiding looking my way. I didn't know how I should read that.

Diverting my attention, I glanced back over my shoulder at Mom and Aunt Wilma and smiled. Then I shifted my gaze back to the jury box and then to Judge Jones and then to the notepad on the table in front of me as I waited anxiously for the trial to begin.

To my amazement, Nancy Shew stood, approached the jury, and began delivering her opening statement. What a sly move, for Peterson to use his female assistant as a sympathy grabber for all of the female jurors. In a meek, mild-mannered way, Shew carefully read the entirety of the charges, then gave a blow-by-blow account of the state's version of the crime, describing in detail how they believed Ronnie and I had allegedly raped and murdered Debbie Carter. Naming witnesses one at a time, Shew highlighted what their testimonies would reflect. She mentioned a few new names, some of whom Greg had told me about, that had been added as witnesses since the second hearing.

There was no doubt about it. Shew was very effective in her role; her fragility and femininity seemed to go right to the heart of every one of the jurors. Her slow and deliberate presentation captured the jurors' attention—all except for one man who appeared to be asleep. As she spoke, she strolled in front of the jury box, pausing occasionally, mostly at spots in front of where the women were seated. There were a couple of times when, as Shew touched upon the more graphic details of the murder, more than one female juror would shift her eyes in my direction. Their cold, judging stares caused me to shiver. Of all the female jurors, Mrs. Flowers seemed the least affected by Shew's lurid descriptions. After a good twenty minutes, Shew finally wrapped up her statement and sat down.

To my surprise, Greg's opening statement was short and to the point and lasted only a couple of minutes. He simply stated to the jury that it was our position that another person had acted alone in committing the murder of Debbie Carter. Pausing in front of the center of the jury box, Greg prefaced the upcoming testimonies of a couple of the state's witnesses and asked the jury to consider both sides and both of the interpretations that would be offered. Apparently, since Shew had already informed the jury as to what each witness's expected testimony would be, Greg must have considered it a waste of time to go through all of the same information again. Looking over my shoulder as Greg sat back down beside me, I noticed that Mom and my aunt had bewildered looks on their faces.

Jones instructed the state to call its first witness. Peterson lunged from his chair and requested a bench conference that lasted every bit of five minutes. When he returned to the prosecution's table, he looked distracted—hardly like his usual arrogant, macho style.

Returning to his seat, Greg whispered to me, "For some reason, Peterson is doing his best to keep Gore off the stand. I don't know why. I talked to Gore last night and he said he would be willing to testify, so let's see what happens."

Glen Gore appeared, followed by the bailiff, from the rear door beside the jury box. He looked very stressed and walked in a rigid manner to the witness stand, where he was sworn in. His testimony was identical to what he had testified to at the hearing— that he had seen Ronnie at the Coach Light Club on the night that Debbie Carter was killed and that he had danced with Debbie for a little bit before closing time, after she had told him that Ronnie was bothering her. But his demeanor toward Peterson had changed.

His answers were not as forthcoming or responsive as they had been previously and he looked at Peterson with contempt.

All I cared about was Gore saying that he had not seen me at the Coach Light on the eve of Debbie's death. Whether he was lying about having seen Ronnie or Ronnie pestering Debbie for a dance was up to him. I had no control over that. Fortunately, Peterson didn't belabor the point and quickly yielded Gore to Greg.

Greg stepped to the podium, took a deep breath as if he was pulling a reserve of energy from down deep, and asked Gore to confirm as he had done previously that he knew me by sight. He also ascertained that Gore was sure that he had not seen me at the club on that night. Greg's questioning also brought out the fact that Dennis Smith and Gary Rogers had lost the three sets of hair samples that Gore had provided and that no one had followed up with regard to the missing samples.

I studied the jurors' faces. Not an eyelash was raised. That worried me. I believed they had already made their minds up that I was guilty.

Another round of re-direct by Peterson and re-cross by Greg gained little. Gore recalled that the Coach Light wasn't very crowded on that particular night and that he didn't remember seeing Tommy Glover. With that, he stepped down. It still wasn't clear to me why Peterson hadn't wanted Gore to testify, unless it had something to do with his attitude. But the jury wouldn't know that. They hadn't seen him at the preliminary hearings. I dismissed the thought as the state called Tommy Glover.

Like Gore, Glover added nothing new in his brief appearance on the witness stand. No, he answered Peterson, he had not seen Debbie Carter in the lounge area of the Coach Light. Yes, he had seen her in the parking lot talking to Glen Gore. No, no one was in her car or got into her car with her that he saw.

"Did you ever see while you were out there at any time in the past, did you ever see Debbie Carter flirt with anybody?" Peterson asked.

"No, sir," Glover answered, like a robot.

"For the jury's benefit, what did you do and what did you see her car do that evening when you left?" Peterson said.

Glover looked at the jury. "I just seen her get in her car and leave."

The courtroom crowd was restless and inattentive while Glover gave his answers; many of them had apparently already heard his testimony at the hearing.

When Greg approached the podium, he had only a couple of things on his mind.

"Mr. Glover, do you recall how many people were in the small bar you described? The lounge, I believe was how you described it," Greg asked.

"I think I was the only one in the lounge side at that time," Glover answered.

"There was nobody else in the lounge?"

Glover apparently had a need to clarify. "Besides me, there wasn't anybody else in the lounge."

Greg turned and looked at me and then back to Glover. "Prior to this time, did you know Dennis Fritz?"

"No, sir," Glover answered.

"You know who he is now? You've seen him in court before, here in court?" Greg pushed.

"Yes, at the preliminary. Yes, sir."

"Did you see him at any time that night out at the Coach Light?" Greg asked.

"No, sir," responded Glover.

And that was it.

Jones looked up, excused Glover, and directed Peterson to call his next witness.

Gina Vietta, a woman in her late twenties, was the first witness that hadn't testified at my preliminary hearings. I hadn't heard very much about her except for Greg telling me that she was a detention guard at a county jail not too far from Ada and that she had been the last person to talk to Debbie on the night before the day when she had been discovered dead. Not knowing what this woman's testimony might include, I felt my breakfast churning in my stomach as she approached the stand.

With his head bowed dramatically, Peterson walked slowly to the jury box and half-turned to the waiting witness. Following a round of introductory questions, Peterson asked Vietta if she had seen Williamson and me together at the Coach Light.

"Objection!" Greg shouted out.

Jones called both attorneys to the bench.

I could hear bits and pieces of Greg's argument to Jones. "Incompetent," "irrelevant," and "immaterial" were some of the words Greg used. I also caught a drift of Greg saying he had previously talked to me about something he used in preparing his motion of limine—establishing a nexus to show a relationship between something or someone and the time and place of the crime. The judge said something I couldn't hear. With an unpleased look on his face, Greg walked back to the table and whispered to me that Jones had overruled his objection. I heard him mumble to himself, "That's a bad evidentiary ruling."

Peterson asked the question again, and Vietta told the court that she had seen Ronnie and me together on several occasions at the Coach Light. I quickly grabbed my notepad and scribbled the words "That's a lie!" and slid it in Greg's direction. He nodded.

In response to Peterson's next questions, Vietta said that Debbie had told her that Ronnie had asked her out for a date, and on occasion he had given her a hard time and she had asked to change stations when she saw us together. I was relieved that my name was left out when Vietta said that Debbie had told her that only Williamson made her nervous. Peterson then asked her to tell the story of her late-night telephone conversations with Debbie on the eve of her death.

Vietta said she received a call from Debbie between two-thirty and three in the morning. Debbie had asked her to come to her apartment and pick her up because there was someone there that she didn't feel comfortable with. When she asked who it was, Debbie told her to hold on for just a moment. She said she heard muffled sounds in the background. Vietta told Debbie that she would be right over to get her, and the conversation ended. Before Vietta could leave the house, though, Debbie called her back and said that she had decided to stay home and there was no need to come and get her. Vietta again asked Debbie who was there. Debbie changed the subject and told Vietta to call her in the morning to wake her up. She didn't seem scared or excited at the time of the second call.

The jury's attention was deeply focused on Vietta's words. Even the juror that had fallen asleep was now alert and listening to everything the witness was saying. Not a word or a shuffle could be heard from the spectators. Even Jones, who had appeared to be in an aloof meditative state, had also come alive and was peering intently at Vietta. And then came the question from Peterson that everyone was waiting to hear.

"Did you that evening, December the 8th, if you recall, did you see either Dennis Fritz or Ron Williamson out there, if you recall?"

"I don't recall seeing them there, sir," Vietta answered in a straightforward voice.

Peterson repeated the question as if he had expected some other kind of response. Vietta looked him straight in the eye.

"I don't recall seeing them there," she answered again.

Peterson stood motionless and silent for just a moment before yielding the witness to Greg.

Several members of the jury shifted uneasily in their seats. I suppose they had anticipated that Vietta was going to say that she had seen Ronnie and me together on that night, but Peterson's theatrics did nothing but add to the mounting tension in the courtroom. The prosecution had gained nothing from Vietta's testimony. Whispers from the gallery permeated the silence as Greg stood and approached the witness stand.

He wasted no time in getting to the point. After ascertaining from Vietta that the club was not crowded on that night, Greg confirmed her testimony that she had not seen either Ronnie or me at the club on that specific night. Moving directly in front of Vietta, Greg changed the direction of his questioning and returned to the telephone conversations she had described. Eyeball to eyeball, he asked her if she had any reason to believe that there was more than one person with Debbie Carter when she called.

"Objection, Your Honor. Speculative," Peterson wailed as he stood up, his chair sliding out from underneath him.

"Overruled!" Jones stated immediately.

Greg repeated his question. Vietta said that she did not believe there was more than one person there because Debbie had only said that there was *someone* there and she felt uncomfortable with *him* being there—emphasizing that the language Debbie had used implied just one man. Greg politely thanked Vietta and requested a bench conference.

This time I could not hear very much of what was being said, but Peterson seemed to be getting the short end of the straw. The jurors' attentions were now focused on stretching, yawning, and situating themselves into more comfortable sitting positions.

For the rest of the morning and into the early afternoon, the state presented a string of familiar witnesses who repeated for the most part what they had said at the first preliminary hearing. Debbie's dad, Charlie Carter, described how he had discovered his daughter's body in her apartment. As I listened to him and watched him, with that look of heartbreak in his eyes, I had an urge to stand and yell out to him that I didn't kill his daughter and that I was sorry for all of the misery that he and his family were going through. Knowing how Charlie Carter must be suffering only stirred up the contempt and rancor that I felt toward Peterson, and I glanced at him. Who the hell was he to put our families through this nightmare without having any real evidence to support his purported allegations?

Greg leaned my way and informed me that Smith and Rogers were next in line on the witness list. Because I had already heard Smith's and Roger's previous testimonies, I concentrated on appearing relaxed and confident before the jury. Without staring at the panel members, I glanced from time to time in their direction to discern their individual reactions while Smith elaborated on the graphic details of the murder. Some of the women jurors looked horrified by his crime scene descriptions. Of course, Smith was trying his best to appear as an angel before the jury and often looked over their way and flashed his smirk so they would notice him even more. His bald head seemed to glow in the glare of the courtroom lights as he rambled on about the array of events that led law enforcement to their suspicions of Ronnie and me.

At the close of Smith's testimony, Jones recessed for lunch. Reminding the jurors of their obligations, he admonished them to not breathe a word to anyone about the case.

While Greg engaged in yet another bench conference with Shew and Peterson, I was escorted by the deputies from the courtroom. As I passed by my mother and aunt, I asked them how they were doing and gave them my love and prayers. I wanted so much to reach out and put my arms around them and absorb every bit of the pain and suffering that they were going through.

Upon my return from the jail an hour later, Greg and I had a few minutes to talk before the jury came in. "Listen, Dennis, we haven't got very much time, and I apologize for that, but I just got through talking to Jones about discharging a couple of the witnesses you had collected statements on to testify against Harjo. Melvin Love and Kenneth Stepp are being held over at the city jail right now, but I don't want to put them on the stand because they are saying some very damaging things about you."

"Well, Greg, don't you have their tape-recorded statements that Westcott left you when he had interviewed them back in December in the county jail? If they lie, can't you play that tape before the jury and let them listen to their original statements?"

"I know what you're saying, Dennis, but it would be too risky if they were to say some bad things about you, and I'm not even for sure whether Jones would allow that in or not since Peterson wasn't at the interview. What I'm trying to say is that, if Jones allowed me to play the tape, Love and Stepp might say that you put them up to it or make any number of excuses. I went over to the city jail this morning to talk to Love. When I got there, Rogers met me at the desk and made the statement that my peckerwood wanted to talk with me, so I went back in the jail and tried my very best to talk with him. He was absolutely going crazy, shouting obscenities that if I put him on the stand, 'he would make me sorry.' Those are his exact words. Then he started screaming that he wasn't going to get killed in the pen for being a ratty snitch, as he called it. Dennis, he was so totally out of control I could barely even hear myself talk. I can't prove this but I believe that Rogers may have said something that caused him to go off like he did. It's the same story with Stepp. You remember the letter that I gave to you that he wrote to me?"

I nodded.

"I'm sorry, Dennis, but we just can't take that chance. It's way too risky."

I didn't say anything, but underneath my disappointment I realized that I would have rolled the dice to see what would happen if Love and Stepp were confronted with their own prior statements.

The bailiff ushered the jury into the courtroom. The spectators settled onto the benches and their chatter subsided as the jury members made themselves comfortable for the long afternoon ahead. Except for an occasional cough or an untimely yawn, the jammed courtroom grew as quiet as it had ever been. Only the voices of Shew and Rogers could be heard, batting back and forth different aspects of the investigation. And even they grew quiet when the judge made his entrance.

The state's next witness was Gary Rogers. Nothing had changed about his courtroom personality. Between his sour expression and his precise, cut-and-dried manner of speaking, Rogers made it clear to the jury that he was above and beyond the normal cut of a cop. Without question, Rogers was there for one purpose and one purpose only—to help convict me of the murder that he and Smith had worked so hard to solve for the past five years. At intervals during Rogers's testimony, I heard Barney in the background mumbling something to his assistant about some of Rogers's responses to Shew.

Greg's cross-examination was very thorough as he covered every point that he had questioned Rogers about in the preliminary hearing—asking him about evidence found at the crime scene, the long drawn-out process of evidence testing, and the slow pace of his investigation in general. With a look of reluctance and a tone of regret, Rogers admitted to the jury that I had repeatedly told him that I was innocent, that I never knew Debbie Carter, and that I had never been in her apartment.

Members of the jury appeared unmoved by Rogers's admission of the truth. The unsettled feeling that I had been having that the jury members had already made up their minds seemed to grow even more disturbing as I watched their stony faces. Shew's re-direct and Greg's re-cross drew forth no new information. The day just seemed to grow longer and more tiring.

During a brief recess, I was left alone at the defense table while the others took bathroom breaks and stretched their legs. As Mom and Aunt Wilma left the courtroom for a moment, my heart cried out on the inside. They both looked so weak and tired. *Oh, God, protect them from any danger or harm and give them the strength and courage to live happy lives if I am convicted.* Then a more agonizing thought entered my mind: *I will never get to see my precious daughter again if I'm convicted.* Tears stung my eyes. I pressed my fingers against the bridge of my nose to stop them. I could not allow my emotions to be seen or misconstrued by these people—especially the jurors, who had already been sneaking peeks at me throughout the trial. I looked straight ahead while I waited for Greg to return from the restroom.

The jurors filed back in, and the judge took his seat. The prosecution called Fred Jordan, the chief medical examiner. She remained in her seat. This time, it was Peterson who stood and walked to the podium. With an air of conceit and overwrought drama in his voice, Peterson questioned Jordan, going over the same points he had presented at the preliminary. As Jordan detailed the extent of the internal and external injuries inflicted upon Debbie Carter, I realized that some of the jurors had turned away from him and were staring squarely at me. Cecil Smith, who sat at the end of the jury box, had the most judgmental look. Rattled, I felt perspiration bead on my forehead. I looked away from Smith and then away from the whole panel. A deathly silence pervaded the courtroom as Jordan's responses became unintelligible mumbles in my ears.

Adding insult to injury, and over Greg's robust objection, Jones allowed Jordan to show to the jury the gruesome photographs of Debbie's tortured body on her apartment floor and, later, in the morgue and, later still, in her coffin after the exhumation. It was clear, after the photos had been circulated through the jury box for closer viewing, that Peterson believed that the momentum had shifted in his favor. He strutted across the courtroom with a cocky look on his smiling face, and in a voice that infuriated me, he yielded the witness as he casually glanced in my direction.

Throughout Greg's cross-examination, the jury seemed listless and inattentive. The devastating impact of the crime scene pictures had gone apparently to the very core of their ability to maintain an open mind. Their frequent glimpses at me told me that. Despite Greg's diligent efforts in questioning Jordan and his all-out attempt to counter the pictures' effects, the damage had been done. There was no doubt in my mind that the jury believed that I was guilty.

After another round of examinations by Peterson and Greg, Jordan was dismissed and left the courtroom. Observant that some of the jurors were in a distraught frame of mind, Jones called for a ten-minute recess and reminded the jurors of their instructions.

Greg and I sat silently at the defense table as the jury box emptied. Cecil Smith was the last to go. As he passed by the defense table, he looked directly at me with a stare that would have melted steel. I glanced at Greg, whose head was lowered, and commented about the way Smith had looked at me. After a moment of silence, Greg sighed heavily and turned his chair to face me. He hesitated briefly, as if to find the right words to say.

"Doggone it, Dennis," he whispered, "every time I take a step forward, Jones puts me two steps backwards. His evidentiary rulings have been completely in Peterson's favor, especially on my motion of limine, which I specifically objected to because the showing of the photographs could do nothing else but inflame the jury. I realize you don't know anything about the law, but Jones is very well aware that it's very hard to overturn a case on appeal based upon the jury seeing these types of photographs. There was absolutely no need for the jury to have seen every one of those pictures, especially the one of her in the coffin."

"Believe me, Greg, I saw the jury and how they looked at me after seeing those pictures. Smith just got through looking at me like I was some kind of demon, and I can tell that many of the jurors have already made their minds up that I'm guilty as hell itself," I responded. We sat in silence for another minute or two.

Greg offered a faint smile. "I just want you to know that I am doing the best I can for you, and we've got a long way to go before that fat lady sings, so try to hang in there and stay as calm and collected as you can. It's very important how the jury views your reactions. I think you're doing a wonderful job, under the circumstances. To tell you the truth, if I was in your position, I might already be as crazy as a loon," Greg said just as the panel of jurors was ushered back into the jury box.

The next two witnesses that Peterson called were my old neighbors—Gary Allen, who had already testified once, and Tony Vick, who had lived in one of the garage apartments. I wasn't worried about Allen's testimony, but I was very concerned as to what Vick's testimony might be.

Almost too nervous to talk, Allen gave the same short, descriptive account that he had testified to at the preliminary hearing. Nothing had changed. He timidly stated that he had heard me and another person having a water fight in my backyard some time between the first and tenth of December in 1982.

His testimony irked me, but I sat still and expressionless. *So what if I wanted to have a water fight in my backyard in the middle of winter*—which I knew I hadn't done. *Why should this even be used as evidence against me, without some kind of proof that it happened on the night of the murder—except maybe to draw some kind of inference that this other person and I were washing blood off ourselves?* Greg and I knew that Peterson wouldn't dare take that kind of long leap, especially in front of Jones, but it was apparent from his line of questioning that Peterson was once again playing to the jury his dramatic buildup of something he knew wasn't going anywhere.

On his cross-examination Greg went straight to the point, asking Allen if he actually saw me or just heard a voice that sounded like mine. Allen insisted that he recognized my voice but as before, he stated that it was too dark to visibly identify me. After Peterson threw in a couple of objections to apparently make himself look good, or perhaps just keep the jury awake, Greg ended his questioning of Allen.

Vick's testimony turned out to be even more meaningless than Allen's. He stated to both Peterson and Greg that he had lived in the ground-floor garage apartment behind my house during the time that Debbie Carter had been murdered and that he had seen Ronnie at my house on several occasions but couldn't remember the exact dates. Vick stated that he had been a lifelong friend of Debbie's and that, following her murder, he recalled a conversation that he had with me in the backyard when he told me of Debbie's death. He said he recalled a few occasions after that when I had asked him if he had heard anything more about whether they had found the people who had murdered her. Vick stated that at times I seemed to be overly interested and concerned about the subject.

Before being dismissed, Vick stated that he had seen Williamson and me at the Coach Light Club on separate occasions but never there together.

I wondered what Peterson's purpose was for using Vick's testimony, other than letting the jury know that Ronnie and I had been friends. Vick couldn't put Ronnie and me together at the Coach Light Club on the night of Debbie's death. Had Peterson tried to insinuate that there was something wrong with having a friend and being seen with him at my own house? Is Peterson trying to show the jury that I'm guilty because I associated with Ronnie? As Vick stepped down, the jury members shifted in their seats. Spectators in the courtroom yawned and coughed, and whispers circulated in the background—all of which told me that people were ready to hear some hard, concrete evidence.

"The state calls Donna Walker," Shew announced in a gentle voice.

Greg had asked me during one of his jail visits if I remembered talking to someone by this name, a Donna Walker who worked as a store clerk at the Love's convenience store. I told him that I vaguely remembered some girl with blond hair and glasses who I chatted with from time to time while having coffee before driving on to teach school in Noble. I immediately recognized Donna as that person when she entered through the courtroom door. I had no earthly idea what she was going to say about me. All I could remember was that she was cute and that she used to flirt with me on occasion, despite the fact that she was married.

After being sworn in, Donna quickly opened up to Shew by telling her that I had been a regular early-morning coffee drinker during the weekdays. Walker went on to say that on regular occasions she would see me in the presence of another man, who became known to her as Ron Williamson. Donna thought it was unusual that, after she heard of the Carter murder, that Williamson and I kind of faded into the woodwork, but she never drew any conclusions from that fact, or from our absence. Later, though, she said, when we reappeared, she noticed that our character and dress had gone completely downhill.

" They seemed kind of nervous and paranoid," Walker said. Shew had no further questions. She yielded the witness.

Greg questioned Walker extensively about her recollections as to the times of the day that she had seen Ronnie and me together. Donna became confused as Greg pressed on. He drew one objection after another from Peterson for being argumentative. Walker admitted that she was unsure of the exact hours due to the amount of time that had passed since being first questioned by the police in August of 1987.

"That's almost five years after the offense, and you were able to recollect all these things we've been talking about here?" Greg queried.

"Objection, Your Honor. It's argumentative!" Peterson roared.

With flushed cheeks and a trembling voice, Walker concluded her testimony by stating that she was as sure as she possibly could be about one thing or the other.

"Call your next witness," Jones emphatically stated.

"State calls Letha Caldwell," said Shew.

As with Walker, Greg had told me that this woman would be testifying, too. But the nature of her testimony left me shocked and dismayed when Greg explained it. He had learned from Peterson's office that Letha was going to testify that, upon opening her door one night at a late hour, Ronnie and I were standing there in front of her and that she had to display a gun to convince us to leave and to not bother her anymore.

As she made her entrance into the courtroom, I shook my head. I couldn't remember any such event ever taking place, but here she was, getting sworn in to talk about it. I sat in disbelief as Caldwell greatly exaggerated the number of times that I had supposedly been at her house with Ronnie. When she mentioned a time when I was supposedly offering her pills, I recalled the incident, and it was she in fact who had asked Ronnie and me if we wanted some Valium or marijuana. Amazingly, everything she said inferred guilt by association—no one was there to corroborate and support her testimony. It was her word against no one's.

As Greg started his cross-examination, I started detaching mentally from the whole proceeding and all of the lies and distortions that were being paraded before the court in an attempt to prove my guilt because I had once been Ronnie's buddy. I felt as though I were sitting in a theater watching a movie about an innocent man going down the tubes on the strength of incompetent evidence. I withdrew deeper into myself, barely hearing the echoes of Caldwell's grating, deceptive clamor as she reinforced the theme: guilt—my guilt—by association. The realization that I would be convicted and never see my daughter or family again roared through my mind, assaulting me with memories of the excruciating pain and suffering that Elizabeth and I experienced as a result of her mother's murder.

Elizabeth was only two years old when Mary was murdered on Christmas Day in 1975. At that age, she didn't demonstrate much emotion over the loss, though she did become somewhat withdrawn and was noticeably unhappy and unsure about what had happened. I was certain that she must have had some memories of seeing her mother's body slumped over in her rocking chair because she had been alone in the house for hours after Mary was shot in the back of the head. And surely, Elizabeth remembered the assailant busting the door open and pulling her mother's limp and lifeless body from the chair onto the floor by the decorated Christmas tree. Surely some of those images had stayed with her.

Six months after Mary's death, Elizabeth and I went on a camping trip to help alleviate some of the sorrow and stress we had been experiencing because of the trauma. We were sitting on folding chairs in a circle of tall trees in front of a crackling campfire some time after supper. The early June evening had turned cool, and the fire's heat was warm and comforting. The glow from the flames illuminated the tree canopy high overhead, and sporadically, insects fluttered into the path of the sparks that rose with the smoke toward the night sky.

"Look, Daddy. Look at what's by the fire," Elizabeth said, her voice nearly a squeal from all of her excitement.

"That's a moth, honey, keeping warm by the fire," I gently replied.

For a moment, the large gray moth circled erratically above the flames. Elizabeth giggled and pointed to it and called it by name as it zigzagged its way in and around and through the smoke and sparks. There was joy in her voice as she spoke. She was having so much fun.

Suddenly, the moth seemed to lose its bearings. It wavered and dropped and flew right into the flames. It did not reemerge.

"Where'd it go?" Elizabeth asked as concern spread over her face.

"Elizabeth, honey, the moth flew into the fire and died," I told her. I looked carefully at her as I spoke in case she was confused.

In seconds, her look of worry changed to a grimace of pain. She began screaming at the top of her lungs. Her little body shook violently. I wrapped my arms around her and held her tightly to my chest. For what must have been several minutes, her piercing screams railed against the night, and her body rocked and trembled. At last, her convulsions began to subside. I held her close as I realized what had happened. All of her tightly held emotions over the months since her mother's death had spilled out all at once.

Greg had apparently leaned toward me to ask me a question that I didn't hear.

"Dennis, are you all right?" he asked.

Snapping out of my memory, I assured him that everything was okay. "I was just thinking about something that happened long ago."

"The state calls Rusty Featherstone," Peterson blared out.

"Okay," Greg said to me. "You just looked a little out of it."

"I'm okay," I insisted, staring at Featherstone as he made his way to the witness stand.

Peterson launched into questioning, asking Featherstone about an event that happened when Ronnie and I were at a Holiday Inn Club in Norman. Greg interrupted repeatedly, asking for relevance, and for once, Jones agreed with him.

Mark one on the chalkboard, I said to myself as Peterson gave up and stormed back to his seat, his face wrought with aggravation.

"I have no questions of this witness," Greg hastily remarked as he glanced at me with a reserved look.

Featherstone stepped down.

"State calls William Martin to the stand," announced Shew.

Martin stated that he was the superintendent of the Noble school system. The sum and substance of his testimony was that I had called in sick on December 8, 1982, the same day that Ms. Carter had been discovered dead. Greg only asked a couple of questions of Martin during his brief cross-examination.

When Shew called James Harjo, I braced for what I hoped might be his come-uppance. I hoped Greg would punch holes in his stupid Perry Mason story.

Harjo, in his mentally retarded way, entertained the jury by doodling his *x*s and *G*s on a piece of paper as he explained how he had determined my guilt through the self-taught analytical methods that he employed while we were in the county jail together. He kept the jury laughing as he answered Shew's questions, describing his Perry Mason techniques over and over again in both the direct- and cross-examinations. Greg did little to shake him from his story.

From a first impression, it seemed like the jury was laughing at Harjo's ridiculous, convoluted testimony. But the longer I studied the jurors' reactions, the more I could see that they were actually being swayed by Harjo's comic demeanor. Everyone in the courtroom could tell that Harjo's elevator didn't go all the way to the top, but that didn't seem to matter to the jury. They were listening and absorbing every detail of what he said, and more so, appeared to believe what they were hearing.

I shrunk back in my seat and bit my lip since there was nothing I could do that would stop this insanity. Harjo had to be a pathological liar because, instead of being normally nervous, he was enjoying every minute under the spotlight of the jury's attention. After forty minutes on center stage, Harjo walked from the courtroom with a proud, pleased look on his face. He had finally gotten the much-needed attention and laughter that his boyish mind demanded. The jurors seemed relaxed and in a good humor as they watched him disappear from the courtroom—that is, until they looked in my direction with cold, humorless eyes and expressions full of suspicion.

Mike Tenney was next. His demeanor and testimony had not changed, either. Answering Shew's questions with a cocky attitude, Tenney spoke right out as to how he had written everything down at the command of Gary Rogers. He acted proud to be representing the state of Oklahoma in this official capacity. It was his big chance to show his superiors that he was much more than just a mere trainee guard. His beady eyes looked alert and eager to please as he read before the jury his written account of my hypothetical conversations with him in the county jail.

Objections erupted from Greg. He moved fiercely for a mistrial because Tenney mentioned that I had said something about a plea bargain. The long stressful day had worn thin on Greg's nerves, and he was noticeably hot under the collar. He accused Shew of floundering around by putting in highly objectionable testimony. Shew's flushed cheeks showed her embarrassment, but Greg didn't care. On his cross-examination, he raked Tenney over the coals by getting him to state fully what he had been holding back during Shew's questioning—that I had always told him I was innocent and never implied my guilt to him in any way.

At the late hour, Jones continued the proceeding until eight-thirty on the following day. After giving his usual cautionary instructions to the jury, he released them with the resounding bang of his gavel. Before I even had a chance to stand, the guards were at my side, ready to take me back to the jail. Despite the guard's persistence, I made sure that I got a hug from my mom and aunt before leaving.

Chapter 21

I found when I was back in the miserable confines of the bullpen that several inmates wanted to talk to me about the trial. I sat down at the table and grabbed the tray of cold food that had been left for me. To my surprise, no one had tampered with it. As I ate, the inmates asked questions. I shared various aspects of trial procedure but I didn't go into much detail. After eating, I excused myself. I was exhausted and had to get some rest. Besides, a big domino game was about to commence, and I sure didn't feel like being involved in that earsplitting fiasco.

As I rested in my bunk, I thought about the day's events. I recalled how Cecil Smith had glared at me so savagely. Then there were Caldwell and Harjo, who lied so viciously against me. I suspected that Peterson, Rogers, or Smith had gotten to both of them in some way. The outcome wasn't looking good, and there was nothing I could do to stop the lies except take the witness stand myself and defend my own life. Greg had warned me about the downside of testifying in my own behalf, but at this point, wild horses wouldn't keep me off the stand. I understood that Peterson would be able to bring up my old felony charge of the cultivation of marijuana, along with any other number of possibilities that could impeach other portions of my testimony, but my mind was made up. There was nothing that Greg could do or say that would change it.

The pained and sorrowful expression on Charlie Carter's face haunted me as I nodded off to sleep. I saw his face in my dreams, and upon waking, I was reminded of my own lingering, terrible hurt over the murder of my wife. I had not forgiven myself for having moved Mary and Elizabeth far out into the country, where our closest source of protection was our neighbor-landlord. The haunting memory that had replayed itself in my mind a thousand times since her death surfaced again in the middle of the night. This time I could do nothing to escape it.

It was bitterly cold that Christmas Eve morning in 1975 when I received a call from the Katy railroad station switchboard that I had to go on a through freight run to Fort Worth. I had been working for the railroad as a brakeman for the past six months. The money was good, but the unpredictable hours had been a strain on our marriage. Mary and I had been having some disagreements on how to potty-train Elizabeth, and as she drove me to the station in the darkness of the night, we didn't say a word to each other. I held Elizabeth tightly in my arms. When we arrived at the station, I set Elizabeth on the seat without saying a word and abruptly got out. There was no "goodbye" or "see you later. I love you"—just my own stubborn silence as I slammed the car door shut behind me. I watched as the tail end of our lime-green Maverick Grabber disappeared from sight and then I went to work.

While awaiting my turnaround freight back to the terminal the next afternoon, I received a call from Mary's sister, Letha, who told me in a trembling, broken voice that Mary had been shot in the back of the head and was in the hospital undergoing surgery. She said that Elizabeth was okay but was being examined for any sexual impropriety. They had arrested a suspect, a seventeen-year-old boy who was our landlord's nephew.

Frantic and in a state of shock, I rushed around until I

was finally able to get a ride to the hospital. I learned from the doctors that the surgery was unsuccessful because the bullet had fragmented into too many pieces throughout Mary's brain. Rushing into her room, I saw my beloved wife lying unconscious in a tangle of instrument wires while she fought for her life. Her face was swollen and bruised from the bullet's brutal impact, and the breaths she took were shallow. With our preacher by my side, and her mother and father in the outer room because they couldn't bear to see their daughter die, I promised Mary that I would always take care of Elizabeth and would never leave her for any reason. I told her how much I dearly loved her and that I was so sorry for having gotten mad and not saying goodbye to her. Holding back my tears to keep my voice strong, I poured my heart out to Mary, telling her that Elizabeth was okay and for her not to worry, that I would always be a good father and that our daughter would be raised to be a good woman before God. Even though Mary lay in an unconscious state, I knew that her spirit heard every one of my words. She took her last breath and let go of the life she loved so dearly, dying peacefully in my cradling arms.

Now, in my bunk in the dead of night on the start of the third day of my trial, those images came back to me again and again. Each time I awoke, I thought they were gone, but they returned when I dozed off again. Eventually, I roused myself from my disturbed sleep, showered, and prepared myself for another day of uncertainty and its grueling stress. After breakfast, I was escorted by a troop of guards up to the courtroom, past the circus of people that anxiously awaited my arrival. My handcuffs were removed and I entered the courtroom to take my place at the defense table alongside Greg, with Mom and Aunt Wilma seated in the row directly behind me.

Greg turned and looked at me with worried eyes. "Dennis, we've got a major problem on our hands. It's come to my attention through numerous sources that the juror, Cecil Smith, was a chief of police here in Ada for forty years."

"He what?" I exclaimed.

"I know, Dennis, it was a complete surprise to me, too. As you are well aware, Smith never divulged that information to the court. Just as soon as I can, which might be more toward the end of the day, I'm going to bring this to Jones's attention and ask for a mistrial on the basis that Smith hid that information from us."

"I couldn't quite put my finger on it at the time, but now that you've told me, I can see why he's been starin' holes through me all through the trial, just like a cop would do. When did you find out about this, Greg?" I asked.

"Just recently. I'm going to try and get Smith disqualified and replaced by one of the alternate jurors. That is, if Jones will go for it."

"What is the chance of that happening?"

"Truthfully, Dennis, I don't know. It's like I told you before. Jones is a tough cookie to deal with, but this is the kind of error that he may not want to deal with if your case goes to the appeal level and is reversed on that issue. Right now, I don't want you to worry too much until I find out what can be done."

"That's fine, Greg. It's not like I don't have anything else to worry about with eight women and an ex-cop being on the jury, and on top of that, having to face the death penalty for the murder of a woman I never met in my life."

Greg ignored my smug, angry tone and changed the subject. "It's going to be another long day," he said. "The state has a long list of witnesses it plans to call. If there's time this afternoon, you might have a chance to make your statement."

That was fine with me. This was a Friday and I did not want to spend the weekend in that hellhole going crazy with the anticipation of testifying hanging over my head. I only wanted to tell the pure and simple truth, no matter how hard Peterson came down upon me.

With the jury in place and Jones perched upon his oversized chair, he opened the proceedings. "Call your next witness," Jones said. He sounded a little more sullen than usual.

"State calls Cindy McIntosh," said Shew, dramatically stating Cissy's name.

In her brief testimony, Cissy explained that she had been locked up right across from me and that she had heard Ronnie ask me if Debbie Carter was still on the floor or on the bed after I told Ronnie that I had viewed the crime scene pictures at the preliminary hearing. Glancing at me before continuing, she said that she could not remember if I made any comment back to Ronnie.

Shew had no further questions and yielded the witness to Greg, who only elicited from her the already-stated fact that she did not recall if I had made any response to Ronnie. Cissy was released and promptly exited the courtroom. I wondered what Peterson had in mind by using her testimony since it was not incriminating toward me. I didn't believe that he was quite that dumb to use a witness who had nothing bad to say against me. I had an urge to lean over and ask Greg if they had gotten my trial mixed up with Ronnie's, but I understood on some level that this was nothing more than yet another attempt to slyly convey my alleged guilt to the jury through my past association with Ronnie.

After Cissy testified, Jerry Peters and Mary Long rendered long-winded expert testimonies about how they had arrived at their conclusions through all of their precise testing procedures and opinions which were, of course, based upon their enlisted qualifications and high-ranked abilities to assess crime scene evidence. I had heard it all at the preliminary hearing. It seemed like such a waste of the taxpayers' good money for the jury to have to sit and listen to testimony that amounted to nothing more than speculation and hindsight. Peters devoted a good percentage of his testimony to telling the jury how he had screwed up by not having obtained a full set of prints from the ridges of Debbie's stiffened palms to be able to make an accurate comparison to the piece of Sheetrock that had been removed from her apartment wall. Likewise, Long's testimony was also a meandering array of opinions based upon percentages. According to her, Ronnie and me were in a twenty-percent class of males who might have committed the murder.

As their words washed over me, I decided that so far this trial had been nothing more than a two-ring circus filled with lies and deception promulgated by a ringleader hellbent on getting a conviction. There was no evidence to prove even the actual elements of those things I was accused of—that I committed the forcible rape or the murder. The record was devoid of any evidence that showed my time and whereabouts on, during, or after the night of the murder. And on top of that, the jury that was intently listening to these experts as if they were gods sent straight from heaven to right the wrongful acts of a murdering madman was, in fact, a jury that couldn't even understand half of what was being said because of the experts' use of highly technical words and scientific jargon. If someone had given me a choice between being here in this cauldron of boiling water that was spewing over in the courtroom and being up the creek without a paddle, I would have opted for the latter. Up the creek, at this moment anyway, looked like the far better option.

During Peters's and Long's turns on the witness stand, the atmosphere in the courtroom shifted. The spectators who had been quiet began to stir noisily in their seats after listening to the tedious testimonies of these two so-called scientists. I could hear whispers and chatter throughout the gallery. I didn't know exactly what that meant, but I suspected that such overblown scientific testimony had not met the observers' expectations in the same way that good old-fashioned, hard-core evidence would have done. Too, it was getting close to lunchtime, and everybody was ready for a break. Even the jury was showing signs of discomfort and anxiety.

I hadn't turned around for quite some time to check on my mom and aunt. When I peeked over my shoulder, I caught a quick glimpse of their haggard expressions. They did their best to smile, which let me know that no matter what the circumstances or outcome might be, they were behind me all the way. Their support gave me added will and stamina to stay alert and receptive, despite the draining effects of the stress I was feeling.

Jones was in a sour mood and rarely lifted his head except to adjust his glasses or look suspiciously around the courtroom when there was an outbreak of noise or chatter. "Call your next witness," he mumbled after Long stepped down.

Peterson called the mysterious Susan Land to the stand.

I didn't want to appear nervous, but the mere mention of her name prompted me to shift to the edge of my chair in anticipation of her testimony. Greg had not filled me in on what she might say.

Land was a slender woman with a professional demeanor whose mannerisms were deliberate and authoritative. Dressed in a blue cotton dress, Land identified herself as a criminalist who worked for the OSBI. Her answers were forthright and precise as she explained to Peterson that she had originally mounted the majority of the collected hair samples before passing them on to Melvin Hett. She had also labeled other articles of evidence that had been removed from Ms. Carter's apartment: the catsup bottle, a western-style belt, a pair of socks, a floral blouse, and other assorted items that she analyzed for evidentiary purposes. She carefully explained to the jury the procedures she used in the process of mounting hairs onto a glass slide.

Following a bench conference, which I strained to hear but couldn't, Jones made an announcement that the court would recess for lunch and gave his usual instructions to the jury. Before I was taken back to the jail, Greg informed me that Land would finish her testimony after lunch and that he had been told by Peterson that Melvin Hett would be the state's last testifying witness. Seeing that the guards were heading in my direction, Greg whispered that there was a good possibility that I would get to testify before the day was over and that he had some information to tell me after lunch concerning the results of our hair expert's findings. I was very anxious to take the witness stand and tell the jurors face to face that I had no knowledge whatsoever concerning the murder of Debbie Carter.

Following lunch, when Greg and I were again seated at the

defense table, Greg told me what he had heard from the hair expert. "Before the jury gets back, I want to let you know that Bisbing, our hair expert, called me last night and said that he had finished his examinations of your hair," Greg said. He seemed nervous as he spoke and kept glancing away. "I've got good news and bad news to tell you. The good news is that nine out of the twelve pubic hairs that Bisbing examined showed no similar characteristics to your pubic hair. The bad news is that the remaining three pubic hairs showed to be microscopically similar to yours."

Greg hesitated and looked toward the rear of the courtroom, where Barney was entering with his female assistant and Frank Baber. Then he turned back to me and started to speak, but I quickly interrupted him.

"What about the scalp hair comparisons?" I asked.

"That's the other thing, Dennis. Bisbing said that he didn't test the scalp hairs because he felt that the pubic hairs would be a good representative sample of the hair in evidence."

"Well, Greg, wouldn't it be important, too, if both of the scalp hairs showed not to be mine? I would think that anything in my favor would go a long way in persuading the jury's minds."

"I know what you're saying, Dennis, and I agree with you, but there was also a consideration made on the limited amount of funds that your family could come up with. With the three pubic hairs going against you, it really wouldn't make that big of a difference if the scalp hairs showed to be dissimilar to yours. Bisbing will be here Monday to testify—that is, if you still want him to come. I told him I would let him know something after I talked to you. Do you still want him to come, under the circumstances?"

"Well, won't it look bad, Greg, if our own expert's testimony coincides with Hett's? Wouldn't that be more damaging to the jury than if Hett just testified by himself, without Bisbing?" I didn't understand Greg's sudden mood of reluctance.

"Dennis, the jury's coming in. All I can say is that it will have to be your choice, and that's something that I can't decide for you. I will just quickly say that the favorable results could have a positive impact on the jury and, at the very least, it would be evidence in your favor, and that's more than we have right now. Think it over for a little while and we'll talk before they take you back over."

Land's testimony was brief. Jones overruled another objection from Greg about the chain of custody of the mounted hair slides. In a tense, aggravated voice, Greg stated that he had no questions and quickly sat down at the defense table, once again mumbling something about Jones's evidentiary rulings. Behind me, I could hear Barney saying something under his breath that was loud enough for Jones to hear. Jones looked up over his glasses in the direction where Barney was sitting, but instead of saying something to Barney, he distractedly told Peterson to call his next witness.

Peterson stood and called Melvin Hett to the stand.

Hett's in-court persona had not changed from the first time I saw him at the preliminary hearing. He walked mechanically to the witness stand in his purpose-driven manner, oblivious to anyone around him. He was a man of authority on a mission. There could be no mistaking that. Behind him, the bailiff followed, his arms loaded with cardboard tube canisters and several wooden frames resembling easel boards.

The panel of jurors reacted to Hett's omnipotent presence by sitting up straight in their seats, with their widened eyes glued upon him. He seated himself in the witness chair and extracted papers from his leather case. There could be no doubt in anyone's mind — Hett was Peterson's top gun, and he was ready to unload his ammunition before the court.

For nearly an hour, Peterson and Hett held sway. Hett was incredibly articulate and pointed in his explanations before the jury and went to great lengths to detail the numerous characteristics found in different types of hair. At Peterson's request, Hett stepped off the witness stand and placed his unrolled charts on the wooden easels and then returned to the stand to continue his testimony, this time using his illustrations. Peterson peppered him with questions: "How many different classifications are there of hair as far as Mongoloid, Caucasian, and that type of thing? What happens when you have a person who is the product of a mixed marriage, say, American Indian and Caucasian? You have different classifications, scale size, cuticle function. What are those? What do those mean to you, sir?"

Hett started at the top of his list, detailing in complicated, drawn-out explanations each and every physical structure found in a single hair. He talked non-stop for a good fifteen minutes before Peterson spoke again, and then he rattled on some more. I glanced at the jurors' faces several times while Hett raced through his recitation of descriptive illustrations while looking at Peterson. The panel members looked bored. A few of them had even started sliding down in their seats.

They weren't the only ones. Greg was tapping his pen on the table. I wondered whether Elizabeth had seen any newspapers about the last two days of the trial. Jones appeared at times to have fallen into some kind of meditative state, with his head hung downward and his eyes closed while he listened. Rustling and the occasional yawn could be heard from the back of the courtroom. The slightly discernible tail end of a remark muttered by Barney was the only sound in the courtroom that seemed to stir Jones into momentarily opening his eyes. What appeared to be dragging everyone down was the complexity of Hett's profound technical wording coupled with the extremely boring subject matter. No one in the courtroom even cared to hear it. What everyone was waiting to hear was, simply, whether or not my hair matched the samples removed from the crime scene.

After another twenty minutes of discussion about cuticle thicknesses, textures, pigment variations, scaling protrusions, cortices, and medullas, Hett got around to telling the jury that eleven pubic hairs and two scalp hairs that he had examined from the crime scene were a consistent match with my characteristics. I had heard all of this before and I was not impressed by his expert findings, because I knew that I had never been in Debbie Carter's apartment. On the other hand, the jury, which had waited through his subterfuge for this precise moment was now absorbing every word of his microscopically deduced opinion.

Greg leaped from his chair and vigorously objected to Hett's use of the word *match*. Jones called a bench conference. By now, Greg had almost worn a path from the defense table up to the bench. This one just dug the path a little deeper. I didn't hear Jones's ruling, but thereafter, Peterson yielded and Greg cautiously approached the witness stand to begin his cross-examination.

Greg wanted Hett to know right up front that he wasn't going to try and trick him, and if there was anything he didn't understand, he should just say so, and he would repeat the question. Greg was well aware that Hett could be a very crafty and a very difficult witness to deal with, and so, like he had done with other witnesses, he tried to soften him up before getting into some of the more controversial issues that they had bumped heads on at the preliminary hearing. He edged in subtly with Hett by asking him questions as to what his thoughts were on the subjective science of hair comparisons. His cross was very short and focused primarily on the generalities of the science of hair comparison.

As Greg yielded and Peterson went into his re-direct, my thoughts drifted to the decision I knew that I was going to have to make about whether or not to put Bisbing on the stand. Finding out that Bisbing, who was supposed to be on my side, had made the decision to not examine the scalp hairs really irked me. I caught bits and pieces of Peterson's grandstanding questions to Hett, and then my mind wandered back again to my unresolved dilemma. If I decided that Bisbing shouldn't be put on the stand, then the jury would have heard only Hett's one-sided damning account. There would be no defense version to counter Hett's opinions. If, on the other hand, I decided to use Bisbing's testimony, wouldn't the jury definitely believe I was guilty after hearing a double dose of highly incriminating hair evidence? Why couldn't Bisbing have allowed my mom and aunt to make some kind of payment arrangement for the additional scalp hair testing? After all, my life was literally on the line. It couldn't have cost but a few hundred dollars more to test two more scalp hairs.

Greg finished his re-cross by asking Hett if he had been directed by anybody to pay particular attention to the hair samples taken from me and Ronnie. Peterson shot up out of his chair and requested another bench conference. Again, I couldn't hear what the attorneys and judge were saying. Upon further questioning, Hett evasively admitted that he had been initially advised that I was a main suspect but that he had examined my hair in the same manner as he did the other samples. Greg had no further questions.

The state rested, Peterson said. Jones called a brief recess.

I would be next to take the stand.

CHAPTER 22

As I sat alone at the defense table and waited, my heart pounded so hard in my chest that I was afraid it was going to leap from my body. Though I was anxious to testify, this was my one chance—my one and only chance—to defend for my life. I wanted to give the best testimony that I could so the jurors would see that I was telling the whole truth about everything. That meant I needed to be calm. I took a couple of deep breaths and tried not to think.

Greg came back to the table, slid his chair over next to me, and told me that Jones had denied his in-chamber motion to disqualify Smith as a juror. The way he explained it was that Jones wouldn't even give it consideration because Greg had made his decision about Smith based on a lack of questions asked specifically about Smith's employment with the police department. Given that, Jones denied the motion on the basis that Smith didn't actually lie about his employment.

"Who was to know that Smith had been a police chief for forty years?" said Greg. "He should have divulged that information to us, because he would've also had to have retired from his chief of police job, just like he had reported about retiring from the

Oklahoma Corporation Commission. I think that was a pretty big error on the part of Jones."

"Smith may not have actually lied but he never divulged that information which, in my mind, is the same thing as lying!" I interjected.

"I agree with you, but you will be able to bring it up on appeal if we don't win this trial, and I'm gonna do everything I can to make sure that we do win. And that takes us to where we're at now. We've spent some time in the past discussing how you should testify. Just remember, don't open any doors that Peterson can expand on because, believe me, he will be trying in every way to get you riled up so you will talk more. Just answer his questions and don't feel the need to add anything else. And don't let him intimidate you. Let him ask the questions, and make your answers as brief as possible. Are we on the same page?"

I nodded.

"One other thing. Try to not look at the jury excessively. It's all right to glance in their direction when you're explaining something, but don't stare at them. It will only make them nervous about you. Okay?"

"Yeah, I'm ready. I'm pretty nervous right now but I will be very careful when answering his questions. By the way, I've decided that I do want Bisbing to go ahead and testify, even though some of his results are against me. At least I will have some kind of a defense to put before the jury."

"I think that's the best decision you could make, Dennis. Under the circumstances we need everything that we can get. Are you ready to give it your best shot?"

I nodded again, looking squarely into Greg's eyes.

"Just answer my questions as straightforwardly as you can," he told me. "I will stop you if you start over-explaining something so that will be your cue to limit your answers. Here comes the jury back. Are you ready?"

"I'm as ready as I'll ever be." I glanced toward the prosecution table. "And I can tell that Peterson is, too, with that big fat grin he's got smeared all over his face."

After the jurors were seated, Jones made the announcement to the panel that the state of Oklahoma had rested its case and that Mr. Saunders would be presenting his defense.

"The defense would call Mr. Fritz," said Greg. He sounded confident as he spoke.

I stood and stepped to the witness stand, where I was sworn in and seated. A long-forgotten feeling came over me as I sat in the witness chair and looked out at all the faces in the crowd. Many people seemed to leer at me, their hostility and aggression clearly showing in their eyes. The situation reminded me of the hot seat, minus the straps and wires, that I had sat in when Smith and Rogers questioned me during their post-polygraph interview. Even without looking in the jury's direction, I was sure that every juror's stare was trying to penetrate deep into my soul. My heartbeat thumped in my ears like drums.

Greg bombarded me with basic questions—"How old a man are you? What high school did you attend, and where did you go to college? When did you come to Ada and how long have you lived here? Have you ever been convicted of a felony, and did you lie on your school teaching application? Why did you resign your teaching position at Konawa, and where did you teach at next?"—and I did my best to answer them.

"Why did you go to Kansas City in 1987 after leaving Ada, and where are you living now, Dennis?" Greg asked.

"Objection, Your Honor. Not relevant," Peterson wailed.

"Overruled," Jones said, raising his voice more than usual.

Greg continued to question me about seemingly everything that had happened in my life. My answers to him were to the point. I offered only minimal amounts of explanation on the responses that needed it. As Greg ventured into some of the more complicated aspects, Peterson's objections grew in fervor and pitch, and Jones appeared to become increasingly annoyed at having to overrule him.

During the bench conferences, I had the opportunity to glance at the jury. What I saw on some of the jurors' faces—that closed, judgmental stare that told me their minds were made up—made me feel uneasy. I made up my mind to do everything I could to soften their attitudes toward me. Greg helped out considerably by asking me a multitude of personal questions that allowed me to relax and build confidence before I underwent questioning by Peterson. I looked at Mom and Aunt Wilma several times. Just the sight of them helped me to relax even more.

With a defiant look directed toward Peterson, Greg inched into the deeper parts of his examination. "When were you married, and how did that marriage terminate?"

"My wife was murdered. She was shot in the back of the head. It was a terrible thing that happened. We had been married from 1969 to 1975," I said with the honesty of regret.

"Where did that happen, Dennis, and was the perpetrator convicted?"

"It was outside of Durant, Oklahoma, in a small community called Mead, Oklahoma, and yes, he was convicted," I responded.

Peterson was fuming with impatience. He tapped his pencil loudly upon the table and glared at me with a look of dissatisfaction. Greg continued his torrent of personal questions: "Did you have any other marriages, and how many children? When you were teaching school in Noble, where did you live? This was a junior high school where you were coaching? Was your daughter living with your mother in Ada?"

I answered honestly. That was all I could do.

Changing the course of his questioning, Greg asked, "During the time you've been in jail, have you had occasion to have some conversations with Mike Tenney?"

I unloaded the whole truth about Tenney to the jury. I found that I was able to make casual eye contact with them and still maintain the detachment that Greg had instructed. It seemed that the jury was interested in what I had to say about Tenney's underhanded tactics, especially Mrs. Flowers, who was actually shaking her head in disbelief.

"How do you know Cynthia McIntosh, and do you recall a conversation she testified to here?" Saunders asked briskly.

As I explained the whole scenario of meeting her in the jail and what she had overheard Ronnie say to me, I could see Peterson rifling urgently through an open binder of papers. More than likely, I thought, they were probably some of the letters that I had written back to Cissy when we were in cells across from each other in the jail.

"How do you know James Harjo, Dennis?" said Greg nonchalantly.

I explained every detail of my association with James in the county jail—from befriending him initially, up and through the series of events that led to the explosive Halloween night when he came into my cell to accuse me of being guilty of having murdered Debbie Carter, and ending with the standoff confrontation and his verbal threats of making up something on me "pure as gold." The jury's stone-faced reactions showed no mercy or understanding. Every word, every sentence, and every detail I described—everything was the total truth but not a single indication came forth that any of the jurors believed me, especially Smith, who never blinked but instead watched me as though I were sitting across from him in an interrogation room.

I felt isolated, resentful, and angry on the inside, sitting up here fighting for my life and telling the honest-to-God truth, while everyone—except my mom, aunt, and Greg—stared holes of contempt through me. But feeling what I was feeling only made me even more determined to take on Peterson and make it clear that I was not going to let him provoke me into showing any weakness or uncertainty about my testimony.

Greg was pumped up and going full steam ahead as he asked me a series of questions that required detailed recollections: "What was the nature of your overall relationship with Ronnie? Do you remember Letha Caldwell pulling a gun on you and Ronnie? Explain to the jury about your conversation with Tony Vick when he told you about Ms. Carter's death. Were you having a water fight the night Gary Allen said that he recognized your voice? Dennis, do you recall where you were on the evening of December 7, 1982? Did you know Debbie Carter and have you ever been in her apartment?"

I answered him as accurately and honestly as I could.

Greg took a breath, and with his hand pressed to his chin, turned from the witness stand and approached the jury box. All eyes were glued to his every move as he strode in measured steps alongside the wooden railing to the far end and then halfway back, where he paused in suspended silence. With his body still facing the jury, Greg turned his head in my direction, and in a serious whisper, asked the question that everyone had been waiting to hear: "Dennis, did you kill Debbie Carter?"

Every sound in the courtroom ceased. Any motion that might have been occurring stopped abruptly and all eyes were riveted on me in a moment that seemed frozen like a photograph. Everyone waited to hear what I had to say.

"No, I did not," I answered without hesitation. "I did not kill Debbie Carter, and I don't know anything about the death of Debbie Carter whatsoever. I've been locked up over in that county jail for eleven months on circumstantial evidence, and I'm the kind of person that would never take a life. I've never thought about taking a life. I've never wanted to rape a woman. I've never had any thoughts of this kind of activity ever in my life."

"No further questions," Greg said in a subdued yet satisfied voice.

Peterson sprang from his chair and was up in my face before Greg even sat down. Bent on making me look really bad before the jury, he started pumping questions at me about how I had falsified both of my teaching applications and state certification documents to conceal my past felony conviction.

I admitted it. There wasn't anything to hide. As I tried, however, to explain the reasons why I had lied, Peterson cut me off and would not allow any explanation besides *yes* or *no*.

"And will you instruct him just to answer the questions, please?" snapped Peterson at the judge. His voice was shrill and belligerent.

"Counsel, approach the bench," Jones ordered.

Because I was sitting right next to the bench, this time I overheard their conversation.

"Okay," said Jones, looking straight at Peterson, "I'm going to instruct him. You may not like the defendant, but you're not to be angry in this courtroom."

"I'm not angry," Peterson retorted.

"Yes, you are. This is the first time you've raised your voice to this bench," Jones said in a voice of absolute authority.

Peterson dropped his head and the words "all right" squeezed out of his mouth like a school kid who had just been disciplined by his principal.

Jones turned to me and instructed me to answer Peterson's questions. As he did so, Peterson maneuvered himself tactfully toward the jury box and flashed the impaneled jurors a wide smile as if he were apologizing to them for his out-of-control courtroom behavior. I was laughing on the inside at how Peterson would instantly employ something from his bag full of theatrics when something didn't go his way.

"Did you ever on any other occasion falsify a record that would be kept by the government concerning your conviction?" asked Peterson in a modified tone.

"Not to my knowledge, other than these two occasions. I don't know," I said.

Handing me a collection of documents from Hill's Pawn Shop, Peterson asked if I had filled those out and answered *no* to a question about any prior convictions. I told Peterson that if I remembered correctly, Mrs. Hill, the owner of the pawn shop, had checked each of those entries when I went in to pick up my property. I explained that it had been a long time—some twelve years ago—but I did not recall marking the back of the form.

There was no doubt about it. Peterson was trying to make me out to be a liar before the jury so they would believe that I was also lying about not having raped and murdered Ms. Carter. It was a Grand Canyon leap for Peterson but he was doing his best to bridge that gap in the jurors' minds. My name had already been smeared all over the media for almost a year, so it wouldn't take much for the jurors to fill in the doubts they might have had in their minds.

The afternoon wore on as Peterson continued to parade before the jury by asking a volley of questions: "Isn't it a fact, Mr. Fritz, that you were fired from the Noble school system?"

"No, sir, I resigned."

"You told this jury that the reason you couldn't remember about a water hose in your backyard is because you had moved eight to ten times since 1982?"

"That was just an expression."

Peterson went on and on about the number of moves I had allegedly made in the past five years. All I could do was answer him until he finally changed topics.

"You told Mr. Harjo whoever did it had to be really crazy and probably wiped their fingerprints down?"

"Something to that effect," I replied.

"Don't you think, Mr. Fritz, that if Mr. Harjo was going to make up a story as 'pure as gold' on you, he could have done a better job?"

"Objection," yelled Greg.

"Sustained."

For ten minutes, Peterson raked me over the coals, asking one question on top of the other about my association with Ronnie. He was trying to get me to say that Ronnie and I had terminated our friendship over some alleged falling-outs.

"Did you all take girls out?" Peterson asked me.

"No, not to my recollection."

Peterson looked at me sideways and tried a different tact. "Okay, let me see if I can refresh your memory then. Do you recall going to Norman, Oklahoma, to the Holiday Inn with Ron Williamson?"

"Objection!" shouted Greg. "May we approach?"

Jones recessed for a short break, reminding the jurors of their instructions before they left the courtroom. While the jury was out, Greg requested to go on the record to clarify the question because he hadn't asked me during direct whether Ronnie and I took out girls, which meant that Peterson couldn't introduce it during cross, or at least that's what I understood while I remained in the witness seat.

Peterson's expression changed when Greg made the request. He glowered at him and at me.

"Your Honor, I don't intend to ask Mr. Fritz if he abducted that woman. I'm not going to ask him that. I'm not totally foolish," Peterson said defensively as he shook his head.

"What is the question about then?" Jones asked.

"The question is, you know, he's denying any kind of close friendship with Ron Williamson, and I can put them in a bar in Norman, Oklahoma, trying to pick up a woman there. And in fact, that's as far as I'm going to go with it at this point," Peterson said, sure that he was on solid ground.

"When was that?" Jones asked, seeking clarification. Something about what Peterson was saying wasn't making sense to him.

"Pardon me?"

"When was that?" Jones asked again.

"It was August of 1982 when this close friendship was supposed to have dissolved," Peterson explained.

Greg wouldn't let him have an inch of ground. "I don't think Dennis ever testified to that. And I didn't ask if they took girls out. I talked about the quality of the relationship. I don't think he ever said. He has used the word *friends, friends and acquaintances,* period. So Mr. Peterson can't open the door. He just can't open it," Greg argued. He glanced over at Peterson and then back to the judge and continued, "The basic problem is that the prosecution has tried to couch its case on guilt by association, and that puts me in a situation to have to explain the relationship. Otherwise, it wouldn't make any difference one way or the other. But that's the kind of problem.... We're off in left field now, where he's trying to bootstrap in some stuff that has nothing to do with the case. We're out here in left field."

Jones was trying to get to the root of the matter, while Peterson was trying to get Jones to buy his argument that I had already stated on direct that I had denied a friendship with Ronnie and that I implied that we had taken girls out just because I had answered that Ronnie and I had never been out on a double date together. Jones wasn't buying Peterson's stretch of an argument, though, and ruled against him on the grounds that it was beyond the direct examination and could result in reversible error. Since the jury was out, I didn't try to conceal the snicker and smile that slipped out as a result of watching Peterson receive another round of deflating defeat.

Peterson acted like he didn't notice my reaction but his tone reflected his irritation. "I've been doing this for ten years," he said to the judge. "I'm not going to ask the man on the witness stand if he abducted—"

Jones interrupted him. "Well, I'm not buying that argument. However many years we've been doing this is totally irrelevant," Jones said.

"He's denying a friendship with this man, Judge," Peterson argued.

"That's my point," Greg exclaimed. "When did he deny it? I'd like to hear when he denied the friendship."

Jones still sounded confused. "But the question we're talking about was, 'did you and Mr. Williamson date girls together?'"

"And he said 'no, this is not a date. I never said I went on a double date. That's not what I did,'" Greg replied.

"So what is the testimony that they dated girls together?" Jones still appeared to be searching for some connection between Peterson's question during cross and whether Greg had asked about any of this during his direct examination.

Peterson was quick to answer, "If he says no, then I was going to ask him, did he ever try to, did he and Ron Williamson ever try to pick up a girl?"

"And that is the evidence that you put in your bill of particulars?" Jones asked.

"Well, not necessarily that evidence, Judge. The evidence in my bill of particulars is that this woman was forced in a car and taken out by this defendant and Ron Williamson."

The judge looked at Peterson and shook his head. "I think this is beyond the direct examination and is a search for something that is prejudicial and would result in reversible error." With that, he sustained Greg's objection and Peterson had to resort to another line of questioning. Peterson didn't look at me as he returned to the prosecution table to wait for the jury to return.

After the recess, Peterson's mighty ego emerged in yet another round of overbearing questions in other areas that Greg hadn't touched upon in his direct. He wanted to know who my friends were back then, besides Ron Williamson.

"My daughter," I replied.

He wanted to know why I didn't have any male or female friends.

I told him that I didn't have time for friends because I was teaching school and raising my daughter. Peterson's invasive questions subsided. He had thrown everything but the kitchen sink at me but he could not get past the door that I would not allow him to enter. His face was taut with frustration but he held his feelings in because he didn't want to cross swords with Jones again.

Before finishing his cross-examination, though, Peterson

took one more stab at me. He wanted to know why I couldn't remember where I was on the night of the murder, and why I didn't think to check my school records to see where I was.

"Didn't it ever occur to you to do that?" he asked.

"No, I didn't have a reason to really have to know where I was at. I know where I wasn't, though," I responded.

"You've never seen Debbie Carter?"

"Yes, sir, this is my testimony," I replied.

"Never been in her apartment?"

"Yes, sir, this is my testimony."

"Never wanted to rape a woman and never had those type of thoughts in your life?"

"That is absolutely correct."

Greg's re-direct and Peterson's re-cross were very brief and covered nothing that hadn't already been asked. Jones stopped the proceedings and gave his usual instructions to the jury to not say anything to anybody over the weekend.

As the deputies approached to escort me back to the jail, Greg and Peterson stood before Jones in another bench conference. Tears were streaming down my mother's face as I passed by her. The guards were not about to let me give my mom and aunt a hug since the Carter family was still seated not too far behind them. They ushered me forward. With my head down, I avoided Charlie Carter's piercing stare.

CHAPTER 23

Without having had a chance to talk with Greg before being removed from the courtroom, I had no idea what was going to come next. I expected that the jury would reach a verdict on Monday or Tuesday because there wasn't much left for us to present, but that was of little comfort on Saturday morning as I sat in the bullpen. Greg had been very good at keeping me informed, though, and I had high hopes that he would pay me a visit before the weekend was out.

Ronnie was acting up again. His blood-curdling screams were so loud it was as if he were right here in the bullpens. After hearing him scream at least thirty times in a row that he was innocent and did not kill Debbie Carter, I quit counting. I stuffed wads of toilet paper in my ears to try to drown out the noise.

Several of the other inmates followed suit and packed their ears, too, in an attempt to muffle the nerve-rattling sounds that radiated from Ronnie's powerful lungs. At one point in late afternoon, I looked around the cell. We were quite a sight to see—all of the guys sitting around the table, slapping their dominoes as hard as they could against the tabletop, talking in loud voices, with ragged strips of toilet paper dangling out of their ears.

Not that our efforts to drown out the noise were very successful. Ronnie's howling continued throughout the night and into the early morning hours. I empathized with him. I knew well the horrific feelings that arose from the pressure of facing the death penalty. If howling would have been part of my nature, I might have howled, too. The stress was unimaginable.

On Sunday morning, while still in my bunk trying to catch up on sleep after missing breakfast chow, I heard my name being yelled out by a guard standing in the hallway. "Get up, Fritz. Your attorney's here to talk. I ain't got time to stand here waitin' for you all day. Come on, let's go," he commanded.

"All right! All right! I'm coming," I fired back.

Someone in the bullpen across from me hollered out for the guard to hold on to his panties because he was waking everybody up. Apparently Ronnie's rants had everyone on edge. The guard ignored the comment and ushered me up the hallway. I entered the visiting room and saw Greg standing by the glass door, looking out into the direction of the courthouse.

"Good morning, Dennis," he greeted. The clarity in his voice let me know that he had gotten a better night's sleep than I had. He seemed to be in a very chipper mood. "There's a few things that I want to talk to you about before Monday. They took you out of the courtroom so fast I didn't have a chance to tell you what Jones and I talked about."

I was still groggy but I listened eagerly.

"First of all, Bisbing will be the only witness that we'll call for your defense. I talked with him yesterday during the lunch break and he'll be here first thing Monday morning. From what I gather, he has known Hett for some time and has had some in-court dealings with him on the witness stand. That in itself will be in our favor since he's familiar with Hett's procedures, so hopefully he may be able to throw a few bricks into Hett's testimony. Secondly, after Bisbing's testimony, the state will put on two rebuttal witnesses to challenge your in-court testimony. They're going to bring Mike

Tenney back up and Norma Hill, the lady who owned the pawn shop that Peterson questioned you about." He paused.

I spoke up. "I was kind of expecting something like that from Peterson. I tell you, Greg, I have a distinct memory that Mrs. Hill checked 'no' to the section about the felony information. As a matter of fact, I'm absolutely for sure that she was the one who checked it because I remember thinking that I would get in trouble if I falsely marked it."

"As you've probably figured out, Dennis, Peterson is trying to paint a picture about you to the jury that you are the world's worst liar, and of course, he's implicating to the jury that you are lying about not killing Debbie, and there's nothing that I can do to stop him except deal with it on my cross-examination. Also, they were wanting to put Featherstone on the stand, and I objected—not only to using him as a rebuttal witness but also to Tenney and the pawn shop lady. Jones sustained my objection for Featherstone, but he wouldn't budge on Tenney and Mrs. Hill."

"Why were they wanting to put Featherstone back on the stand?" I asked.

"Featherstone said that you told him in your post-polygraph interview that you and Ronnie had it in mind to rape Lavita Brewer, the girl that they're saying you and he abducted at the Holiday Inn in Norman."

I was jarred to wakefulness in a hurry by his answer. My anger rose. "Boy, that really pisses me off, Greg," I sputtered. "Featherstone knows very well that I didn't say that. What I told him was that she thought she was going to be raped. I never said anything whatsoever about me having any intentions of raping her. I tell you what, Greg. I hate those lyin' bastards for setting me up like this. I specifically told Featherstone, Smith, and Rogers that I didn't have any thoughts about raping that woman. They've got a tape of that interview, don't they? Can you get hold of it?"

"Calm down, Dennis," Greg said. "I'm not in your position but I understand how I would feel if I was. And that brings us to the harsh reality that we have to talk about. If the jury does, God forbid, find you guilty, then we will go into the second stage of the trial called the penalty phase, where the state will be using Featherstone's and Brewer's testimonies to try and get the death penalty on you. As far as getting hold of the interview tape itself, I don't think that would be much of a problem since I could use it for the purpose of impeaching Featherstone's testimony, but what I'm more concerned about is not exposing the jury to anything that has to do with the lie detector examination, which they are claiming that you failed. For this reason, Dennis, and this reason alone, I have a bad feeling about getting into the post-polygraph interview, which could invariably open the door and allow Peterson to expose parts of the polygraph interview itself. Anyway, Dennis, I think there's better than a fifty-fifty chance that you'll walk out of that courtroom."

"Well, I'm glad that you think so, Greg. Personally speaking, I don't think that I have a snowball's chance in hell of walking free from that courtroom. There's just too many things that I've been feeling and seeing that tell me differently."

As I was being led from the visiting room, Greg came back into the doorway and hollered at the deputy. "I forgot to give these to Dennis. Is it all right if he has these earplugs?" Greg asked.

The guard took them and handed them to me.

Back in the bullpen, I recalled the look in Greg's eyes when he told me that I had a fairly good chance of being found not guilty. That look told me a much different story—his worried look didn't match up with his bridled sense of confidence.

Monday morning arrived. As I entered the courtroom, I instantly spotted my mom and aunt as they sat with their heads turned toward the courtroom entrance. Their facial expressions were lined with furrows of worry from the tension that the past few days had imparted. If the grim looks on their faces were an indication of what was to come, my life would be totally changed on this day to a life of misery and pain, either on death row or a lifetime in the state penitentiary.

The jurors, on the other hand, looked rested and anxious to get on with the day's proceedings. Jones gave Greg the go-ahead to proceed.

"Thank you. The defense calls Richard Bisbing," Greg announced.

All eyes gazed on Bisbing as he entered the courtroom. He walked briskly to the witness stand, his precise gait and astute look conveying an energetic air. After being sworn in, Bisbing described his background in the microscopic identification of hairs, fibers, serology, and some drug identification. After a lengthy description of his earned credentials, Bisbing settled back into his chair and conveyed to the court how Mr. Hett had provided him with the mounted pubic hair slides of my hair and the crime scene hair samples.

Greg went to the heart of the matter and asked Bisbing what his hair examinations revealed. Bisbing told the jury what Greg had already informed me of—that three of the pubic hairs he had examined showed to be microscopically consistent with the characteristics I possessed, with the remaining nine hairs showing dissimilar characteristics to mine.

With eyebrows raised, several jury members shifted uneasily in their seats.

"Just going by Mr. Fritz's known samples, is there anything about those that is unusual in any way, just in and of themselves?" asked Greg.

"They're normal pubic hairs. There's nothing specific, nothing particularly unusual about those pubic hairs, no," Bisbing replied.

Greg shifted then to the subjective science of hair comparison, and Bisbing repeated what Hett had already testified to—that it depends a great deal on the skill, expertise, and experience of the examiner.

I looked over at the jury box. Some panel members fidgeted in their seats, I presumed because Hett had already pounded them with this kind of talk during his testimony and they were wary of having to listen to more of the same.

"Can microscopic hair comparison ever be used for positive identification?" Greg asked.

"It can never be positive, never like fingerprints. You always have the possibility that there are other people in the world that have hair that looks just like this hair," Bisbing said.

"Is it possible or usual that two qualified individuals in the science of microscopic hair comparison could arrive at entirely different conclusions as in this case?" Greg continued.

"Well, I don't think that two people who are qualified and equally experienced and have performed the same test ought to arrive at different conclusions. There has to be some difference in the process, and that difference in the process is probably the individual."

"Does that occur where two individuals will arrive at different conclusions?"

"Certainly it occurs, yes," Bisbing concurred.

"And we're all human beings and perceive things differently. Isn't that correct?" Greg said as if he were gaining momentum.

"Yes."

When I glanced at the jury a second time, my heart sank. They looked like they had completely lost interest in what Bisbing was saying. They had already heard from the very beginning of Bisbing's testimony the words that they needed to hear—that three of my hairs matched. Everything else was beside the point.

"Can anyone positively identify the source of the evidence hair?" Greg asked.

"No," answered Bisbing.

The jury's attentions were turned to someone coughing loudly in the back of the courtroom. I doubted that any of the panel had heard his response.

"No further questions," said Greg.

It was Peterson's turn. The D.A. came at Bisbing with a

barrage of technical questions as to the makeup and physiology of hair, followed by another volley of queries about how hair is lost from the head.

Bisbing explained that hair is shed or lost naturally and that most people lose over a hundred hairs daily.

What was Peterson building up to? I guessed that he was just trying to build himself up for the jury, to impress them that he wasn't as stupid about the science of hair comparisons as he had been before Hett took the stand.

Peterson asked Bisbing why he did not look at the known and unknown hairs that were associated with my head. Before Bisbing could answer, Peterson wedged in a couple more questions. "Wouldn't it have been highly more significant to also look at Mr. Fritz's head hair? Don't you think that has any bearing on the source of those hairs to also examine the head hair, too?"

Bisbing was not bothered by Peterson's over-eagerness to ask multiple questions. He simply stated that he didn't think that head hair comparison has any bearing on the source of the pubic hairs.

Peterson wouldn't give up trying to use this as a ploy in an attempt to show that our defense expert hadn't done a thorough job in his examinations. "And from what you testified about, you spent approximately six hours examining these hairs. Is that correct?" Peterson asked.

"Yes," Bisbing answered outright.

"And Mr. Saunders asked Mr. Hett the other day, and I feel obligated to ask you this same question, does not the mental attitude or the way a person feels that day have a lot to do with the result?"

"It may, yes."

"Uh-huh. And would you tell the jury, if you will, whether or not you had a head cold that day?" Peterson reverberated.

"Yes, I did," Bisbing said with indifference.

"Thank you," said Peterson like he had just won a blue

ribbon in a sixth-grade sporting event. "And did you feel pretty good that day?"

"I had a head cold and a cough. I didn't feel real well, no," Bisbing stated with honesty in his voice.

"Thank you," Peterson repeated with childish sarcasm in his voice. "And you understand, do you not, that Mr. Hett spent not just five or six hours looking at these particular hairs and all of the hairs involved in this case, but several hundred hours?"

"I would believe that, yes."

Peterson rambled on for a few more minutes, asking Bisbing about some articles that he wrote in which hair examiners are trained to minimize their answers on cross-examination. Bisbing agreed, and Peterson yielded the witness. Greg had no further questions.

The rest of the day unfolded itself as predicted. On Peterson's rebuttal, Tenney testified that he had never mentioned or threatened me with the death penalty and that he never tried to influence me in any way to plead guilty.

Mrs. Hill's testimony was simple and to the point. She had aged considerably since I had seen her last, and her frail physical appearance in the courtroom solicited empathy from the jurors. She stated that, on several occasions, I had pawned the same pistol at her shop and that she had never filled out the questionnaire that asked whether or not I had ever been convicted of a prior felony. There was nothing that Greg could do or say in his cross-examination of Mrs. Hill that could rectify her truthful manner of speaking. To the jury, I was nothing but a flat-out liar when, in fact, I was almost positive that I had not misrepresented myself on the felony checklist information.

The state of Oklahoma rested its case, and Greg moved the court for a directed verdict. Jones quickly denied his motion.

As the proceedings shifted gears, Jones initiated his jury instructions, which contained all of the rules of the law that the jury had to be told in order to reach a fair and impartial verdict. After giving a lengthy recitation on several different points of the law, Jones informed the jury about finding me guilty beyond a reasonable doubt, reading the elements of the offense, what *drawing reasonable inferences* meant, the differences between direct and circumstantial evidence, determining the credibility of each witness, and the procedures of reaching a unanimous verdict. It seemed to me that the jury had heard most of these instructions during *voir dire*. Whether Jones realized it or not, the effect of his dry monotone came close to putting the jury to sleep as he rambled on in his lengthy recitation. Heavy sighs and long drawn-out yawns could be heard from the rear of the courtroom as the aftermath of Jones's instructions put everybody in a relaxed state. Then it was time for Shew's closing argument, which amounted to nothing more than a repeat of her opening statement—this time, with a little more lace and glitter wrapped around the package.

As Greg rose slowly from his seat for his closing argument, I broke out all over in a nervous sweat. Greg approached the jury. With a look as grim as death on his face, he began delivering his remarks. As he spoke, he walked the length of the jury box, pausing to explain critical issues that the jury needed greatly to hear: how it was unfair that I had had to recall events that happened over the extended period of seventeen years, and how the state's lack of evidence necessitated their only ace in the hole—guilt by association.

"Where's the evidence?" Greg exclaimed, extending his arms as he held out his open, empty hands.

After reading verbatim the instruction on circumstantial evidence, Greg turned square-faced to the jury and quoted another interesting idea concerning the law: "'All of the facts necessary to such proof must be consistent with each other and with the conclusion of guilt the state seeks to establish.' I mean, it's got to fit together. You can't have a bunch of loops in the thing, a bunch of holes in it. The state's witnesses got up there, and just said, well, I saw Williamson and I saw Fritz. That's all they talked about. They had to put that on because there was so little evidence going to the real fact. The real fact is, whether or not, if you buy the state's approach to this thing, they were together on the evening of December 7 and the morning of December 8. That's what they're trying to prove and they don't have any evidence on that. The only thing that makes any difference is whether they were together on the day in question. So, consequently, they try to overcome you with volume what they lack in substance. Where is the evidence of that association the day of the crime? Where is the evidence of that association the week of the crime? They've kind of glossed over that. They kind of forgot about that somewhere along the line."

One by one, Greg tore down the testimonies of every one of the state's witnesses, emphasizing that there was no degree of evidence that showed any involvement on my part.

"Glen Gore? Nothing to do with Dennis—just consistent with Ronnie Williamson. Gina Vietta? She wasn't concerned about Dennis—just Ronnie. Cindy McIntosh? Nothing to do with Dennis Fritz—only consistent with the guilt of Ronnie Williamson. Gary Allen? Certainly not the kind of evidence that proves anything, certainly not by a reasonable doubt. James Harjo? Said Dennis had told him 'we wiped everything clean.' Remember Jerry Peters's testimony? He said twenty-one prints had been found on various items. Is that consistent with what Harjo wants you to believe? What about the expert's opinions? Mary Long said Dennis is a non-secretor; so was Debbie! Melvin Hett? 'Could have been' were his words. Dennis Smith and Gary Rogers? They both said that Dennis had always told them he was innocent and never knew Debbie Carter and had never been in her apartment. And Rogers said — he talked about 'a great struggle.' Remember? More consistent with one or two attackers? Again, I feel like that's more consistent with a single attacker than two."

As Greg spoke, I watched the jurors' faces as closely as I could without drawing attention. It looked as though they were disengaged from everything Greg was saying. Why? I was sure that everyone except maybe Mrs. Flowers was convinced that I was guilty. Cecil Smith wasn't even really paying attention. The foreman, Wayne Sanders, was listening all right, but was he really weighing what Greg was presenting? The other seven women jurors were looking at Greg like he was talking nonsense. Why? My guess was that they couldn't get the horrific impact of the duplicitous crime scene pictures out of their minds.

Greg paused in front of one of the women on the panel. "I'm going to ask you to do this. When you hear Mr. Peterson's argument, where he says something, I'm going to ask you to do this. Say, 'What would Saunders say about that? How would he respond to that?' If you'll do that in your mind, then it will make it a fair deal. I mean, I don't get another chance to talk to you, but if you'll just ask yourself, 'What would Saunders say if he had another opportunity?' it will be a fair deal.

"Ladies and gentlemen of the jury, this is an extremely serious case. I ask you to give it your serious consideration. You responded to Mr. Peterson during *voir dire* examination—most of you—that you wouldn't guess things that aren't there. You wouldn't guess somebody in trouble. If the state hasn't proven it to you beyond a reasonable doubt, by your instruction, by your oath, you must acquit. I appreciate your time. I appreciate your efforts. Thank you," Greg concluded.

With a look of indifference upon his face, Peterson placed his hands upon the prosecution's table and hoisted himself to a standing position, as if he were the king of Sheba looking over at his flock of jury servants. With his flamboyant arcade of gestures, he moved to and fro in front of the jury, presenting his closing arguments in a slapdash charade of orchestrations of how Greg had understated the magnitude of the case against his client.

"Defense counsel wants you to guess his client not guilty. He wants you to assume a lot of things, but there's only one eyewitness that could tell you exactly what happened to her, and she's dead. Counsel wants you to think that there was one person involved in this."

Peterson knew that he had the full attention of every juror and he was doing everything he could do to take advantage of that opportunity by tearing down Greg's closing argument.

"There's things that defense counsel forgets. You know, we want to put this behind us. We don't want to look at this right up front. Remember the testimony of Mary Long? She examined her fingernails—no skin, no debris, no nothing. Think about that. A woman will use her fingernails. I don't care who they are," said Peterson, pausing at a section of the jury where four female jurors were sitting together.

"There would have been blood of the donor. There would have been skin of the donor. There wasn't any. No marks anywhere on her wrists, her ankles, and Dr. Jordan concluded that the bruises here might be defensive wounds. Defense counsel wants you to assume that Debbie Carter fought for her life against one person. You know, when I was a little boy and I'd tell my daddy a lie, he'd look me right in the eye and say, 'son, that's hogwash.' And that's what we've got here."

Greg sprang from his chair and exclaimed, "Excuse me!"

"Counsel, approach the bench," Jones instructed with irritation in his voice for having been drawn out of his meditative state.

"I'm not going to allow that!" Greg demanded, his voice loud enough for most of the courtroom to hear him. "He cannot do that. He changed the burden of proof already. He's changed the burden of proof by talking about me having to—asking them to assume anything. That isn't the law."

Jones sustained Greg's objection in part and addressed the jury.

"Ladies and gentlemen of the jury, credibility of the evidence that you've heard is not for the attorneys in this case, and there's wide latitude in discussing the evidence, but it's for you to determine credibility, and personal opinions by counsel are not a proper part of this case." After a brief pause, Jones lowered his head and returned to his meditative state.

Peterson continued in his purposeful ploy to undermine Greg's rationale that the state had failed to put me and Ronnie together on the night of the murder.

"Counsel says the state's case is guilt by association. Well, to a certain degree that's true, but not the whole case. The only thing that is relevant in defense counsel's idea of guilt by association is that we're able to show: one, that these two people aren't strangers. They knew each other very well, very well, that it was a continuing relationship from 1981 to 1983. Why?" Peterson gestured with his arms stretched out wide, as if he were telling the jury a yarn about the size of a catfish he had once caught. "Why would we want that kind of evidence to show this association and friendship, longstanding friendship between this defendant and the defendant, Ronald Williamson? Because there was hair found in Debbie Carter's home that matched these two defendants. That's why."

Peterson hammered the stake deeper and deeper, always reminding the jury of his own reasonable theories that were always just the opposite of what Greg had presented. The jury's attentions hinged upon every word, every pronunciation, every emphasis that Peterson used to sway the jury to his way of thinking. On and on he went, parading back and forth, downplaying the believability of Greg's remarks. I could sense Greg's irritability building as he fidgeted in his seat with every little jab that Peterson used to belittle him.

"You know, counsel has got to jump on James Harjo. He's got to push James Harjo behind him somehow. He's got to get rid of him. Can't believe James Harjo. Can't do it because, if you do, he's made a very incriminating statement," Peterson ranted on.

Greg mumbled a few choice words under his breath, unable to do anything but sit and watch the mounting humiliation.

"Tommy Glover didn't see Debbie Carter there that night in the bar, but does that mean that she wasn't in the bar? Of course it doesn't. Counsel's asking you to abandon your common sense and say that because nobody saw Dennis Fritz, he wasn't there.

Nonsense," Peterson conclusively stated. "Ron Williamson lived a block away from Debbie Carter, and Dennis Fritz lived six blocks from her and drove a car. Do you think he could have driven up there to Ron Williamson's house, went in the back door to Ron Williamson's bedroom, said 'Let's go get a beer at the Coach Light?' Also, counsel says that because Cindy McIntosh can't remember what Dennis Fritz's response was to Ron Williamson's statement, 'Was she still on the floor or on the bed,' Dennis Fritz didn't have anything to do with this," said Peterson. He turned from the jury and pointed in my direction, displaying his usual smirk.

Greg lowered his head. I heard a faint chuckle in the gallery.

Peterson continued, "Gary Allen's testimony is, to say the least, interesting. He's heard his voice on numerous other occasions, if you'll recall. And he hears this same voice at three o'clock in the morning. And I think he used the words 'cussing and laughing,' and he looks out his window. There's a porch light down there, and he sees two people with their shirts off, washing themselves off."

I immediately grabbed my notepad and scribbled down that Allen had never testified to any washing having ever taken place. Greg glanced downward and nodded as Peterson continued.

"I recall Mr. Tenney's testimony that this defendant said 'suppose it happened this way.' And then, after he gets through with what this defendant said, the questions are asked to him, how many people over there tell you they're innocent, and he says every one of them."

"Objection!" Greg said in a strained voice. "May I approach?"

I could only hear a part of Greg's argument, saying something along the lines of misconduct or mistrial or maybe both, with his voice ringing out a continuing objection near the end. I barely overheard Jones overrule his objection. Jones thereafter instructed the jury that they weren't allowed to consider Peterson's last statement.

For the next twenty minutes, Peterson went on and on about Hett's testimony, explaining to the jury that his expert had tested all the hairs, whereas Bisbing had only tested the pubic hairs. "You know, counsel wants you to disregard the hair evidence because it's not fingerprints. That's what he wants you to do because it doesn't fit with his reasonable theory. You can't accept the hair evidence because, if you do, then his client is in trouble. But he wants you to not consider that hair evidence, but even his own expert testified, if you recall, the question was asked to him—and it's the most recent thing in my memory—so, 'what you're saying is it's not like fingerprints that eliminate everyone else in the world but that one person. Is that right?' 'Yes, that's right," Peterson mimicked in an exaggerated tone followed by a pause as he stared into each juror's face.

Greg strenuously objected, and at a bench conference, renewed his motion for a mistrial based on prosecutorial misconduct after Peterson commented about what the likelihood was of two people out there in the great wide world with similar hair that didn't know each other showing up at Debbie Carter's apartment. After the conference, the proceedings continued and Peterson made the same statement a second time to the jury. Greg objected again, this time his face flushed red with impatience. The courtroom was quiet as counsels and the judge sorted out Greg's objection.

Peterson then spent twenty more minutes attacking the credibility of my in-court testimony, pitting my alleged misrepresentations before the jury and using them as a foothold to convince the jury that his witnesses had no reason to lie, and therefore I was lying about having not raped and murdered Debbie Carter.

The whole courtroom was ready for Peterson's closing argument to end, including the judge, jury, bailiff, and court stenographer—all of them had looks of browbeaten exhaustion. But Peterson was not through as he went another round by explaining to the jury how he had proven the elements of murder in the first degree in both of the charged counts against me—"the evidence indicates that he was an active participant," Peterson emphasized with great confidence. "But, of course, no one saw anybody stick their penis in Ms. Carter, did they? On defense counsel's theories, then it didn't happen because nobody saw Dennis Fritz in Debbie Carter's apartment, so therefore it's not Dennis Fritz," Peterson whimsically offered.

After going into a drawn-out explanation over Jones's previous instruction on circumstantial evidence and its implications as to how it related to the totality of evidence against me, Peterson finally got around to giving his summation to the jury.

"Ladies and gentlemen of the jury, Debbie Carter was brutally murdered on December the 8th, 1982, and the evidence in this case is overwhelming that Dennis Leon Fritz and Ronald Williamson took her life the evening of December 8th. I've done my duty. The witnesses for the state of Oklahoma have done their duty. And I'm going to ask you to do your duty and return a fair and just verdict in this case. Thank you."

In attempting to decide if there was any further need for the alternate jurors, Jones immediately asked the impaneled jury if they had any health problems or any concerns about their ability to continue with the case. From the jury's silence, Jones separated the alternates and told the jury to go on into the jury room and, after lunch, begin their deliberations until reaching a verdict, whereupon they would advise the bailiff and their verdict would be announced in open court at that time. Jones expeditiously excused the alternate jurors and also the attorneys for the state of Oklahoma. While Greg renewed his objections to Peterson's closing argument and moved once more for a mistrial, a team of guards surrounded me to escort me back to the jail. My mom and aunt patiently waited in the seats as I attempted to stop in mid-aisle to hug them. With looks of sorrow and humiliation on their faces, my mother lunged forward to hug my neck with one of the flanking guards nudging me onward, out of my mother's clinging embrace and back to the jail to await the jury's verdict.

Instead of being placed in the bullpen, I was put into my old isolation cell adjacent to Ronnie's. I could not sit down and just do nothing. I dropped to my knees on the dirty floor and prayed for divine intervention that the Lord would fill each juror's mind with the knowledge that I was innocent and bring forth from them a verdict of not guilty. I humbly asked the Lord for protection over my daughter and family. I could hear Ronnie calling out to me, wishing me luck as I prayed.

A couple of hours dragged slowly by before a guard appeared at my window and informed me that the jury was ready to come back into the courtroom. My heart beat wildly as I made the long walk back through the courthouse and up to the third-floor courtroom. The jury filed in with looks of frustration upon their faces. Mrs. Flowers had her head bent over. Her open palms covered her face. She looked as though she had been crying. She also looked like she was being put under an intense amount of pressure. Wayne Sanders, the jury foreman, informed the court that the jury had a question that was reduced to writing. Jones instructed Sanders to hand the paper to the bailiff, who handed the paper to Jones.

"Is this a request to hear testimony again?" Jones asked the jury foreman.

"Yes, sir," replied Sanders.

Following a bench conference, Jones explained to the jury that the court could not read back certain portions of the testimony, and that they would have to go back and consider the evidence and use the instructions he had previously given.

I was returned to my cell. The minutes seemed to tick ever so slowly into hours before I was called back into the courtroom.

Everyone in the courtroom was already in place. I asked Greg the time.

"Six-thirty," he said as he nervously awaited the jury's entrance.

I immediately noticed that Mrs. Flowers was visibly upset

and hid her face in her hands again. This time, Jones wanted to know if the jury was making any progress toward reaching a verdict. He cautioned the jury foreman to not say anything about how the jury stood as far as finding a verdict of guilty or not guilty. Jones wanted to know if the jury had taken any kind of poll to indicate whether they could reach a verdict, or were they still discussing the evidence?

Sanders indicated to Jones that the jury had been split 11 to 1 for the past hour and a half. There was no question in anyone's mind that the juror who was holding out was Mrs. Flowers. Jones ordered that the deliberations be continued. Wiping the tears from her eyes, Mrs. Flowers stood with the rest of the jury and walked back into the jury room.

Again, I was taken back to my jail cell. I was in no mood to talk to Ronnie as he offered his consolations. I tried to stay deep in meditation and prayer.

"Come on, Fritz, let's go," a guard's loud, unnerving voice yelled into the bean hole window. "The jury's reached their verdict." The guard unlocked and opened the cell door and I stepped forward. I was ready for whatever lay ahead. I could do no more. I realized that my life was now in the hands of God as I walked that long sacrificial walk back to the courtroom where the jury of my peers would shortly render judgment upon me. I held my head high as I entered the courtroom and took my seat beside Greg, who put his arm around me and wished me the best. He sounded sincere but tired.

While we waited for the jury to come in, Jones spoke to everyone in the courtroom who was observing the trial. Looking beyond me in the direction of my mother and aunt, Jones announced that the jury had reached a verdict and that if anyone wasn't sure whether they could control their emotions, they should go ahead and step out of the courtroom. No one budged. Jones told the bailiff to bring in the jury.

With their eyes and heads held low, the jury walked in and

somberly took their assigned seats. The majority of the female jurors starred downward with a blank expression upon their rigid faces. Three of the four male jurors gazed straight ahead. Just as Jones asked the jury foreman if the jury had reached a verdict, Cecil Smith arched his head in my direction and looked squarely at me, as if to let me know that I was getting what I deserved. I didn't have to hear the jury's verdict being read. I already knew what the outcome was going to be—just as I had known from day one of the trial.

"Mr. Sanders, would you please hand the papers to the bailiff, please?"

"Read the verdict, please," requested Jones.

"Verdict Criminal, State of Oklahoma, County of Pontotoc in District Court, the State of Oklahoma versus Dennis L. Fritz, Defendant, Case Number CRF-87-90. We the jury drawn, impaneled and sworn in the above entitled cause do upon our oaths find the defendant guilty of Murder in the First Degree. Signed, Wayne Sanders, Foreman."

Though I had mentally prepared myself for a guilty verdict, I wasn't prepared for the torrent of feelings that swept through me. I lowered my head and remained seated, feeling for the first time a sense of paralysis as I listened to the muffled sobs of Mom and Aunt Wilma behind me. The lights in the courtroom swirled and spun as I grew weak and numb with the reality that I had just been found guilty of a murder that I knew nothing about. I had no reserve of energy or passion left to stand and shout to the jury that they had made a terrible mistake. Instead, my thoughts shifted to more immediate questions: How would Elizabeth react after hearing this news, how would Mom and Aunt Wilma deal with this decision physically and emotionally, and finally, how would I face this same panel of strangers as they decided whether I lived or died? I didn't look at Greg. I couldn't.

Jones's voice brought me back to the present. He read down through the roster of jurors and polled their verdicts one by one.

Greg had said this would happen as a matter of procedure. No one faltered as they each stated their verdict: "Guilty." "Guilty." "Guilty...." Their words of finality pounded against my eardrums.

"State has nothing further," said Peterson in a throttled voice.

"Defendant has nothing further," Greg replied without emotion.

"All right," said Jones as he spoke to the jury. "As you have been told, there's another part of this trial, and we will commence that at nine o'clock in the morning. Remember your instructions I've given you. Do not let anyone attempt to talk to you and do not discuss this with anyone when you're outside the courtroom." Jones banged his gavel and released the jury.

Greg put his arm around my back and helped me up out of the chair to release me to the clutches of the deputies that surrounded me. The whole courtroom seemed to be spinning out of control. I heard the clicking of the handcuffs and felt the cold steel meshing tightly around my wrists as I was led away from the defense table and up the aisle where my mother and aunt stood. Tears flowed from their swollen eyes and dripped from their cheeks. Without asking the guards for approval, I went straight to Mom's and Aunt Wilma's open arms. Nothing else mattered right now except being near them and allowing them to embrace me. One of the guards nudged me to move forward, but when it became obvious that I was not going to move until my family had their opportunity to console me with their hugs and kisses, all of the guards backed off and allowed us some time to say our goodbyes. When I was ready to go, I stepped back from Mom and nodded.

The bullpen was unusually quiet as I walked down the corridor of the jail. I was emotionally crushed and in a state of shock as I entered. The other inmates gave me space as I changed out of my suit back into my jail clothes and slid into my top bunk. Without a word, I stuffed in my earplugs and turned toward the wall. I tried not to think of tomorrow.

Chapter 24

I awoke the next morning from an agonizing sleep. I could barely remember what had happened yesterday after the verdict was read. Everything seemed so suddenly surreal. It wasn't like I didn't have any indication or perception that this was going to happen, but now, the stark reality of conviction was knocking at my door. All of my hopes that I might be found not guilty had shattered, and all that remained were fragments of what I had imagined might be freedom and happiness. Everything was changed.

How could this happen when there was absolutely no evidence that showed my actual involvement in the alleged rape and murder? How could I have been convicted upon the strength of uncorroborated lies and misrepresentations? And now, some girl was going to testify that Ronnie and I had abducted her when in fact she had voluntarily gotten into the backseat of my car because she wanted, or so I had thought, to cruise around and listen to some music. Just the thought of Featherstone taking the witness stand and telling the jury that I had admitted to him that I had intentions of raping her was more than I could swallow. I loathed him. A man who had taken an oath to uphold the law and protect the innocent

was now going to swear in open court before God and man that
I had said something that went against my very nature and my
interviewing statements.

Anger and resentment surged through me as I pictured his
rosy cheeks as he took the witness stand. I was not going to sit here
in a pool of pity and lose all of my determination and fight because
someone might distort the truth, my truth. That had already been
done once. I wasn't about to let them do it again without letting it
be known that I wasn't some weak, whimpering shell of a man. I
wanted the interview tape to be played before the jury to show them
that I had not made any such guilty statements to Featherstone. I
wanted the jury to hear what I had said — that the girl thought she
was going to be raped and that I stopped the car to let her out!

I pulled myself out of the bunk and got showered and
dressed, anticipating that the day held little hope for anything
besides despair but prepared to fight in whatever way I could. I
drank a cup of coffee and waited for the guards to arrive.

The courthouse atmosphere was electric. Onlookers in tight
little groups spoke in whispers about the possibility of observing
firsthand a convicted criminal about to receive the death penalty. I
met their stares and nods with my head held high. Ernie, the guard
who had always seemed a bit more human than the rest of them,
made a few jokes to me on the elevator as we ascended to the third
floor of the crowded courthouse.

"Good luck, Dennis," he said with a smile as we walked
from the elevator to the courtroom.

The looks on Mom's and Aunt Wilma's faces as I neared
them expressed the sheer horror and confusion brought on by the
tremendous stress of their worry about the death penalty. Their
eyes brimmed with wetness, and they struggled to hold back their
tears. As I passed, I paused to speak to them.

"Everything will be all right," I said. "I love you both very
much."

Before the jury was ushered in, Greg requested a bench

conference and moved the court for a directed verdict on the issue of the death penalty for the reason that there was no evidence that indicated that I was the perpetrator. He further indicated that the state's best evidence only tended to show that I was there.

"And if you believe that, you're just cold. I'm dead serious about it. I don't think that the jury can be asked to speculate as to what role he would have under this evidence, and there is no evidence whatsoever that he was a direct participant," Greg argued in an excited voice that I could hear from where I sat at the defense table.

Peterson quickly responded by saying that there was evidence that I was a participant in the sexual intercourse of Ms. Carter because my pubic hair was found in her bedroom.

Jones disagreed. He said that he was going to overrule the objection, but there had to be more proof than what Peterson just mentioned because rape does not necessarily lead to death. Peterson stood still and said nothing.

Greg then objected to the presentation of evidence in the bill of particulars for the reason that the alleged abduction occurred prior to the charged murder. He used the example that, since the statute of limitations had expired on the underlying felony of rape, then the prosecution could not use the abduction evidence as an aggravating factor.

Leaning forward, Peterson put both of his hands on Jones's bench and refuted Greg's argument by saying that defense counsel was entitled to go back to my childhood and put on mitigating circumstances, so therefore, the state of Oklahoma was entitled to put on any and all aggravating circumstances with no restrictive time limits.

Jones overruled Greg's motion and told Peterson that he was relying on his argument. "Are we ready to proceed at this time?" Jones asked.

Greg said that he was.

"Bring the jury in," Jones ordered.

With their heads hanging low, the jury members filed to their seats. With a look of duty on their faces, they awaited the proceeding to begin. This time, instead of trying to avoid looking at the jury, I maintained a proud and dignified expression as I looked at each juror to let them know that I still had nothing to hide and that they had made a terrible mistake in having found me guilty. No one returned my glances. They kept their eyes focused on the judge.

Upon Jones's permission to proceed, Peterson read to the jury the bill of particulars in *rem punishment*. It stated that I had committed the charged murder and should be punished by death due to the following aggravating circumstances: One, the murder was especially heinous, atrocious, or cruel; two, the murder was committed for the purpose of avoiding or preventing a lawful arrest or prosecution; and, three, there was the existence of a probability that the defendant would commit criminal acts of violence that would constitute a continuing threat to society. Peterson read his name at the end of the statement, "William M. Peterson, District Attorney," and then added, "To this bill of particulars, the defendant has entered his plea of not guilty."

Then he began his opening statement by telling the jury that the prosecution would adopt and reintroduce the evidence from the first stage, and then present the defendant's prior conviction for unlawful cultivation of marijuana, and, finally, present the testimonies of Rusty Featherstone and Lavita Brewer. His voice was particularly enthusiastic as he gave a brief description as to what Featherstone's and Brewer's testimonies would encompass and then he asked the jury to recommend to this court that I be put to death.

"Mr. Saunders," Jones said with expectation.

"I'll waive," said Greg without emphasis.

"All right, Mr. Peterson, call your first witness."

Before calling Featherstone to the stand, Peterson moved the court to reintroduce and reaccept the evidence that was presented in the first stage of the trial.

Jones advised the jury that the evidence that they had previously heard would be considered as a part of their penalty phase decision.

Followed by the bailiff, Featherstone entered the courtroom and took his place on the witness stand. Featherstone recalled having an interview with me on June 6, 1983, wherein, he told the jury, I had relayed to him that Ron Williamson and I had gone to the Holiday Inn Club in Norman, Oklahoma, and begun drinking and dancing with girls. The defendant, Featherstone said, befriended a woman and asked her to go out with him and told her that he had a portable bar in the back of his automobile. The defendant and Ron Williamson accompanied the female to his car, Featherstone continued, and as she entered the vehicle, Mr. Fritz sped away from the parking lot.

I started writing notes to Greg, hand over hand, that I had never danced with this girl and never asked her out or told her that I had a bar in the back of my car. Peterson pumped Featherstone for details, and as he continued to testify, I scribbled comments on my notepad for Greg.

"At first, he told me that at one intersection he was afraid for her safety, and he stopped and let her out," Featherstone said, his expression serious and focused. "He later told me that was not true, that she had gotten out of the car as he slowed at an intersection."

"Lies! Lies!" I scribbled on the tablet and pushed it in front of Greg.

He looked at my words but did not respond.

"Did he ever mention to you his thoughts that he was having about this young lady?" Peterson asked Featherstone with a tinge of mocking in his voice.

"Yes, sir, he did. He stated that the thought of rape had entered his mind, primarily because of the proximity of the girl in the vehicle with him, the circumstances of her being with the two of them. He stated that he hoped that wouldn't have to happen, that once they got to wherever they were going, she would become willing."

"Yield the witness," Peterson stated abruptly.

I grabbed my notepad and started to write a message to Greg that that was a bald-faced lie that I had never said under any circumstances, but Greg bounded from his seat before I could finish and began questioning Featherstone.

He was brief with his cross-examination. He asked Featherstone when this alleged incident occurred, and Featherstone said he was not sure of the date.

"Dennis did say he was concerned about her safety because she became excited? Is that your testimony?" Greg asked.

"At the initial part of the interview, yes, sir."

"This idea—this thought of rape—wasn't that as a result of the conduct of Ronnie Williamson? Isn't that why Dennis said that he became concerned, because of the conduct of Ronnie Williamson in reference to this girl?"

"That's not the way I recall his statement, sir," voiced Featherstone with a little sarcasm. He admitted that he had taken notes and that there was a report made but didn't know if they still existed.

Greg wanted to know if the interview had been recorded. Featherstone said that it had been and that there was a video made of that interview.

"No further questions," said Greg.

"Call your next witness," Jones said in his methodical way.

"State calls Lavita Sue Brewer," Peterson announced.

Asked why she went to the Holiday Inn Club on the particular night in question, Brewer said that she had known the band that was playing there, and that, due to her recent divorce, she decided to go out by herself and be among her friends in the band. Peterson was noticeably anxious and wasted no time in getting to the point.

"And did anyone talk to you or come around you that evening?"

"The defendant asked me to dance a couple of times," replied Brewer.

"I couldn't tell at first, but later on, a guy that he was with came by the table, and there was a short introduction, but he didn't stay long," Brewer recounted.

"Could you describe him for us, please?"

"The other man?"

"Yes."

"He was a tall, big man, and he had bushy hair and a big nose. That's really all I can remember."

Quickly, I fumbled for my pen and wrote Greg a message that she was getting me and Ronnie mixed up. He didn't look at it immediately, so I reached over and put my hand on it again and moved the note back and forth so he would notice. He acknowledged me with a nod, then continued to listen intently to her testimony.

As I well knew, Brewer was mistaken because Ronnie was well over six feet and I was only five feet, nine inches tall. And Ronnie had the bushy hair, and I had the big nose.

Brewer continued to answer Peterson's questions, stating, "The defendant asked me out, but I told him that I wasn't really interested in seeing anybody at this time and that I also had plans. And when the lights came on, he came up to me and told me about the bar in the back of his car and asked me if I would like to see it. And I said no, I told him I already had plans, but when I walked out of the club, their car was parked in front of the doors. They told me again about the bar, and I—"

"When you say they, are you talking about both of them?" queried Peterson.

"No, it was mainly Mr. Fritz I talked to all night."

This time I didn't write a note. I leaned over and told Greg that was another bald-faced lie. "Greg, did you hear me?" I asked emphatically.

"Yeah, I read your note and heard what you said, but I need to listen to her testimony," he quickly answered with a slight turn of his head.

"What happened then?" Peterson asked, practically drooling to get to this point in her statement.

"He repeated again about the bar, and I stupidly sat down in the backseat and that's when they took off with me "

"Would you describe for the jury, if you would, the trip that you had with this defendant and his passenger."

Brewer, in her fragile way of speaking, told the jury that she had became hysterical and started crying and begging to be taken back, and shortly thereafter, she felt the car starting to slow down, so she was able to open the car door and she jumped out and ran between houses and down alleyways before calling the police.

"Yield the witness," Peterson said as he hastily turned and walked to his table.

As I was about to tell Greg to ask Brewer about her confusion over our identities, Greg lunged from his chair and began his cross-examination of Brewer.

"Ms. Brewer, you were in a highly excited state?"

"Yes, sir."

"Is it possible that Mr. Fritz stopped the car in order to let you out or slowed the car in order to let you out?"

"No, sir, I'm sorry," answered Brewer with an unequivocal response.

"That's not what happened?"

"No."

As Brewer stepped down from the witness stand, Peterson announced with a plastered smile that the state of Oklahoma rested its case. Still standing, Greg informed the court that he would waive his opening statement and that he, too, rested.

Jones gave lengthy and complicated instructions to the jury regarding their duty in determining which penalty to impose. With a look of seriousness, Jones explained to the jury that the phrase *especially heinous, atrocious, or cruel* as described within the bill of particulars is to be directed to those crimes where the death of a victim was preceded by torture of the victim or serious physical abuse. Without inflection or a change of pace in his delivery, Jones carefully clarified the meanings of aggravating and mitigating circumstances and how they were to be considered in arriving at a verdict, and how the circumstances should be weighed to decide which of the three punishments they opted to impose. He was meticulous in his delivery, going over every little detail, looking over his glasses as he spoke, eyeing the jury with looks of expectation as he rambled on to the end of the assigned instructions. He qualified to the jury that they must not use any kind of chance in reaching a verdict.

"It must rest on the belief of each of you who agrees with it," he advised. Finally, in closing, Jones reminded the jury that their verdict must be unanimous upon either the death penalty, life imprisonment, or life without parole, and that proper verdict forms must be filled out and individually returned to the open court.

Jones looked at Peterson, who then rose from his seat and walked slowly to the jury box with a gleam of confidence in his eyes. After looking at each of the jurors, Peterson began his closing argument: "Ladies and gentlemen, I think the evidence shows in this case overwhelmingly that Debbie Sue Carter was murdered in an especially heinous, atrocious, and cruel manner. Her young life was taken from her, and I think you can see from the photographs and pictures that she received serious physical harm to her body from the beating that she took and the instruments placed in her body. And if you recall, the doctor said that those injuries were not committed after her death. They were committed while she was alive.

"The evidence shows that there was a sexual attack on her body. And the evidence shows also that there was no need to take her life. The murder was committed for the purpose of avoiding or preventing a lawful arrest or prosecution. They eliminated an eyewitness. She could no longer go to the police."

Peterson took a breath and moved slightly away from the jury and then turned, as if he was giving the jury time to digest what he had just said, then walked slowly back toward them. All eyes were riveted upon him.

I waited anxiously, fully expecting to hear his final words that he hoped would condemn me to death. My palms were wet and clammy, and my heart was racing wildly as the intensity of Peterson's statements mounted.

"And number three, the existence of a probability that the defendant would commit criminal acts of violence that would constitute a continuing threat to society. You heard Ms. Brewer's testimony. You heard Rusty Featherstone's testimony as to what was going through this defendant's mind as he was racing through Norman. I'm going to ask you to recall the testimony at trial where the defendant tried to mitigate his involvement in this crime by telling James Harjo 'we didn't mean to hurt her.' Ladies and gentlemen, recall the photographs," said Peterson as he gestured open-handedly to the jury and awaited their reactions. "If, 'we didn't mean to hurt her,' I don't know what would be meaning to hurt someone after reviewing those photographs. Not only was his head hair found but his pubic hair and semen was found in the vagina of Debbie Carter. I don't know how more major of a participant you can become in the rape of somebody.

"Ladies and gentlemen, the evidence in this case cries out for the death penalty, and the state of Oklahoma is going to recommend to you that you recommend to this court that this defendant be sentenced to death. Thank you." Peterson returned to the prosecution table without looking at me.

Greg then stood, approached the jury, and gave his closing statement. "I'll be very brief. I've never stood before twelve people and asked for a gentleman's life. Each one of you, when you entered the jury box, carried with you your own set of values, your own conscience. I think it would be highly improper of either the prosecution or me to tell you what your conscience would indicate and what your conscience dictates.

"Some of you voiced reservations about imposing a death penalty. I ask you to review those reservations for the reasons that are inside you, not the reasons I would give you. I'd ask you not to violate your own conscience because, when this case is over, you're going to have to live with yourself either way you decide. You're going to have to look in the mirror and say, I participated in that verdict, and you ought to be able to feel good about it, no matter which way you go. So, I'm not going to tell you which way to go. That's not my place; that's not my part. You have your own set of values, and you have to live with yourself. So, I would ask you to search your soul and come forward with a verdict that you can live with. Thank you very much."

As Greg was seating himself, Peterson popped out of his chair and told the jury in a dramatic voice not to let defense counsel place the burden of guilt on them for something I did. He told the jury that it would take courage for them to recommend the death penalty and asked them to come back in the courtroom and say, "Dennis Leon Fritz, you deserve to die for what you and Ron Williamson did to Debbie Sue Carter." His finger was pointed directly at me.

"I didn't kill Debbie Carter," I exclaimed.

Jones and the jury made no response. I might as well have not said it.

Following the jury's departure to the jury room, Greg once again motioned the court for a directed verdict on the same basis as before—that there was not one bit of evidence that showed my involvement, only with the possible exception that I might have been there.

In a single breath, Jones denied the motion, announced a recess, then told the deputies as I was being handcuffed that the court would call for me when they were ready for me.

The spinning motion in my head gained intensity as I was removed from the courtroom and taken back to the isolation cell. I had difficulty breathing. I felt weak all over. I nervously paced the floor waiting for the jury's life or death decision. I despised Peterson, despised him in every way one man can despise another whose disregard for the truth and the value of life was so blatant and evil.

I dropped to the floor and began praying for divine deliverance to not receive the death penalty. I was beyond caring about anyone seeing me on my knees, pleading to the Lord for my life. I heard Ronnie speak my name. He sounded as if he were a great distance away.

I don't know how long I prayed. Time no longer had definition or meaning. With only the smell of concrete to remind me where I was, my mind whirled with disbelief and thoughts of escaping. I prayed for deliverance. I prayed for a miracle. After a time, I felt a warm and relaxing sensation spread over my chest and throughout my body. I couldn't be sure how long that feeling lasted.

The slicing, rough sound of the guard's voice calling to me jarred me from my deep state of prayerful meditation. "Come on. It's time to go back," he said.

I went, relaxed yet uncertain. In the courtroom, the jury foreman handed his written question to the bailiff as I looked at each juror's hardened set of features and melodramatic straight-ahead stare. As before, Mrs. Flowers was bent over with her head in her hands, quietly weeping.

"For the record," Jones said, "the jury states, 'We are 11 to 1. What happens if we cannot be unanimous?' Mr. Sanders," — the judge directed his gaze to the foreman — "has the jury reached the point that no progress could possibly be made toward a unanimous verdict?"

"Yes, sir," replied Sanders.

"Was the jury ever divided in any other way than 11 to 1?"

"No, sir."

Jones advised the jury to go back into deliberations and reconsider the evidence available to them with the instructions he had given and to take one more opportunity in considering this matter.

Again, the handcuffs were slapped around my wrists and back to the jail I went, the memory of Mom's and Aunt Wilma's ashen, fearful faces in my mind. I hadn't been back in my cell half an hour when the guard returned and took me back to the courtroom.

"The jury has reached a verdict," Greg said as I was seated at the defense table.

I braced myself for the worst.

Jones repeated his announcement to the viewing courtroom that anyone who could not control his or her emotions should leave. No one budged. The jury members entered the courtroom and took their assigned seats.

"For the record, the jury has returned to the courtroom. Mr. Sanders, has the jury reached a verdict?" asked Jones without emotion.

"Yes, sir."

"Would you hand the papers to the bailiff, please?" ordered Jones.

I took in a deep breath and looked over my shoulder at Mom and Aunt Wilma, who were nervously shifting in their seats. I crossed my fingers underneath the table where my hand rested upon my trembling legs.

After a deafening silence, the bailiff began reading the verdict: "We, the jury, drawn, impaneled, and sworn in the above entitled cause do upon our oaths, having heretofore found the defendant, Dennis Leon Fritz, guilty of murder in the first degree, fix his punishment at life in the state penitentiary. Signed, Wayne Sanders, Foreman."

I could not contain myself any longer. I stood and let the words flow, "Ladies and gentlemen of the jury, I would just like to say to you—"

"Excuse me," Jones said, raising his voice as he looked over the rims of his glasses at me.

"Dennis, you can't do that," Greg warned as he stood in his seat and faced me.

I ignored them. "My Lord Jesus in Heaven knows that I

didn't do this. I just want you to know that I forgive you and I'll be praying for you," I blurted out.

Jones's instructions to me to be seated barely registered. I sank to my chair and listened as the judge told the jury that they were excused. Pandemonium erupted as the spectators clamored their approval of the verdict. Amid the racket of their spirited jubilation and the jostling of the deputies as they snapped the handcuffs around my wrists, I heard the painful, heartfelt cries of my mother and aunt. I couldn't look at them. I couldn't look at anything as I was escorted from the courtroom. I could only imagine what lay ahead.

Chapter 25

The agony of not knowing whether I would live or die was at last behind me. Now I knew that I would not have to spend the next years of my life suffering on death row while awaiting appeals. Though I didn't know very much about the system, I had heard that most of the medium-security prisons had law libraries that would allow inmates the opportunity to work on their own cases. I didn't know where I would be sent, but if I was lucky enough to get into a medium-security facility, I would have a fighting chance to reverse my case and prove my innocence.

The sight of my suit hanging at the end of my bunk triggered thoughts of Mom and Aunt Wilma and their physical safety while they were in Ada. I figured that since I hadn't gotten the death penalty, there might be some crazies out there that might want to get more revenge than what the jury had meted out. And then, too, there was the possibility that the Carter family was bent out of shape over what they might have considered was too lenient a sentence. Who knew if they might decide to take matters into their own hands? After all, I couldn't discount all of the death threat rumors I had heard.

After a long and worrisome night, I was allowed to visit with Mom and Aunt Wilma the next morning before they went back to Kansas City. It was a miracle in itself that Ron Scott granted them permission to visit me, especially since I had just been convicted and this was not a regular visiting day. Although the ten-minute visit was brief and a plastic shield divided us, we had a wonderful, close visit that ended as others had—with our hands to the plastic, followed by a prayer for strength, faith, and thanks for allowing me to get a life sentence instead of death or life without parole. We reassured each other that everything was going to be all right and that they would come to see me when I was assigned to my new prison home. My mother informed me that Peggy Carter, Debbie's mother, had fainted on the courthouse lawn while I was being brought back to the jail after receiving my life sentence.

Almost before the visit had really started, the guard knocked upon the door. With Mom's and Aunt Wilma's hands still lingering on the plastic shield, I reluctantly left through the rear door while looking back over my shoulder. My last glimpse of their tearful expressions caused my heart to ache. It would probably be several months before I would get to see them again.

Ron Scott escorted me back to the bullpen and took my suit to give to Mom. He came back and asked me whether I wanted to waive the ten-day waiting period and go on to the penitentiary, or wait, which might take up to two weeks or longer. I told him that I wanted to stay. I didn't give him any reasons why. He couldn't have cared less anyway. The main, underlying reason that I wanted to stick around for a while was to hear the outcome of Ronnie's trial. The trial date was scheduled for April 21, which was a little over a week away.

I had heard from the other guys in the bullpen many wild tales about the bad things that happen in prison. The stories about rapes and stabbings didn't scare me as much as the thought of having to be locked down 24/7. I couldn't imagine anything much worse than where I was right now, with the disrespectful farting, slapping and slamming of dominoes, and earsplitting snoring. The idea of being unable to retreat to a little privacy now and then gave me the creeps.

Then there was the matter of being confined and what it was doing to me physically. Not only had my mind slowed, I had gotten a little on the fat side and always felt sluggish and sleepy. What else could be expected after eating stale doughnuts every day for almost a year? They were always there and probably didn't cost the jail any more than the gas to go get them. It sure wasn't out of the kindness of their hearts that they gave us doughnuts, especially since the meal portions had gotten smaller and smaller. Aside, though, from wanting to know how Ronnie's trial would play out, I was more than ready to get out of this hellhole.

The plan, Scott told me, was to transfer me to the Lexington Assessment and Reception Center (LARC), where I would be emotionally and physically evaluated before being assigned to a penitentiary to start serving my sentence. I was filled with a lot of apprehension about how the new surroundings would be. Everyone I talked to said that the amount of time that anyone ever spent at LARC was less than a month. In my mind, that was lost time; I wanted to get to the penitentiary as quickly as possible so I could start work on my appeal. I was a good reader, and I was sure that big mistakes had been made at my trial that I would be able to challenge before the courts.

The days crept by. I slept a lot to pass the time. Ronnie's trial started, and everyone kept their fingers crossed in hopes that he wouldn't start yelling again. He had not made much noise for a while from up in his cell toward the front of the jail. On occasion, he had bellowed the first few bars of a hymn with great zeal, but then he would stop just as abruptly as he had started. We kept hoping the quiet would continue.

The silence lasted for only a couple of days. On about the third day into his trial, after he was brought back to his cell, Ronnie ranted, raved, shouted, and screamed well into the night, until everyone was delirious with fatigue and anger after listening to his wailings. Ronnie's trial lasted eight days and those were eight days of sheer pain and torment for me, knowing that Ronnie was closer than he had ever been to cracking up.

At the end of the last day of trial, word came back to the bullpen from one of the trusties that my old buddy had been found guilty and that the jury had given him the death penalty. That evening, everyone waited for Ronnie to begin his vigorous screams. Not a peep came from his cell—not just that night but for several days. At the end of the weekend, he was moved into my bullpen, where he silently paced the length of open area throughout the day and evening hours. His unpredictability had everyone in the cell on pins and needles. We all seemed to be waiting for the moment when Ronnie might go off.

On a few occasions, I tried to talk to him but he was totally oblivious to anything I said. At times, he would stop pacing and stand in a stationary position and stare up in the corner of the bullpen in a trance for several minutes. Then he would start pacing again. He was in a world of his own. Nobody wanted to encroach upon or disturb that place for fear that he might get caught in the web of Ronnie's dark and secret hideout, wherever that was, where his wrath and fury festered.

It was late afternoon in the middle of the week when Ronnie's moment arrived. We had more or less gotten used to his pacing, of his passing by the picnic table as he walked from the front of the cell, where the bars were, to the back wall. I was in my bunk. The other guys were sitting at the table, starting a game of dominoes. We were all waiting for chow to be served. I was watching the game mostly for self-preservation purposes; I didn't want to be caught off guard by the irritating sound of a domino being slammed to the table.

Ronnie stopped at the picnic table for an instant but he didn't speak. He just raised his fist suddenly and crashed it down with all his might onto the table's metal surface, causing dominoes to bounce and scatter. Several fell onto the floor. The players looked at him with fear, surprise, and shock upon their faces. Ronnie turned and continued his pacing as if nothing had happened. In the bone-chilling silence that followed, each of the players got up from the table and guardedly returned to their cells. So did Ronnie but without any measure of caution.

Shortly thereafter, one of the inmates who stayed on the top bunk across from Ronnie in the rear cell came into my cell at the front of the bullpen and asked me if I would consider changing places with him. He said he didn't want to be that near to Ronnie if he were to go off again. I agreed to do so and moved my mattress and belongings back to the top bunk in the darkened cell. Ronnie sat in an upright position at the rear of his bunk, staring up at the ceiling in a hypnotic state. He seemed totally unaware of my presence.

After climbing up into the bunk, I let a few minutes pass, and then I spoke. He and I were the only ones in the cell. "Ronnie, did you kill Debbie Carter?" I softly asked as I stared straight into his eyes. There was no response. I hesitated and then continued. "Ronnie, if you did kill Debbie Carter, I have a right to know. I've also been convicted of this murder and I think it would only be fair of you to tell me since I now have to endure a life sentence."

Again, there was only silence, as if Ronnie never heard a word I had said.

Just as I was about to speak again, Ronnie lowered his gaze from the ceiling and stared into my eyes. His lips barely moved as he said: "I don't want to talk. I want to go to sleep and die."

Those were the last words he spoke to me. I was called out of the cell the next morning for the sixty-mile ride to the Assessment and Reception Center in Lexington, Oklahoma. With apprehension, I sat silently in leg shackles and handcuffs in the presence of two other inmates as the squad car sped toward its intended destination. When I had taught school in Noble, I had passed by the prison every day, never thinking in my wildest dreams that I would one day be a prisoner in such a hellish-looking place.

The greenery of the rolling countryside mocked the gloominess of the reality that awaited me. Unwanted feelings of desperation and sorrow unleashed pangs of doubt and fear as the harsh sight of the razor-wire fences around the lifeless, dreary, concrete structures came into view. A suffocating feeling came over me, and my heart pounded heavily and fast in my chest.

The gates opened as we drove up to the receiving center. We were unloaded and immediately taken to the commander of operations, where we were processed in. We were given clothing, a mattress, bed supplies, and an issue of personal hygiene products. I was then escorted to an area that looked like a huge gym, where there were tables in the center and closed-door cells that opened and closed electronically. I was assigned to a two-man cell. My cellmate was a man who looked like he might be from Mexico. It didn't bother me that he couldn't speak any English. I wasn't in any mood to talk, anyway. He kept to himself, and so did I.

Feeling alienated and unsure about what I could expect in this place, I sat in the cell and gazed out the slit of a window at the radiant sunshine—something I had not been exposed to for almost a year in the county jail except for those infrequent walks between my cell and the courtroom. The sunlight, and the window, gave me a sense of openness and that allowed me to relax somewhat. I scanned my new surroundings and for a moment felt as though I had just come straight out of hell itself and was now cast into an intermediate level of Hades while awaiting my assigned prison.

During the course of the day, the cell doors were popped open automatically four times—three times for chow and once for an hour of daily exercise and a shower before being locked back down. Medications were made available for the inmates who had health issues. What a difference this place was—compared to the county jail.

On the second day, I was assigned a counselor who informed me that I would have to undergo a series of emotional and physical tests that would have a direct bearing on which prison I would be sent to. I told the counselor that I was innocent of the charged crime and wanted to get in a prison that had a good law library. The counselor seemed uninspired by my declaration of innocence and simply said that a reviewing committee would determine my assigned placement. She also informed me that I would be required to attend an upcoming orientation where someone with the prison would present an overall listing of all the rules and regulations for any and all prisons in the state of Oklahoma.

After asking her what prison was the best one to be in, she said in a frank tone of voice that I was very lucky to have not gotten the death penalty and that I would very likely be assigned to a medium-security prison, but there was always the chance that I could be placed in maximum security at McAlester. She went on to say that the Joseph Harp Correctional Facility was considered to be the Cadillac of the state's prison system because it had an open yard where visitors could come inside the prison and have dinner with their incarcerated family members. She gave me the names of some of the other medium-security prisons: Mack Alford in Stringtown and the Dick Conner Correctional Center in Hominy. Lexington itself, she said, had its own medium-security facility.

That night, for the first time since my arrest, I was able to see the stars and the moon from my cell window. I longed to feel the cool spring breeze blow across my face and hear the sounds of summer crickets following a rainstorm. As I peered through the heavy molded glass into the darkness outside, I realized how much I missed so many things that I used to enjoy: the weekend camping trips, driving down the freeway on a summer night with all the windows down, playing guitar, the excitement of dining at a nice restaurant, being able to go anywhere at any time the urge struck.

Most of all, though, I dearly missed my family and all the good times that we used to have together—the laughter and joy of sharing birthdays, helping Mom plant her spring garden and dig through the soil for worms for a fishing trip, spending time with Elizabeth and hearing her call me "Daddy." All of that was gone. I had been thrown into a world of madness and turmoil, with strangers who could care less about my feelings or my dreams to be free again. The unbearable pain of having to withstand the torment of no one believing in my innocence, or even caring, was almost more than I could fathom.

Why had this happened to me? What had I done so wrong in my life that I should deserve this kind of punishment? My cellmate ground his teeth and mumbled something in Spanish in his sleep. A guard came by and shone his flashlight in on us and then moved on without a word. How much more of this madness lay ahead of me?

A lifetime, Dennis, my inner voice rudely reminded me. I answered in a whisper under my breath, "However long it takes to prove my innocence, I will not give up—I will not give up."

The next morning began with the long, tedious process of getting a physical exam. I stood in what seemed like a never-ending line for hours among noisy, cocky inmates whose constant babble made the day even more nerve-racking as it wore on. Everyone referred to the attending doctor as "Goldfinger" due to the fact that, at the end of the physical, he checked everyone's prostate by ramming his finger up where the sun didn't shine. That seemed to be the high point of humor for the day, and everyone made a big deal that the doctor's fingers were large. Without wanting to get off into that idiosyncrasy, I kept to myself and tried to be friendly but without the horseplay and games.

A guy directly behind me who looked to be about my age started up a conversation. He had tattoos on both of his arms and his accent was decidedly southern.

"Man, where'd you fall out of?" he said in a quick-witted voice.

"Pontotoc County," I replied.

"Yeah, I've heard some stories about that place. Been through there a couple of times and there wasn't really much action going on, so I had to split and get on back to Bob Macy Land in

Oklahoma City. How much time did they give ya?" he asked after enjoying a big yawn.

"They gave me a life sentence for something I didn't do," I remarked.

"Well, this is my second hitch in Oklahoma after I got through doin' a couple of small hitches in Arkansas. Believe me, man, you sure don't wanna get busted in that state. Oklahoma's not much better but those hillbillies in Arkansas wanna keep you down as long as they can."

"Where did you do your time at in Oklahoma?" I asked.

"Bob Macy Land, bro. Oklahoma County, and that's not no joke. All I pulled was some short time at Jess Dunn outta Tulsa," he proudly replied with a restrained laugh.

"Next to Joe Harp, what other medium prisons do you think would be acceptable?"

"Man, don't get me to lyin' cause there ain't none of 'em that I wanna be in. I hear that this place ain't bad for the chow but they are really strict in enforcin' every little rule you can think of. They say that Stringtown used to be the place to go, but the place is on lockdown now after they burned it down last week. The worst place of what I hear is Conners. It's named as the dumpsite of all the mediums in this god-forsaken state. Anybody that can't make it in the system always ends up at Conners."

The line started moving as a burly guard announced that chow bags would be passed out shortly.

"Ain't nothin' but bologna anyway, and I've had my fill of that shit to last me a lifetime," the tattooed guy said. "Naw, man, they tell ya that you can put down where you wanna go but you'd be real lucky to get into Harp. More than likely, it'll be either this place or those other two dumps. Who knows, I may be there with ya. I scratched out a couple of twenties this go-round, and they're both runnin' consecutive so I'll be pullin' about fourteen years before I can be a good citizen again."

I grew quiet again. After several hours, I was finally ushered into the exam room, where I met Goldfinger, who was indeed a very large man with very large fingers. Now I understood why everyone was so excited when they came out from the exam room. Before being taken back to my cell, I had to give blood to be tested for HIV and other contagious diseases. After having visited Goldfinger, a needle in the arm definitely didn't warrant a complaint.

During the rest of the week, I took a battery of tests that were required for the emotional evaluation that would help the committee decide which penitentiary to send me to. The days passed by very quickly. In the middle of the third week, while on lockdown, I was informed by one of the guards that my counselor wanted to speak with me. After all the doors were opened, I quickly made my way to her assigned area and anxiously awaited her arrival. I had stressed to her that I wanted to get into a penitentiary that had a good law library and one without too much violence. Because of what I'd heard, I was very apprehensive about having to go behind the walls at the state penitentiary in McAlester. I had chosen Joe Harp as my first option and Lexington as the alternative, in the hope of staying as close to my daughter as possible. Harp and Lexington were both in central Oklahoma, only a couple of hours away from where Elizabeth resided in Duncan.

The counselor wasted no time by informing me that I would be going to the Dick Conner Correctional Center in Hominy. My heart sank as she spoke the words. She further stated to me that I had scored favorably on my emotional tests and that the committee's decision was based upon the population needs of each penitentiary. Being the pleasant person that she was, she smiled and told me that the Dick Conner facility had a good law library and that its bad reputation was overrated. She wished me good luck in proving my innocence and said that I would probably be shipped out some time around the first of the week.

Chapter 26

Not a soul on the old green and white-striped Department of Corrections bus spoke as we rolled through the dreary, gray afternoon toward our first stop—the state pen at McAlester. Departure from LARC had been swift and without warning. I had heard the sound of cell doors popping open, followed by a guard at my doorway telling me to pack my gear and meet in the gym. When all of us were assembled, we were told to follow the officer in command to the property room where we would identify our belongings, and then, after being handcuffed and shackled, we would proceed to the bus for transport to our assigned prisons.

I was so relieved that I hadn't been assigned to the Oklahoma State Penitentiary — or Big Mac, as many of the inmates called it. On the long bus ride, my mind wandered through the complex situation that had now become my life. I thought of Elizabeth and how she must have reacted when she found out that I had been convicted. I recalled our one and only visit in the county jail. The vivid memory of Elizabeth's horrified look when the guard announced that the visit was over and I was led out the door made me shudder with sadness. Why was my daughter being punished, too? Wasn't it enough that Mom and my aunt had to endure this nightmare, let alone my thirteen-year-old daughter who had been through so much already? And now I was en route to the worst medium-security prison in Oklahoma, staring at a life sentence. A cold, sickening feeling flushed over me as I glared out the bus window at the gloomy day that was fading into darkness.

The old bus roared up the prison entrance road, past the eerily illuminated walls toward the entrance of the Oklahoma state pen. None of us said a word as the bus groaned and bounced with every bump and ridge in the road. Maybe we understood that the jarring and jostling that we were feeling would be the last such experience we would have for a long time.

Several of the inmates who had been involved in the fires at the Mack Alford center were unloaded at Big Mac. As I looked out at the lonely perimeter surrounding the prison, my thoughts turned to Ronnie. Shortly, he would be taking his last bus ride to this same prison to begin his sentence of death. I believed that Ronnie would probably never make it to the death chamber, not with the amount of inner suffering that he had already been through. With his family's history of health problems, he would probably die of a massive heart attack just from the sheer stress of being on death row. Ronnie's tormented screams echoed through my mind as I looked out at the harsh, strife-filled reality of the towering white concrete walls interlaced with tangled strands of razor wire that glimmered in the dewy night. The handcuffs and shackles dug deeper into my flesh as I shifted in my seat.

Within thirty minutes, the bus was rolling again along the darkened highway toward its final destination—the Dick Conner Correctional Center. Apprehension gave way to boredom, and I dozed as we forged steadily ahead. I wasn't sure how much time had passed when I awoke to the sight of a tall, foreboding chain-link fence surrounding the perimeter of the correctional facility. This sight was vastly different from that of the O.S.P. The Conner facility was situated in a valley and looked like it was surrounded by wooded areas. Its housing structures stood a couple of stories tall and looked like they might be made of stone or stucco. It was hard to tell at this distance. In front of the housing complexes stood an irregularly shaped building.

The blinding brilliance of the perimeter floodlights cast a forbidding and lonely aura around the heavy fencing and the area beyond it, toward the woods. I could feel myself growing smaller with each second that passed. A rush of excitement pulsed through me and my heart pounded as the brakes of the bus squealed to a stop at the clearance gate. The attending guard motioned us on. The bus lurched forward past the gates, and the numbing silence that had traveled with us for hours gave way to sighs, yawns, and rustling as we prepared for the next stage of the trip. The air grew thick with apprehension and tension.

I didn't know the exact time but I guessed it had to be somewhere around midnight. My ankles and wrists had numbed from the steady pressure of the restraints. Whatever lay ahead had to be an improvement over my present state of emotional and physical distress. The bus turned sharply to the right and sped a short distance through a parking lot to get into a drop-off position in front of the illuminated double doors. At last, the bus rumbled to an abrupt halt.

"Stay in your seats and refrain from any talking," the female guard rasped. The doors of the bus flapped open as the attendant guard stepped down and rang the buzzer on the outside of the building. The double doors swung open wide, and we were instructed to slowly stand and walk single file off the bus into the semi-lit building. Once inside, we were further ordered to a waiting area where we—six other inmates and I—sat in a half-darkened room. We waited in silence for what seemed like an hour until two guards arrived, switched on the lights, removed the handcuffs and shackles, and ordered us to go to another section off to the side of a rotunda, where we were processed in.

We then changed into the orange jumpsuits that they provided and received a mattress, blanket, and pillow. We were then escorted out of the rotunda through the main compound, where the guards ushered each of us up to our prospective units. Two other inmates were alongside me as we walked up a sloping sidewalk to the last building unit at the top of the hill. The guard announced that this was the V and W unit, where we would be housed. Another guard inside the unit unlocked the door gate, and I was taken inside the V unit up to cell number 213, where another inmate lay asleep in one of the beds. I set my mattress down softly and walked back to the locked door and switched off the light. The sleeping inmate never budged. The remainder of the night was extremely hot. Despite the open slit of a window, no air circulated in the cell.

I awoke to the sound of the door being opened, just like the doors had been opened at LARC. I had barely slept. The heat had caused me to perspire to the point that my body was sticky with sweat against the plastic mattress. My cellmate shot out of bed without saying a word and vacated the cell. I sighed deeply at the prospect of having a little privacy to relax and investigate my new surroundings. The cell was approximately twelve feet by fifteen feet with a double locker attached to the wall, a commode, a sink, and a mirror made of plastic. I ventured to the door and looked out, not wanting to be seen by anyone that might be outside. Several inmates dressed in street clothes were seated on a concrete bench on the lower level as if they were waiting for chow to be called out.

All in all, it looked like a fairly clean place. There was a telephone, and I could see a double set of showers on the top and bottom floors. The thought of calling Mom and Aunt Wilma and my daughter came to mind, but I felt awkward in the jumpsuit when everyone else was wearing normal clothing and didn't want to venture out where the others would gawk at me.

"Chow out! Chow out!" the guard on duty shouted at the top of his lungs.

I peeked out the window and saw a herd of other inmates

hurriedly making their way out of the unit and down the sidewalk. I noticed one of the other inmates that had come up to the unit with me. He was making his way with the rest of the group in his orange jumpsuit, acting like it was no big deal. He and the others broke into a downhill run.

I was starving, so I decided to follow the crowd and get something to eat and see what the place looked like in the daylight. Waiting until most everyone had left, I followed the last inmate down the hill and around the corner of what appeared to be a gym that extended to the side of the centrally located chow hall. The first thing I noticed when I walked in was that the blacks were seated on one side and the whites were on the other. I went through the serving line, got my tray, and sat down at a table by myself on the whites' side. Sitting among all types of criminal offenders in this harsh and chaotic environment caused me to feel awkward and alienated. The realization sprang forth in my mind that I could never under any circumstances accept these surroundings that I was now being forced to live in.

No one appeared to take any notice of my presence so I finished eating and made my way out to the compound area. I was looking for the law library. I walked past what appeared to be the kitchen, then the laundry room, and back toward the left where I had been brought in the night before. I tried to act nonchalant, like I had been here for a while, as I made my way back up towards my unit. I peered into all the windows as I made my way around the circle in the compound. At a building set back from the other structures, I peeked inside, and behold, I saw volumes of law books on floor-to-ceiling shelves against three walls. The room looked fairly spacious, with three long tables and three manual typewriters. For the first time in months, I was excited. I couldn't wait to begin to work on my case.

In the afternoon, one of the unit workers knocked at my cell door and relayed a message that the unit manager, Linda Lazelle, wanted me to report to her office for further assessment and orientation. I combed my hair, splashed some cold water on my face, and left immediately. Her door was open but I knocked anyway. She invited me in and I was introduced to a case manager and a unit counselor. They all seemed very friendly as they took turns explaining to me the rules and procedures that each inmate was expected to follow on the unit and in the prison. They informed me that I would have to attend an orientation, then get a job, and that I would be expected to attend several classes dealing with rational behavior and stress management over the course of the next several years. After thoroughly looking over my jacket review that had been forwarded from LARC, Ms. Lazelle looked up at me with her dark, sparkling eyes. I guessed her to be somewhere in her mid-thirties.

"Mr. Fritz, I see that you were convicted of first-degree murder," Ms. Lazelle candidly commented.

"Yes, that's what I was convicted of but I'm totally innocent of having murdered anyone," I matter-of-factly stated. "I have no knowledge whatsoever of who committed this murder."

I waited for a response. There was none. The silence in the room was offset by the sound of a small oscillating fan in a far corner. Ms. Lazelle quickly glanced at the other two team members and then looked back at the file in front of her.

"I see here, Mr. Fritz, that you were a junior high science teacher before your arrest?" asked Ms. Lazelle, breaking the uncomfortable silence in the room.

"Yes, ma'am, I taught seventh-, eighth-, and ninth-grade science at two different schools here in the state."

"Mr. Fritz, would you be interested in being a tutor on the unit? We would like to build up our G.E.D. program on V and W, and we would welcome you if that's what you would like to do. If not, then you will have to get another job on the unit or on the yard sometime within the next two weeks."

"Yes, ma'am, I would be very interested in the tutor position," I replied after a moment of thought. "What would the pay be?"

"Mr. Fritz, all of our jobs, no matter what they are, start out at $7.20 a month. If you stay with the job and do well, we could probably get you raised up within a year to the highest pay scale, which is fifteen dollars," Ms. Lazelle said with a smile.

"Isn't there any jobs at this prison that pay more than fifteen dollars a month?" I respectfully asked.

The case manager spoke up first. She was about the same age as Ms. Lazelle and spoke with a very soft and kind voice.

"Mr. Fritz, the only other job that you could apply for that would pay more than the fifteen per month would be out at the Oklahoma State Industries. There are two factories out there. One makes license plates, and the other one produces garments for the entire prison population within the state. But you would need to be here for at least six months of clear conduct before you would be able to go outside the main gate."

"Do you know how much I would make out there on starting pay?" I asked. "The only source of income that I have right now is through my mom and aunt, who make very little cleaning houses."

"I'm not exactly sure what their pay scale is out there, but since you would have to be here a little while before applying for that job, it might be in your best interest to take the tutor job or some cleaning job on the unit."

I knew right off that I didn't want to be a janitor so I told the unit team that I would accept the tutor position and start whenever they were ready for me. Before the meeting ended, I asked when I would be able to get out of the orange jumpsuit and back into regular street clothes. Ms. Lazelle informed me that my property was on the way up as we were speaking but that the unit team would have to inventory it before releasing it to me.

I left her office with a good feeling. I had a job, I still had my sanity, and soon I would get my property—what little there was—and be free of this Easter bunny suit that made me feel conspicuous and paranoid. I only had one purpose in my mind as I returned to my cell. As soon as possible, I wanted to get to the law library and begin studying the law — to do everything I possibly could to legally prove my innocence and rightfully reclaim my stolen freedom.

But, before anything else, I wanted to give my mom and aunt and my precious daughter a call and let them know that I was all right and that there was nothing for them to worry about, that I would be back home sooner than they might believe. That sense of urgency to talk with them was delayed, though, after I found out that I had to put their names and numbers on my calling list and that it could take a month for approval before I could place any outgoing collect calls.

My property arrived, and I was wearing my normal clothes before the late afternoon lockdown for the 4:15 count. My cellmate was very shy and seemed to sleep the majority of the time. At least, he didn't snore or pace the floor during the night. I was quite satisfied that he never wanted to talk or have anyone else over to the cell. I took full advantage of the quiet and was looking forward to what the unit staff had told me when I had picked up my property, that sometime next week I would be assigned a permanent cell on either one of the units.

The unit manager also informed me that the ball field and walking track would be open on a daily basis in the afternoons and evenings, with movement times every fifteen minutes on each hour of the day. I quickly mentioned to her that I wanted to work on my own case and asked about the operation of the law library. She didn't know the exact times but believed that inmates also had access during the afternoons and evenings. She added that the institution had a leisure library that was open during the same times.

The first day had been long and tiring. So far, it wasn't as bad as I had imagined. After eating chow, I discovered that the law library was open until nine o'clock. I spent the remainder of the evening browsing through the library, marveling at how many books I had access to, and daydreaming of the time that I would be free again.

Chapter 27

Most everything about Conner was a drastic improvement over the miserable and suffocating confines of the county jail. During the weekend, I ventured out onto the ball field and walked the unpaved track without any guards watching over me. I visited the leisure library and discovered that it was air conditioned, and it had many different books to choose from. The law librarian was a strict disciplinarian and kept the noise level at a minimum, which made for a much more relaxed environment.

It felt so wonderful to have the freedom of movement with a variety of choices. I could now breathe fresh air and feel the radiant sunshine on my skin. When I compared this to what I had endured for nearly a year in Ada, it was as though I had entered the gates of heaven. Even the food was tastier and offered more variety. We could go to the canteen once a week, and televisions and radios were allowed in our cell—if a man was fortunate enough to have money on his books to afford such luxuries. We were allowed visitors during the week and on weekends, and we had daily access to the gym and nightly access to the chapel. We could also receive Christmas packages from our families that could include clothes and all sorts of fresh-baked goodies.

There was also a downside to the pleasantries at Conner. The units were extremely noisy and chaotic in the evenings after the staff left for the day. Only one guard remained on each of the two units to maintain order. It was a never-ending battle to have any privacy in the cell, as inmates would rove from door to door, searching for cigarettes or a handout of something to eat. The short-timers—guys with sentences of twenty years or less who were called "youngsters" by the older inmates with long sentences—would play little grab-ass games and wrestle on the floors outside the cell areas, begging for attention. They were incredibly inconsiderate. Loud noises and cussing always accompanied such events and usually resulted in a fistfight to establish who was the toughest.

Homosexuality and drugs were rampant on the units. There were the so-called "girls"—guys who would dress in short-shorts and shirts cut and pulled down around their shoulders and wore lipstick and makeup that had been smuggled in by visitors. They would stealthily make their way around the unit, staying out of the guard's sight as they went from room to room. They smoked pot and performed sexual acts for favors or cigarettes, which were the main currency used to buy drugs or food from inmates who ran "stores" and sold food or stored-up canteen out of their cells.

The inmate motto was to beat the system in any way that they could. Their livelihood depended upon their prison smarts and their ability to smuggle whatever they could get, whether it was food from the kitchen or drugs through the visiting room. The latter always required a "packing mama," who was usually a large, fat woman that nobody was interested in physically who would cram her vaginal cavity full of marijuana or pills bound in a baggie and tightly wrapped with black tape that was lubricated for easier insertion. After waiting in the long line for visitors, the mama would make her way into the visiting room, where she would meet her man, wait for a while, and then proceed to the restroom. There, she would expel the taped wad of drugs and inconspicuously pass it to the waiting inmate upon leaving the restroom. He in turn would use the bathroom and insert the taped wad as far up his rectum as he could get it so that it wouldn't be detected when he was strip-searched by a guard with a high-powered flashlight who looked directly at the bent-over inmate's fully exposed anal area. He would then return to the unit and remove the drugs. My first class in Drug Smuggling 101 was bestowed upon me by my second cellmate during a late-night lockdown, appropriately while we were watching a rerun of "Friday the 13th." Fortunately for me, the cellmate's best friend, Louie, wanted to become roommates with my cellie—which was short for cellmate—so I graciously obliged him and put in for a room change within the week.

Within a month or so after arriving at Conner, my nerves were completely shot. I could not handle the loud, disruptive noise within the units. I spent most of my time tutoring on the unit in the mornings, studying in the law library in the afternoons and early evenings, and visiting the leisure library where I read and wrote letters to my family. All of these things were worthy causes that allowed me to be able to get out of the maddening units and, at the same time, do something that kept my mind off my ever-present problems.

I began to familiarize myself with the different state and federal law book editions that the library had. It was a slow and complicated process to learn the legal terminology and know how to cross-reference from the state to the federal levels. I read everything that I could get my hands on that pertained to my case. With the help of inmate law clerks in the library—most of whom had been doing this for years— I gradually gained a small amount of confidence about accessing the available legal materials. I was still a long way from being able to successfully argue my case in the courts, but I was learning.

Daily, mail was called out shortly before the 4:15 lockdown. All the inmates huddled around while the officer shouted out the names of those who had mail. On several occasions, the inmates made so much noise that the guard handing out mail had to stop and order everyone to lockdown immediately. Later in the evening, If everyone was cooperative, he would again attempt to call out the mail.

Within a couple of months, I received a handful of much-welcomed mail from Mom and Aunt Wilma, and Elizabeth, whose first letter created a warm glow of happiness within me, and an unexpected letter from the law firm of Cole, Huff and Davila. A twinge of excitement skittered down my spine as I rushed to my cell and hurriedly opened the envelope. The letter was from Rolando Davila, an attorney out of Oklahoma City, who stated that he and his firm had been selected to represent me on my direct appeal into the Oklahoma Court of Criminal Appeals. Additionally, Mr. Davila informed me that he and Robert Cole were going to come to the prison for a visit just as soon as they could get approval from prison officials. My heart leaped with joy at the prospect of having a firm of appellate attorneys working on my case. With the eagerness of a kid, I tore into the letter from Elizabeth. It read:

Dear Daddy, I miss you and love you so much. I'm sorry I didn't say much to you when Me Ma and I came to the jail and visited with you. I was so scared and I didn't know what to say to you. I have been so sad without you and I wonder how long it will take you to get out of there. Daddy, I don't believe that you did what they said. I'm going to be starting to school in a little over a month and I miss you so much. I wish you were here with me so we could be together and go to the park and play on the swings, like we used to. I love you, Daddy. Lisa

About halfway through her letter, tears gushed from my eyes, and I could barely see to finish reading. My heart throbbed with the pain of hearing her tender words as she called me *Daddy* and said that she didn't believe I did what they said. I stopped my tears but cried within, never making a sound. I did not want to be overheard by my cellie down on the bottom bunk. I was too upset to even read the letter from my mom and aunt. I needed to go somewhere and have a good cry and get the pain out of my stressed-out mind, but there was no such place to go to in here. There was only mass confusion and somebody always around who was always watching, always on the prowl for what they could steal or bum. I could see why they called Conner the bottom of the barrel.

I had to get out of the cell. If my macho cellie caught me crying, he could make my life miserable by telling the other inmates that I was a weakling. When the doors finally popped open, I climbed off my bunk and left the cell, taking Mom's letter with me. Elizabeth's letter had cut me to the quick. I felt so stressed.

While waiting for evening chow to be called, I went to the unit day room, which was miraculously unoccupied, and read Mom's letter. She and Aunt Wilma gave me their love, prayers, and encouragement that they were doing everything possible to help secure my release. They had good intentions, but I knew they didn't have the necessary funds to make it happen. I could feel my mother's frail spirit as I read how she would always be there for me, no matter what the outcome might be. Mom was the kind of woman that would give her shirt to someone if they were stranded somewhere in sub-freezing temperatures. She and Wilma were still cleaning houses and barely making enough money to live on, but inside the envelope was a prison receipt for $50 she had sent to me so I wouldn't be without canteen. Mom stated that they were going to come down from Kansas City the next weekend to visit with me. I was excited at the thought of getting to see them and wrap my arms around them and tell them how much I had missed them. I felt so all alone and separated from the world I once knew.

Not long after arriving and getting settled in at Conner, I began to experience bouts of stinging, prickling sensations all over my body. Some days the prickly feeling was bad enough that I wanted to tear my shirt off just to get a little relief from the torment. At night, the heat within the cells was unbearable. Combined with the pin-stick feeling, I felt like I was in agony. I didn't know what was happening to me, and I didn't mention the sensations to Mom.

I didn't want her to worry. She and Wilma already had enough on their minds. Before the week was out, though, because I was worried that this might be something that needed medical attention, I went down to sick call to talk to a physician's assistant.

"What can I do for you today, Mr. Fritz?" the P.A. mumbled. He didn't seem at all concerned about why I was there.

"For the past couple of weeks, I have been experiencing pin-prick sensations over my body. It's getting so bad that it is affecting my concentration and my ability to go out anywhere, because I want to take my shirt off and get relief. It feels like I'm almost on fire," I explained.

"Mr. Fritz, are you receiving any psychological treatment at this time?" the P.A. asked, turning his back to me so he could write something on a prescription pad on the counter.

"No, and I don't need to see any shrinks because I don't have any mental problems," I snapped. "I have been wrongly convicted for a crime that I know nothing about and I've been under a lot of stress, but I've never experienced anything like this ever before."

"Mr. Fritz, I'm going to prescribe some Benadryl for you and set you up for an appointment with one of our psychological doctors that comes in every Monday." His voice was flat and disinterested.

"Doc, I told you that I don't require any mental help. I have a physical problem, and this is not my imagination. I resent it very much that you are treating me like some kind of nut case when I'm trying to tell you that I have severe physical symptoms that might be a very serious problem," I blustered.

"The visit is over, Mr. Fritz, so please leave my office or I will be forced to call the shift officer and have you taken out."

"I'm going. When will my prescription be ready?"

"You can pick it up in the morning at med call. If you are late getting down here, you will lose the prescription," he told me.

His arrogance made me furious. I wheeled around and walked out of the office, thinking all the while that he was a real asshole for a wannabe doctor. I wasn't about to agree with seeing a shrink. I had already heard that they had a unit at Joseph Harp Correctional Center called Fantasy Island where they kept all the psychos. I sure wasn't going to take a chance and get a jacket like that on me that would follow me around forever. As I walked back to the unit, I wondered if maybe the pores in my skin were closed since I didn't get any sunshine while I was in the county jail and that maybe it would just take some time to acclimate to the outdoors. I decided to continue with my exercise program of walking the track regularly and try to stay away from as much stress as I could. I sighed when I realized that staying away from stress was totally out of the question.

As part of my daily routine, I dialed Mom and Aunt Wilma's telephone number to see if my calling request had been approved by the prison officials. For several weeks, each call was terminated before it was completed, which resulted in a feeling of great disappointment. On one particular mid-morning, though, things were quiet on the unit, so I decided to give the phone another try. This time the call went through. My breath quickened as I waited, and a feeling of exhilaration tingled throughout my body.

Mom answered. Upon hearing my voice, she began to sob, releasing her pent-up emotion, worry, grief, and elation all at once. She relayed to me in her broken voice that she had called and talked to Elizabeth on a couple of occasions and that Elizabeth was unusually quiet and seemed very distraught when she had asked her how she was feeling. At one point, Mom said, Elizabeth had cried so hard that she couldn't finish their conversation. Mom said that Elizabeth's maternal grandmother had informed her that Elizabeth was in a state of shock after having been told that I was convicted and would not be returning home. That bit of news was heart wrenching.

I wanted to tell Mom about the recent letter from my appellate counsels, but I was distracted by several prison guards charging through the front gate towards each of the two units. I paused, wanting to spare Mom whatever trauma was about to take place. The unit's inside doors suddenly flew open and one of the guards approached me. His face was flushed and red.

"Lockdown! Lockdown! Lockdown!" he commanded in a loud, impetuous voice. "Get off the phone."

I told Mom that I had to go and that I loved her. I didn't wait for her to say goodbye.

The sounds of doors popping as inmates scurried into their cells intensified the pandemonium. I didn't know what had happened but whatever it was, it seemed very serious. I ascended the stairs two at a time, well aware that the guard was watching my every move. I entered the opened cell door and closed it behind me. My cellie was already inside with a worried look on his face.

"What's happening?" I asked, a little out of breath but trying not to sound too excited.

"Oh, I forgot. You haven't been through a lockdown, have you?"

"What are they locking down for? Have you heard?"

"I didn't get a chance to hear the full details, but there was a stabbing on one of the other units. This means we'll be locked down for two or three days, until they finish their investigation. It could take up to a week. And before they let us out of lockdown, they'll shake our cell down for shanks and anything that they can get their grubby little hands on that they don't want us to have. And for me, that means trouble, 'cause I've got over a half ounce of weed on me that I've got to figure out what to do with."

"Have you ever been in this situation before?" I asked, concerned that I might end up paying some of the price for his possession of drugs.

"Just one time at another facility, and I had to end up eating my stash. I stayed high for a week. But the weed I had before wasn't as near as good as what I've got now. If I eat all of this, I might not wake up for several days or I'll be so fucked up that they'll bust me by just lookin' at me."

"Well, there's one thing for sure. You can't keep it in here because they will find it, won't they?"

"It just depends on whether or not they bring the dogs in. I can't risk taking that chance. Do you want to help me eat some of this?" he said, grinning a little to conceal the underlying worry that showed in his eyes.

I didn't want to appear weak or non-compliant because that would probably result in being labeled, which would put me at odds against the other inmates, so I agreed to help out if there was no other alternative. On the other hand, because I sure didn't want to be subjected to a urinalysis if the guards got suspicious, I suggested that maybe he could hide it the same way that he acquired it in the first place. Fortunately for me, he liked the idea, and he had kept the black tape that it originally had been bound in.

But he didn't have any lubrication, he said. I reached into my locker and pulled out a bottle of baby oil that I had bought at the canteen and used to get relief for the prickling feeling in my skin. I handed him the bottle. He re-taped the baggie, smeared baby oil over its surface, and put the wad in a secure hiding place until the time might come when we would have to undergo his prediction of being shaken down.

The next few days were very uncomfortable and stressful. Every fifteen minutes, my cellie would go to the door and check to see what was going on. His anxiety nearly drove me to the edge.

On the fourth day, it happened. We heard the commotion of the shakedown team entering the unit. My cellie leaped from his bed, made a dash for his stash, and successfully stuffed the wad in his anal cavity by using additional baby oil. When the guards got to our cell, we had to strip to our birthday suits and be checked from behind with the flashlights. My cellie passed the test; he showed his moon to the guards without being busted. We were released and ordered to stand outside on the run while they turned our cell upside down and inside out, maliciously dumping everything on the floor and on the beds. Then we were ordered to return to the cell. No further instructions were given.

I was upset when I saw all of my law work papers scattered

on the floor in a crumpled pile. For four hot, miserable days, without a shower and nothing to eat but the bare necessities in sack lunches from the chow hall, we had endured the stress of not knowing why or when things might change, only to be rewarded by having our cell ransacked. Late that afternoon, after the regular 4:15 count, the doors all popped in unison and we were finally free to take showers, which meant standing in a long line, and then get ready for chow to be called, which took longer than usual because the chow hall had to be cleared before calling the next unit.

Fortunately, the lockdown was not extended into the weekend, so I was able to have a wonderful visit with my mom and aunt, who arrived the next evening. The visiting room was very noisy and crowded with kids running amok. Hostility was so thick in the air that I tensed up with anxiety when I heard laughter or other outbursts that interrupted the normal flow of conversation. A few inmates had oral and standup sex with their visitors while the guard was distracted or preoccupied in another area. I hated that Mom and Aunt Wilma had to be exposed to these sights. I made up my mind that I would never allow Elizabeth to be exposed to any encounters such as these.

Because Mom and Aunt Wilma were from out of state, they were allowed to visit on Saturday and Sunday, too. Despite being totally worn out from the three-day visit, they were the last ones to leave, waving goodbye and blowing kisses through the outer glass while I stood in line to be strip-searched before returning to the unit.

Feeling sad and empty inside, I hesitantly made my way into the strip-searching room to undergo the humiliating experience of bending over and spreading my buttocks as wide as I could before a flashlight-toting guard who then released me to return to my unit. Immediately, I said a silent prayer, thanking the Lord for the fulfilling visit and asking that He provide a safe journey home for my blessed mother and aunt. Upon walking further up the hill, I overheard a couple of inmates talking about last week's murder.

I could only catch part of the conversation, but what I heard was that it had been a gang-related killing because of a drug transaction gone sour; some inmate had lost his life over a few dollars because his greed had taken over his common sense.

CHAPTER 28

The agonizingly hot temperatures of summer slowly faded into the crisp, cool days and nights that signaled autumn. The inmates' attitudes cooled down, too, as the sweltering heat disappeared, with only a minimal amount of aggression openly displayed. A renewed briskness appeared in everyone's stride as they made their way from the limited leisure activities provided within the prison. The sounds of the locusts humming out in the trees beyond the perimeter also signified change.

The tormenting pins-and-needles sensation continued to plague me. It could happen at any time without any warning and was definitely getting worse. Could it stem from my mental state, after all, since my increased exposure to the outdoors seemed to have had no apparent effect on the recurring episodes? Maybe the horrendous stress that I had been harshly exposed to had caused me permanent injury. There had been a few improvements—I was moved to a cell where my cellmate was gone all day for work, and I had talked to my family members on several occasions—but the insidious feeling of turning into a human pincushion was emotionally and physically abominable. Above anything else, I was not going to jeopardize my situation with the prison medical people, only to end up being sent to Fantasy Island or be scrutinized as a full-blown mental case. Something had to change, though, or I would be in a straitjacket if these stinging sensations kept up.

In a desperate attempt to try anything, I quit smoking and started doing deep-breathing exercises for relaxation. I could not let anything, no matter what it was, get in my way of going to the law library at every available opportunity, even if it meant having to suddenly rush out the door with a trailing excuse that I had to get some fresh air. There was nothing more important than obeying my own expectations of doing everything legally possible to prove my innocence.

I had not heard a word from my appellate attorneys since the initial letter, and I was beginning to wonder if I had been shuffled under the pile. I wrote several letters to them with attached legal cases that I felt were pertinent to my case. Every day, upon entering the law library, I heard the same old response from the law librarian—"No mail today." I was very disappointed and felt dejected that they had not even bothered to respond. One of the inmate law clerks suggested that I write a letter to the state bar association to find out what was causing their delay.

"Joe, if I write and complain to the bar association, don't you think that would be starting off on the wrong foot with them?" I asked.

"I wouldn't say so," Joe responded without looking at me. After a few moments of silence, he looked up from the law book that he was reading and said, "Listen, man, you need to understand that you're fighting for your life and that these people who represent themselves as attorneys wake up every day and they're free men who get their paychecks and then go home at night. It's no sweat off their balls if you spend the rest of your life in here suffering because of their unconcern."

"I can understand that, but I just don't want to make a bad report on them if they could otherwise do a good brief for me."

"Man, you've got to wake up and realize where you're at and what you're in for. The courts in the state of Oklahoma are so backed up right now and under fire because of the extended delays that have already been occurring in answering the direct appeals. There's a lot of people in here that have been waiting for over three years to have their appeals heard. What I'm tryin' to say to you is that you should not cause any further delay yourself just because you don't want to step on these people's toes."

"Can I file anything myself into the courts on any of the issues that they might not raise?"

"No, you can not. Once they have entered their appearance, you are prohibited from doing any filing yourself. If they fail to raise an issue that is warranted by the record, you can later raise an ineffective assistance of counsel claim in the post-conviction process. Until then, the only thing you can do is to assist them in the preparation of your upcoming direct appeal. Just a word of caution: Be sure that you get everything notarized that you send to them and always keep a copy for your own records. Listen, man, I've got to get busy. I'm workin' on several class-action lawsuits on these delay issues."

"Just one other thing, Joe, and I'll leave you be. Can you help me when it comes time to do my post-conviction?"

"Do you have any money comin' in on your books?" Joe whispered as he moved closer to me.

"I get a certain amount of money every month, but it's not that much," I replied.

"When you're ready, we'll talk."

I had heard from other inmates in the law library that Joe was one of the best in the system in researching and writing briefs. I didn't want to appear totally dumb to him, but at the same time I wanted to establish an association with him if I ever needed someone to help perfect my post-conviction—if it went that far. I still felt inadequate in trying to understand how to recognize and frame the mistakes that I believed had been made, even though I had read the transcript record several times. In my mind, the fact that they had allowed Harjo's testimony, uncorroborated as it was, to stand alone in fulfilling the bind-over requirements at the remanded preliminary hearing was unbelievable in itself. I also believed that it was a big mistake when Judge Jones allowed Cecil Smith to stay on the jury after he had failed to state his full employment record. More importantly, I wanted to overturn my case on the insufficiency of the evidence since that issue was the only one that would result in an all-out release. I was sure, after having read most all of the precedent-setting sufficiency-of-evidence cases, that the evidence required to establish guilt beyond a reasonable doubt did not exist at my trial.

I immediately started working on perfecting my complaint to the Oklahoma Bar Association. After the final lockdown for the night, I usually stayed up late and finished writing the complaint, which took a shorter amount of time since I had obtained the necessary forms.

I was very fortunate to have a cellmate that was a sound sleeper and didn't mind the small reading light I used during the late night hours. We had a mutual respect for each other. Since I had the privacy of the cell throughout the day, I would give him his privacy at night by leaving the unit and going to the law library. I wanted out of the units anyway, and my cellmate wanted his earned privacy. It was as simple as that.

Once a week, the men in our unit went to the canteen where we could purchase different items ranging from snack cakes to chips, prepared sandwiches, ramen noodles, tobacco, and personal hygiene items. Cigarettes and Lil' Debbie cakes were the most popular because they could be used to buy hamburgers that were smuggled out of the kitchen or small amounts of marijuana that a large percentage of the inmates smoked. Purchasing items from the canteen could also be a risky venture, especially if you were a new inmate and were seen carrying several sacks up to the unit. Often, inmates who never turned in a canteen list would stand around the canteen among the large group of inmates to watch for the unsuspecting newcomer. Later, they would show up at his cell with a mask on, and brandishing a shank, steal every stitch of food and cigarettes the new guy had purchased. To further complicate matters, if the inmate reported the strong-armed robbery, he was taking his life in his own hands because now he was a snitch. The consequences that he might suffer ranged from "catch out," which was a stay in protective custody until he could get transferred, to death. Catch out was no assurance of safety. A snitch's reputation could follow him from prison to prison.

I rushed down the hill with my canteen slip in hand amid the mass of eager, running inmates who flew by me so they could be the first ones in line to receive their canteen. I turned my slip in at the canteen window and then proceeded to the law library to get my bar association complaint notarized. As I opened the door and walked inside, the law librarian held a long narrow envelope out in front of her.

"Guess what I have here?" she taunted.

"My release papers?" I said with a flash of humor.

"Could be, could be," she said as she persisted in her play-acting mood.

But when she saw that my facial expression was changing to a look of impatience, her disposition abruptly changed to one of indifference. She handed me the envelope and said gruffly to take my legal mail and either sign in or leave the law library. Since this was her usual personality, I took no offense and thanked her for my mail. Her semblance of a smile disappeared with a blink of an eye.

I left the library and immediately tore open the envelope. My excitement collapsed into disappointment when I saw a single short paragraph and hurriedly scribbled signature. The letter stated that the attorneys' visit had been approved and that they were scheduled to come to the prison the following Thursday. I was instructed to bring any paperwork or files that I had in my possession. Not a reference or a word was said about the legal cases I had sent them that I had spent hours researching. I was pleased that I had finally heard from them, and at the same time, I was greatly relieved that I would not have to file the bar association complaint.

Since the last major shakedown in the unit, I had been able to talk with Elizabeth only a couple of times over the phone, largely due to the expense of placing a collect call. While walking back to the unit with the sack of canteen in my hands, the memory of Elizabeth's voice sounded over and over in my mind as I heard her assuring words telling me that she loved me and believed in me. The most important thing to me in the world was to know that my daughter stood behind me with a strong belief in my declared innocence. The only other things that were of even near-close importance were my mom and aunt's welfare and being able to prove my actual innocence.

In our first conversation, Elizabeth had been very shy and not sure of what to say. It was important for me to ascertain the strength of her belief. Even though she had conveyed to me in her letter that she didn't believe that I had done what they had said, I was still unsure that she might have some unsettled doubts that she was not expressing to me. Since Elizabeth and I always had an upfront ability to communicate, I had spared no words and asked her directly if she truly believed in my innocence. Her response was silence, which ripped to the core of my heart as I awkwardly held the phone to my ear and tried to think of what to say next.

"Elizabeth, I love you with all my heart and I want you to know that I would not lie to you in any way, especially about what they said I had done. It's important for me to know what your true feelings are concerning your belief in my innocence."

The silence swelled to deafening proportions.

"Please believe me when I tell you that I didn't do that," I said, breaking the stillness. "I have been falsely convicted of something I know nothing about. Elizabeth, a big mistake was made, and only the Lord God in heaven can bring forth my innocence. I know that you believe in the Lord and believe that He is capable of bringing forth a miracle of helping me prove my innocence, but it is so important that you believe in me with all of your heart for that miracle to take place. Do you believe what I'm telling you to be the truth?" I fervently asked.

I became aware that the palms of my hands were clammy with perspiration as I tightly clasped the telephone.

"Yes, Daddy, I believe you," Elizabeth said in a soft, subdued voice.

Without warning, a flurry of pin pricks suddenly engulfed me, but Elizabeth's spoken words of trust and faith overrode my urge to say goodbye and run for the door.

"I want you to pray for me, Elizabeth, and ask Jesus to prove my innocence. Will you do that, sweetheart?" I asked, trying to conceal the exasperation and mounting tension in my voice.

Her response flowed forth without hesitation or thought. "Yes, Daddy, I will pray for you every night before I go to sleep." Elizabeth imparted as she began sobbing. Gasps and sighs punctuated her attempts to complete her statement. "I miss you, Daddy. I miss you so much."

"I pray for you and Me Ma Mary every day, Elizabeth, and I will always be there for you, just like Me Ma Fritz and Aunt Wilma are there for you, too. I better go, sweetheart. We're just about out of time, so I'll say goodbye. I hope you have sweet dreams tonight and a good day at school tomorrow. Tell Me Ma Mary I said hi, and give her my love. I'll write you soon. I love you with all my heart."

"Bye, Daddy. I love you, too," pronounced Elizabeth with sadness in her voice.

I returned to the unit, passing the guard in the control booth and calling out my room number for the door to be popped open. I went into the cell, closed the door, and with tears of happiness and sadness in my eyes, lay down and drifted into an undisturbed sleep.

At last, Thursday arrived. All week the unpredictable pin-prick sensations had occurred, driving me to the point of near-madness as I tried to prepare for the visit from the attorneys. I tried doing extra sets of breathing exercises to relax as I made my way down the sidewalk toward the visiting room. The deep breathing seemed to hinder the regularity and length of the attacks, and in the back of my mind, I resisted the thought that I might actually have to see the psychologist. I didn't want to, partly because he looked like he had just graduated from college, but more so because, if I did let my guard down and ultimately schedule an appointment, I took the risk of being singled out as a guy with a mental condition.

"Oh, God, please help me not have an attack while I'm talking to my attorneys," I prayed. I had taken an extra amount of time to look as good as I could under the circumstances. Dressed in my blue prison shirt and best pair of Levis, I entered into the visiting room with my legal papers in hand and spotted the two attorneys sitting at a long table.

"Are you Dennis?" the slender man asked.

"Yes, I am," I answered.

"My name is Rolando Davila and this is my partner, Robert Cole. Have a seat. There are lots of things to discuss in the two hours that they've given us. First of all, Dennis, I would like you to know that Robert and I have been in the appeals business for a long time. As you are probably aware, our office is located in Oklahoma City, and you may or may not know that we specialize in appeals, and we have been looking forward to meeting with you and discussing the parameters of your case."

"I don't mean to interrupt you, Mr. Davila, but I want you to know upfront that I am an innocent man. I have been falsely convicted on evidence that was far short of what it takes to convict someone on."

Having said that, I felt like I had opened up the can of worms in the direction that I wanted the conversation to flow. The two attorneys shifted positions in their seats and awaited anything further I had to say. I remained silent.

"Mr. Fritz, I take it that you are being totally honest with us, but I should point out to you that our responsibility is to review the entirety of the record and then determine what issues are the strongest in your favor."

I interrupted. "Did you and Mr. Cole receive the legal cases that I sent to you?" I said with sternness.

Mr. Cole spoke for the first time. "Yes, we did receive your work and we greatly appreciate what you sent. I apologize for not getting back with you but we were already aware of the line of cases that you sent, and we felt that we would wait and discuss these with you today. Out of my own curiosity, Mr. Fritz, could you give me a single explanation why you believe that you were wrongly found to be guilty?"

"That's an easy question to answer, Mr. Cole. The main reason that I was found guilty was that the district attorney totally camouflaged his lack of evidence with the so-called evidence of my alleged association with the co-defendant, Ronnie Williamson. Have you had a chance to read over the transcripts?"

"As a matter of fact, Mr. Fritz, we have just obtained your full record and have been reviewing the preliminary hearing and some of the trial," said Davila, with his glance projected downward toward the table. Clasping his hands together, he inadvertently looked sideways and asked me what I thought about the representation that my attorney had rendered.

I hesitated before speaking: "Well, to be honest with you both, I feel that he did a fairly good job after taking into consideration that he was a civil attorney who had only handled a few criminal cases before taking mine. But you have read the preliminary hearing, so you have probably seen this. I feel that Mr. Saunders should have provided me a better defense against the state's main witness, James Harjo. I had handfuls of statements that I had collected from other inmates who had been in jail with me who stated that I never made any kind of confession to Harjo. I mean, they were there and they knew what the truth was. Some of them backed out at the last minute because they didn't want to be involved in a murder trial, and some of the others allegedly could not be located. From my point of view, though, I felt that some of these witnesses should have been put on the stand because they had given prior, tape-recorded statements to a private investigator that my family had hired, and if any of them lied on me while they were on the witness stand, then Mr. Saunders would have had the tapes to refute their testimonies. In my opinion, that would have been better than having no defense at all, don't you think?" I asked, looking squarely at Mr. Cole.

"Dennis, you may or may not realize this but preliminary hearing matters are not very ripe for review, primarily because they are not correlated with a determination of guilt and are subjected to a different analysis by the appellate courts that usually don't reverse upon such issues. I know that may be difficult for you to understand, but the magistrate judge has wide latitude in his determination as to the type and amount of evidence that constitutes probable cause bind-over. I say that because it's very rare that an appellate court will reverse on issues such as a magistrate's determination to bind a defendant over on trial."

The remainder of the two hours was spent answering the attorney's trial-related questions and giving them a complete history of my adult life up to the time that I had first met Ronnie, and then a recap of the years that transpired before my arrest. I emphasized several times that it was my desire for them to argue a strong sufficiency-of-evidence claim and show the appellate court that the jury reached their verdict without the needed evidentiary support required to find guilt beyond a reasonable doubt. Upon leaving, Davila and Cole assured me that they would do a thorough and adequate job on perfecting my appellate brief and would keep me posted on the progress of their work. I left the visiting room with the refreshed feeling that I was in good hands and there was hope that I might be vindicated.

Chapter 29

The once-unfamiliar clatter of daily penitentiary life gradually cascaded into monotonous, resounding routines that I resisted with every breath. Prison became a relentless bombardment to the senses.

Every morning, noon, and evening, some guard bellowed "Chow out!" to get the inmates to their feet and in a mad dash to the chow-hall line. Three more times a day another guard shouted out "Lockdown!" to get the men back to their cells for a head count. Yet another guard delighted in cell shakedowns, where he could rummage through every personal item in a cell in his random search for an infraction. When he found something, no matter how slight, he wrote it up—thereby meeting his monthly quota while keeping everybody on edge.

Most of my aggravation and frustration grew from the unrelenting noise from the inconsiderate inmates in my unit. Every time I tried to talk on the unit telephone to my mom, aunt, or daughter, there was something or someone that caused a disruption. In the chow line, when someone standing behind me would suddenly yell to someone on the other side of the hall, my nervous system frayed just a little bit more. Every loud, unexpected noise seared through me like lightning, reminding me of how much I hated these surroundings and the loss of my precious freedom that I had once taken for granted. At every opportunity, I tried to avoid noises and the unpredictability of my situation.

Often, I would stay in my cell following the call for chow just to experience the welcome sound of quiet and to escape the disruptive crash of some new disturbance or commotion. Other times, I found myself dashing to the chow hall with the rest of the inmates—not so much because I was hungry but so that I could eat some food and return to the unit well ahead of the other inmates, just so that I could enjoy a few minutes of longed-for solitude.

I also had to adjust to the depersonalization. When I first arrived at Conner, I was assigned an Oklahoma Department of Corrections number—173018—and that was who I was in the system. Guards and inmates still called me by name, but my identity became more and more wrapped up in that number. When I went to the law library and signed in, I signed in by number, so everyone else who signed in behind me knew how long I'd been in prison. Incoming mail had to have my DOC number on it. Medication was dispensed according to number. Over time, that number became me.

As days drifted into months, I focused more and more on the law. I studied and familiarized myself with the complicated procedures and standards of review that the state appellate court would employ in deciding my case. I was convinced that the evidence used against me was truly insufficient and without the indicia of reliability that was necessary to uphold my conviction. Each time I found a good line of cases under state and federal law that supported my developing issues, I enthusiastically typed a letter to my attorneys to let them know of the research I had discovered and to make it clear that I was doing everything possible to help with my case. They responded to my letters, although sometimes weeks would pass before I received their correspondence. Joe had been right. It seemed that the notary seal on each outgoing letter stimulated the attorneys into keeping me informed in a timely manner.

As long as I was researching and writing letters, I felt fairly good. But the pin-prick sensations continued, their occurrence increasing to about eight times a day. As December progressed, the irritation grew unbearable, and after the holidays I broke down and made an appointment to see the psychologist. In his docile and shy way, he invited me into his office. His lanky body and effeminate mannerisms made me uncomfortable immediately, but I was stressed and I had already taken the step to see him. At that point, there was no turning back.

I went in and sat down. He opened the conversation by asking me what the purpose of my visit was. I shared with him the fact that I was innocent of the crime that I had been convicted of, and that for the past several months I had been suffering greatly from frequent stinging sensations all over my body. He seemed to have difficulty in maintaining eye-to-eye contact with me and acted nervous that I was in his office, which made me feel all the more that I had made a big mistake by coming to see him.

"How long have you been locked up?" he asked. His voice was gentle, but his eyes looked past me as he spoke.

I hesitated before answering. He seemed bothered by my silence as I counted up the months that I had been in prison.

"I've been in since May," I replied. "So, that would be eight months now since this is already January." I felt uncomfortable in the silence of his non-response and continued talking to fill the gap. "The stinging sensations have gotten worse, and now it's to the point that I'm reluctant to even go anywhere on the yard because when the flurries—that's what I call them—when they come upon me, I want to immediately rip my shirt off. I can't begin to describe how bad they have gotten. Sir, I know I'm not crazy, but I don't know what's causing this to happen, and I just thought I would see if you could help me out in some way."

He said nothing. An unusually long silence enveloped us, but I sensed that I had said too much already so I stayed quiet.

"Is your father still living?" he asked with a glimmer of interest in his eyes.

"What does that have to do with the stinging I'm having?"

Another uncomfortable silence followed.

"Did you and your father get along very well?" he asked.

"Listen, I think I have made a big mistake by coming down here. I thought you might be able to help me out, but I have gained a much different opinion now that I've visited with you. I thank you very much for your time, and I will manage my own problem in the best way that I can." I stood and calmly walked toward the door. The young psychologist said nothing as I quickened my stride toward the exit and left as fast as I could without revealing any apparent anxiety.

Out in the hall, I took a deep breath and expelled it. I decided to stay away from the medical facility as long as I had to. There was no need to provide the young psychologist with any reminders to reinvestigate my case. Maybe my own efforts at exercise and deep breathing would resolve the situation. Maybe if I learned to relax a little, the stinging sensations would go away. Maybe something would happen with a change in seasons.

Temperatures that winter were almost as extreme as the summer heat had been. Although my cell was on the top run, it was at the far end, and little or no heat reached us through the air ducts. The inside of the cell window froze over for weeks at a time, and layers of ice accumulated around its bare metal frame. Extra blankets were distributed to every cell during the coldest times. Still, my cellie and I shivered day and night.

I wore my long johns, coat, and stocking cap when I sat up late at night writing letters and working on my case. In the mornings when the guard popped the doors to let the Industries workers out to go to their jobs, my cellie moaned and groaned about having to wake up to near-freezing temperatures. He mumbled vulgarities about the prison staff, about how they were heartless and without concern for our welfare. Under the thick pile of blankets where I lay as if wrapped in a cocoon, I sometimes chuckled to myself at my cellie's complaints. When he left and shut the door behind him, I relaxed, knowing that I had the cell to myself for the entire day. On those cold, frosty mornings, I sometimes skipped breakfast and slept in.

It took some time to get comfortable with my tutoring responsibilities, though I enjoyed helping the inmates to obtain their G.E.D. diplomas. Ms. Lazelle, the unit manager, provided me with a small desk in my cell that I reserved for the students—whenever they showed up. My assignments varied but at no time did I have more than five students, and I tried to schedule all of my sessions with them in the mornings so I could work in the law library during the afternoons and evenings. The majority of my students, however, liked to sleep late and would come to my cell well after their scheduled time with some big made-up story as to why they were absent.

Being a tutor under these conditions put me in a bind with Ms. Lazelle and the inmates. On the one hand, I risked being labeled a snitch and putting myself in harm's way if I told Ms. Lazelle that the students weren't showing up, because she expected to know about their progress. On the other hand, the inmates did not want to be told what to do by another inmate so, instead of acting authoritatively, I could only encourage them to schedule a meeting time that was comfortable for us both.

Gradually, I changed my tutoring schedule to include weekend hours, requiring the student inmates to show up at least twice a week in the mornings and attend a two-hour session during the weekend. I warned them, and they had to agree to the stipulation that if they did not show up on their scheduled morning hours, I could knock on their cell doors and wake them up.

Several of them tried to bribe me with cigarettes if I would falsify my reports to say that they were showing up every time and doing well in their sessions. I never agreed to such deals because I knew that word would eventually get back to Ms. Lazelle that I was not doing my job. If that happened, I'd get stuck with some awful unit-cleaning job that would interfere with regular daily access to the law library. If that happened, I might be stuck here forever.

At the end of my first year at Conner, I received a letter from the appellate attorneys. They had perfected my direct appeal and filed it in the court of criminal appeals on April 24, 1989. In addition to the notification of the filing, Davila informed me that the attorney general's response brief would most likely be filed within a three-month period barring any time extensions, and that I would be receiving a copy of their direct-appeal brief within a few days. I was very anxious to see what issues Davila and Cole had raised and to what extent they had been argued.

A copy of the appellate brief arrived within the month. After mail call, I locked down for count and began scanning through the proposition of error that the attorneys addressed. They had listed nine points, each one elaborated with paragraphs of explanation, but I summarized as I read it to be sure that everything was there: (1) withholding exculpatory evidence, (2) prosecutorial misconduct in the closing argument, (3) evidence insufficient to sustain a verdict of guilty, (4) plea negotiations that resulted in reversible error, (5) denial of a fair trial due to a juror's concealment of his past employment, (6) trial court erred in the admission of cumulative and gruesome photographic evidence, (7) delay in bringing the case to trial violated rights to due process, (8) trial court erred in failing to give the requested jury instruction concerning the weight and credit to be given hair and body fluid evidence, and cumulatively, (9) denial of a fair trial due to the accumulation of errors.

My primary concern was with the third point, the insufficiency of the evidence. After evening chow, I reread the entire brief. I couldn't help but feel very disappointed that the appellate attorneys had not argued the insufficiency issue as thoroughly as they should have. For all that it had, their argument lacked any clear emphasis on my actual innocence, which was critical to my case. Their argument did not encompass the crucial details of what the prosecution had failed to prove—the necessary elements of first-degree murder—and that was what made it weak.

During the next few months, as I waited for the appellate court's opinion, I felt like I was in limbo. Because post-conviction—appealing directly to the court that convicted me—would be the next step if I was denied at the direct appeal level, I could do nothing more than continue in my research efforts and learn everything I could about legal procedures and concepts under state and federal law. If my appeal was rejected, I would not be afforded any further representation by the state, and I would be solely responsible for representing myself in the courts. If that time came, I wanted to be at a level of competency that I would be able to write my own briefs to further challenge the issues at hand.

In the meantime, I contended with the hassle of simply living. One of the more uncomfortable things about prison life was getting a new cellmate or being uprooted from your own cell and placed randomly with a stranger. The unwritten law between inmates was that, if you were in the cell first but had a particularly difficult cellmate that you wanted to replace, you had to find someone compatible to replace him with and then make a formal request. All of the parties involved in a cell change had to sign the form to show that they were in agreement. If any one of them disagreed, the cell transfer couldn't happen.

I'd learned to live with the quirks of my cellie. He'd learned to live with me. But three days before my birthday, on a hot August day, my cellie told me during the 4:15 lockdown count that within ten days he would be transferred to a minimum-security facility. With barely more than a week to find someone to cell with in a place where I'd made few associations and really didn't want to, I knew that if I couldn't find someone to my liking, I faced the prospect of a total stranger moving in. The only positive aspect about this circumstance that I could see was that I had squatters' rights to the bottom bunk. It wasn't much consolation but it was my only bit of control over my space. The more I thought about it, though, the more I resisted the idea of having to find someone to live with. It was going to be difficult to find a person that I could not only get along with but who also had a job at the Industries so I could have the cell to myself during the day for my tutoring sessions.

Toward the end of the month, I received word that Ms. Lazelle wanted to see me in her office. I had no idea what she might want to talk to me about. I had completed all the tutoring paperwork. Things seemed to be going smoothly. Hoping that her summons was nothing bad, I knocked on her office door and she invited me in. The unit case manager was seated alongside her desk. They asked me to sit down. I immediately read their expressions and noted that the mood in the room was upbeat. For a moment, I enjoyed the cool air that flowed from the air conditioner that was in the rear of the room.

"How are you doing, Dennis?" Ms. Lazelle asked with an excited smile.

I could sense something out of the ordinary was going on. I politely responded, "I am doing all right. Thank you for asking."

With a sparkle in her eyes, Ms. Lazelle told me that she had some good news to share with me that she believed would make my day. Both she and the unit case manager stared straight at me with beaming smiles, and that made me a little nervous. I didn't know what on earth to expect, but I listened intently.

"Dennis, as you know, I am adamant about our literary program here on our unit. Your tutoring work has set an exemplary example of achievement above and beyond normal expectations. I have had discussions with the warden and respective prison officials, and they have backed me up in my decision to single-cell the tutors here on V and W."

My heart began to flutter.

"This will be a pilot program in which we will monitor the results of the overall achievements of each of our on-unit tutors.

What I have decided to do—that is, after your present cellmate transfers—is to let you stay single-celled so you can have the privacy to continue working with your students. If you keep setting a good example, as you already have been, it is my plan to then single-cell all of our unit tutors in a grouped number of cells all lined together. We are going to name it 'Tutor's Row' since it will be the first time that any facility has ever initiated such a program. What do you think about what I've just said, Dennis?" Lazelle asked with a gleam in her smile.

Jubilation welled up inside of me and for a moment I was at a loss for words. When I spoke, I was so excited that my sentences blurred: "First of all, Ms. Lazelle, I want to thank you so much for this opportunity to have the privacy that I need to effectively work with my students, and secondly, I am so happy right now I can't even begin to express my overall feelings, but I will try to live up to your expectations and will continue helping the students get their G.E.D. diplomas."

"Well, Dennis, we appreciate your outstanding efforts and have really enjoyed reading your very comprehensive reports. As a matter of fact, I showed some of your reports to the education people and they were really impressed with the detail you have described on the progress of each of your students. Right now, we are ahead of any of the other units on having the greatest number of total G.E.D.s , so," she paused and nodded her head, "keep up the good work."

I left Ms. Lazelle's office with a smile of my own and was floating on Cloud Nine by the time I returned to my cell. I was so excited that I danced around the cell and tried to imagine what it would be like to have the privacy that I so dearly needed, not only for tutoring but to ensure my continued sanity. The overwhelming sense of alienation that was embedded deep within me and the accumulated depression and anger that I had stuffed down inside me since the beginning of this ordeal suddenly diminished as I stood alone in my cell. I felt like I had been bestowed with a new lease on life.

I realized that the reason that I had not allowed myself to become closely associated with the other inmates was because I had been fighting the powerful effects of institutionalization. The clues had been there all along, but now I could visibly see my feelings, as if I were watching them on a movie theater screen. The repulsion that I had felt while watching the silly inmates with all their foolish games and horseplay made perfect sense to me. Some were short-timers, some had longer sentences; it seemed to make no difference to them. They had succumbed to the deceptive effects of being institutionalized. They were guilty of the crimes that they had committed. They knew they were, so there was no reason for them to separate themselves from the masses they tried so hard to impress. They had given in to their circumstances, and in all appearances, were actually enjoying the prison environment, as if they had arrived at some place in their minds where they had become accepted and had found their niche. I had held myself apart from them and that mindset because I wasn't guilty and because I knew I deserved the life of a free man.

The months flew by after my cellie's departure. Mom and Aunt Wilma visited with me on regular intervals every two to three months. I continued writing to and talking with Elizabeth over the phone. I continued going to the law library to amass information and absorb knowledge. I put more time and concentration into my tutoring responsibilities, even during the afternoons, which always seemed to interfere with being at the law library.

The days passed quickly, turning into weeks and months that never seemed to change, as if the passing of all that time was like one long, never-ending day filled with a never-ending series of tiring routines and conformity. My single cell became my refuge, a place where I could feel emotionally protected and sheltered from the constant flood of noise and disruption. Alone, I could stay up as long as I wanted. I could comfortably study or write letters without having to tiptoe around. Most comforting was the privacy of using the toilet. Just waking up every morning and realizing that I had the freedom of doing what I wanted to do without the intrusion of another person being in the cell provided an atmosphere of tranquility and relaxation, and I had so desperately needed it.

The stinging sensations subsided eventually, occurring only once or twice a month. The harshness and confusion of prison life still existed, but at least now, it existed beyond me. I could escape the madness by being alone in the privacy of my single cell.

Chapter 30

A day of reckoning arrived in May 1991. One of my tutoring students was scheduled to take his G.E.D. exam on Friday, and I was helping him in the areas where he showed the most weakness. Usually, I had to hunt Darrell down for his tutoring sessions, but on this day he was eager and anxious to pass his upcoming exam, and he was surprisingly on time and in a good frame of mind.

I had taken a personal interest in Darrell because his life and mine seemed somewhat similar. He was a good kid, even if he was a little rough around the edges. Unlike the majority of the inmates, Darrell had a good head on his shoulders and seemed to set himself apart from the other young men, who boasted an attitude and fancied themselves as criminally clever. Darrell had grown up in a large family, and his mother had remarried several times. He had often felt left out and insecure about his place in the family and his position in life. He said he went in the wrong direction by overusing drugs and alcohol. Often, he and I talked at length about our past good times and mistakes. I related to Darrell in a lot of ways, even if I had been an only child.

We had just ended our session and were talking when

someone rapped at my door. It was Dale, an inmate who I associated with at the law library.

"Hey, what's going on?" I greeted him.

With his law work tucked under his arm, Dale stepped inside. His expression was serious, and he stammered and stalled until Darrell finally caught the hint and left the cell.

"Did you know that your case has come out in the bar journal?" Dale asked.

"What? No, I didn't," I responded. The muscles in my throat began to tighten.

Dale stood silently, with a look of foreboding in his unyielding stare. I knew what his answer was going to be before I asked.

"I was denied, wasn't I?"

As he glanced downward for a brief moment, I drew in a deep breath. I wasn't sure I wanted to hear his crushing words.

"I'm sorry to have to tell you this, Dennis, but they affirmed your case without any dissenting opinion by any of the judges."

A feeling of lightheadedness came over me, and the familiar sting of despair and hopelessness crept into my mind. "Did you have an opportunity to read the full opinion?" I asked, my stomach tensing as I spoke.

"Yeah, I got to read it. The full opinion was almost ten pages long. They didn't cut you any slack at all. Believe me. It was a total washout of a ruling, with all of the judges concurring to deny you relief."

From elsewhere on the unit came the sound of a guard yelling "lockdown." Dale turned to leave, and I quickly asked him one more question.

"Do you think there are any grounds to base a rehearing on?"

"I can't say for sure. Meet me at the law library after chow," he said as he rushed toward the stairwell.

I slammed the cell door with a jolt of trailing anger and then threw the full weight of my body onto the worn-out mattress covering my bunk. Nausea churned in my stomach. *Those dirty bastards have done it to me again.* I covered my head with the scratchy blanket and cried out from within—*How much longer can I take this suffering and shame, Lord? Impart to me your strength and perseverance to not give up, and fill me with the fight to move ahead and claim victory over these wrongful circumstances.* My voice went from a whisper to a shrill screech that sounded funny even to me as I spoke. I curled up and turned to the wall.

A minute later, the damned guard was knocking on my door. He wanted to see some sort of movement. *Go away and leave me alone, you persistent asshole!* On hearing the rustling of keys, I kicked one of my legs outward so I wouldn't have to uncover my head and expose the mat of tears that stained my face. I wept until exhaustion swept over me.

An hour later chow out was called, and I hurriedly made my way to the hall, where I ate unusually fast. Then I went to the law library and began reading the twisted court opinion. I was sickened even more after seeing the verbiage of the court's unanimous refusal to reverse my case. Dale came over and sat at my table and asked me what my thoughts were concerning the opinion.

"Nothing but trash!" The words exploded from my mouth. "I want my appellate attorneys to file a motion for a rehearing, but I'm not sure that they will do that. I'm so angry over this bullshit. It doesn't even cover a lot of the material facts that were brought out in my trial. And the facts that were brought out by the assistant attorney general— They were totally erroneous. She even claimed in her response brief that I had been seen with the co-defendant at the nightclub on the eve of the woman's death. Do you think that any of these misstatements might be grounds to base a rehearing on?" I ruefully asked Dale.

"The only thing I know concerning rehearings is that there has to be something that was either overlooked by the court or the attorneys of record. Other than that, I'm not very knowledgeable about what it takes to get a rehearing," Dale told me.

I left the law library that evening with my mind made up that I was not going to let the court system do this to me again. I was not going to lie down like a whipped pup and let the state argue facts that were not in evidence. I was furious over the outright injustice of being sucker-punched by more lies on top of the ones that already existed. I went back to my cell and immediately wrote a letter to my appellate attorneys, requesting that they file a petition for rehearing based upon these misrepresentations. I spent the entire night organizing the structure and flow of how I was going to argue my issues in the post-conviction process.

Night after night, with sweat dripping from my body due to the extreme temperatures within the cell, I gradually shaped my issues, alleging mostly ineffective assistance of counsel claims that had not been raised on my direct appeal. I had learned enough about the law to know that these claims had to be exhausted at the state level before a federal court would even consider them. Within the post-conviction process, I would first have to file my petition back into the Pontotoc County District Court and, if denied, appeal it onward to the Oklahoma Court of Criminal Appeals.

Within a month or so, I received a response letter along with a copy of the appellate attorney's brief in support of their filed petition for rehearing. The thrust of the petition was predicated upon questions of law and facts that the appellate court had seemingly overlooked. The petition was short but to the point. Before I could file my near-completed post-conviction brief, I had to wait for the determination to be made on the petition for rehearing.

Sometime in July, I received confirmation from the attorneys that the rehearing was denied on June 26, 1991. I wasn't surprised. Some of the inmates in the law library had told me, and I'd read, that rehearings were very difficult to obtain. For the next several weeks, I diligently focused on the perfection of my first brief. As a novice at brief writing, I capitalized every letter I typed to be sure that it captured the court's full attention.

After waiting for over two months without getting a

response, I filed a petition for writ of mandamus into the state appellate court for a directive to be issued to the district court to order them to rule upon my post-conviction. A few weeks later, I received a very short order of denial from the district court, with very few findings of fact or conclusions of law to base an appeal upon. It was obvious that the court in Pontotoc County was not going to do me any favors, nor were they ever going to admit that they had made a huge mistake in wrongfully convicting me.

The never-ending strife and confusion of prison life provided the impetus that sparked my full devotion and directed my energy toward doing everything possible under the law to fight my way out of the penitentiary. Everything I did was totally centered in and around the law. When I ate, when I walked, when I talked, when I slept—I would dream about the law and how I would someday beat my case and walk from the prison gates as a free man. Every day I would learn something new that would spur me onward toward the realization that I could succeed in proving my innocence.

The wheels of justice, however, turned slowly. The last weeks of summer faded into autumn and then winter. After having been granted two extensions of time in which to perfect my post-conviction appeal, I walked to the mailbox on a cold, snowy day shortly before Christmas in 1991 and dropped my completed brief into the outgoing mail slot with the proud feeling that I had done the best possible job that I could do. Snowflakes fell from the gray, darkened sky. It was quiet outside. My shoes left gliding tracks in the powder as I made my way back up the long stretch of sidewalk to the formidable-looking unit that bore the unwanted status of being my home.

The stinging sensations on my skin had finally ceased. I was now free of the anxiety of the excruciating distress that had accompanied the unpredictable attacks. I felt as though a great weight had been lifted from me. I was able to experience and enjoy the semblance of some sort of inner peace, at least enough to move forward and participate in my daily activities.

Because I was caught up as far as I could go in my law work, my focus shifted. I felt a strong need to spend more time writing letters and communicating over the phone to my family members. Occasionally, I received a letter from Elizabeth's maternal grandmother, Me Ma Mary, who was overseeing Elizabeth's custody and care. Many years ago, before my arrest and conviction, Mary and I had been close but everything changed after I was charged with murder. The times that I had written letters to her and talked with her on the phone, I always mentioned that I was not guilty and knew nothing about the crime. Her reactions were always evasive, which gave me the impression that she was not convinced of my innocence. Within her letters, she talked mostly about Elizabeth and how she was getting along.

At first, she was rather reserved in letting me know the extent of Elizabeth's actual feelings concerning my conviction. Over the course of time, though, Mary gradually opened up to me about how Elizabeth felt and conveyed to me that Elizabeth was very scared about the thought of coming to see me. Elizabeth's fear had a lot to do with television shows that she had seen that depicted the most dangerous and vulgar scenes of jailhouses and visiting areas. Mary always indicated that Elizabeth missed me dearly but was very nervous of having to go inside the prison, and then, of having to leave me behind. Mary believed that Elizabeth was very resentful because she had lost both her mother and father and didn't believe she had a normal family life like the other kids at school. Mary reassured me that Elizabeth was doing well but still experienced grief and sadness over my absence. Her disbelief and shock after having received the initial news of my arrest, and later the conviction, seemed to be leveling off.

Each time I received a letter from Mary explaining Elizabeth's inner thoughts and feelings, I would experience a prolonged, deep sadness because my little girl was being tormented emotionally by something that wasn't true. I would get so angry and frustrated about trying to understand why all of this had happened, but there were no clear-cut, soothing, reassuring answers. There were only unanswered questions, and after that, my unwavering faith in the Lord I wanted resolutions but none could be found; only the intelligence of the Lord knew the answers. I dared not to invade or question His purpose for me being here but instead rendered my humble thanks for providing me with His miracle of helping me to prove my innocence. I knew He was there. I could feel the presence of His Holy Spirit guiding me onward when there were times that I had nothing left to give—out of nowhere, a renewal of energy and strength would always refuel my mind and body.

Springtime arrived. The assistant attorney general assigned to review my post-conviction appeal had filed successive motions for extensions of time in which to complete her reply brief. I was disgusted with the slowness of their inaction and believed that it was merely a delay tactic, at my expense, to catch up on their overextended workload. I waited.

On a perfect day in early May, when there was not a cloud in the sky and the humidity was low, I met a new inmate on the unit. Our unit was not scheduled to draw down at the canteen for another two days, and I had run out of Redman chewing tobacco, a habit I had picked up after I quit smoking. I was suffering the pangs of withdrawal. I checked with everyone I knew that chewed any kind of tobacco at all and they were either out or not interested in parting with their remaining amount. I still had a pack of cigarettes in my locker that I had saved back—not to smoke but to use to buy hamburgers or Lil' Debbies. But after exhausting every possible source in a long line of tobacco chewers, I was nearly at the point of firing up a cigarette and smoking again. I wanted a chew so bad I could almost taste it.

That's when I met the new man. While standing out in front of the unit offices, I noticed an unfamiliar inmate entering the front gate. He walked directly toward me.

"Say, man, I'm new here on the unit and I was wondering if

you knew anyone that would be interested in buying a fresh pouch of Redman for a pack of cigarettes?" he said.

I was astonished by the coincidence—his coming to me first, out of all the people on the unit he could have approached, and wanting to sell me the very thing that had been on my mind for the past couple of days.

"Sure," I exclaimed. "I would be very glad to take that off your hands. As a matter of fact, I have a pack of Marlboro Reds in my locker. Follow me to my cell and I'll get them for you."

In a matter of minutes, the transaction was made. From that moment on, I was certain that it wasn't just happenstance that had brought the inmate my way. As we stood in the corridor, I got a feeling in a gut-level kind of way that defies common sense that this man was brought to me by the good man upstairs. We talked for a couple of more minutes.

"Just out of curiosity, I was wondering what made you decide to ask me?" I asked after he said that he had just been transferred from another prison.

"Well, for some strange reason, they must have ignored the pouch of Redman because it was in my property when I picked it up here. I found that to be somewhat of an oversight on their part. I don't know the answer to your question. I just had a feeling that you might be a chewer, so I checked you out. You were actually one of the first ones that I asked since bringing my property up not too long ago." He sounded like it was no big deal.

I thanked him again and wished him well.

Not long after that incident, I received the attorney general's reply brief. Because I was the defendant and had initiated the petition, I had the opportunity to further file a response to the state's response. I was all for hammering as many nails in the coffin that I could, due to the fact that this assistant A.G. had surreptitiously misstated material facts against me. I perfected my detailed response and slipped it into the mail.

After a couple of months of waiting, I got the bright idea to file a petition for writ of mandamus into the Western District Federal Court to order the court of criminal appeals to fairly re-adjudicate their overreached sufficiency of evidence claim in my previous direct appeal. I was itching to get into federal court anyway, and this seemed like the perfect opportunity to initiate my claim of not having had a fair and meaningful appeal under the due process protection of the law.

While waiting for the attorney general's reply brief on my filed writ of mandamus petition, I received word that my post-conviction appeal had been denied on September 16, 1992. It was now time to move fully into the federal courts and generate a petition for writ of habeas corpus. I felt very comfortable and confident that I had fairly raised all issues in my case at the state court level and that I would be able to defeat any procedural arguments that the attorney general's office would surely allege.

The long hot summer had been such a drain on my energy reserves that I literally sweated out night after night in the locked-down confinement of my cell. I was tired and needed a break from the law, but I could not allow myself any slack because it would impair the progress of my fight for my long-sought-after freedom. Having been in prison for a little over four years, I had gotten used to its unpredictability—all the major lockdowns; the periodic, random shakedowns after someone was stabbed or murdered; the way that the guards left my cell in disarray after a search; and the never-ending influx of new inmates—with their varied personalities—arriving daily at a steady rate on the unit. But getting used to something was not the same as being comfortable with it. Becoming comfortable in prison was not a good thing, I had to remind myself regularly. Just when I felt like everything was beginning to moderate and become tolerable, something awful would happen that would reel me back into the reality that prison was an extremely dangerous place.

In the mid-morning hours on a chilly day in November of

1992, I had just left the unit manager's office after my six-month review, a situation that was required of every inmate. I quickly made my way across the unit lawn to go back to my cell and get some much-needed rest but as I opened the side door to my unit, I froze at what I saw. Slumped against a wall on the concrete slab floor was an inmate with a hole in his forehead the size of a hardball. Blood spurted out with every beat of his frail heart. The sight of his exposed skull and glassy, sunken eyes held me motionless. I was horrified. I couldn't speak.

Guards rushed into the unit screaming, "Lockdown! Lockdown! Now! Get to your cells!"

I hurried to my cell, along with the inmates who wasted no time in getting to their cells. Doors slammed hard, and shouts of "lockdown" echoed sharply through the building. From the small, rectangular glass in my door, I saw the medical staff people sprint into the unit with oxygen canisters, a stretcher, and other resuscitation equipment. This situation was more serious than any I could recall, and I knew that this lockdown was going to last for more than a few days. As I watched, like everyone else around me who peered out their cell-door windows, members of the medical team, each one holding dearly to a side of the bouncing stretcher, ran from the unit as fast as they could on their way to the medical building a quarter mile away.

I spent the next six days in lockdown writing the rough draft of my petition for writ of habeas corpus. The image of the wounded inmate clung to me like death. I couldn't get it out of my mind. I desperately wanted out of this place. I couldn't live like this forever. One by one, every inmate was called to the unit manager's office and questioned about the horrible event. On the seventh day, a major shakedown took place. That evening, the doors all popped open at once and we were freed, to again stand in long lines while we waited for the shower, then wait for the hours to pass before we were finally ushered to chow under tight security—waiting, waiting, to start it all over again.

Chapter 31

Rumors floated around like dust in the air after the brutal attack on the inmate. Some said that the man had snitched to the cops before coming to prison about the relative of someone who lived on the unit. Another rumor was that the violent attack occurred because of the inmate's refusal to pay up on a drug deal that went sour between the Bloods and the Crips—the two black gangs that existed in the prison. Later, I heard another rumor that the inmate had died as a result of his skull being smashed in.

Speculation on the subject faded, however, as the routines of prison life returned. For me, it was a wake-up call to not allow myself to ever get too comfortable with my environment. Anything could happen at any time and in any place, so it was in my best interest to steer clear of forming any close associations with anyone—especially when it came to owing money to any of the inmates that ran stores out of their cells. On those rare occasions that I did charge a box of Debbies or some other canteen-related item, I always made sure that I had the money on my books to pay off the debt at the agreed-upon time.

At mail call, I received a letter from a woman named Kim

Marks, who stated that she was a private investigator for the Oklahoma Indigent Defense System. She explained that she had been keeping up with my case because she knew Ronnie's appellate attorneys, and they had mentioned my name several times. The substance of Kim's letter was to notify me that she was going to call the warden and schedule a time in the near future that she could come to the prison with another woman by the name of Leslie Delk and show me the videotaped confession of Ricky Simmons. She asked me to write her back immediately and let her know of my decision. That evening after lockdown, I wrote Kim back and gave her my permission to come to the prison and show me the tape. I mailed it off before going into the law library the following afternoon.

Except for having to endure the freezing temperatures in my cell, I looked forward to the dismal, cloudy days of winter. As a general rule, the inmates became more docile during the winter months, and I enjoyed the privacy of walking around the ball field with the handful of other inmates brave enough to bear the cold. Even during the most extreme conditions, I fled to the solitude of the ball field for at least one hour a day, where I could relax completely and envision being a free man again some day.

The rough draft of my habeas corpus petition was a long way from completion. I had been told by the inmate law clerks that the greatest chance for getting a reversal in my case was at the federal district court level. As they explained to me, federal court was a whole new ball game when it came to the complexities of the standards used by the reviewing court to reach its determination. It became much more difficult to gain relief at a higher federal level due to presumptions of correctness in previous proceedings that had to be overcome before a reviewing court would reverse on any or all issues on which the lower district court had denied granting relief. And now I had to frame my issues into constitutionally based allegations. So the first hurdle that I had to overcome was learning how to federalize my state-exhausted issues into ones that conformed to the federal court's requirements.

I intensified my research efforts. Day in and day out, when I didn't have tutoring responsibilities, I focused on the law. I was the first one at the law library in the morning and the last one to leave at the end of the day. I wanted my district court petition for writ of habeas corpus to be perfect, down to pinpoint accuracy of dotting all my *i*s and crossing all my *t*s.

After an exhausting afternoon at the law library, I walked back to the unit with my mind still deeply absorbed on my case. At mail call, I received notice that Kim Marks and Leslie Delk would be at the prison at ten the next morning. I greatly anticipated their arrival. I had always wanted to see Simmons's confession.

The next morning I met Kim and Leslie in the visiting room. Prison officials had provided them with a video player. Before beginning, they talked a lot about Ron and how he was doing. They seemed highly interested in my case and promised to help out with anything I needed in a legal sense. Leslie and I sat down while Kim started the tape. Upon its completion, we talked about the numerous times that Agent Rogers tried to convince Simmons that he surely couldn't have murdered Debbie Carter. Each time, Simmons would say that he knew he had killed her and would start crying with remorse. Rogers would tell Simmons again that he didn't believe what he was saying because it sounded too made up. Simmons repeated over and over that in fact he had murdered Debbie because he was in love with her and she wouldn't have anything to do with him.

When our time was almost up, we said our goodbyes and promised each other that we would stay in touch. Kim and Leslie were one of a kind. Their hearts were full of compassion and deep devotion in their own fields of the law. As I walked back to the unit, I felt a great sense of satisfaction that I had finally gotten to hear Simmons's confession—it sounded to me like he was telling the truth. I would keep Kim and Leslie in my mind as good friends and good sources for helping me in my search for justice.

On November 13, 1992, after laboring for weeks to get

everything just right, I filed the habeas corpus petition into the Western District Federal Court in Oklahoma City. As I expected, the assistant attorney general put up a fight. In the first part of 1993, I received a copy of her reply brief with a motion to dismiss, in which she argued that I had not fairly exhausted some of my claims at the state level. She specifically argued the claim of not receiving a just and meaningful direct appeal and then mentioned other claims based on my trial and the appellate attorney's ineffective assistance of counsel. I was more than ready for her resistance. I had already sketched out a rough draft of the corresponding line of cases I would present to counter her arguments. In a matter of days, I perfected my reply brief to the Western District court to demonstrate that I had in fact fairly brought these issues to the attention of the state court, and I filed it. There was no sense wasting time.

Although I didn't expect it, the escalating battle seemed to chip away at my emotional and physical stamina. While working in the law library or in my cell, I found myself getting sleepy and nodding off from time to time. The strain was taking its toll. To alleviate the stress of working ten to twelve hours a day on my case, I occasionally played a guitar that I checked out down at the gymnasium. I even played a few games of chess when the occasion arose.

In the spring, Unit Manager Lazelle okayed my request to start a very small garden space outside the unit near one of the fence lines. I made my way over to the horticulture building that the prison used to supply the compound with flowers and shrubs and obtained a few bootlegged strawberry plants and some pepper seeds and ushered them into my worked plot of ground. The three-by eight-foot space was something that I could call my own—at least I laid claim to it—and it gave back to me a much-needed diversion and the relaxation that I craved. Every day, before going to the law library, when there weren't many other inmates around, I would venture toward my garden and enjoy the sanctity of viewing the thriving results of my efforts.

Like everything else in prison, though, my plot of ground gradually became the object of interest of numerous curious inmates, which annoyed me, but I had a far greater plan in mind. Little did the unit manager know that when she and the unit staff were gone on the weekends, I stealthily enlarged my small garden plot by a few feet in width and length. My secret project became even more adventurous when I used the unit wheelbarrow to go out onto the ball field and gather symmetrical stones so I could create an eye-appealing border. By early summer, my garden had not only quadrupled in size but was also filled with a variety of garden vegetables that soon became a popular commodity on the unit.

By the middle of August, Ms. Lazelle hadn't said a word, and while I kept hoping for the best, I was expecting the worst. One very hot afternoon, I was pulling weeds in the garden after having left the law library because it had closed early when, to my surprise, I looked up and saw Ms. Lazelle walking directly toward me.

"Hi, Linda, how are you doing?" I stated.

Without speaking, Lazelle eyed the full circumference of the newly modified rock border that had been extended numerous times.

"I really like what you have done to your garden, with the added dimension of the rock inlays," Linda said as a smile crept across her face.

"Thank you, Linda, for the opportunity that you provided," I graciously responded.

"Well, you did all the work. It looks so good. Even some of the other shift office personnel down front have made some favorable comments about the beautiful border you constructed. You've added a new look to our unit, and I like that," Lazelle said enthusiastically. With that, she turned to leave.

A wave of joy swept over me as a sense of relief danced through my mind. My bold and unauthorized initiative to enlarge the garden had paid off. The garden plot soon gained the attention of other enthusiastic inmates who also shared a green-thumb interest in gardening. On weekends, they helped me load numerous wheelbarrows of sand at the faraway horticulture building and push them all the way up the long and grueling incline of the sidewalk that led to our unit. Word quickly got around to the other prison units that the V and W inmates had a garden. In a short time, almost every unit at the prison allowed interested inmates to dig up a plot of ground and share a garden.

The latter half of 1992 and much of 1993 were filled with many blessings to be thankful for: My family was safe and in good health, I still had my single cell on Tutor's Row, the ungodly stinging sensations had ceased, I had helped several more inmates attain their G.E.D. certifications, I enjoyed the fulfilling rewards of our new garden spot, I had weathered the first go-round in the federal court system, and I had gained a new friendship with an inmate named Mickey, who became my walking and gardening buddy. Mickey and I had met on the ball field, where we walked for exercise and to get out of the unit. He had graduated from Oklahoma University in Norman. Sometime after graduation, he leased a sporting goods store and was doing quite well for himself—until the eventful day of his arrest. Like me, Mickey didn't react well to stressful situations and usually separated himself from the prison masses. Our jobs were both in the education field of helping inmates get their G.E.D.s, but he worked at the education building under the principal's thumb, while I soloed in the unit.

Although Mick was nine years younger than me, I called him "Old Man" due to the fact that when I had first met him, he was very lethargic and timid about opening up to people. In turn, he called me "Old Man" because I had graduated from high school before he had finished fifth grade. He, like me, had gained weight in the county jail, where he had spent nearly two years before entering prison. We walked and jogged on the ball field to get back into shape.

On August 30, 1993, I received a letter that made me

whoop for joy. The Western District court's initial report and recommendation denied the attorney general's motion to dismiss. This paved the way for me to continue to pursue the arguments about issues concerning ineffective counsel that I'd presented in my original petition. I had already started working on my main brief in support of the habeas corpus petition, but the court's report gave me the go-ahead to get it finished and get it filed. Maybe there was hope on the horizon, after all.

Fall dwindled and winter arrived, and the decrease in overall activity among the inmates helped my concentration immensely. I was in the middle of the most important legal battle of my incarcerated life. Not a minute went by that I didn't think about the successful completion of perfecting my brief in support. I was obsessed with the belief that my case was going to be reversed, and I was reasonably assured that I would either be granted a new trial or an outright dismissal. After spending hours rereading and reediting what had taken weeks to research and write, I decided the document was as complete as it would ever be. I was precisely on point in arguing the substance of my issues with supporting case law. As I prepared the materials for mailing, I found comfort in believing that I had done the best I could do.

In the mailroom, I confidently handed the thick manila envelope through the window to the clerk. As she flung it into the outgoing mail bag, a thought came to mind that, if she only knew the importance of what she had just carelessly tossed, she would have surely handled it with the same amount of care that it had taken me to prepare. Holding back my annoyance, I simply said, "Thank you, ma'am, and have a wonderful day."

With a feeling of deep satisfaction in my heart, I walked the short distance to the leisure library and took the liberty of reading the newspaper before returning to the unit. It was all about waiting now before determining what to do next. I was ready mentally and emotionally for the paper battle headed my way, but physical exhaustion dogged me. Evidently, the stress and all the time I had spent working on my case were catching up with me. A couple of months earlier, I would have exercised and physically engaged myself to keep my body and mind as relaxed as possible, but now I had to fight the unusual urge to sleep. As I entered my cell, I decided I would stay out of the law library and take a few days off and catch up on some jogging.

At some point during early December, I realized that I was losing some of my memories. Recollections of how it felt to reel in a fighting largemouth bass or times when I spent a Halloween evening taking Elizabeth door to door in her costume had begun to fade, as if they had been a part of some dream from which I'd been interrupted and now remembered only vaguely. At night, after I turned out all the lights, I spent hours looking out the window at the trailing razor-wire fence and imagining myself floating over it and flying away like a bird.

Other times, I went outside on the basketball court at night and caught myself daring to think what it would be like to be on the other side of the fence, with the freedom to go and do as I pleased without having to be locked down every night of my life. I felt disdain toward the system when my imagination faltered and couldn't put me on the other side of that fence, in that outside world filled with the bright lights of pleasure and discovery, full of shopping malls and candy stores and restaurants—the world I had once known that I was now having trouble remembering. Was that world still out there for me, or would I forever remain in my present world of torment and pain? I wanted to yell out as loud as I could so that at least the sound of my voice would experience the freedom of breaking out over the tops of the distant, darkened fences. But then, dragging me back to the reality of where I was but shouldn't be, I could hear the faint, repeated calls of "lockdown," and I knew I had to head back. I closed my eyes for a few seconds more to etch the fleeting feelings upon my mind and then slowly made my way back into my unit. More than once, I met the counting guard just as he arrived at my door; he had to use his keys to unlock it to let me in.

"A little late there, aren't you, Fritz?" he grumbled one night.

"Sorry about that. I was outside getting some air and didn't fully hear your lockdown call."

"Well, let this be the last time, or I will have to write you up. Are we on the same page about that, Fritz?"

"Yeah," I half-heartedly replied, not wanting to say what was really on my mind.

I shut my door and lay down on my bunk. I sighed deeply, and a feeling of extreme sadness crept over me. I instantly recognized where the feeling was from. For the last few days, I had been tossing an issue over in my mind and had come to the conclusion that Elizabeth would be better off without having to worry about me. As a little girl, she had possessed the rare qualities of keeping her composure and showing patience in whatever she attempted to accomplish. It was so unfair that she had to continue to be emotionally burdened with the hardships that go along with having a dad in prison for such a heinous crime as murder. She should go on with her own life and be happy without having to contend with the constant reminders of the nightmarish ordeal that had been forced upon her.

I had received a letter from her the day before that had really shaken me up. In it, she had sent a print of her high school senior picture. Elizabeth had blossomed into a beautiful young woman. I couldn't get her resemblance to her mother out of my head. I had looked at the photo countless times during the past two days, and sometimes old memories surfaced about Mary—things that I hadn't thought of in years. Elizabeth had the same look in her eyes as her mother—a free-flowing sweetness that radiated from inside, with an innocence that opened up to everyone she came in contact with. Seeing that in my daughter made me realize that my pain over the loss of Mary was still wedged deep inside me. I reread Elizabeth's letter for the umpteenth time:

Dear Dad, I hope you are doing well and you are making

progress in your case. I believe with all my heart that you will win your case and be free again! I haven't heard from you lately. Is there anything wrong? I miss you so much and pray for the day that you will be released. Dad, I'm going to be graduating from high school shortly. I have a boyfriend whose name is Clay. You would really like him. He's very nice and reminds me a little of you. I hope you like my senior picture. I don't think it's very good of me but everybody else disagrees. Dad, I want you to know that I will never forget you. I remember all the good times that we used to have. Most of all, I especially remember the holidays where we would decorate the house and celebrate with so much excitement. I recall going on trips to the lake and enjoying a lot of activities outside that we used to do together. I also remember living in our house in Ada, OK, and the summers where I would play outside until the sun went down, and having you around to teach me new things. So, don't ever feel that I have forgotten you. I will stand behind you all the way, no matter what. Dad, I better close and get this in the mail. Write to me and let me know what is going on in your case. If you need for me to do any legal things, just let me know. Miss you and love you very, very much. Your loving daughter, Elizabeth

The more I read her letter, the madder I got. I had missed out on years of watching her grow up. Now, she had matured into a young woman and I still had no guarantees of whether or not I would ever get out of here to see her. All of the years that I could have been with my family had been lost. I hated everything that the system stood for and for every way that it had stolen my precious freedom.

Mom and Aunt Wilma visited me in the interim between Christmas and the start of the new year. The holidays had been especially gloomy because of memories of Mary and the tiredness I'd been feeling, and I had exercised more to be in the best possible spirits. Several times during their visit, however, I had trouble keeping my eyes open and had to lay my head down on the table to rest. Mom and Aunt Wilma found it peculiar that I was so sleepy.

I simply told them that I hadn't rested very well for the past few nights. Looking at me suspiciously, they asked me if I had been taking any drugs. I assured them that I had not and made a self-conscious effort to keep from getting sleepy in front of them by drinking a lot of coffee. The last thing I wanted to do was to worry them.

As January progressed, however, I felt more and more depressed. On some days, I didn't even want to leave my cell because I didn't want to deal with all the noise and disruption from the other inmates. I became aware that my eyes were more sensitive to bright lights and that I was acting more withdrawn. I knew that the holiday season had been a source of depression for many years, but this went beyond that. I didn't understand the tiredness. Maybe the sleepiness and lethargy were associated with some form of depression that I knew little about. I tried to put it aside and replace it with more exercise.

Some time in February, I met Mick out on the ball field. We were both enjoying the cooler temperatures of early spring.

"Hey, Old Man, what's going on?" I said, extending our usual greeting.

"Not too much, Old Man. How have you been doing? I haven't seen you in a few days?"

"Same old same old," I replied in an effort to stimulate some humor. "What's been going on in your side of town?" I asked, as if I didn't know better.

"Oh, just tryin' to put up with my youngster cellie."

"Rick is still your cellie, isn't he?"

"Oh, yeah. He's quite the singer, as you well know. The trouble is that he sings to himself during the times we're locked down, and it's starting to drive on me. He told me the other day that he is going to try and go professional when he gets out. When I asked him if he could practice on his own time, he acted like he didn't know what I was talking about. You know how those youngsters are—you have to spell everything out to them before they have a clue of what's really being said," Mick said with a chuckle.

"Well, Old Man, knowin' how those youngsters are, he'll probably be wanting to move to another cell anyway before too much longer."

"Yeah, that's probably what will happen, and I'll end up getting someone from some motorcycle gang with tattoos from his ankles all the way up to his neck and then back down to his ass again."

Mick and I had a good laugh over the way he had coin-phrased his concern. We were pretty equal as far as letting each other talk. Sometimes he would let me ramble on, and other times, once he got wound up, he would take up some of the slack. That's the way it was between me and him. We didn't talk much at a serious level. He had thirty years to do, I had my life sentence. There wasn't any sense in hearing complaints.

"Well, Old Man, you ready to run?" asked Mick.

"Let's do it. I'm ready to put you in the dirt today, so let's see what you got," I told him.

Mick and I had been running for the past several months and had gotten up to a pace that we were timing ourselves on both the shorter and longer distances. Today, though, I didn't feel like exerting much effort, but the challenge was there and I wasn't about to let Mick beat me. There were only a couple of guys on the running track, so I relaxed and set my stride to a steady tempo and stayed even with Mick. I did that a lot, and then, usually right near the end, I would sprint toward the finishing line to put another victory under my belt. But today was different.

Panting like a stuck hog after he finished the race, Mick walked back to me where I still stood on the track, stooped over, with my hands on my knees while I labored to catch my breath.

"Hey, Old Man, kind of lost you back there," he chided me. "It's been a while since I've tasted this sweet a victory. What's the matter with you? You've been enjoyin' that single cell too much, haven't ya? Eatin' all those ramen noodles is kind of slowin' you down a little, Old Man," he taunted and let go a big, gusty laugh.

"Well, you got me this time," I told him when I had caught my breath, "but you just wait. Next time I'll be lookin' back at you in a trail of dust."

CHAPTER 32

I opened one eye. Sunshine spilled in through my cell window. I didn't know the exact time, but I was too tired to get off my bunk and look at my watch on the top of my locker. I felt confused and a little disoriented. From somewhere on the unit, I heard the voice of who I thought was the night guard calling "chow out" again and again.

I tried to move my head, but the ache in my neck stopped me. The same dull pain in my upper torso and neck had been hurting for weeks, but I had associated it with neck strain from the extended amount of sitting I'd done while working on my case. I tried to move again because I needed to get up and use the toilet, but my mind was in a daze and my body was so weak that I could only roll over and face the wall. Something was seriously wrong. I had never felt like this in my life—even with the worst case of flu I had ever had when I was a kid. I closed my eyes and drifted back into a hazy sleep.

Much later, my bladder awakened me with such urgency that I felt a small amount of urine drip into my underwear. With every ounce of energy I could find, I pulled myself up and sat on the edge of the bed. Weak and dizzy, I felt as though I would topple to the floor. I stood up unsteadily and looked at my watch. It was two thirty in the afternoon.

"Oh my god," I said aloud. The chow call that I had heard had not been for breakfast but for noon chow. I clumsily staggered to the commode and urinated, and then sat down at my desk, where I plugged in my hot water pot to make a cup of instant coffee. I noticed a piece of paper on the floor by my door.

"Oh, shit," I muttered, hoping that it wasn't a note from the unit manager, who might have seen me sacked out in my bunk when I was supposed to be tutoring. I steadied my hand against the wall, picked up the note, and read the handwritten message. It was from Dale, telling me that I had legal mail at the law library. I hurriedly gulped down my coffee and with a monumental amount of effort made my way to the library.

The unpredictable overseer of the law library gave me a strange look.

"You look like you just came out of the grave," she said.

"Yeah, I feel like it, too."

"I hope you're not drinking any of that home brew that you all make up there on the units," she said callously. Her point-blank manner and overbearing stare rankled me, and I looked away from her to glance at her desk. "No, no, I don't touch the stuff, ma'am. I'm just not feeling so well. Do I have any legal mail?"

"As a matter of fact, you do, but you don't need to stay in here and spread around whatever you got. You need to go to Medical if you're feeling that bad," she insisted. "Here's your mail. You better get somewhere real quick because you've only got less than five minutes till movement is over with."

I exited the library and hurried as best I could toward my unit. I snuck a peek at the envelope and saw that it was from the Western District court. I had planned to open it in the privacy of my cell, but I couldn't wait. I tore into the envelope. Sure enough, it was the report and recommendation I had been awaiting. I wasn't quite sure what day today was, but the stamped "filed" date on the document was May 31, 1994. I immediately flipped to the back page, foregoing the report and going right to the recommendation. The words jumped off the page and hit me squarely between the eyes: "In accordance with the foregoing, it is recommended that the petition for writ of habeas corpus be denied."

Another denial, but this time, the news was more than devastating—it crushed me. By the time I got back into the cell, I felt so weak and upset that I didn't even want to read the report. I was stunned and too tired to care. I put the letter on the desk, fell onto my mattress, and escaped into a haven of confounded sleep.

That evening after skipping chow, I forced myself to go down to the law library, where I began typing my objection to the district judge in response to the magistrate's report and recommendation ruling. As I typed, a whirling, sickening feeling in my stomach replaced any thoughts of being hungry. I realized that, for the past few weeks, I had been having difficulty urinating and that my bowel movements had become ashen in color. I had no idea what was wrong with me, but I knew that if I went to Medical and someone there determined that I needed to be hospitalized, I would have to abandon my legal fight—and I was not about to take that chance. I rationalized that whatever I had would soon clear up and I kept typing.

Over the course of the next month or so, my symptoms intensified. I was exhausted and sleepy all the time, and the squeamish feeling in my stomach wouldn't go away. My bowel movements grew paler, the back of my neck ached constantly, my vision was blurred, and bright lights bothered me. I felt like a walking zombie, barely able to hold my head up when I was at my desk writing or at the law library researching and reading. I was so close to being finished with my objection to the district judge, though, that I was certain that in just a couple more days, the notice would be ready to mail out and then I could recuperate. Then I could get ready for the battle with the Tenth Circuit Court of Appeals, if God allowed it to go that far. That was my plan.

There were moments, however, when I didn't know how much longer I could keep going in my frazzled state of mind and this horrible physical condition. In the heat of the night, while being locked down, I fervently prayed to God to heal me of whatever I had contracted. Sweat ran profusely down my face as I kneeled in my cell and asked the Lord for the strength of mind and body to continue and to fill me with the power of the Holy Spirit to withstand all obstacles.

Before the week was out, and with hardly an ounce of energy to spare, I finished typing my objection. I lay my head on the top of the typewriter to rest, just for a moment, just to recoup the energy I needed so I could return to my cell.

"Fritz, wake up!" The law librarian's shrill words jolted me like an electric current. I sprang from my chair, from the fog I had drifted into. "You know you're not supposed to be sleeping in my law library. What's the matter with you?" she demanded. "Have you got some kind of sleeping sickness? I don't know what your problem is, but you're breaking my rules by sleeping in here, and you know I won't put up with that."

Still in a stupor, I looked at her blankly. "I haven't been getting much sleep at night from working on my case," I replied, not wanting to lie but hardly telling the truth.

She hesitated before walking away and then announced to everyone in the library that it was time to get back to the units. From now on, I would have to be very careful in not allowing myself to fall asleep again, or it could jeopardize my law library privileges.

I mailed my objection to the court, and after that, sank into a funk that I just couldn't shake. I felt as though I had entered the realm of the non-living. Sleep was my only ally. I befriended it daily. Much of the time I existed in an odd, lulling sort of slumber, where nothing had significance and I didn't feel any concern. Even the extreme temperatures of summer in the cell didn't affect me. It took every bit of energy I had to stay awake during the daylight hours as I attempted to keep up with my tutoring responsibilities and law work. I had to literally force myself to stay awake long enough to write letters to my family members so they wouldn't think that there was something wrong. I saw very little of Mickey—not because of any lack of effort on his part but because, in my sleepy haze, I simply did not hear his knocks upon my door.

When I found out that my objection to the magistrate's report and recommendation was denied, I wasn't sure if the news was even real. Was it a dream, too, like so many things seemed to be? I had just awakened from a trance-like sleep when I got the letter, but I was too tired to even look at the date of the denial. For that matter, I really wasn't sure if this was May, June, or July. For some reason, the last day of May stuck in my memory—what little memory I had—as the date of the report and recommendation. Maybe that was the first one, though? And this was the second? Just the thought of having to engage in another round of battles in the court of appeals seemed suddenly overwhelming, and I fell back against another wave of drowsiness and drifted back to sleep.

On a sultry late summer morning, I realized that I had no other choice but to seek help from Medical. I had to risk dealing with their attitudes and indifference. If I had cancer, what difference would all my legal work make, anyhow? I wouldn't be around long enough to enjoy my freedom—if that ever did happen—so all of my research would have been in vain, anyway. But I had to find out what was wrong with me! I couldn't stand feeling this way.

I stumbled up to the Medical window and asked to see a doctor. I described my symptoms and said that I thought it was urgent that I see a physician ASAP. The nurse on duty expressed no sense of alarm or emergency, which I was fully prepared for. After a lengthy wait, I got in to see the physician's assistant. Unfortunately, it was the same man with whom I had a bad experience during my visit regarding my stinging sensations. I already knew where things were headed before I spoke.

"What can I do for you this time, Fritz?" he asked without looking up from my medical file.

"I'm very sick," I said. "All I want to do is sleep and I can hardly hold my head up, even during the day."

He made no effort to sustain eye contact.

"I'm listening, Mr. Fritz," he remarked without a thread of concern in his voice.

"Listen, I'm trying to tell you that I am seriously ill, and I want some tests done to try and find out what's wrong with me," I insisted.

"I see here, Mr. Fritz, that you did not complete your appointment with the psychological doctor that I set you up with."

"Sir, I'm not talking about my emotional state. You don't seem to understand what I'm trying to tell you. I need help because of my present physical condition, not my emotions. Are you going to order some tests for me or not?" I demanded.

"Mr. Fritz, there is no need for you to be hateful with me. It is my prognosis that you need a psychological evaluation before any consideration is given on running any tests."

"I'm out of here! No thanks for your recommendation. Let it be known, though, that if I'm permanently injured over your refusal to run blood tests on me, I will file a lawsuit on you for your malpractice," I advised him as I walked defiantly out of the exam room. I despised this P.A. In my opinion, he was nothing more than a quack that couldn't make it as a doctor on the streets. Why else would he be practicing medicine in a prison?

At the same time, I was very worried. I had no other options to resort to, except to keep on sleeping and try to eat as well as I could. A formidable thought surfaced. *Am I going to be able to do this Tenth Circuit appeal with the way that I'm feeling? If I'm ever going to regain my freedom, I cannot allow myself to give up at this point. I must force myself to find a solution to what's making me feel this way.*

After the disaster in Medical, the days and weeks swirled together in confusion as I applied pressure to crank out a whole new round of pleadings. I typed out my notice of intent to appeal and filed it back into the Western District court to the Tenth Circuit. Fortunately, I had prepared myself by learning the extensive rules and procedures for formatting my brief properly, and I had already gathered the additional line of cases that were pertinent to my issues. Although I would not have to file my main brief until the attorney general's office had filed its reply brief to my initial pleadings, I wanted to be ready, considering the fast and furious pace that would follow after the reply brief was filed. I could start working on both the opening brief and the main brief now, confronting the arguments that the assistant attorney general had initiated in her past pleadings. Time, I had to remind myself, was of the essence.

I closed myself off from the unpleasant world of mass confusion and distraction by isolating myself in my cell as much as I could without attracting suspicion. My condition worsened. The debilitating fatigue I experienced every minute of the day showed no mercy. My concentration dwindled into fragments. I was lucky if my attention span lasted thirty minutes at a time. The hazy, distant world in which I existed moved through my mind like a feather on a windy day, without direction or structure as I struggled with the two choices in my life—completing my brief or succumbing to the whispered invitations to close my eyes and drift off into blissful sleep.

After what seemed like months of work, the near-impossible task of having perfected my opening brief was completed. The document was ready for typing, which meant using the typewriter in the law library, where I had to be on my guard against the ever-vigilant law librarian's suspicion and scrutiny. She had already warned me that she didn't tolerate sleeping.

Two long grueling days later, I was sick, aching, and exhausted but the opening brief was typed and completed. I requested the necessary number of copies to be made, and came back the next day and made sure that it was mailed. "Thank you, God," I muttered as I headed back to my cell. It would only be a matter of time until I heard back from the assistant attorney general. In the meantime, I decided to continue working on my brief in support and spread out my stress to a manageable level. As I entered my cell, however, I was overwhelmed by the desire to sleep for a long, long time. I fell onto the mattress, and the clutches of sleep embraced my depleted body.

For the next week or so, I made myself eat even though I wasn't hungry. I forced down six to eight glasses of water every day. I even dared to go back down to Medical and got some prenatal vitamins—leftovers, I figured, from some storeowner's discarded inventory.

While I was waiting at the window for my vitamins, I noticed a new face behind the glass. The man had to be a doctor. He was ushering in some of the seated inmates from the outer waiting room. The possibility of trying again to get some blood tests done flashed through my mind, rekindling the thought that maybe I could eventually be well again. I filled out a medical request, stating that I was very ill and needed some help, and handed it to the nurse behind the glass.

"Mr. Fritz, I may be able to get you in to see the doctor if you've got time to wait. There's quite a few patients in front of you, but I might be able to squeeze you in. Would you like to wait, or would you like for me to make an appointment for you?" she explained.

"Is there a new doctor here that I would be seeing?" I asked, mindful of my two run-ins with the physician's assistant.

"Yes, he's been here for a couple of weeks. So, do you want to wait around?"

"Sure," I replied.

I took a seat, and just for a moment closed my eyes. I awoke some time later to the sound of my name being called. I was directed to an examination room.

Without much delay, the doctor entered the room and introduced himself. He seemed to be quite mannerly and receptive to a discussion about my problem. He didn't interrupt as I described my many symptoms. I told him about the other doctor and how he had denied my request for a blood test. He continued to listen without comment.

"I just can't keep going on like this," I pleaded. "I know that there is something seriously wrong with me, and nobody wants to listen. I have been wrongfully convicted of a crime I did not commit, and I'm feeling so bad that I can barely hold myself up to work on my case. I want to get some blood tests to find out what's wrong with me."

The doctor glanced from me to the open file in front of him.

"I see here, Mr. Fritz, that it's almost time for your annual physical, anyway, so I'm going to order some blood tests. I'll schedule an appointment for you to come back and see me in a week or so. You'll receive notice through the mail on your unit. Is that all I can do for you today?"

"What type of blood tests are you going to order?"

"Well, from what you have told me, I'm going to order a CBC, which is a complete blood count, and a liver profile to check your liver function. Once we get the results back, we can go from there."

I thanked the doctor for extending to me his patience and I meandered back up the hill to the unit.

Two weeks passed without a word from Medical. I wondered if they had forgotten about me or whether there had been some mix-up at the testing laboratory. I made another trip back down to the facility to try to find out the reason for the delay. The nurse on duty informed me that I had missed my appointment. I explained to her that I had never received notification but that I was here now and wanted to know what my test results were. She became defensive, but I stood my ground. My persistence paid off. She told me to come back in an hour and she would try to work me in to see the doctor.

Instead of waiting, I walked the short distance over to the

leisure library to try and relax, and maybe even catch a few winks of sleep. As I entered, however, it occurred to me to look for a book on nutrition and health. There were only a few books in that category, and I quickly scanned their titles. One book in particular, *The Zone,* by Barry Sears, caught my eye. I pulled it from the shelf, sat down at a nearby table, and skimmed the book's contents. I found myself becoming absorbed in what he had to say—that proper ratios of protein, carbohydrates, and fats would help to activate the immune response with any given disease. With great excitement, I checked the book out and made my way back to Medical. A new ray of hope entered my mind, no matter what the test results might show.

I went straight to the nurse's window and asked when the doctor would be ready to see me. He appeared at the side door and motioned me to enter. In his office, he opened my medical file and read over the test results to himself.

The silence was overwhelming, and beads of perspiration appeared on my forehead as I imagined that the tests had uncovered HIV or something worse. I recalled the time that I caught one of my previous cellmates stealing a pack of cigarettes from my locker. If he had taken those, it was possible that he'd also used my razor, which could have put me at risk.

After a moment, the doctor raised his head and spoke: "Mr. Fritz, I'm happy to inform you that your test results, with the exception of your cholesterol being a little on the high side and a slightly elevated white blood cell count, are completely normal."

I could not believe what I was hearing—not with the way that I was feeling. My pulse quickened as I searched for something to say. "That's impossible," I exclaimed. "I know that something is bad wrong with me. Are there any other tests you could run to see if I have mononucleosis or some kind of fatigue syndrome?"

"As a general rule, Mr. Fritz, if you had those types of diseases, your CBC would have shown some indicators reflecting your body's immune response. I'm not saying that is always the case, though. Why don't you give it another month or so, and see how you feel then? If your symptoms persist, come back and we'll run some more tests."

Blood rushed into my cheeks. I was dumfounded, but I couldn't think fast enough to talk him into changing his mind. Questions dribbled out of my mouth as I shook my head in disbelief, but the doctor had no answers. He eventually dismissed me. With my head lowered to hide the look of rejection on my face, I walked up the long, steep hill to my unit, carrying my new book in my hand.

The next month was a blur. I made repeated trips back down to Medical, begging as my condition worsened for additional blood tests to be run. The mononucleosis test showed negative. I waited a few weeks and demanded that the doctor run a test to see if I had hepatitis. Tired of hearing my pleas, the doctor ordered the test and advised me that I would have to wait at least a couple of weeks for the results.

I saw Mick from time to time. He was the only one I had talked with about my illness, and his response was generally the same: I was turning into an old man and had to have some excuse to keep from getting a whuppin' out on the ball field. He always followed his remark with a hearty laugh. Little did he know that, at times, I barely had the strength to walk, let alone think about running, and that after reading some of the Sears book, I decided that my over-expenditure of energy in racing with Mick had weakened my immune system and some dormant virus had attacked my body.

One morning I received a note to go to Medical immediately. When I got to the window, the doctor was waiting. He ushered me into his office, where he didn't mince words as he spoke: "Mr. Fritz, your blood test came back. It shows that you have hepatitis C."

I sighed heavily, and an odd sense of relief lifted from my shoulders. At last, the enemy had a name. My next step was to figure out what it was and how to beat it. I studied everything that I could get my hands on about hepatitis C. The definition of chronic hepatitis was a persistent inflammation of the liver, which in a large percentage of cases could lead to other severe problems such as cirrhosis. I learned that it was called the "silent killer" and that symptoms might not appear for as long as ten years from the time of first exposure. I was clueless as to how I had come in contact with it, but that was of no consequence to me now.

I wrote to several organizations mentioned in different sources in the leisure library: the American Liver Foundation, Hepatitis Foundation International, and the National Hepatitis C Coalition, Inc. The literature they sent back described the same symptoms that I had been experiencing: low energy, fatigue, withdrawal and/or irritable behavior, changes in sleeping patterns, significant weight loss, loss of appetite, tearfulness, depression, and the persistent feeling that things would not get better. According to the literature, there was only one accepted standard of treatment available—interferon injections that were not only very costly but also very debilitating to the body. The percentage of people who received an overall sustained cure from the use of interferon was very low, with further relapses usually occurring.

When I read that treatment for one year could cost as much as $20,000, I knew without asking that Medical would not provide for any such treatment. It was solely up to me to do whatever I could do to fight this disease, along with the other deadly disease I'd been fighting for seven years—wasting away in prison for a murder I did not commit.

Something about knowing at last what I was up against made the prospect of fighting two foes at once less menacing than it had been, and I set into motion a newly formed plan. I had studied the requirements and measurements for the Zone diet. I would rigorously follow and practice its regimen and try to heal myself. In addition, now that I understood that consistent exercise would increase my chances for recovery, I would force myself to walk every other day on the ball field. I would not sleep my life away when there were so many more important things to accomplish.

CHAPTER 33

As 1995 began, I found myself mired in the ever-present chill in my cell and a dismal depressive mood that pushed me deeper into a sense of doom and gloom. My spirit was at its lowest point since I had found out about my illness. Often, I spent hours in my bunk, dressed in long johns and with layers of covers over my body, thinking and wishing that things would change.

Over the course of several months, the assistant attorney general had filed for ongoing extensions to gain additional time so she could complete her reply brief to my opening brief to the Tenth Circuit. When I felt like it, I pushed myself to work in the law library to stay one step ahead, furthering my research on the requirements for filing a petition for rehearing should the Tenth Circuit deny me. The pressure mounted with every day that passed that I didn't receive a response. All I lacked in completing my own reply brief was some restructuring, but the waiting was wearing me down. My body and mind ached to move forth in the course of my legal proceedings.

One afternoon, I was called into the unit manager's office, where Ms. Lazelle informed me that the single cells on Tutor's Row would be discontinued due to the diminishing number of credited G.E.D.s that had been earned. My heart sank as she slowly chose her words: "The program here on the unit has not produced up to our expectations, and I have been fighting a lot of pressure about needed space for incoming inmates. I had high hopes that our unit would set a precedent for other institutions to become more deeply committed to the prospect of educating a greater number of inmates through the G.E.D. program."

I shifted uneasily in my chair as Ms. Lazelle opened a folder in front of her.

"Dennis, as I have mentioned to you before, your work on the unit has been exemplary, and you have continued to steadily help several inmates get their G.E.D.s. I see here that you have had nine students so far who have received their G.E.D. certificates. For this reason, I have made a decision to keep you single celled. Also, within the next few days, I am going to relocate you to another cell over in the V unit, just as soon as some transfers can be made. What are your feelings about this?"

I studied my thoughts before I spoke: "I feel extremely honored, Linda, that you have again given me such a high compliment. I just try to do my best when I find someone who wants to put forth the amount of effort it takes to get their G.E.D. I want to thank you very much for allowing me to keep my single cell so I can have the privacy to properly tutor my students."

With that said, Ms. Lazelle excused herself and I went straight back to my cell. Fortunately, there were no questions regarding my health or comments about the number of times that I had more than likely been spotted lying in my bunk in the mid-morning hours. I was so very thankful that I would be able to keep my single cell. "Thank you, God, again," I whispered as I crawled into bed to go to sleep.

The call of chow out shattered my slumber. The mere thought of having to get out of my warm, cozy bed and go out into the cold of the day made me shiver with disdain. I rolled away from the wall and caught a glimpse of a piece of paper that had been slipped under my door. I pondered its possible content for several minutes before dragging myself out into the cold air. The message stated that it was important to call my mother ASAP, and that alarmed me. I dressed and went to the near on-unit phone and called. Mom answered immediately.

"Son, I got some bad news to tell you," she said somberly.

"Oh, god. What is it, Mom?" I replied, thinking that something had happened to Aunt Wilma.

"Son, your dad died on December 3. I just got word from Amelia Kay not too long ago. She said that he passed away at the Veterans Hospital from complications of diabetes and congestive heart failure."

"Oh, Mom, I feel so bad that I didn't ever have the chance to really get to know him. Was he in a lot of pain?"

"I don't know, son. Amelia was shaken up and didn't talk long. It's so hard for me to believe it, too. As you know, he was in bad health for a number of years, after both of his legs were amputated because of the diabetes. He was seventy-two years old. I'm sorry to have to give the news to you over the phone but I knew that you would want to know as soon as possible."

"That's okay, Mom. It just tears my heart out to think that I'll never have a chance to get to know him like I had always wanted. Did Amelia say anything about how his wife was taking it?"

"No, son, we just talked for a minute before she broke into tears and said goodbye. Are you going to be all right? I know you cared about your dad."

"Yeah, I'm going to be all right, Mom," I lied. "How about you? You loved him for a long, long time, and I know that this will be hard for you underneath."

"Don't worry about me, son. Just take care of yourself and watch your back in that place. I will send you the clipping from the newspaper when it comes out. I love you, and I pray for you daily. Write me when you can."

"'Bye, Mom. I love you with all my heart and I also pray for you and Wilma. 'Bye."

An overwhelming wave of sadness swept through me for the next several days. At the same time, I was assigned to my new cell, which turned out to be much colder because it was on the lower level. I didn't really care one way or the other. I was distracted by the pain of losing my dad.

Without having gotten to know him, I understood that the void inside me would never be properly healed. Even though I had been around him for a short period of time as a teenager, I had never felt comfortable in his presence because I didn't understand that he kept his emotions hidden away. I knew, though, that he was a good man who barely ever missed a day's work, and now I missed him so. With tears dripping from my eyes, I prayed that he might rest in peace for eternity. My tears of sadness carried the brighter reality that he would never be back for me again.

Between sleeping and shuffling back and forth to the law library, I became obsessed with the progress of the O.J. Simpson trial on TV. Watching it gave me something to do during the winter months. I could stay in bed and watch the powerful Dream Team attorneys at work. Sometimes I caught myself daydreaming about hiring Johnnie Cochran or one of the other defense team members as my attorney. I imagined them in the Pontotoc County courtroom, retrying my case and bringing forth my innocence. I visualized the expression on Peterson's face during confrontations with the likes of Barry Scheck and F. Lee Bailey. I played out scenarios in my mind where I was the one that was actually on television, watching and listening to the various courtroom maneuvers that the Dream Team would employ on my behalf. Just the thought of having an attorney like Barry Scheck, reportedly the best DNA attorney in the world, made my imagination tingle with wishful thinking. I considered the possibility of making contact with Mr. Scheck but I was on my own, and there was no way that I could ever afford the representation of someone so monumental. The daydreams also helped me to absorb some of the pain over the loss of my dad. So what if it was a form of escape? It was better than just sitting around and feeling sorry for myself.

On a dark and rainy day, I dragged myself back down to the law library, if for nothing else than to break the monotony of hanging around the unit and wasting an afternoon by sleeping. For the most part, the suspicious law librarian had ceased to watch me like a hawk. She now nagged other inmates to no end. That was just fine with me, as long as she stayed off my back. When she saw me enter the library, she held out her arm stiffly, clutching a large brown envelope tightly in her hand. I approached her. Neither of us said a word. I accepted the mail and signed in.

I carried the envelope to a nearby table, sat down, and tore into it. It was the assistant attorney general's reply brief, stamped that it had been filed April 3, 1995. A quick read through her responses indicated that they were nearly identical to previous briefs she had filed. I took a deep breath, sensing a new air of optimism, hope, and excitement regarding my tactics. Once again, she was misrepresenting pertinent record facts that were not in evidence, just as she had done throughout the past proceedings. While that meant there had to be a considerable amount of restructuring done on the reply brief I had been working on, that was all right with me. Her continued misrepresentation of material facts gave me the ammunition and proof that my previous arguments in the earlier appeal proceedings had been wrongly overlooked by each court. For the first time in a year, I felt a surge of energy flow through my veins. I went right to work, and within three weeks, I finished typing my reply brief. I mailed it out at the start of May.

The cool, crisp, early evening air brought forth an abundance of fresh fragrances and brightened colors as I eagerly made my way from the chow hall toward the adjacent law library. As I was walking, I recognized immediately—having walked from the law library to the unit earlier that afternoon—that something was new and different in the way that I felt. It was more than just a sense that

I was starting to understand how the law worked. It was a feeling that I hadn't experienced in well over a year—a fragment of energy, once lost and now renewed, that seemed at the same time foreign and yet so desirable to my worn-out mind and body. A twinge of apprehension struck me. "Please don't let this trace of a feeling leave me, Lord," I said to myself as my soul once again embraced my trembling body. As I grasped the handle of the library door, a thought flitted through my mind that I should flee to the asylum of my cell and avoid any thieves who might want to steal this healthy feeling.

Alone in my cell a while later, I put up the jigger curtain—the cardboard piece that fit snugly within the frame of my cell-door window—and basked in my privacy. I dropped to my knees and held my hands high, giving praise and thanks to the Lord for having helped guide me to the one book in the leisure library that was meant for me to discover. I was still a long way from feeling as healthy as I had before the onset of the ravages of the hepatitis C virus, but I was certain that I was on the road to a slow but sure recovery.

Throughout the summer months, my physical health inched its way up the scale toward feeling better. I was still weak and could not race with Mick, but he was delighted to have a walking buddy back on the track and someone to chat with while enjoying some gardening.

In September, I received a mail-call message that I had legal mail in the law library. After the call for evening chow, I rushed down to get it, hoping that this legal mail might be the Tenth Circuit ruling. There was no one else around except for me and the law librarian.

"I guess you came for this," she said as she held a bulging envelope close to her.

"Yes, ma'am," I replied politely.

"How much is it worth?" she taunted with a half-grin on her face.

I could play her game. "Oh, what about a pack of cigarettes and a case of ramen noodles?" I countered with a little humor of my own.

"Here!" she grunted, thrusting the envelope at me suddenly. "Now either sign in or get over there in that chow hall and eat some food that will put some weight back on you."

Her abrupt change of mood didn't bother me. I took the letter and left the library. Sure enough, it was from the Tenth Circuit. I quickly stepped to the concrete slab in front of the chapel and opened the bulging envelope. I flipped to the last page and my heart dropped to my feet as I read the denial, stamped September 11, 1995. My stomach reeled, and bitterness welled up inside of me. My physical hunger for food vanished completely, replaced by a desire to throw up. All of the pain and suffering that I had gone through to get to this point was now smeared with rejection and humiliation. With the Tenth Circuit's decision to deny me, I was almost at the end of my rope. The only option left to me was the United States Supreme Court.

Chapter 34

For several days after I received the denial from the Tenth Circuit Court of Appeals, I turned the sting of defeat over in my mind. The only option left to me should the Tenth Circuit reject my request for rehearing was the United States Supreme Court, and the chances of an ordinary inmate winning there were almost nonexistent. Even a skilled attorney who specialized in cert briefs got a run for his money in the highest court.

I faced a crossroads: Should I throw in the towel, or reach deep within and pull together my shattered confidence and hope and keep on going? The monkey on my back wouldn't leave me alone, chattering in my mind to let go and be like everybody else — the guilty! Its presence was powerful and strong as its deceptive whisper commanded me to break my grip from what I thought was the end of the rope: *Come with me. You can't win anyway. Nobody cares. This is your home now. You know you are defeated so let go and give up the fight. This is where you belong. You are INSTITUTIONALIZED!*

I knew, however, that I had come too far to call it quits. I rejected the seduction and stepped from my mood of despair with renewed zeal, determination, and fight. I would not give up, not now, not when hope remained that the Tenth Circuit might reverse its decision if I filed a petition for rehearing.

During the next two weeks, I struggled with the pressure of writing a petition that had to be flawless and contained an argument so compelling that it would overcome the presumption of correctness of the most recent ruling. I studied night and day to come up with an idea that might be recognized by the reviewing judges. I searched for the weakest link in all of my past proceedings. In the early morning hours, while I sat in my cell poring over notes and documents, an idea came to me.

Over the course of previous proceedings, I had always argued that the sufficiency of the evidence did not go beyond a reasonable doubt in proving all the elements of first-degree felony murder, but now the thought occurred that I should focus on the felony murder statute and determine whether it had been sufficiently proven in my case. After all, Barney and Greg had said before and during my trial that felony murder had not been adequately proven to have been used as a predicate for proving first-degree murder. What if, instead of arguing that the predicate felony murder had not been sufficiently proven to charge first-degree murder, I could argue that the essential element of intent on the underlying felony of forcible rape was never proven beyond a reasonable doubt? Even though I had not raised that exact issue in the state courts, or in my federal pleadings for that matter, it should be considered as an overall part of the sufficiency claim, which had been fairly exhausted at both the state and federal levels. As daylight shone through the narrow cell window, I danced around like an excited kid. This, I believed, was the key to the locked doors. This was the argument that would set me free.

Everything that I researched for the next two days told me that I was headed in the right direction with my new plan of attack. It was not as if I had a landslide of options to choose from, but because every other argument had failed, this one was worth at least giving a try. With purpose in my mind and spirit, I completed my brief with the additional argument that the court's review concerning my Sixth Amendment claim of the right to enjoy counsel free from any governmental interference was improperly denied through the adoption of the lower magistrate's incorrect understanding of the issue on review. The thrust of my argument was based upon the magistrate's misinterpretation of my right-to-counsel claim as a Miranda issue.

With a level of energy that I hadn't felt for a year, I skipped noon chow and rushed to the law library to be the first in line to get a typewriter so I could spend the full afternoon typing my brief. With only a limited number of typewriters, the library was first-come first-serve, and I only had a matter of days to meet my deadline. I even disregarded my normal routine of looking at the legal journals to see if any new cases had come out that might have some bearing upon my case. I had no time for such luxury.

I gained speed on the typewriter with every key I struck. I had plenty of correction tape with me, and the library was unusually quiet. Dale sat down at the typewriter next to me and started to work; he had only a limited amount of time while he was on break from his job in the chow hall. Sounds of other inmates filing into the library went on around me. Out of the corner of my eye, I noticed that Dale momentarily left his seat, but I paid no attention to his whereabouts as my fingers moved like magic over the keys.

Dale returned to his seat and exclaimed, "Dennis! Dennis!"

I glanced over at him and saw that he was holding an open three-ring binder in his hands. "What, Dale?" I responded without missing a beat as I typed.

"Stop! Stop typing. You won't believe what I've just discovered."

"What is it?" I asked, a little annoyed that I had been interrupted.

"Your co-defendant has been ordered a new trial."

"What are you talking about?"

He handed me the binder and pointed to the open pages.

I couldn't believe my eyes as I read, "Ronald Keith Williamson v. Dan Reynolds."

"Look at the back page. Read the back page," Dale insisted.

On page 86, staring out at me as big as life itself, was the epilogue of Frank H. Seay, United States Eastern District Judge. With a sense of disbelief and a look of shock that surely must have contorted my face, I slowly read:

While considering my decision in this case I told a friend, a layman, I believed the facts and law dictated that I must grant a new trial to a defendant who had been convicted and sentenced to death.

My friend asked, "Is he a murderer?"

I replied simply, "We won't know until he receives a fair trial."

God help us, if ever in this great country we turn our heads while people who have not had fair trials are executed. That almost happened in this case.

ACCORDINGLY, the Writ of Habeas Corpus shall issue, unless within one hundred twenty (120) days of the entry of this Order the State grants Petitioner a new trial or, in the alternative, orders his permanent release from custody.

IT IS SO ORDERED this 19th day of September, 1995.

I felt so disoriented that I didn't know whether to laugh or cry. The significance of the order resonated in my mind. I sat speechless as I scanned the lengthy opinion. A rush of elation charged through me.

"You know what this means, don't you, Dennis? It means you're going home, too—that is, if they don't retry him, which they may very well do," Dale said. He looked at the clock on the wall. "I got to get back to work. See you later."

For several minutes after Dale left, I just sat—the notebook sprawled open on my lap, my rehearing petition still in the typewriter. My silence attracted the attention of the law librarian, who began to stare in my direction. With great displeasure, I closed the binder and continued typing. Regardless of this news, I still had to finish my brief.

After evening chow, I hurried to the library and checked out the wonderful, wonderful opinion. I wanted to be able to read it thoroughly that night and for days to come. I called Mom and Aunt Wilma and Elizabeth to share the good news with them. Mom and Wilma were elated after I explained to them that Williamson's reversal could very well affect my case in a positive way. Elizabeth was also excited but she understood very little about the law. She told me she loved me and supported me and wished me the best on my petition for rehearing. Just hearing their voices gave me the confidence and enthusiasm I needed to continue my pursuit of freedom.

Shortly thereafter, on September 25, 1995, my rehearing brief was filed by the Tenth Circuit. As I read the Williamson opinion more closely, I was overwhelmed to discover that several of his overturned issues were close to or identical to mine: that the jury was never exposed to the exculpatory videotaped confession of Ricky Simmons, that there was some unreliability of microscopic hair analysis comparison due to its imprecise and speculative foundation, and that the closing argument of the state prosecutor also denied the appellant his right to have received a unanimous verdict. In a rush of excitement, I prepared a judicial notice of adjudicative facts that noted the inconsistencies and stated that it was an absolute necessity to have a full court hearing to prevent a fundamental miscarriage of justice from occurring.

From my perspective, the Williamson opinion was new evidence that should be applicable to my companion issues that had already been denied. I also included within my additional pleadings a motion for appointment of counsel under the Criminal Justice Act based upon the fact that, since these companion issues existed within the Williamson case and were indistinguishable from mine, I should be afforded the right to have counsel appointed to challenge the validity of my denied issues in light of the Williamson opinion. In addition, I also typed a motion to stay the issuing mandate, which would preserve my right to due process in that I would not be denied the opportunity to benefit at the Supreme Court level, since the Williamson opinion had not been decided until after my denial in the Tenth Circuit.

There was nothing more that I could do at this point. I had included everything that I could think of, with the exception of the kitchen sink. It was just a matter of time until the Tenth Circuit ruled upon my belated motions.

The Williamson opinion sent a ripple of legal shock waves throughout the prison system. Not only had Ronnie's conviction been overturned but the extent and magnitude of the reversed issues greatly affected numerous other inmates whose cases had either been finalized or were in the ongoing judicial pot. Judge Frank Seay's bold reversal was the focus of talk within every prison law library in the state of Oklahoma. His opinion breathed new hope in the efforts and aspirations of many inmates.

Without delay, I wrote letters to Ronnie's habeas attorneys, Janet Chesley and Vicki Werneke, at the Oklahoma Indigent Defense System in Norman. I was interested in finding out what their legal opinions were as to how the Tenth Circuit rehearing judges would react to my included use of the Williamson opinion. Within a few days, I received word back from Randy Bauman, deputy division chief within the Appellate Indigent Defender Division, stating that he was hesitant to comment further without knowing more about my case. He did state, though, that it was unfortunate that my case was at such a late stage and that I had had to undertake this endeavor without counsel. After reading his short letter, I felt disappointed that his words were not very encouraging. Nevertheless, all I could do was pray that Judge Seay's opinion would go in my favor on my rehearing determination.

The days passed slowly as the chill of winter again invaded my cell. Thanksgiving was just right around the corner, and the blue holidays of Christmas would follow. To the prison inmates, the holidays represented a time when the two best meals of the year were served. It was also a time when annual inspections occurred.

The big boys from the state Department of Corrections toured the facility with their clipboards in hand and their fingers pointing in several directions. The warden walked around the yard amongst the group, dressed in his best clothes in an attempt to make a good impression on the visiting officials.

During this time, inmates were expected to be on their best behavior; the well-prepared Thanksgiving and Christmas dinners were points of encouragement. Of course, not all of the inmates shared the same perspective of thought. It was a period of time, too, that the majority of the prison staff became more concerned about inmates' needs—granting more cell moves, allowing the inmates a little more leeway if they were late for a lockdown count, and extending communication between unit staff and inmates by going from cell to cell to talk to the inmates about their gripes and complaints. After having survived the crunch time of early fall, when audits were taken and the quality of food was at its worst, the inmates were appreciative when Thanksgiving and Christmas arrived. While I appreciated the good dinners, the sadness I associated with the holidays greatly outweighed any happiness that the prison could provide.

During the early months of 1996, rumors circulated rampantly among the inmates about private prisons that were being built all over the state. As the oil boom of the late seventies and early eighties diminished as a source of revenue for Oklahoma, prisons became the economic moneymaker, supplying jobs within communities and meeting the growing need for housing an ever-increasing population of unlawful citizens. Unless an inmate lived in another county where a private prison was being built, no one wanted to be uprooted and forced to be moved away from family and friends. The stress due to the possibility of relocation wore on me, and I became fearful that I would be among the list of selected inmates that would be transported without notice.

As I lay in my bunk contemplating in my mind how the Tenth Circuit would handle the Williamson decision in the supplementations that I had appended to my rehearing brief, I heard a soft knock on my cell door. I got up. Linda Lazelle was outside. This was the first time that she had ever come to my door unexpectedly. I popped my door open.

"Dennis, I'm sorry to disturb you but an emergency call just came in and you are supposed to call your mother immediately."

"Okay," I responded, detecting a bit of alarm in her voice. "Did she say anything about what the emergency was?"

"From what I understand, Dennis, your mother-in-law passed away just recently."

"Oh my god, it can't be!"

"I'm sorry for your loss, Dennis. If there's anything I can do, please let me know."

I rushed to the telephone and dialed Mom's number. She told me that Mary had died a couple of days ago, on December 10, in the hospital. "I've talked with Elizabeth and she is terribly upset, as you can well imagine. I could barely understand her over the phone because she was hysterical and crying and I couldn't hear the full details of how she died. What do you want me to do, son?"

"I don't know, Mom. The only thing I can do from here is to call her at her school number to see if I can get ahold of her in the dormitory."

"From what I could understand, she told me that she wouldn't be in the dormitory because her classes had ended for the semester."

"Well, did she say where I could find her?"

"She gave me a telephone number where she would be at, and she wanted for you to call her as soon as possible. I don't know if I wrote it down right because she was so upset and I couldn't understand her."

Panic set in when I realized how complicated this could become. "Mom, I can't call on the pay phones because this number won't be on my list. It would take probably weeks to get it approved. Maybe I can get the prison people here on the unit to let me use their phone somehow."

We talked a little longer. Mom sounded as stunned as I was over Mary's death. I told her that I would call her back later, that I was going to try to get permission to use the unit manager's office phone. After saying goodbye, I rushed to Linda's office and explained the situation to her. She said that she could call the number I had, and if my daughter was there, she would give her the message to call her office phone where I could talk with her in privacy. She dialed the number. Someone else answered. There was a pause, then Linda talked to my daughter and told her to call the number she gave her. She called back. Linda handed me the phone.

"Elizabeth, I am so sorry to have heard of your grandmother's death."

There was a short silence on the other end. In a low whisper, Elizabeth said that Me Ma Mary had passed in her sleep and that she was not in any pain at the time.

"Are you going to be all right, Elizabeth?" I asked, already knowing the answer.

"Daddy, I loved her so much. She was so good to me and she never raised her voice at me one time."

The line went silent and I knew that Elizabeth was in agony but was trying to be strong for my benefit.

"Elizabeth, I know how much you loved your grandmother, and there's not much I can say to make you feel better, but I want to tell you that Me Ma Mary is in heaven right now and she is happier than she has ever been in her life. I'm so sorry that you have lost Me Ma. I loved her so much, too. She was a very good woman, and I know that she is looking down upon you right now and smiling a big smile because she wants you to go on and be the kind of strong person that you are. She would want that for you, Elizabeth."

"I know Daddy, but I loved her so… I don't know what I'm going to do without her," Elizabeth mumbled. Then she burst into hysterical sobs.

"Please, Elizabeth, stay strong and take it to the Lord and

He will help you to ease your pain. The Lord will also give you the strength to make it through this as He has been doing for all of us since I've been locked up."

"I love you, Dad. Don't worry about me. I will be okay. It will just take some time for me to be able to get back to myself."

"I will be praying for you, Elizabeth, with all my heart. I love you and I'll be with you in spirit. I better get off this phone, so take care of yourself and give this to the Lord. Okay?"

"Okay, Dad, you can call me at my school number after I get back in early January."

"Goodbye, sweetheart. May God go with you."

Throughout the weeks that followed, I wrote to Elizabeth as often as I could. The sadness that was left behind over Mary's death was a huge blow to me. I did love her. She had always treated me with respect and kindness. She was such a gentle woman who had no bad thoughts about anyone. In my mind and heart, I had a feeling that Mary now knew for sure that I was innocent after all.

With very little to do besides prepare my arguments for the United States Supreme Court, I balanced my time by working more with my students, writing more letters to my family, and continuing to follow the strict Zone diet. Although I still had hepatitis, I was slowly starting to feel better. If my petition for rehearing was turned down and I had to file an appeal in the Supreme Court, I wanted to be as healthy as I could be to wage that battle. I knew that the highest court wasn't likely to consider an appeal unless it affected the law in a major way.

By March 24, I still hadn't heard anything from the Tenth Circuit. I was strung as tight as a fiddle with anticipation. That evening before lockdown, Mick knocked upon my door for a visit.

"Hey, Old Man, come on in."

Mick stood in the doorway. "Old Man, I got some news for you that you might be interested in hearing." He was the kind of guy that never wasted time in getting to the point.

"Oh, yeah. What's goin' on?" I replied, leaning toward him to find out what he had to say.

"Listen, you know Timothy Durham, don't you?"

"I've seen him down at the law library on a few occasions but haven't really talked to him. He's usually very quiet and doesn't talk very much to anyone."

"Well, we were talkin' yesterday, and he was telling me about a place in New York City called the Innocence Project. Have you ever heard about it?" Mick looked at the stack of papers on my desk.

"Not really. I wrote some time ago to a place in New Jersey called the Centurion Ministries, and they wrote back and told me that I was too far away for their budget to extend to."

"Well, you've heard of Barry Scheck. I remember you talkin' about him when the O.J. trial was going on. That's who is over the Innocence Project. With another guy by the name of Peter Neufeld, if I remember correctly. I'm gonna talk to Tim tomorrow and see if I can get that address for you, and you can write and find out some information about what they have to offer."

"That would be great, Mick. I vaguely remember someone mentioning something a while back in the law library about some project in New York that had just kind of started up. Thanks, Old Man, for the thought."

"Don't worry about it. I better get goin'. It's getting close to lockdown," Mick said as he turned to leave. "I'll get back with you on that address."

I didn't wait for Mick to get the address. By the time lockdown count was finished, I had written a letter to the Innocence Project, stating my plea for help:

> *...I have been wrongly incarcerated for the last nine years for a murder and rape charge that I know absolutely nothing about. I have continuously proclaimed my innocence in both the state and federal courts of Oklahoma. Likewise, I have been indigent and without the proper representation to fully assist me in the preparation of my case. In both the state and federal*

*courts, I have continuously motioned for DNA testing to be
done on the existing crime scene samples. All of my attempts
have been denied without sufficient reasons being given.... At
this time the state has appealed Mr. Williamson's case to the
Tenth Circuit. In both the co-defendant's case as well as mine,
the entire strength of the state's case rested on the examination
of class characteristics of hair and body fluids evidence... I'm
going to close for now with the hope that you will contemplate
my situation and need for help. I am truly an innocent man who
has suffered greatly over the state's need to convict someone. If
you could help me in any way, I would be at a loss of words to
express my appreciation. Thank you.*

Sincerely,

Dennis

I didn't know if my letter would be acknowledged, but it
was like a dream come true. *The* Barry Scheck, the same one who
I had watched on television during the Simpson trial, would be
getting a letter from me! It sounded unbelievable. During the night
my previous daydreams resurfaced. I was so excited I could barely
sleep. I would be the luckiest man in the world if I could get Barry
Scheck and the Innocence Project to take my case. I was up at dawn
the next day to get things started.

I met Mick out on the ball field at midday, and as promised,
he handed me a paper with the address of the Innocence Project on
it. After our workout, I hurried back to the cell and completed the
letter, and then rushed to the mailroom and mailed it.

Not many weeks after that, Dale told me to come up to his
cell, which was above mine, and get some Supreme Court cases
that he felt were pertinent to my case. As soon as chow was called,
I rushed to the law library, where I was greeted by the librarian,
who held a legal-sized envelope in her hand. It had to be the
determination on my rehearing petition. Instead of going outside,
I sat at a table and opened the envelope. "Rehearing denied"—the

familiar words bounded from the page. I sat there nearly numb and tried to prepare myself for the inevitable; surely the other motion rulings had been denied, too.

"Good news?" the librarian asked with nonchalant disinterest.

"Just the same old thing—one denial after the other," I replied.

"Well, at least you tried and that's what important."

"No, ma'am, that's not what's important. Getting out of here is what is important," I blurted out, thinking that I didn't want to hear her comments.

"Well, where do you go next?" she continued.

"Next?" I snapped. "I'll be going to Fantasy Island if I don't ever get out of this hellhole." I wanted to run and hide somewhere where I couldn't be found, somewhere that was a million miles away, someplace uninhabited where I was totally alone. "I'm going back to the unit, ma'am," I said as I walked to her desk and signed out.

I had to get away from everyone. I needed time to think about the nagging doubt of whether I was ever going to get out of here. But instead of going straight to my cell, I wandered out to the ball field and began walking. There had been a rain shower earlier that day and there were only a few other inmates on the track. I heard a familiar voice hollering from behind me.

"Hey, Old Man, did you get that letter in the mail to the Innocence Project?"

I hadn't bumped into Mick for a couple of weeks, and it was good to talk to him again. "Yeah, Old Man, I got it out the very same day you gave me the address," I told him.

"What's the matter? You seem a little under the weather."

"I just got my rehearing denial in the Tenth Circuit. I don't think I'll ever see the light of the day outside of this place. It's the same thing, over and over again."

"Oh, don't worry about it. The Innocence Project will take

your case and help you prove your innocence. You've got to believe in that or it won't happen."

We walked on for a short distance in silence. Mick stopped. "Are you ready to get a whuppin' or do you want to just do some walkin'?"

"Yeah, let's just do some fast, hard walkin' so I can get all of this out of my mind," I said. As we walked, I thought about what he'd said. Maybe he was right. Maybe the Innocence Project would take an interest in my case. After all, they dealt with DNA cases, and that's what my case was all about.

Chapter 35

Never before had the pressure been as great as it was now as I realized that I had only ninety days to finish my research and complete a perfected petition for writ of certiorari for the Supreme Court. Despite the agonizing thought of having to endure the hot, brutal summer ahead, I psyched myself up. This was my last chance to try to win my freedom. Neither hell nor high water was going to get in my way.

I studied at the law library at every available opportunity. The Supreme Court cases that Dale gave to me were of tremendous help. Many of the cases resulted in either remands back to the lower judicial districts or vacating the judgment and sentence altogether, although those were few and far between. And Dale showed an avid interest in helping me with my case, which I appreciated. After evening lockdown, I fought off the urge to sleep and slaved away through the night till early morning came. With each passing day, I built momentum. April was gone before I knew it. The only thing that could stop me now was time itself.

From out of nowhere, though, in mid-May, the worst thing that could have happened did. The bottom fell out from underneath me. It had been an unusually hot month, with temperatures soaring well into the nineties. I had just returned from the law library and was standing among the inmates as the guard called out mail. All of a sudden, the guard's walkie-talkie blared out the command for an immediate lockdown. The urgency of the voice on the walkie-talkie conveyed that someone must have been brutally beaten or murdered. Everybody stood dumfounded as the guard threw down the mail and roared out the command, "Lockdown! Get to your cells now!"

My heart sank. At a time when every second counted, lockdown meant that I would not be able to do any research for several days. Depending on what had taken place, it could take as long as a week. Adding insult to injury, I would be confined in the unrelenting heat in my cell. Things could have been worse, though, I decided as I headed to my cell. At least I didn't have to put up with a cellie, who would have completely disrupted any and all efforts toward what I needed to accomplish.

As I suspected, the lockdown lasted for nearly a week, followed by individual interrogations and an intense shakedown, after which we were released. Rumors flew afterwards that an inmate who lived on another unit had been stabbed multiple times right outside our unit beside the basketball court. Supposedly, he was killed because he refused to take some dope from a couple of inmates from our unit who were being pursued by prison guards in the yard compound. The inmate came up to our unit and got mouthy with the two inmates that had tried to give him the dope. He had no protection from the shanks they were packing, and they stabbed him over fifty times in the body and neck.

For me, the inmate's death was a resounding message to not become overly involved in anyone else's business. The second message I received, this time in the mail, brought better news. A postcard from the Innocence Project had been slipped under my door during the lockdown. It read that they were considering my case and that I would receive further correspondence shortly. While that was a good sign, it still wasn't a definitive *yes*. I climbed back into the saddle of my legal work and regained my momentum.

The end of May brought surprise and delight into my life, when I received a questionnaire from the Innocence Project concerning the history of my case. I completed the forms and mailed them back the next day. That form, and my anticipated completion of the writ of certiorari petition, buoyed my excitement, and for the first time since my arrest I experienced renewed hope, along with feelings of happiness, rejuvenation, confidence, and composure. My innate sense told me that the Innocence Project would take my case and initiate the testing on the long-forgotten crime scene samples, but I had some doubts. What if Peterson had messed with the samples and switched some of my offered hair samples over to the crime scene samples? *Don't even go there, Dennis. You don't even know for sure that the Innocence Project will take your case. What is important now is that you do the best job that you can on the cert petition and go from there. If I am fortunate enough to get Barry Scheck and the Innocence Project to work on my case, I can cross that bridge if and when it comes about.*

Because the lockdown had set me back severely in the amount of research time I needed, I stepped forward in June and motioned the high court for a sixty-day extension of time in which to file my cert brief. I had to properly frame my issues in a context that would get the judges' attention—abandoning my weaker claims that could not meet the court's stringent provisions, and instead, concentrating on presenting my issues as uncommon and in direct conflict with the law of the land. I needed time to develop that strategy and get the research done.

Within days I received word from the court that they had granted my requested motion. They gave me until September 8, 1996, to file my cert brief. Because the brief would be in the neighborhood of forty pages, with approximately thirty case citations, I realized that it would take me every bit of that time to perfect my writing and get it properly formatted and typed.

From the sweet gates of heaven on a bleak and lonely day, a letter floated through the mail from the Innocence Project to my hand. My heart raced with exhilaration as I hurried back to my cell. When I got there, though, I found that I was scared to open the envelope because then I might discover that my request for help had been turned down. Anxiety mounted as I stared at the all-important letter. After several minutes, I ripped open the envelope and read a request for copies of the lab serology and hair reports.

My heart fluttered like a kid on Christmas morning. I paced the floor, eagerly waiting for count to clear. Never in my wildest imagination would I have believed that Barry Scheck and his Innocence Project would be involved in my case. The truth was too surreal to fully comprehend. It was as if an angel had been sent my way to prove to the world that I was truly an innocent man.

The door popped open for count clear. Out of a dire need to hear someone else agree with me that the Innocence Project was near the point of taking my case, I made an excited dash upstairs to Dale's cell, taking the steps two at a time. At the landing, I paused to catch my breath. Then, trying to appear as if I weren't too excited, I stepped into Dale's open doorway and asked him to read the letter and give me his thoughts.

"Well, what do you think?" I ask, trying to sound nonchalant.

Dale read every word very carefully but hesitated to speak.

Again I stated, "Dale, what's your read on that? Does it sound like they are interested in taking my case?"

Still looking at the letter, Dale said slowly, "I don't necessarily think that they are telling you in so many words that they are going to take your case."

Disappointment stung me. Dale wasn't saying the words that I wanted to hear.

"Well, don't you think, though, that after they get the lab reports and it meets with their expectations, wouldn't it be favorable to think that they might take my case?" I asked, prodding, hoping he would be in agreement.

Looking up from the letter, Dale said calmly, "I think it depends greatly upon the totality of the circumstances of your case, and until they see everything, including the transcripts, they won't be in a position to decide one way or the other. Sorry I can't be any more in agreement with what you want to hear."

"That's quite all right, Dale. I always respect any opinion that you might have, so thanks for sharing your thoughts with me. Let me know if I can do anything for you. All you have to do is ask." I left his cell feeling like a deflated helium balloon drifting back down to earth. I had always joked with Dale that he would make a better prosecutor than a defense attorney. He didn't seem to understand my humor, but he always gave me his undivided attention and honest responses. I mailed copies of the reports out the next day.

Kim Marks and Leslie Delk, who by now had moved on from the Oklahoma Indigent Defense System, wrote me often, keeping me abreast of the ongoing progress in the Williamson case. They informed me that an attorney by the name of Mark Barrett had been recently assigned to Ronnie's case, and they included his address. Kim and Leslie also stated that, at this point, there had been little or no communication between the prosecution and the defense. They were sure that Peterson would surely initiate the DNA testing in the proper sequence of time. They said that Ronnie was in very poor condition—that he had lost a lot of weight and that the majority of his mental faculties had faded from the horrific stress of being on death row for eight years. Kim also mentioned that she had learned that the guards on death row had spoken over the loudspeaker into Ronnie's cell, taunting him with voices that they claimed to be that of Debbie Carter.

There was absolutely nothing that I could do to help Ronnie out. After all, he had gotten a new trial and I was still fighting to stay afloat in the swirling legal quicksand. According to Kim and Leslie, Ronnie was still screaming out his innocence at the top of his lungs day in and day out. For this, they said, and for other reasons related to his physical health, Ronnie had been moved on numerous occasions in and out of the Special Care Unit within "Big Mac." The mere reminder of Ronnie's continued screams opened a flood of unwanted memories about the torment and the stressful times when I had been in the county jail. I shuddered to think that, after all these years, Ronnie was still screaming at that level of heightened intensity. I drafted a letter to Mr. Barrett to express my concerns over the probable DNA testing for Ronnie that would eventually be initiated by District Attorney Peterson.

By the end of August, I was exhausted. The lingering heat of summer had drained me emotionally and physically. My body, mind, and spirit felt as though I had been through a trauma of incredible proportions. I received a letter from the Innocence Project requesting copies of all state appellate briefs written by me and the assistant attorney general. With perspiration dripping from my brow, I had to tell Mr. Scheck in a letter that my appellate brief had been stolen a couple of years ago, but I could send a copy of the state's appellate brief along with a rough copy of my cert brief that was due on September 8.

I was satisfied with the completed draft of my cert petition, to which I had devoted several hundred hours of researching and rewriting. All that was left was the final phase of typing my masterpiece. The filing date was drawing near, and the thought of another lockdown made me cringe with desperation. A little more than a week was left, and everything seemed to be flowing smoothly—that is, until the law librarian abruptly decided to close down the law library for a two-day inventory. The sense of desperation I had felt was acute and frightening.

For two days I stayed in my cell, mentally preparing a strategy to be one of the first ones to get to a typewriter when the library reopened. Since our unit alternated with other units regarding which was first to leave for evening chow, I had to devise a way to get the on-duty guard to let me out first on an early pass. It would not be an easy thing to do. The only solution I could come up with was to have a talk with Linda Lazelle.

It was on a Friday not long before she would leave for the weekend that I approached her office and knocked on her door.

"Come in," she called out from behind her desk.

"Hi, Linda. I need to talk with you about something very important. Do you have a minute?"

"Yes, as a matter of fact, I do. I'm glad you came by because I also need to discuss something very important with you," she told me.

There was a fleeting awkwardness as we both started to speak. Then she nodded for me to go first. I conveyed the whole story to her, about the sudden inventory and the dire and legal importance of getting my brief completed and mailed by the due date. Linda was all ears. I concluded by asking her if she could give me permission to leave early for evening chow on Wednesday, Thursday, and Friday during the next week.

"I have no problem with that, Dennis. I will prepare a memorandum and have it put in the guard's control room, so you will have no problem in getting out early. Now, there is something that I need to talk to you about that you are not going to like." She sounded apologetic as she spoke.

"I don't know how to tell you this in any other way, so I'll come right out with it. I received word from the warden that all single cells in the prison will be terminated by the end of next week. I'm sorry that it has to be this way. Your success with having helped thirteen inmates get their G.E.D.s has been remarkable, to say the least. So, with my gratitude of thanks and a job well done, I will make the necessary arrangements for your early outs for next Wednesday, Thursday, and Friday."

That next week, I managed to successfully type my cert brief and get it mailed on the due date with ten minutes to spare before the mailroom closed. At last that pressure had been lifted from my shoulders. My spirit was now soaring with eagles. So far, the Innocence Project had not denied my request for their help. The crisp days of fall allowed me the comfort and opportunity to enjoy long walks and good conversation with Mick out on the ball field. On each of these occasions, Mick assured me that I would be going home shortly. I played devil's advocate with him by asking why he was so sure.

Mick's response never varied: "I feel it on the inside, Old Man. That's how I know. You're going home." He tended to repeat this several times during our daily walks.

"Time will tell, Old Man," I almost always responded.

The weeks of autumn were filled with the unpleasant task of having to adjust to several different cellmates who stayed for short periods and then decided to change cells, leaving me with the stressful options of trying to find someone else suitable to move in with me or roll the dice and get the draw of the straw. Living with another person in the close quarters of a small cell would be very difficult to adapt to after having lived by myself for almost four years, but I accepted my fate and was introduced to my new cellie. I also spent more time outside while the weather was good.

On November 6, 1996, I walked another lap after Mick left, which made me a little late getting back to the unit for the afternoon lockdown. The guard had just finished passing out legal mail and was preparing to enter his control booth to pop open some doors for some waiting inmates. I asked him if I had gotten any mail. He motioned me into the control room. Reaching into his mail sack, he pulled out a letter and then told me to get on to my cell.

The letter was from the Innocence Project. In my mind and heart, I knew that this had to be the one that I had been so eagerly awaiting. My cellie was asleep as I sat down on my bunk and tore into the envelope with a do-or-die attitude. Dale's words came to mind as I realized there was nothing left they could ask for except for my transcripts.

I read slowly in anticipation:

Dear Mr. Fritz:
Based upon the information you have provided us, we are
prepared to work with you in your efforts to prove your
innocence. Your case will be assigned to a third-year law
student who will attempt to locate the evidence in your case and
arrange to have it submitted for DNA testing. This student will
write you shortly. I wish to assure you that all of our student
interns are closely supervised by a staff attorney and professor.
Furthermore, any conversation or correspondence you have with
the student, or anyone else in our office, is confidential and fully
protected from disclosure. Please send your trial transcripts. We
look forward to hearing from you soon.

Yours sincerely,
Barry C. Scheck
Director, Innocence Project

I bounded from my bunk. I wanted to jump into the air and shout for joy that Barry Scheck had committed himself and the Innocence Project to take on my case. I paced the floor as my cellie slept. At last, I had the greatest DNA attorney in the world representing me in my struggle to my innocence. The harder my cellie snored, the faster I paced. Visions of courtroom scenes and joyous expressions on my family's faces flooded my mind.

I thought about running up to Dale's cell to tell him the great news, but a burst of cautiousness flashed in my head, and I heeded it. If I told Dale, then everyone he might tell would tell other inmates who might ultimately become jealous and try to manipulate some situation that could cause problems. I needed to keep this to myself. I had to remind myself that the best-kept secret was the one that was untold to anyone—with the exception of my family.

As soon as count cleared, I made my way to the telephone before the waiting line grew too long and called Mom and Aunt

Wilma to tell them the great news. They were ecstatic. As we talked, I visualized the gleam in their eyes and the long-lost expressions of happiness that must have radiated from their faces. I could practically feel their tears of joy. We celebrated in the reunion of our longstanding faith and perseverance. We celebrated our love with the confidence that the whole truth would surely follow. I said goodbye to them and immediately called Elizabeth to share the wonderful news with her. She asked a plethora of questions about the scientific aspects of DNA testing. I assured her that, as soon as I gained more of the technical information, I would let her know. Goose bumps appeared all over my arms as I listened to the happiness and enthusiasm in her voice. We had to cut the conversation short because she was running late for an appointment. Her last words to me—"You are going to be set free, Dad. I know you are!"—rang in my ears well into the night.

Since the completion of my cert brief, I now had time to spare, which was a foreign feeling. I had worked for so long, and now there were no other courts to prepare for. I had climbed to the top of the legal proceedings ladder, where I perched without a safety net should my cert petition be denied. In addition, because Aunt Wilma was experiencing an illness, Mom was not able to send me any money, and I was having great difficulty in procuring the funds I needed to get my 1,200-page trial transcript copied and mailed to the Innocence Project.

The solution to my problem came in the form of an introductory letter from my newly assigned third-year law student, Seth Kirschbaum. Out of sheer necessity, I placed a collect call to him and shared my financial difficulty with him. He put me on hold momentarily. When he returned, he said he had gained approval from a staff attorney, Gille Ann Rabbin, for me to go ahead and mail my transcripts to the Innocence Project, and they would cover the cost of copying and mailing. I was so grateful for their courtesy and professional attitudes.

As Thanksgiving passed, the telling blues of December descended upon me. I still held myself accountable for the death of Mary. Why had I not foreseen so many years ago the possibility of something going wrong during my work-related absences? With that foresight, I imagined, things would have been different. Nothing would have been like it was today. As I walked listlessly to the law library, I asked myself why this month was always the one in which I felt the terrible agony of self-persecution. December was supposed to be a time of joy, a time of celebration, and here I was, struggling with depression.

"You've got legal mail," the gruff librarian announced as I approached the desk. "If you're going to stay, sign in. Otherwise, there will be no dilly-dallying."

I had no idea what she was talking about. I took my mail and left. As I headed back toward my cell, I looked over the envelope. The return address read "United States Supreme Court." I opened it. I couldn't believe what I was reading: The Supreme Court was ordering the Oklahoma attorney general's office to file a reply brief to my petition. *My* petition. The chances of receiving this kind of ruling from the Supreme Court were next to none. Evidently, I had struck a nerve during the high court's review. Exactly which nerve I did not know. The court provided no factual indicators in their order.

Chapter 36

Despite the court's initial response, my petition for writ of certiorari was denied by the Supreme Court on February 18, 1997. All of my legal endeavors had failed me. The hundreds of hours that I had spent throughout my long legal battle as I endured the obstacles of prison life were finally over. The crush of defeat swept over me.

Frustration and bitterness set in. I withdrew into myself and talked to no one for several weeks while I struggled with the fact that my legal fight had ended. All that was left were the DNA tests. If they showed inconclusive results, I was as good as guilty. An exclusive DNA test result, on the other hand, would clear me, but my distrust of Peterson kept coming back. I was afraid someone might tamper with the evidence and mix my proffered hair samples with those from the crime scene. That fear, and my disappointment, nearly sank me. I grew even more depressed when word came from Mom that Aunt Wilma had been in and out of the hospital for congestive heart failure. She could not and would not give up the cigarettes.

Every night shortly before lockdown, I ventured outside to

the basketball court. This was my place of solace, where I could get out of my cell and imagine the feelings of sought-after freedom that lingered in my mind. The forlorn silhouettes of the bare trees on the far side of the fence etched a deep sense of loneliness in my soul. I wanted to reach out and embrace them, but I couldn't. I could only imagine what might be, what could have been, what wasn't.

The beauty of spring arrived without meaning or significance. As I passed by my garden spot, it became a sore reminder of what I had once created with the hopes of one day having a garden of my very own—in the free world. I continued to tutor, but my heart wasn't in it.

In late March I began to ascend from the depths of self-pity and depression. I made up my mind that I couldn't give up after all this time and after all this work. I would start anew and review all of my judicial pleadings. Maybe something was in there that I'd missed. Maybe something would surface that would open a new path. I prayed to the Lord to give me the determination and strength of mind to bear the painful reminders of the numerous failures that I had encountered.

Daily, I forced myself to sift through the enormous stack of paperwork that represented my pleadings. I read and reread the documents countless times without finding any kind of handhold that I could latch onto for the renegotiation of my case, but nothing appeared.

With great reluctance, I conceded that there was nothing else that I could do. I began to bundle up the documents to store them away. As I was sorting, a thought occurred to me that I had contemplated in the early phase of my legal work, when I wasn't sure what I was doing. It concerned a jurisdictional issue that had been raised when my case had been remanded back for further preliminary hearing. It had intrigued me because I maintained that the Pontotoc County District Court lacked the scope of evidentiary facts to have predicated their arrest and bind-over order on the issue. Recalling that it had something to do with subject-matter jurisdiction, I relocated the law book where I had found the information and began reading. Something of interest hit my eye concerning territorial jurisdiction, but I read on. I ran into a line of cases that I quickly Shepardized over to the Westlaw series in the F.2d's.

As I skimmed through the sections covering subject-matter jurisdiction, my excitement soared nearly through the roof. The book stated that the prerequisite for filing a petition for writ of habeas corpus had to be initiated into the same confining jurisdiction from which an inmate had received his judgment and sentence. I had found it odd that the Williamson case had been filed into the Eastern District Federal Court when I had filed into the Western District Federal Court. We had both been convicted in the same court, after all.

I brought this to the attention of Dale. His conclusion, as mine, was that I had filed into the wrong federal court and they had accepted wrongful jurisdiction over my case. I researched more to be absolutely sure that the Western District had erred in accepting my case. After confirming my suspicions, I prepared and filed a motion with supporting case authority back into the Western District court, alleging that they had wrongfully accepted jurisdiction over my case.

While awaiting the court's response, I received a notice letter from District Attorney Peterson informing me that on or after the 23rd day of May, 1997, the crime scene evidence in both the Williamson case and mine would undergo DNA testing. I was appalled at the thought of having the crime scene samples partially or wholly destroyed through the testing process, rendering nothing available if and when it came my time to have my own independent testing done. As far as I was concerned, they had already falsely convicted me. I had no trust or faith in their abilities to not botch the DNA testing, as well.

Sometime back, I had helped another inmate to prepare an uncontested divorce against his unfaithful spouse. I took my cue from that experience, and after a few hours of research, prepared a motion for a temporary restraining order against the OSBI and the state of Oklahoma to cease and desist in any and all DNA testing until I could fairly alert my representative, the Innocence Project. With a stroke of luck from above, I got it mailed on the very same afternoon that I finished typing it. I sent letters and copies of the motion to everyone that was involved in my case—Barry Scheck and the Innocence Project, and Ronnie's attorney, Mark Barrett.

These accomplishments gave me a wonderful feeling of satisfaction and confidence. At least, if everything else failed and I had to end up doing a life sentence, I would not have to look back over my shoulder and feel regret for not having done everything humanly possible to secure my release. I waited with rising anticipation for the Western District Court to admit fault—that is, if I was right about my allegations.

Having been in prison for ten years, I could not remember a month of April that had been this hot. The heat was nearly unbearable within the cramped confines of the cell, and I searched for reasons to go to the law library, where it was air conditioned.

On one of those extremely hot days, I received legal mail from both the Western District Federal Court and from Mark Barrett. I relaxed in the chilly air of the library and read. The court had ordered the attorney general's office to file a brief in support of my allegations. I knew without a doubt that I had hit the nail on its head. Otherwise, the court would have automatically denied my complaint.

In the other letter, Mr. Barrett introduced himself by stating that he had been assigned to work on Ronnie's case as it progressed toward a new trial. He explained to me that Ronnie's condition had deteriorated to the point that Ronnie was in a delusional state about Ricky Simmons, who he adamantly believed had killed Debbie Carter. I could sense his agitation between the lines of his handwritten letter. He also informed me that Judge Landrith, from the Pontotoc County District Court, had given orders for

Ronnie to be transferred off of death row to a mental facility at the Eastern State Hospital in Vinita to await his upcoming competency determination. He awarded me high praise for having filed my restraining order against the state officials. I could tell that Mark was a nice person who possessed the much-needed compassion and professional character to handle Ronnie's legal interests.

The assistant attorney general's reply brief arrived a week or so later. This time there was a new name on the document—someone rumored to be the "top gun" in the attorney general's office. Her brief with all of its supporting case law totally refuted my simple argument, but because I preferred the cooler air in the law library to the heat of my cell, I took my time and thoroughly read every one of the cases she had cited in support of her opposing stance. Her brief read as though I was totally out in left field about my allegations, but I quickly realized that her supporting case law was not about subject-matter jurisdiction, after all. It focused solely on territorial jurisdiction, which was a completely different subject.

I stuck to my guns and fired back a three-page response brief on May 12, 1997, to reassert the gist of my initial petition. I knew now that I was totally in the right and her argument was nothing more than a tightly concealed smokescreen. On May 27, I received word back from Western District Federal Court. Never before had I felt the amount of excitement as I did now. I didn't want to stay in the law library to open this very important letter so I walked over to the leisure library, where it was also air conditioned. I found a vacant table and opened the envelope.

As I read, I felt the blood rush to my head. When I finished reading, I started giggling like a little kid that had just been given his first bicycle. I was so excited I nearly peed my pants as I read: "The motion to vacate judgment is granted, and this Court's order and judgment of July 29, 1994, denying petitioner's habeas relief, are hereby vacated." All of my habeas corpus rights had been fully reinstated and were transferred to the Eastern District Federal Court in Muskogee, Oklahoma.

I floated on air as I walked back to the law library. I showed Dale the district court's ruling. His jaw dropped as he read the back-page conclusion of the judge's order. I immediately began to work on my newly accorded petition for writ of habeas corpus by typing one motion to amend the transferred petition in its entirety and a second motion to exceed the twenty-five page limit in support of the opening brief.

Correspondence was as spotty as rain all summer long. I received one letter in June from Kristina Cross, who was my newly assigned law intern at the Innocence Project. The substance of her letter was that the DNA testing in my co-defendant's case was being put off until a determination of his competency was made by the district court in Pontotoc County. Shortly thereafter, I was contacted by a law student by the name of Ali Khorasanee. He extended an open invitation to call him at any time during normal business hours. It was not until the early part of November that I heard from Ali again. He informed me that he had talked to District Attorney Peterson and learned that he had intentions of testing my DNA samples along with Ronnie's. Peterson had assured him that some of the samples would be saved for retesting, if it proved necessary. It seemed that my restraining order motion hadn't been in vain after all.

I continued onward with the long and tedious process of perfecting my opening brief to the Eastern District Federal Court, but this time I had the advantage of having already done this once, which greatly helped me minimize my mistakes. The months flew by as I diligently worked toward its completion. After filing several motions to amend, delete, and abandon some of my grounds for relief within my amended habeas corpus petition, I filed the brief into the Eastern District court on December 3, 1997. Thereafter, I received a copy of the magistrate's order by the Eastern District court, which was directed to the attorney general's office to show cause why my petition for writ of habeas corpus should not be granted and to file a reply within thirty days. I had a much better feeling with this court, especially since it was the same court that had reversed Ronnie's case.

With the holiday season nearing, I learned through a copy letter sent by the district attorney's office that Ronnie was to go before his competency hearing on December 10. I called Elizabeth, Mom, and Aunt Wilma with every piece of news to let them know of the new developments. They were thrilled to hear that the time of the DNA testing was drawing near, since it was contingent upon hearing if Ronnie would be found competent to stand trial.

The spring months rekindled my desire to be free. I began making weekly telephone calls to Gille Ann Rabbin, the executive director of the Innocence Project. She was a nice person who had a gentle way about her. Every week she would tell me to try to be patient, that it would not be too much longer until a determination would be made in Ronnie's competency hearing. I felt as though I was starting to unravel at the seams, not knowing the exact length of time to expect before the DNA testing commenced. I tried to relax by playing chess on the unit during the evening hours, but nothing seemed to help. The underlying fear that Peterson had somehow switched my hair samples with those from the crime scene evidence wouldn't give me a moment's peace. I prayed through the day and through the night, thanking the Lord for His intervention of bringing about His miracle of truth.

On an uneventful, rainy day in May, I went to the law library and began typing a motion to the Eastern District court to advise them that the attorney general's office still had not fulfilled the court's previous show-cause order. I felt a peck on my shoulder. There stood the librarian with a legal letter in her hand. I read the contents: The magistrate judge was reissuing an order to the attorney general's office, telling them that they had failed to comply with the previous order, and were further ordered to show cause by May 27 for their failure to comply with the order of the court. Now, they were under the judicial gun.

Not long after, I received the assistant attorney general's

long-awaited dismissal brief for my alleged failure to have properly exhausted my state remedies. I had already anticipated her argument. Within a few days, on July 13, 1998, I mailed my reply brief into the court on the respondent's motion to dismiss. Two days after that, I received a letter from Kim Marks, who shared with me the long-awaited information that Barry Scheck and Mark Barrett were making arrangements for the DNA testing to be done. Kim's words flooded my soul with joy. I felt like I could fly.

The next four months raced by. I motioned the court to allow me to further amend my existing petition with the deletion of several other issues that were being challenged by the assistant attorney general. I had been through all of this before. It wasn't that I was afraid that the abandoned claims would be dismissed if I carried them onward, but rather, I elected to take my two strongest claims before the court in anticipation that I might obtain an outright dismissal. The magistrate granted my motion to amend, and I brought forth the following issues: that the evidence was insufficient to support my conviction and that trial counsel was ineffective for having failed to properly investigate and present to the jury the fact that another man had confessed to the charged murder.

A new law intern at the Innocence Project made contact with me. As soon as I got his letter, I called and talked with Sonny Chehl, who said that he had been assigned to my case after Ali graduated. He said that he was going to make contact with Mark Barrett and that, as soon as he found out about the status of the joint DNA testing, he would get back in touch with me. I asked him if he could be more definite but he said he couldn't, because he had just started working on my case and had not completely reviewed my file.

The stress of waiting continued to mount. I couldn't sleep. I didn't want to eat. Something had to happen soon or I might have a full-scale anxiety attack, though there were times when I wasn't certain that it wasn't already happening. As the holidays approached, I made up my mind that this December was going to be different. I was going to stop tormenting myself with memories of Mary. That was something that was out of my control. As the new year arrived, I worked to gain my composure and prepare for the legal battle that was at last starting to heat up.

In January I placed a call to Gille Ann Rabbin and found out that she had been replaced by Jane Siegel. When Jane came to the phone, she shared with me the wonderful news that the DNA testing was about to begin. She hesitated before telling me that Barry was in the process of preparing a motion to dismiss on both Ronnie's and my convictions based on the expected results of the DNA testing.

I was flabbergasted. I had some difficulty expressing my questions about the testing process. She sounded embarrassed when she replied that the testing on the body fluid samples had actually already gotten under way. She apologized and said that, as a general rule, they did not notify the defendant or their family until the final results came in. I was almost to the point of jumping up and down when Jane told me that Barry wanted to talk to me and that I should call him back tomorrow morning around nine my time.

I tossed and turned all night and was out of bed before dawn. At nine sharp, I made a collect call to the number Jane had given me. I was trembling over the prospect of talking to Barry Scheck. I had a zillion questions to ask but realized after I had dialed the phone that I had left my list of questions in the cell. I took a deep breath and focused on composing myself. On the second ring, a man with a distinct New York accent answered the phone.

"Hello, this is Barry Scheck," he announced in a clear, bright, cheerful voice.

"Hi, Mr. Scheck, this is Dennis Fritz. Jane Siegel told me yesterday that I could give you a call," I said, surprised that I was already starting to feel relaxed.

"Jane told me that she broke the news to you yesterday about the initial testing procedures on the body fluid samples.

Sorry we had to make you wait, but it's in our best interests, and in yours, too, to wait until we have some DNA markers to indicate what the probable results will be. So far, there are some promising indications that the tested samples do not match yours, but we won't know until the lab does some further testing."

"Who is doing the testing?" I asked.

"We agreed with Peterson to use Labcorp, which was his choice, but I am keeping in close contact with them on the progress of the testing. Brian Wraxall of the Serological Research Institute is doing oversight. How are you holding up, Dennis?" Barry inquired. He sounded compassionate and concerned.

"Well, to tell you the truth, Mr. Scheck, I feel like a tightly strung rubber band about ready to snap."

"Call me Barry, please. That's understandable. I know it's hard for you right now, but try to stay as calm as you can. We should know something definite in a matter of days. When I get word, I will let you know what the results are. But remember, if these tests are favorable, we will begin the slower process of monitoring the hair testing, so it's going to be a couple of months before the results are finalized on all of your questioned hair samples."

"Barry, I know that I mentioned this to you in a letter, but I strongly feel that Peterson may have switched my hair samples with the evidence samples. Is there anything that you can do to detect any foul play on his part?" *There. I'd said it.*

"Don't even worry about that. There are some control measures that I can implement that will show any tampering if any of the samples have been switched. Do you have any more questions that I can answer for you?"

"I have one more question. If all of my samples turn out to be exclusive, indicating that I had nothing to do with the crime like I've said all along, how long will it take you to get me out of here?"

"Dennis, if the tested samples are all in your favor, it shouldn't be more than a week before you will be exonerated."

CHAPTER 37

I went to my cell, turned on the television, and sat down on my bunk. Immediately, my mind went into a tailspin. Barry's words turned over and over in my head, and I experienced a flood of emotions as I reminded myself that it could be several more weeks until the final results were in. Unable to relax, I got up and paced the floor, my mind overflowing with thoughts about the likelihood of the preliminary tests proving ultimately favorable. I resisted the urge to call my mom and aunt to share the news with them. I didn't want to get their hopes up, and then later, if the results were unfavorable, crush them with bad news.

That afternoon, because I felt like I was carrying the weight of the world on my shoulders, I went to the ball field in hopes that Mick would be there. He wasn't. I started walking anyway—my jumbled, perplexing thoughts following me with every step that I took. I spotted Mick just entering the gate.

"Hey, Old Man, how come you're not in the law library?" Mick asked me with surprise.

I told him about the conversation I had had with Barry.

He clapped his hands. "Old Man, you are going home! If

some of those tests were already showing in your favor, then mark my words, they will turn out favorable for you."

"I don't know. The next few days are going to be like a living hell for me while I'm waiting to hear something back."

"Old Man, just remember, you've got Barry Scheck on your side. What more could you ask for? He will make sure that the lab doesn't screw anything up. So, do like he said and try and think about something else—like maybe getting a whuppin' from me on a couple of laps," said Mick, laughing.

"I think I'll pass, Old Man," I told him. "I'm goin' on back to the unit to see if I have any legal mail."

I didn't. As expected, over the next several days, sleep was disrupted by tossing and turning. There was no way that I could concentrate on moving ahead in my law work. Instead, I did everything I could do to relieve the stress that rumbled within me— I played chess, I walked, I played my guitar—but I failed miserably. I couldn't relax. Barry's words wouldn't leave me alone.

By the middle of the week, I had received no mail at mail call. I was disappointed. I was exhausted. I wanted to know whatever there was to know about the testing. I fell onto my bunk and tried to sleep. I was awakened sometime later by the sound of knocking on my cell door. It was Homer Purcell, the unit counselor. I arched myself up out of bed, stretched, and walked to the door.

Homer was hollering something that I couldn't understand. A flash of irritation flitted through me. Why didn't he just unlock my door and tell me what was on his mind? This was prison, after all.

"I can't hear you. What did you say?" I shouted back. I could see him in the window but he was bending over toward the crack in the door.

"You are ...nt!" he yelled one more time.

"I can't hear you? What did you say?" I asked again.

He bent closer to the crack in the door and yelled louder: "You are innocent! The Innocence Project called and said that you have been found to be innocent!"

I couldn't believe my ears. I asked him to repeat the message.

"The Innocence Project called and said you are innocent."

This time I heard him clearly. For a second, I was stunned, and then the message hit squarely in the core of my brain. I put my hands in the air and danced across the cell, shouting, "I'm innocent! I'm innocent!" Over and over again, for several minutes I shouted and danced. Then, with weak knees and a shaking body, I dropped to the floor by my bunk and cried out my praise and thanks to the Lord.

My cellie, who was by now wide awake, listened to me jabber as I told him what Homer had said. His reaction was flat and unenthusiastic. I sensed that he was feeling a little jealous, due to the fact that he was doing a very long sentence. I couldn't dwell on that, though. This was my moment. My jubilation soared up and out of the building and over the razor-wired fences that had long encircled me.

After count cleared, I rushed to the phone and called Mom and Aunt Wilma. Luckily, they were home. After exclaiming to them the wondrous news, I listened to their cries of happiness and joy for several moments. After they settled down, I explained to them that there would be another round of testing on the hair, and Barry had stated that it would probably take a couple of months. We said our goodbyes wrapped in the love of our trust and faith in the Lord.

Time seemed to stop after that. Even the year that I had spent in the county jail seemed like a short-distance drag race compared to the turtle's pace that was now occurring as I waited for the hair sample test results. I tried to call Barry, but he was out of town, so I talked with Jane Siegel. She told me that Barry would be back within the week.

I asked Jane how Ronnie's DNA tests turned out. With an expression of joy in her voice, she told me that Ronnie's tests had been one hundred percent favorable for him. I expressed to her my happiness for Ronnie after acknowledging the amount of suffering that he had been through. She informed me that, despite the fact that Ronnie had not been found competent to stand trial, Peterson had elected to forego that requirement and proceed with the DNA testing. She told me to hang in there as preparations were being made on the upcoming testing of the hair samples. I thanked her for her kindness and thoughtfulness in keeping me updated.

By early April, when I hadn't heard a word from anyone on the status of my case, I decided to call Barry again.

"This is Barry." His voice sounded lively as he picked up the phone. "Sure, I'll accept a collect call from Dennis anytime," he said following the operator's inquiry.

"Hello, Barry, how are you doing?" I cordially asked.

"I'm doing absolutely wonderful, Dennis, and you will be feeling the same way after what I have to tell you. First of all, the tests on the hair are showing greatly in your favor, as well as Ron's, as to specific markers that have been isolated in making this determination. Everything looks most favorable for you at this point. Of course, there will be some additional testing that needs to be done to verify the accuracy of these preliminary findings."

A lump formed in my throat that caused me to stammer momentarily before I found my voice again.

"How much longer do you think it will be, Barry, before the final results are complete?" I asked, trying to sound calm when I wasn't.

"Very soon, Dennis. I can't give you an exact date but it shouldn't take over two weeks to clarify these results. Congratulations, Dennis. It's looking very favorable for both you and Ron at this point. I know I need not ask you this, but are you ready to be a free man again?" Barry asked with enthusiasm.

I took a deep breath and said, "I will be always grateful for what you have done for me. I will never forget this moment for the rest of my life. I am so happy right now, it is beyond description."

"How are your mom, aunt, and daughter feeling over all of this good news?"

"Barry, they are just as excited as I am, maybe even a little more. My aunt has been in the hospital for a little over a week but I'll send word through Mom to let her know that you asked about her. Both of them have been anxiously waiting to hear the final results, so I'll give them a call and let them know what you've said."

"Is your aunt all right?" asked Barry.

"Yeah, she's been having some problems with her lungs because of smoking but she should be out of the hospital within the week."

"Well, give them my best, and I'll keep in touch with you on the final results."

Through the days that followed, I found myself being overly cautious around the other inmates. I was careful about what I said and I tried to act as normal as I could. However, one evening while I was playing chess below the cell-run area, an inmate stepped out of his second-floor cell and called down to me that my case was being broadcast over the television news with regard to the favorable preliminary test results. He congratulated me and went back into his cell. A few other inmates heard his announcement and looked my way.

I thought that the weekend would never end. On Sunday, I called Mom so I could tell her and Aunt Wilma of the recent news from Barry. I was anxious to talk with them, especially Aunt Wilma, who should be out of the hospital by now. The last time they had visited me, Wilma had gotten unusually irritated when I made a joke about her card-playing ability following a game of rummy. If she had been feeling better, she would have laughed it off, but on that day she was a little under the weather.

On the fourth ring, someone picked up the phone. "Son," Mom said in a whisper.

"What's the matter, Mom?"

She began sobbing.

"Mom!" I pleaded in panic. "Please tell me what's wrong. I need to know why you are crying. Please tell me what's wrong."

"Son, Sis— passed away this morning."

Sorrow stabbed me to the core. Mom's words echoed within my brain. I tried to say something but nothing came. I felt faint and leaned against the wall to steady myself. For several moments, I let the news find its way to every part of me. My body and mind absorbed the news by becoming numb. Hot tears spilled from my eyes as I fought to regain my ability to speak and get a grip on my senses to comprehend the excruciating reality of what Mom had said. Then I realized I had to make every attempt to sound as strong as I could, to comfort her against the pain of having lost her sister of sixty-nine years.

"Mom," I said, "I don't know how to say this, or even if I can, but Aunt Wilma is with the Lord right now, and she is happy. I'm going to be back home with you in a little while, and I will take care of you and be there for you, just like you and Aunt Wilma have always been there for me. Mom, are you going to be all right tonight? Is there anybody with you right now?"

"Your cousin Sherry was here for a couple of hours and she wanted me to go with her, but I told her that I needed to be by myself."

"Promise me, Mom, that you will not try to harm yourself in any way. Okay?"

"Don't worry, son. I just need time by myself. Are you going to be okay?"

"Yes, Mom," I replied. "You know how much I love Aunt Wilma, and it's going to be hard on us both, but I will pray for you throughout the night."

At that moment, we were cut off. Wiping the tears from my eyes, I walked out onto the basketball court and lifted my head to the sky. The shock of Aunt Wilma's death would linger, but I had to stay strong.

By April 12, I still hadn't heard a word from Barry or any

of his staff personnel. I had been staying in my cell to thwart any possibility that a jealous inmate might initiate a confrontation. This was a critical time. I didn't want to be put into a tight situation. I had enough on my mind as it was. I stayed in my cell and tried to sleep and watch television. After the final lockdown, I fell to my knees and gave praise and thanks to the Lord for bringing me to this point, even though I was still not totally sure that the final tests would be conclusive. That night a peace came over me that I hadn't experienced in years. I fell asleep and slept soundly till early the next morning.

I rolled out of my bunk after my cellie left for work. I had only one thought on my mind—to call the Innocence Project and find out what was going on. I went to breakfast chow and took my time eating. I felt refreshed and of a clear mind as I made my way back to the cell. As I was collecting my thoughts as to what I would say to Barry on the phone, the morning guard keyed my door and stepped inside the cell. He held a huge cardboard box in his hands.

"Fritz, pack your shit," he said. "You are being transported this morning back to court. Be ready within the hour. You're scheduled to leave at ten this morning."

"Back to court? What do you mean? Back to court for what?" I declared with surprise.

"I have no idea, Fritz. All I know is that you are being transported back to the Ada, Oklahoma, court and they want you at the shift captain's office at ten sharp. You better get a move on it because it's almost nine now." He handed me the box.

"Oh my god," I said aloud. *Is this what I think it is, or has there been some kind of problem with the DNA testing that they will surprise me with when I get to Ada?* Surely Barry would have called me to let me know if this had anything to do with my release. My body was shaking violently as I packed my belongings. By 9:45, I retrieved the wheeled cart outside the unit manager's office and was ready to go. There were not too many inmates within the unit as I wheeled the cart out of the unit to the gate. Neither Dale nor Mickey was in sight but a few inmates standing at the gate, including Darrell, said their farewells.

I was so nervous as I rolled the cart down the long decline toward the shift captain's office that I wasn't sure my feet ever touched the ground. A couple of guards inventoried my property as I anticipated the ride back to Ada. When the guards were finished, they summoned the driver. It was John Christian, the Ada jail guard who had testified against Ronnie at his trial. He looked much fatter and had more gray hair than I remembered.

"You ready to go, Fritz?" he grumbled.

"Sure am, John. Picked up a little weight since I seen you last," I shot back at him. His eyes were still as cold as I remembered them, I realized, as I was shackled and handcuffed for the trip back. All the security made me even more nervous that maybe this transport wasn't about my release after all. During the drive, there wasn't much communication—just some small talk about the weather. Instead, I stared at the countryside with wonderment.

It had been a long time since I had seen civilization. The drastic changes that I observed made me feel as though I had just emerged from a time warp, where I had been stuck for a long time. One of the first things that I noticed were the colors and styles of the cars. They were much smaller and sleeker, with a wider variety of colors than there had been back in 1987. As we slowed to travel through some of the small towns along the way, I noticed that clothes were different, too—with more pastel colors. Another difference that I noticed was that people moved about like they were in a bigger hurry to get here and there. I got the extraordinary feeling that I was watching a futuristic movie in a world that was strange and yet extremely fascinating. Was this world a world I could become a part of again?

More than halfway there, Christian spoke up: "Say, Dennis, if you don't mind, I would like to ask you a personal question."

"My ears are open, John," I told him.

"I would like to know if you and Ron really killed Debbie Carter," he said. He glanced at me in the rear-view mirror.

"Well, John, DNA tests don't lie, do they?" I replied in a belligerent way.

"Off the record, Dennis, did you kill Debbie Carter?" Christian asked again.

I told him that I would have never been convicted if it hadn't been for the outright sloppiness of the police department with their half-assed, so-called investigation that overlooked the real killer. I took it a step further by reminding Christian that he had wrongfully testified against Ronnie and asked him how he felt about that. He shrugged it off by saying that he told the whole truth and had nothing to feel ashamed of. That was where the conversation ended.

As we pulled up to the entrance of the Pontotoc County jail, old memories of contempt and anger resurfaced. I detested these people and everything they stood for. They were without conscience. I was led inside. I recognized a few of the old faces. They greeted me dryly, their heads lowered. When I maintained my composure and behaved like a man of strength and maturity, they hung their heads even lower.

After I changed from my clothes into a worn white jail jumpsuit, Christian led me back to the cell where Ronnie had been housed for almost a year, the cell where his screams of desperation and fear had ricocheted outward into the jail. Another inmate dressed in whites was on the bottom bunk. We exchanged greetings, and I climbed onto the familiar, hard, steel-framed upper bunk. He immediately told me that I was all over the news and extended his hearty congratulations for beating the system.

It was a long, uneasy night of nothing but bad reminders. I didn't sleep a wink; I was wound up as tight as a ball of twine. Everything appeared that I was soon to be released, but a seed of doubt still lingered that something had gone wrong with the DNA testing.

Nothing had changed in the jail since I had left. When they served morning chow, I noticed that they were still using the same metal serving trays. I ate very little; the quality of food was another thing that had not improved. I hadn't seen or heard a word out of Ronnie since I had been here, but I suspected he was around somewhere. Maybe they were keeping him over in the city jail. I was very anxious to see him and to catch up on old times. Maybe he knew more about what exactly was going to happen and when.

I got back up in my bunk and pondered the many questions that plagued my mind. When I awoke to the jangle of keys in the door, I realized that I must have dozed off for a while. The guard said that there were some people there to see me. I followed him to the visiting room.

As I turned to enter, I saw a beautiful young woman standing in front of me. In a split second, I realized that this radiant woman with the beautiful smile was Elizabeth. My blessed mother was standing by her side. An uncontrollable feeling welled up in my chest and I began to cry. In that very same visiting room years earlier I had last seen Elizabeth as a young girl. Now she was grown up. She looked so much like her mother. We stood for a moment, uncertain about what to do as we stared at each other, our faces quivering with emotion. Then we lunged into each other's arms, embracing each other with every ounce of emotion that had been locked away inside us for the past twelve years. With our hearts, minds, and bodies united, we embraced for what seemed like a lifetime — the lifetime that we had been cheated out of.

"Daddy, you are going home tomorrow," Elizabeth said, her voice trembling. I could feel her hot tears falling on my neck and shoulders. "I've missed you and love you so much, Dad."

"Are you sure I am going home tomorrow, Elizabeth?" I asked as I parted our embrace and wrapped my arms around my loving and most dedicated mother. The long and hard road that we had been through together was nearing the end. Her excitement was like an electric current. Then, as a mother would do, she reminded me that she had brought my suit and had left it at the front desk.

"Yes, Dad," Elizabeth told me. "I talked with Barry not long ago and he assured me that without a doubt, you are going home. You are going home, Dad!"

We all joined in a tight circle and wrapped our arms around each other and sobbed like newborn babies. We laughed and we cried as we shared our joy. When the guard came to tell us that time was up, he noticed the drops of tears on the floor and called out for a trusty to bring the mop. As Elizabeth was exiting the room, she turned and told me once again that she loved me and would see me in court tomorrow. Mom blew me a kiss goodbye as she followed Elizabeth from the room.

As I followed the guard back to my holding cell, an unmistakable voice rang out.

"Hey, Dennie Leon, come here and talk to me," Ronnie beckoned.

"Ronnie Keith, where have you been hidin' out at? I was beginning to think that you didn't wanna leave death row with all of that good company down there," I kidded him.

"They just brought me in, Dennie Leon. You are a sight for my sore, weary eyes to look upon. How has that exquisitely tasteful food at Conner's been treatin' you?" said Ronnie. When he smiled, I noticed that he was missing several of his front teeth.

"Surely not as good as this place, Ronnie Keith," I joked, which sparked a round of long-forgotten laughter.

The guard allowed us to talk face to face without locking me back down. Before locking the outer, steel door behind him, the guard mentioned to us that the local affiliate of the television show *Dateline* would be coming to the jail around two in the afternoon to interview us. Ronnie and I roared with laughter at the prospect of being on national television in this broken-down county jail. We also talked about our freedom and all the things that we were going to do upon being released.

It was so good to be with Ronnie again and to talk about the good times ahead. His hair had turned snow white but he still had that distinctive smile and his eyes sparkled when he laughed. After eating lunch, we were allowed to take showers, and the guard provided us with brand new black-and-white striped jail clothes to wear during the *Dateline* interview. The jail officials didn't miss a beat when it came to putting on a show to look good for the public.

My head was still reeling over the glorious visit with my mother and daughter. I was a little nervous about doing the television interview. When the crew members finally arrived, Ronnie and I were led out in the hallway, where we sat side by side as we gave our interviews. It was much easier than I thought. They told me and Ronnie that they wanted to have another interview at a later date, after we had settled down in our new lives of freedom, and we agreed.

Later in the afternoon, Ronnie and I were led from our cells and ushered to the side-entrance visiting room. Inside were three men and a woman. I didn't recognize them, but my heartbeat quickened when I wondered if I was about to meet Barry Scheck. They introduced themselves. Along with Barry were Mark Barrett, Sara Bonnell, and a man named Jim Dwyer, a Pulitzer Prize winning columnist for a New York newspaper. Getting to meet Barry Scheck was an honor in itself, let alone being in the presence of a writer who said that he was interested in writing a book about our case. Mark Barrett's stature and friendly presence imparted his intelligence and compassion, and that had a calming effect on me. Sara, a friend of Mark's who was an attorney in Purcell, seemed like a very nice woman.

A serious look came over Barry's face. He hesitated and then gave Ronnie and me the shock of our lives: "Glen Gore's DNA samples were identified and matched all of the crime scene samples found in Debbie Carter's apartment. Not only will you be exonerated tomorrow but with the actual perpetrator behind bars for having

449

committed this murder, there will be little or no speculation as to yours and Ronnie's guilt. That's as good as it gets." He laughed a little, which made me smile. He continued, "Not only will you and Ronnie be free men but now you won't have to contend with those hanging-around doubts from the community that always seem to accompany cases like these."

As Barry talked about tomorrow's courtroom agenda, the door that led to the sheriff's office suddenly swung open and Christian motioned for Mark Barrett to come with him. I was seated at the table, Ronnie was sitting on the floor with a mesmerized look on his face, and Jim Dwyer was shuffling his notes as Barry continued the forecast of tomorrow's events.

When Mark returned several minutes later, he had a huge smile.

"You will never believe what I just heard," Mark exclaimed. "I just talked to Chris Ross from the district attorney's office and he informed me that Glen Gore has escaped from the minimum security facility in Purcell."

"You mean he ran away?" I exclaimed. "All that he's doing is just showing how guilty he really is."

"Yeah, people don't run unless they're guilty of something," Ronnie remarked.

Everyone exploded into laughter over hearing of Gore's perfectly timed escape—right before we were to be released.

"Ross additionally informed me that there is a state-wide manhunt in hot pursuit of Gore," Mark added.

"This is perfect," exclaimed Barry. He raised his hands into the air.

Ronnie wheezed with laughter as he rolled onto the floor. A few minutes later, he crawled over to the side-entrance glass door and lay flat on his stomach as he glared out through the glass at the floor.

"What are you looking at, Ron?" Barry asked.

"I'm waitin' to see that snake Peterson walk from the

courthouse," Ronnie said with passionate curiosity. He reminded me of a cat waiting for a mouse to scurry out from underneath the fridge.

"There he is! There's that dirty rascal walkin' out with his big fat belly hangin' to the ground," Ronnie blared with his lower legs extending into the air.

After the visit was over, Ronnie and I were locked back down. I was dead tired but much too excited to sleep. I stayed awake for much of the night, trying to imagine what the morning would bring.

In the morning after chow, Ronnie and I walked side by side in our best clothes to the courthouse which was flooded with people, photographers, and cops. Memories of the trial emerged as we made our way to the front defense table where Barry was seated.

The proceedings commenced with Peterson calling Mary Long to the witness stand. I felt a twinge of panic as Peterson stood and approached Mary with his usual conceited mannerisms. That old, tense feeling crept back into my body, and I froze in my chair. Recollections of the past trial flashed before me. I leaned close to Barry and nudged his arm.

"What is this all about, Barry?" I asked with alarm in my voice.

"Don't worry, Dennis. This has all been taken care of. You're going home," Barry reassured me. He stayed seated while he asked Long a few qualifying questions about her testimony.

She made a few comments about the testing results that sounded nearly identical to what she had said at trial. Then she was dismissed, and Peterson rose to his feet.

"Your Honor, this is a very trying time for this criminal justice system. It is my moral, ethical, and legal duty to ask that this case be dismissed," said Peterson.

Judge Landrith cleared his throat and then spoke: "What you've seen is what I believe to be a truly non-adversarial search for the truth. We cannot replace the twelve years these defendants have been incarcerated, nor can we forget Debbie Carter. All we can do is move forward. What this day is is a day of freedom. Mr. Williamson, Mr. Fritz, you are free to leave this courtroom." A smile crept over his face as he banged his gavel.

As his words were being spoken, I closed my eyes, lifted my head to heaven, and said the words, "Thank you, Jesus." When I opened my eyes again, my mother and daughter were rushing to my side, where they wrapped their arms tightly around me. Their tears flowed freely as we embraced. "Oh, Dad, I love you so much. Don't ever leave me again," Elizabeth cried from the bottom of her heart. My mother softly kissed my cheek with the tenderness that only a mother could impart. "Son, I love you so very much. You are going home to stay and I will always be there for you, no matter what," she said in my ear.

Before he was swept into a swarm of people who wanted interviews and pictures, Barry hugged me with all the love and compassion that he had to give. He had come to my rescue and saved my life.

My head was spinning, not unlike the feeling that I had experienced when I had heard the slap of the jury's decision a long time ago. This time, though, I was caught up in every joyous second of the whirling ride toward my newly gained freedom. I was caught up in a swirl of emotion the likes of which I had never felt in my life. I hugged everybody that was near. Kim Marks, Janet Chesley, and other people from the Oklahoma Indigent Defense System embraced me as I experienced my first taste of freedom.

We made our way from the courtroom down to the lower landing outside. A woman that I didn't recognize approached me and extended words of congratulations. She was Sherry's sister, Donna. I hadn't heard from my ex-wife since before my arrest. I asked Donna how Sherry was doing. A pained look crossed her face as she told me that Sherry had passed away two years earlier from a massive stoke. I was saddened by the shocking news. I had loved her dearly but it had not been in God's plan for us to have stayed together. Donna and I promised each other we would stay in touch.

After leaving the courthouse, Mom, Elizabeth and I checked into a hotel to rest before going to eat. I went to the front desk to get the keys for our rooms, and the clerk handed me pieces of plastic. Without wanting to sound dumb by asking her what they were, I walked outside and told my daughter that they never gave me the keys. I held up what the clerk had handed me.

Elizabeth laughed.

"Dad, that is the key," she said. Her laughter subsided as tears formed in her eyes.

"The key? How can a piece of plastic open a door unless you are a burglar?" I said with a laugh. I didn't want to sound embarrassed.

"Come on, Dad. I'll show you how it's done."

Elizabeth slipped a card into the door slot, and amazingly the door opened. She hugged me and then found her grandmother, and they went to their rooms for some rest.

I wasn't sleepy. I wanted to be out there in that great big world where all of the excitement awaited me. Barry had asked after leaving the courthouse where I wanted to eat. Mexican food, I had told him. For twelve years I had daydreamed about sitting down to a big plate of tacos and enchiladas with good cold Mexican beer. I couldn't wait. I paced until it was time to go.

Our evening of celebration began at Polo's. I stuffed myself. I found myself glancing at my watch while we were in the restaurant with an odd feeling that I was supposed to be somewhere where I wasn't. I realized it was lockdown I was missing. For a moment I felt awkward, and then I let the feeling go.

The festive celebration was an absolute dream-come-true. I was actually sitting in this beautiful eating establishment as a free man. Everyone around the table made toasts laced with laughter and hoorahs. My heart bubbled over with elation. The feeling was something that I could come nowhere close to describing. Following our celebration, we drove to Ronnie's sister's house. Annette Hudson opened her doors to us and we continued the freedom party well into the night. We sang, Ronnie played his guitar, we laughed, we cried, we danced, and we gave thanks to the Lord for helping Barry and the Innocence Project bring forth our innocence.

The next morning we ate breakfast and traveled to the nearby Holiday Inn, where Barry had arranged a satellite interview on *The Today Show*. I was very nervous, but after following Barry's lead, I was able to relax and convey a few segments about my nightmare in hell. I had the opportunity to tell how the district attorney had so wrongfully railroaded both me and Ronnie through his vindictive prosecution. My spirit soared as I told the whole truth on national television.

From there, we traveled to the Channel 9 television station in Oklahoma City and another satellite interview with *Burden of Proof*. I was in a moment of pure rapture as Barry, Mark, Ronnie, and I gave our interviews. Next, our entourage proceeded to the Capitol in Oklahoma City, where we participated in a press conference concerning the question of post-conviction DNA testing, and afterwards spoke out in support of legislation to compensate the wrongfully convicted. I was exhausted to the bone, but Barry had the energy of a raging bull as he sought out everything he could find to promote the Innocence Project's cause of freeing the wrongly convicted.

By late afternoon, it was time to say our goodbyes. Mark, Sara, Ronnie, and his family left first. We hugged each other warmly. Together, we had been to the deepest valleys of despair, and now we were a united family that could never be torn apart. As Barry, Elizabeth, Mom, and I walked silently together down the long corridor within the Capitol, hurrying so Barry could catch his flight, I turned my head slightly towards Barry, who was on my right, and saw a tear on his cheek. Deep within me a feeling welled up that told me that I truly loved Barry, as a human being first and for all the magnificent and wonderful accomplishments that he had made, sacrificing his time and limitless energy to free the wrongfully convicted. When we got outside, we took photos and hugged each other several more times before Barry turned to go.

"Thank you," I said to him. "I appreciate everything you've done."

He nodded, and while waving his hand as if what he'd done were no big deal, he said, "Dennis, justice has been served. Today you are free to start a new life with Elizabeth and your mom, so get out there on this clear, beautiful day and enjoy it to the fullest. You have my greatest blessings upon you and your wonderful family."

"I'll never forget what you and the Innocence Project have done for me," I told him. "I want to thank you from the bottom of my heart for being there for me and my family and helping me to win my freedom." I shook his hand.

Barry said, "All of us at the Innocence Project are so happy that we could be there for you."

Mark was waiting in the car to take Barry to the airport. Elizabeth hugged Barry's neck another time and told him she would never forget what he had done. Mom gave Barry a final hug and said, "Thank you, Mr. Scheck, for giving me the greatest gift of all—having my son back again as a free man."

"Take good care of him, Mom, and make sure that he stays a free man," Barry said with a gleam in his eyes and a big smile on his face. He turned and rushed toward the car.

At last Elizabeth, Mom, and I were together again, our minds and spirit stronger than we had ever known, to go forth in this world and build upon our love, knowing that we had been through the greatest battle of all and won.

Dennis Fritz and Ron Williamson react to judge's ruling
dismissing murder convictions against them
4/15/1999

EPILOGUE

After I was exonerated of all charges and released from the Pontotoc County jail, I returned to Kansas City, Missouri, where I lived with my mother. The first few years posed considerable challenges concerning readjustment and my return to society. I underwent psychological treatment for post-traumatic stress disorder.

Due to the state's failure to provide medical treatment for hepatitis C while I was incarcerated, my health deteriorated following my release. I successfully defeated the virus by implementing total body cleanses, along with a strict diet, interferon treatments, and a unique blend of Chinese herbs from a well-known alternative medicine liver specialist in New York. I have maintained good health ever since.

In 2003, with the help of Barry Scheck, Cheryl Pilate, Mark Barrett, and Dan Clark, I successfully sued the state of Oklahoma and received a financial settlement that has allowed me to provide a quality life for me and my family. I have devoted my energies to serving the Innocence Project in New York and Kansas City. I have continued in my alternative healing studies and have shared their positive effects with many people. My relationship with my daughter and mother continues to grow. Not only did DNA testing make it possible for me to regain my freedom, it also made it possible for me to discover that I have a second daughter, Misty.

My dear friend, Ronnie Williamson, died in 2004.

It was through my strong faith in God that I survived this ordeal. To this day, my freedom has allowed me to be a whole person again, and I am so thankful for the miracle that brought me out of the gates of hell into the light of the day. I am still overly cautious when a police car drives by my house or when the phone rings and no one speaks, but I know now that I am still under a very special blessing that breathed life back into my once-broken body.